The EU, NATO and the Integration of Europe

Why did Western European states agree to the enlargement of the EU and NATO? Frank Schimmelfennig analyzes the history of the enlargement process and develops a theoretical approach of 'rhetorical action' to explain why it occurred. While rationalist theory explains the willingness of East European states to join NATO and the EU, it does not explain why member states decided to admit them. Using original data, Schimmelfennig shows that expansion to the East can be understood in terms of liberal democratic community-building, but attempts to take sociological institutional theory a step further. Drawing on the works of Jon Elster and Erving Goffman, he demonstrates that the decision to expand was the result of rhetorical action. Candidates and their supporters among member states used arguments based on collective identity, norms and values of the Western community to shame opponents into acquiescing to enlargement. This landmark book makes an enormous contribution to theory in international relations, and to the study of European politics.

Themes in European Governance

The evolving European systems of governance, in particular the European Union, challenge and transform the state, the most important locus of governance and political identity and loyalty over the past 200 years. The series *Themes in European Governance* aims to publish the best theoretical and analytical scholarship on the impact of European governance on the core institutions, policies and identities of nation states. It focuses upon the implications for issues such as citizenship, welfare, political decision-making, and economic, monetary and fiscal policies. An initiative of Cambridge University Press and the Programme on Advanced Research on the Europeanisation of the Nation-State (ARENA), Norway, the series includes contributions in the social sciences, humanities and law. The series aims to provide theoretically informed studies analysing key issues at the European level and within European states. Volumes in the series will be of interest to scholars and students of Europe both within Europe and worldwide. They will be of particular relevance to those interested in the development of sovereignty and governance of European states and in the issues raised by multi-level governance and multi-national integration throughout the world.

Other books in the series:
Paulette Kurzer *Markets and Moral Regulation: Cultural Change in the European Union*
Christoph Knill *The Europeanisation of National Administrations: Patterns of Institutional Change and Persistence*
Tanja Börzel *States and Regions in the European Union: Institutional Adaptation in Germany and Spain*
Liesbet Hooghe *The European Commission and the Integration of Europe: Images of Governance*

The EU, NATO and the Integration of Europe

Rules and Rhetoric

Frank Schimmelfennig

CAMBRIDGE UNIVERSITY PRESS
Cambridge, New York, Melbourne, Madrid, Cape Town, Singapore, São Paulo

Cambridge University Press
The Edinburgh Building, Cambridge CB2 2RU, UK

Published in the United States of America by Cambridge University Press, New York

www.cambridge.org
Information on this title: www.cambridge.org/9780521828062

First published 2003

A catalogue record for this publication is available from the British Library

Library of Congress Cataloguing in Publication data
Schimmelfennig, Frank, 1963–
The EU, NATO and the integration of Europe : rules and rhetoric / Frank Schimmelfennig.
p. cm. – (Themes in European governance)
Includes bibliographical references and index.
ISBN 0 521 82806 6 (hard.) – ISBN 0 521 53525 5 (pbk.)
1. Europe – Economic integration. 2. North Atlantic Treaty Organization – Membership. 3. National security – Europe. I. Title. II. Series.
JN30.S338 2003
341.242′2 – dc21 2003046173

ISBN-13 978-0-521-82806-2 hardback
ISBN-10 0-521-82806-6 hardback

ISBN-13 978-0-521-53525-0 paperback
ISBN-10 0-521-53525-5 paperback

Transferred to digital printing 2006

Contents

Figures

Tables

Acknowledgments

This book was originally written as a German *Habilitationsschrift.* The obsolescent *Habilitation* has the doubtful reputation of being an anachronistic initiation rite to the higher ranks of academia, which forces scholars to work on oversize and widely unread manuscripts in personal dependence on a university professor for a period of five years and more, during which they "tend to 'disappear' from the surface of the earth" (Jørgensen 2000: 31).

Under the circumstances, I consider myself lucky. I am particularly grateful to Klaus Dieter Wolf who helped me at a critical juncture in my academic career and gave me the freedom and support I needed to complete my research in a reasonable time period. The *Deutsche Forschungsgemeinschaft* (German Research Foundation) funded me and my project on the "Enlargement of the Western International Community" between 1998 and 2002, thus giving me the opportunity to conduct my own, independent research. The Faculty of Social and Historical Sciences at Darmstadt University of Technology provided for a quick and smooth *Habilitation* procedure. Cambridge University Press agreed to publish the manuscript and forced me to shorten it. Finally, my wife Beate and my children Philipp, Paulina and Laura prevented me from "disappearing from the surface of the earth." At the same time, they considered my work sufficiently boring to leave me alone in my study. I dedicate this book to them.

Many others have supported me and the project in various ways. Tanja Moehle and Johanna Möhring assisted me during the preparatory stage of the project at the University of Konstanz. At Darmstadt University, Stefan Engert and Heiko Knobel were extremely helpful in collecting and processing the data for the quantitative analysis of enlargement reported in chapter 6. Furthermore, I benefited from a NATO-EAPC Individual Fellowship for the period 1998–2000 to conduct the research that went into the NATO enlargement decision-making case study (chapter 10). I am highly indebted to my interview partners (see list in Appendix) for sharing their precious time and insights with me. I further thank Karen

Donfried, Chris Donnelly, Gunther Hellmann, Johanna Möhring and Frank Umbach for helping me to get in contact with the interviewees and Thomas Risse and Klaus Dieter Wolf for supporting my application for the fellowship. Finally, Thomas Risse, Rainer Schmalz-Bruns, Klaus Dieter Wolf and Michael Zürn were reviewers of the thesis in my *Habilitation* procedure and made excellent suggestions for improving the manuscript. Special thanks to Thomas Risse: although we keep failing to persuade each other, his work and criticism have always been a stimulus and a challenge for my own.

I presented earlier versions of several parts of the study at the Institute of Political Science at Darmstadt University of Technology, the European University Institute in Florence, the Mannheim Center for European Social Research, ARENA at the University of Oslo, International Relations research seminars at the Universities of Konstanz and Tübingen as well as the Queen's University Belfast, the German–Japanese Symposion on Comparative Foreign Policy in Tübingen, the 1999 ECSA 6th Biennial International Conference in Pittsburgh, and an international workshop on "Governance by Enlargement" at Darmstadt University of Technology sponsored by the Volkswagen Foundation in June 2000. I thank audiences, discussants and other readers for their critical and helpful comments, in particular Josh Busby, Jeff Checkel, Beate Kohler-Koch, Thomas Plümper, Guido Schwellnus and Uli Sedelmeier.

Some parts and results of this study have been published as journal articles. In the order of publication dates, these are "Rhetorisches Handeln in der internationalen Politik," in *Zeitschrift für Internationale Beziehungen* 4:2, 1997, 219–54; "Liberal Norms and the Eastern Enlargement of the European Union: A Case for Sociological Institutionalism," in *Österreichische Zeitschrift für Politikwissenschaft* 27:4, 1998, 459–72; "NATO Enlargement: A Constructivist Explanation," in *Security Studies* 8:2–3, 1999, 198–234; "The Community Trap: Liberal Norms, Rhetorical Action, and the Eastern Enlargement of the European Union," in *International Organization* 55:1, 2001, 47–80; and "Liberal Community and Enlargement: An Event History Analysis," in *Journal of European Public Policy* 9:4, 2002, 598–626. I greatly appreciate the comments I received from the editors and reviewers of these journals.

In the end, for better or worse, I decided myself how to use the information, comments and advice I received during my work on this study. Thus, as usual, the author alone bears responsibility for its contents and any mistakes of fact, inference and judgment.

Abbreviations

ASEAN	Association of South-East Asian Nations
CAP	Common Agricultural Policy
CBO	Congressional Budget Office
CEE	Central and Eastern Europe(an)
CEEC	Central and Eastern European Country
CIA	Central Intelligence Agency
CIS	Community of Independent States
CMEA	Council for Mutual Economic Assistance
CoE	Council of Europe
CSCE	Conference on Security and Cooperation in Europe
C^3I	Command, Control, Communication, and Intelligence
EAPC	Euro-Atlantic Partnership Council
EBRD	European Bank for Reconstruction and Development
EC	European Community
ECSC	European Coal and Steel Community
ECU	European Currency Unit
EEC	European Economic Community
EFTA	European Free Trade Association
EHA	Event History Analysis
EMU	European Monetary Union
EP	European Parliament
EU	European Union
FAZ	*Frankfurter Allgemeine Zeitung*
FBIS	*Foreign Broadcast Information Service*
FT	*Financial Times*
GDP	Gross Domestic Product
GDR	German Democratic Republic
GNP	Gross National Product
IHT	*International Herald Tribune*
IPE	International Political Economy
IPP	Individual Partnership Program
IR	International Relations

MAP	Membership Action Plan
MDF	Hungarian Democratic Forum
NACC	North Atlantic Cooperation Council
NAFTA	North American Free Trade Association
NATO	North Atlantic Treaty Organization
NERO	NATO Enlargement Ratification Office
NGO	Non-governmental Organization
NSC	National Security Council
NYT	*New York Times*
OAU	Organization for African Unity
OECD	Organization for Economic Cooperation and Development
OEEC	Organization for European Economic Cooperation
OSCE	Organization for Security and Cooperation in Europe
PACE	Parliamentary Assembly of the Council of Europe
PARP	Planning and Review Process
PfP	Partnership for Peace
SAA	Stabilization and Association Agreement
SEA	Single European Act
SZ	*Süddeutsche Zeitung*
TEU	Treaty on European Union
UK	United Kingdom
UN ECE	United Nations Economic Commission for Europe
US	United States
USCEN	United States Committee to Expand NATO
WEU	West European Union
WTO	World Trade Organization

Introduction

The study of enlargement: political relevance and theoretical neglect

Eastern enlargement is a defining process in the international politics of the New Europe. Since the end of the Cold War, the major West European regional organizations – the European Union (EU), the North Atlantic Treaty Organization (NATO) and, to a lesser degree, the Council of Europe (CoE) – have become the fundamental institutional structures in the "architecture" of the new Europe. They have developed into the centers of gravity in pan-European institution-building and into the dominant loci of decision- and policy-making for the entire region. The borders of these organizations have replaced the East–West line of the Cold War as the central cleavage in the European system. "Europe" has increasingly come to be defined in terms of these organizations, the "Europeanization" or "Europeanness" of individual countries has come to be measured by the intensity of institutional relations with these organizations and by the adoption of their organizational values and norms.

Immediately after the dissolution of the Eastern bloc, all European organizations began to create a diversified array of institutional relationships with the Central and Eastern European countries (CEECs) – reaching from observer status to some form of association.[1] A few years later, the Western organizations set out to expand their membership to the East in the biggest enlargement rounds in their history. The membership of the Council of Europe grew from fourteen to twenty-two members between 1950 and 1988. Since then, it has doubled. Both the EU and NATO made their principal decisions on Eastern enlargement in 1997.

At its Madrid summit in July 1997, NATO invited the Czech Republic, Hungary and Poland to become members; they joined in May 1999. At its November 2002 Prague summit, NATO embarked upon a further

[1] The "Central and Eastern European countries" are defined here as the European successor states of the Soviet Union and the other formerly communist states in Europe.

round of enlargement to seven new members: the three Baltic countries, Slovakia, Slovenia, Bulgaria and Romania.

Also in July 1997, the European Commission presented its Agenda 2000 in which it recommended accession negotiations with the Czech Republic, Estonia, Hungary, Poland and Slovenia. In December 1999, the European Council meeting in Helsinki decided that the other five associated CEECs – Bulgaria, Latvia, Lithuania, Romania and Slovakia – would join the fast-track group for accession negotiations in February 2000. Accession negotiations with eight CEECs (excluding Bulgaria and Romania) were concluded at the end of 2002. The seven new NATO members and the eight new EU members are expected to join the organizations in 2004. This will not be the end of Eastern enlargement, however. Three further countries – Albania, Croatia and Macedonia – are preparing themselves to join NATO under the Membership Action Plan and, in addition to Bulgaria and Romania, the EU offered the remaining Balkan countries a general "membership perspective." Thus, enlargement will remain center stage for many years to come.

In addition, enlargement has arguably been the most consequential political project for the European organizations in the last decade. For the EU in particular, enlargement has made it necessary to reform major policies (such as common agriculture and structural funds) and decision-making procedures.

Given the political relevance of enlargement, it is striking that it has been a largely neglected issue in the theory of international institutions and regional integration (cf. Friis and Murphy 1999; Wallace 2000). The classical approaches to the study of integration like neofunctionalism and transactionalism only mentioned the geographical extension of international communities in passing (see Deutsch 1970: 4, 43–44; Haas 1968: 313–17; Schmitter 1969: 165). This is not surprising: first, analyzing the establishment and stabilization of regional organizations logically precedes studying their territorial expansion. Second, the heyday of regional integration theory had come to an end before the European Community's first enlargement in 1973. In addition, the subsequent move toward the analysis of material policies and the adoption of theoretical frameworks from Comparative Politics (e.g. neocorporatism, network analysis, multi-level governance) did little to further research on such a polity-building issue as enlargement (see Friis and Murphy 1999: 213). It is more surprising that the revival of International Relations regional integration studies at the beginning of the 1990s and the theoretical debate between "intergovernmentalism" and "supranationalism" still focused exclusively upon issues of "deepening" like the Single European Act, the currency union, or legal integration.

While the increased salience of enlargement since the end of the Cold War has given rise to a sizeable body of literature, the theoretical neglect of this subject resulted in a number of weaknesses in the study of enlargement. First, the bulk of the enlargement literature consists of descriptive and often policy-oriented studies. This situation is changing. Probably, both the indisputable political relevance of enlargement and the lack of theoretical work in this area provided a strong incentive for theory-oriented studies on the EC's (second) Northern enlargement and on the Eastern enlargement of all Western regional organizations. Second, however, most of these studies still focus on single cases – typically, analyzing single enlargement rounds of single organizations, single member or accession countries, or even single policy areas in the enlargement process.[2]

This book makes a contribution to this emerging literature. Its basic goal is to explain the principal enlargement decisions of the EU and NATO in 1997. The central research questions are: why did the CEECs want to become NATO and EU members? Why did both organizations decide to expand to Central and Eastern Europe? How did they arrive at these decisions? And what accounts for their selection of new members among the CEECs? In order to answer these questions, I specify and test theory-based hypotheses about enlargement and use them for comparative and statistical analyses. Moreover, I show that the analysis of enlargement not only benefits from theoretical input from the general literature on international institutions and regional integration but also makes a valuable contribution to it. Eastern enlargement constitutes a puzzle for both rationalist and sociological theories of international institutions and lends itself to exploring novel ways of conceptualizing institutional effects and actor behavior in international politics.

Rules, rhetoric and enlargement: the argument

Explaining enlargement

The book makes two main arguments. First, the constitutive liberal rules of the Western international community – rather than constellations of material, security or economic, interests and power – are the most important explanatory factors in the expansion of NATO and the EU. Second, it is through rhetorical action – rather than a logic of appropriateness – that these community rules have had an impact on enlargement.

[2] For an analysis of the state of the art in the enlargement literature, see Schimmelfennig and Sedelmeier (2002).

It is the first basic argument of this book that we can best explain the enlargement of the EU and NATO if we conceive both regional organizations as community representatives and community-building agencies. The international communities they represent are the European and, in the case of NATO, the Euro-Atlantic community of states. Both "Western" communities define their collective identity not merely by geographical location in a certain region of the international system (Europe or the Euro-Atlantic) but mainly by *liberal values and norms*. The belief in and adherence to liberal human rights are the fundamental ideas and practices that constitute these overlapping communities. In the domestic sphere, the liberal principles of social and political order – social pluralism, the rule of law, democratic political participation and representation as well as private property and a market-based economy – are derived from and justified by these liberal human rights. In the international sphere, the liberal order is characterized by the "democratic peace" – non-violent conflict-management between liberal democratic states – and multilateralism. The liberal identity, values and norms of the Western international community are formally institutionalized in the community organizations as *constitutive organizational rules*.

The policies of the EU and NATO toward non-member states are governed by these liberal community rules. Both organizations seek to disseminate liberal principles of domestic and international conduct in their international environment. They socialize outside states into the liberal order and thereby seek to expand the European or Euro-Atlantic liberal international community. If European non-member states are successfully socialized, that is, they adopt the collective identity of the liberal international community, share its values, and follow its norms, they are both willing and entitled to join the international organizations of the community as full members.

Based on this hypothesis, we can explain Eastern enlargement as the admission of former communist countries that have successfully democratized and adopted the constitutive rules of the Western organizations. By and large, the EU and NATO invited those CEECs to become members that had progressed the most on the path of democratic consolidation. This finding can be generalized to the entire enlargement history of the major West European regional organizations since their foundation: more democratic states are more likely to enter into institutionalized relationships with the West European organizations, to apply for membership, and to be invited to accession negotiations than less democratic states. Conversely, the less democratic a full or associated member of these organizations, the more likely it is to be excluded from the organizations, or its membership frozen or suspended.

It is the second basic argument of this study that the process by which Eastern enlargement came about was characterized by *rhetorical action.* Rhetorical action is the strategic use and exchange of arguments to persuade other actors to act according to one's preferences. In the enlargement process, neither member nor applicant states acted appropriately, that is, on the basis of rule-based enlargement routines or internalized membership norms. They neither took the membership rules of the community organizations for granted nor as moral commands. Rather, *enlargement preferences reflected material environmental conditions and egoistic interests.* However, whereas the CEECs generally expected to reap net security and welfare benefits from joining NATO and the EU, *Eastern enlargement was not a rational, efficient institutional arrangement for the Western organizations.*

First, in a collective perspective, the expected transaction, autonomy, and crowding costs of Eastern enlargement were higher than the expected benefits of admitting the CEECs as full members. Second, both organizations had more efficient institutional forms for their relations with the CEECs – association in the case of the EU and Partnership for Peace in the case of NATO. Third, whereas individual member states, above all Germany and other Western states in the vicinity of the CEECs, supported enlargement as an instrument to control the effects of negative interdependence and to increase their gains from positive interdependence with their neighboring region, neither they nor the CEECs possessed the bargaining power to impose enlargement on the reluctant majority of member states. In this asymmetrical constellation of preferences and power, both the EU and NATO initially rejected the CEECs' demands for full membership.

In order to overcome this unfavorable constellation of preferences and power, *the CEE governments and their supporters in the Western organizations turned to rhetorical action.* They based their claims for enlargement on the collective identity and the constitutive liberal values and norms of the community organizations to which the member states had subscribed. They exposed the inconsistency between the organizations' reluctance to enlarge, on the one hand, and their membership rules, past rhetorical commitments to a pan-European democratic community and past treatment of outsider states, on the other. Their goal was to shame the reticent member states into complying with the community rules and honoring past commitments. As a result of these arguments, *the opponents of Eastern enlargement found themselves rhetorically entrapped.* They could neither openly oppose nor threaten to veto enlargement without publicly reneging on prior commitments and damaging their credibility as community members in good standing. In the end, they acquiesced in enlargement.

Rethinking institutional effects

The book follows constructivist or sociological institutionalist work on international politics by showing that the community-based rules institutionalized in the Western organizations effectively governed their policies on such a fundamental issue as membership and that their impact was strong enough to bring about rule-conforming enlargement decisions despite an adverse distribution of enlargement preferences and bargaining power. The argument deviates from standard sociological institutionalist work, however, in that it rejects the claim that collective identities and rules *constitute* the issue-specific *interests* of state actors and that, in their decisions and actions, state actors follow a norm-guided "logic of appropriateness" or a communicatively rational logic of arguing. By contrast, the analysis of enlargement preferences and politics revealed the dominance of egoistic interests and instrumental action.

To account for the causal link between rule-ignoring individual preferences and a rule-conforming collective outcome, the study introduces the mechanism of *rhetorical action.* It conceives Europe as a *community environment* for state action, specifies the constraints under which states act in such an environment, and describes how the rhetorical use of arguments can result in rule-compliant behavior. Whereas the rule-based explanation of enlargement is the main empirical result of this book, the mechanism of rhetorical action is its main theoretical contribution to the analysis of international institutions and to the debate between rationalism and constructivism.

The analysis of Eastern enlargement provides new insight into the possibility and the conditions of normative international order. According to the standard account of rationalist institutionalism, compliance with international rules depends on individual cost-benefit calculations. In the absence of centralized enforcement – the typical condition in international politics – international rules must be self-enforcing, that is, states comply if the costs are lower than the benefits. By contrast, constructivist institutionalism assumes socialization effects of international rules. To the extent that state actors are convinced of the appropriateness of international rules, they comply even in the presence of net costs to themselves. But what if an international rule is not self-enforcing on the basis of self-interest or internalized beliefs as was the case with the membership rules of the EU and NATO in the case of Eastern enlargement? I argue that even in the absence of self-interest and internalization, compliance is likely if the international environment is characterized by "international community" and if the rule in question is constitutive, legitimate, and salient.

A community is characterized by two core characteristics: its ethos and its high interaction density.[3] The ethos refers to the constitutive values and norms that define the collective identity of the community – who "we" are, what "we" stand for and how "we" differ from others. Moreover, communities are tightly knit, with frequent direct and relevant interactions between members, and membership is permanent for all practical purposes.

A community environment affects interaction and outcomes in four ways. First, it *triggers arguments about the legitimacy* of preferences and policies. Actors are able – and forced – to justify their preferences on the basis of the community ethos. Second, the community ethos is both a resource of support for rule-conforming actions and a constraint that imposes costs on rule-violating actions. It *adds legitimacy to and thus strengthens the bargaining power* of those actors that pursue preferences in line with, although not necessarily inspired by, the values and norms of the community. Third, the permanence of the community *forces actors to be concerned about their image*. This image depends not only on how they are perceived to conform with the community ethos but also on whether they are perceived to argue credibly. Finally, high interaction density reduces information asymmetries, increases the likelihood that argumentative inconsistencies are detected, and thus makes it difficult for actors to argue opportunistically.

Thus, community members whose preferences and actions violate the community ethos can be shamed into compliance by other community actors who (threaten to) expose the inconsistency between their earlier commitment to the community ethos and their current actions. Because rational members of a community are concerned about their image of legitimacy, a community environment has the potential to modify the collective outcome that would have resulted from the constellations of preferences and power and the formal decision-making rules alone. In other words, in a community environment, norm-based collective outcomes are possible even among strategic actors and, in the absence of deep socialization, coercive power or egoistic incentives to comply.

However, even within the same community, community effects vary across policy issues. First, the more *constitutive* a policy issue is or the more it involves fundamental questions of community purpose, the easier it is for interested actors to bring in questions of legitimacy, to frame it as an issue of community identity that cannot be left to the interplay of self-interest and bargaining power, and to shame other actors into compliance.

[3] See, e.g., the conditions of a pluralistic security community analyzed by Deutsch *et al.* (1957).

Second, community effects differ with regard to the *legitimacy* of the rule in question (see Franck 1990). The more clearly a rule is formulated, the more consistently it is interpreted, the more coherently it is practiced, and the more firmly it is integrated into the community's rule hierarchy, the more legitimate the rule is and the more difficult it becomes for a shamed member of the community rhetorically to circumvent and evade its practical implications. Finally, *salience* matters. International community values and norms, which match domestic values and norms or the fundamental beliefs of state representatives, will have stronger community effects than those which are in tension with values and norms at the domestic level and with the fundamental beliefs of policymakers.

The enlargement of the EU and NATO was not only the enlargement of two community organizations. It also represents an issue-area in which the conditions of strong community effects were present to a large extent.

Increasing leverage in problem-driven research: a note on methodology

My initial interest in studying the Eastern enlargement of NATO and the EU was to explain a major development in the international politics of post-Cold War Europe and in the politics of its regional organizations. What mainly aroused my curiosity was the hunch that Eastern enlargement might be a puzzle for the rationalist theories that dominated the study of international institutions and regional integration in IR. In pursuing this hunch, I found out that theory-based work on enlargement was virtually non-existent and proceeded with specifying and testing theory-based hypotheses about the conditions of enlargement. The test showed that Eastern enlargement constituted a puzzle for rationalist institutionalism, indeed. I then turned to sociological or constructivist institutionalism which had emerged as the major (meta)theoretical challenge to rationalist institutionalism in the mid-1990s. The "liberal community hypothesis" derived from sociological institutionalist assumptions accounted fairly well for Eastern enlargement and the selection of new members among the Central and East European aspirants.

Two important questions and puzzles remained. First, was this explanation specific to Eastern enlargement or could it be generalized to earlier enlargement rounds of the EU and NATO and to other Western organizations? I therefore set out to test this hypothesis in a statistical, large-*n* study of enlargement events. Second, the process of how Eastern enlargement came about did not seem to correspond to standard sociological accounts of habitualized or internalized rule-driven behavior. I therefore specified alternative process hypotheses, and their observable implications for enlargement, and analyzed the collective decision-making processes that led to NATO and EU enlargement in order to find out *how*, if at all, the rules of the Western international community drove enlargement.

The structure of the book closely mirrors my research process (see Table 1.1). It is typical of *problem-driven research*, which starts with a *perceived lack of knowledge about a real-world phenomenon* – like an ill-understood, new and/or puzzling event or pattern in international politics – and then *repeatedly moves back and forth between theory and data* in order to fill this gap. In these moves, I was guided by the principle of maximizing or, more modestly, *increasing leverage*. King, Keohane and Verba define "maximizing leverage" as "explaining as much as possible with as little as possible" and suggest that "the primary way is to increase the number of observable implications of our hypothesis and seek confirmation of those implications" (1994: 29). The rationale behind this principle is to explore and assess the quality of an explanation, hypothesis or theory as thoroughly and systematically as possible. I take this principle to imply three basic elements: specifying (alternative) theory-based hypotheses, deriving numerous and varied observable implications, and combining different methods and data.

Specifying (alternative) theory-based hypotheses

Leverage increases with the level of abstraction and generality of a scientific proposition. In contrast to *ad hoc* explanations based on the interaction of concrete factors present in the context of a single event, theories potentially contain numerous observable implications across time and space, actors and social contexts. High leverage thus requires the explanations sought in problem-driven research to be derived from theory-based hypotheses. In addition, in order to assess the quality of an explanation more precisely, it is necessary to confront it with alternative explanations derived from other theory-based hypotheses. Alternative explanations may fail, thereby underlining the strength of the original hypothesis. They may, however, also provide equally or even more convincing accounts of the phenomenon to be explained, thereby putting the original explanation in perspective. In sum, the systematic inclusion of alternative hypotheses gives us a broader and more balanced picture of the causal relationships in a given field and of the explanatory power of the main hypothesis of interest.

My analysis of Eastern enlargement is theoretically embedded in the current debate in International Relations between "rationalism"

Table 1.1 *The structure of the book*

Chs.	Theory	Data	Leverage	Result
1	Rationalist institutionalism on enlargement outcomes		Specification of theory-based hypotheses	
2–3		NATO and EU Eastern enlargement	Two parallel case studies	Puzzle
4	Sociological institutionalism on enlargement outcomes		Specification of alternative theory-based hypotheses	
5		NATO and EU Eastern enlargement	Re-analysis of the two case studies	Confirmation
6		All major enlargement events of NATO, EU and CoE	Additional kinds of observable implications, large-*n* statistical analysis	Confirmation
7	Sociological institutionalism on enlargement process		Additional kinds of observable implications, specification of theory-based process hypotheses	
8	Habitual and normative action	State enlargement preferences	Small-*n* comparative analysis	Puzzle
9	Rhetorical action		Alternative process hypothesis	
10		NATO decision-making process	Process-tracing	Inconclusive
11		EU decision-making process	Contrast case study, process-tracing	Confirmation

and "constructivism," that is, in alternative theories at a high level of abstraction and generality.[4] For all the sterile debates and false dichotomies they have produced, and for which they have been rightfully criticized, it has been a virtue of the recent "great debates" in International Relations that they have opened IR to theoretical imports from neighboring disciplines. Whereas the debate between neorealism and neoliberal institutionalism has been strongly influenced by economic thinking, the debate between rationalism (which comprises both neorealism and neoliberal institutionalism) and constructivism has benefited additionally from sociological approaches. As a result, IR researchers now have at their disposal a broad spectrum of theoretical approaches to the study of institutions and are able to use a rich set of alternative hypotheses about institutional effects. Moreover, these theoretical imports and debates have strengthened the awareness of IR scholars for the theoretical and metatheoretical assumptions on which their work is based.

I do not suggest, however, that it makes sense to test "rationalism" against "constructivism" in the study of enlargement. Both rationalism and constructivism are social *meta*theories defined by a set of assumptions about the social world and about theory-building rather than by specific hypotheses (cf. Risse and Wiener 1999: 778; Wendt 1999: 5–6). They do not provide us with elaborated and internally consistent competing hypotheses on enlargement that we could rigorously test against each other. First, there is a variety of substantial theories and hypotheses based on each metatheory. Theories with the same metatheoretical background may attribute preferences and outcomes to different factors and lead to different and even contradictory expectations about enlargement. Second, the differences between rationalist and sociological theories of institutions are multidimensional and often a matter of degree rather than principle (see Fearon and Wendt 2002). I therefore use rationalism and constructivism as partially competing and partially complementary sources of hypothesis construction for the study of enlargement. Thanks to their high level of abstraction, their transdisciplinary origins and their foundations in social theory, they enable us to deduce a great number of alternative hypotheses and observable implications covering all dimensions of the enlargement of international organizations. Finally, as Paul DiMaggio suggests, "The most productive forms of cross-pollination . . . are those that follow from common attempts to address significant problems of explanation that prove intractable from any single perspective" (1998: 703).

[4] For a first overview, see Katzenstein, Keohane and Krasner (1999).

Deriving numerous and varied observable implications

To "evaluate as many observable implications of your theory as possible" (King, Keohane and Verba 1994: 195) is the core of maximizing leverage. This precept applies both to the number of observations of one kind (cases) and to different kinds of observations.

Generally, the *more cases* taken into account, the better we are able to assess the explanatory power and scope of our hypothesis of interest. Unfortunately, as I have mentioned above, the study of enlargement is dominated by analyses of a single country (or a few countries) in a single enlargement round of a single organization.[5] The single-case design not only leads to the proliferation of *ad hoc* explanations and findings the explanatory power and scope of which is hard to assess; but, it fails to generate knowledge about different patterns of organizational size and national membership, about time-dependent and dynamic effects of enlargement for which we would need a longitudinal study of several enlargement rounds, or about the effects of organizational characteristics on enlargement for which we would need to compare the expansion of several organizations. In three ways, this study increases leverage.

(1) I set out, from the start, to analyze the Eastern enlargement of *two organizations*, the EU and NATO. On the one hand, this choice was motivated by considerations of real-world relevance. NATO and the EU are the most important European organizations. In other words, they allocate the most relevant political values in the issue-areas of security and welfare. Two points follow from this relevance: first, the EU and NATO have been more discriminating in their enlargement decisions than other European organizations (such as the CoE, to say nothing of the OSCE). Second, their enlargement has been more strongly contested than that of the other organizations. For both reasons, findings about the enlargement of these organizations will be most meaningful.

Moreover, a comparison of both organizations enables me to test whether different organizational and context characteristics have an influence on enlargement. First, each organization specializes in different issue-areas, military security in the case of NATO and economic welfare in the case of the EU. Second, NATO has a more hegemonic structure than the EU, whereas, third, the EU is more supranationally organized than NATO. Comparing the enlargement of both organizations will make it possible to find out whether US dominance in NATO or the role of the

[5] There are a few exceptions only, most notably Mattli (1999).

Commission in the EU have really been as central for their enlargement decisions as single-organization studies claim (see, e.g., Goldgeier 1999; Sedelmeier and Wallace 1996).

(2) In a statistical, event-history analysis of the enlargement of West European regional organizations, I included, first, a *third organization*, the Council of Europe, second, the *entire period* since the three organizations came into existence and, third, *all countries of Europe* (defined as the OSCE region) in order to evaluate the liberal community hypothesis. Moreover, I not only looked at enlargement in the narrow sense, that is the accession of outside countries, but extended the analysis to *other events of enlargement* in the broader sense of horizontal institutionalization: the first establishment of institutionalized relations between an organization and an outside state, the non-member state's application for membership, and the exclusion or withdrawal from membership. This statistical analysis considerably improves "the ratio of the body of facts explained to the theoretical concepts employed" (King, Keohane and Verba 1994: 195).

(3) I further increased leverage by not only analyzing *correlational* implications of the theory-based hypotheses but also looking into the *causal process* that links independent and dependent variables (George 1979: 46; King, Keohane and Verba 1994: 225–27). Or, in the terminology of Dessler (1999: 129), I complemented the *generalizing* explanatory strategy with a *particularizing* or *reconstructive* strategy "in which the researcher explains an event by detailing the sequence of happenings leading up to it."

To find out *how* liberal community rules have brought about enlargement, I specified (alternative) causal mechanisms based again on rationalist and sociological institutionalist assumptions. In addition to the hypotheses on enlargement *outcomes*, I formulated five hypotheses about the characteristics of the enlargement *process* – habitual, normative, communicative and rhetorical action (plus rule-independent action as the null hypothesis) – and tested their observable implications. These hypotheses specify the way in which rules affect the actors, their behavior and their interactions.

The analysis of the EU's and NATO's collective decision-making processes not only produced additional evidence that the constitutive organizational rules based on liberal community culture, values and norms did indeed matter in the development and implementation of the enlargement policy of both organizations. More importantly, process-tracing made it possible to determine more precisely at which point in the process and by what means the organizational rules had an impact on enlargement.

Although correlational analysis had provided strong evidence in favor of a rule-based, sociological explanation of enlargement outcomes, process-tracing analysis showed that decision-making deviated significantly from the standard sociological hypotheses of habitual, normative or communicative action. Instead, it supported the rhetorical action hypothesis.

Combining methods and data

Each research design and social science method has its specific strengths and weaknesses. The same is true for different kinds of sources of evidence and data used for testing hypotheses. The combination of different designs, methods, sources and data in one's research can therefore help to add their strengths while compensating for their weaknesses and problems. This will once again increase leverage.

For instance, single-case or small-*n* studies enable the researcher to examine the historical evidence intensively, to employ concrete, historically appropriate concepts, to trace the process of causation carefully, and to analyze complex causal configurations and relationships. Yet the problems of generalizability, control, indeterminacy, and selection bias loom large. Large-*n* statistical studies can reduce these problems considerably. In turn, however, it is difficult to check the reliability and validity of the concepts, indicators and data as carefully as in small-*n* studies. It is impossible for the individual researcher or a small research group to complement correlational analysis with intensive process analysis in a large number of cases. Finally, statistical analysis requires a much higher degree of simplification of the causal relationships than case studies, and their results do not go beyond probabilistic statements.[6]

In this book, I start with two intensive case studies on the decisions of the EU and NATO to expand to the East. These case studies were necessary in order to cope with the complexity of rationalist explanations of enlargement. They were also helpful in generating initial support for the liberal community hypothesis. In order to test this hypothesis more thoroughly and systematically, I then turned to a statistical analysis which was greatly facilitated by the simple causal structure of the hypothesis. For the more time-consuming process analysis, I originally planned to do a single case study of NATO's enlargement decision-making. When it became clear, however, that the results would be as inconclusive as they

[6] See, e.g., King, Keohane and Verba (1994: 210–11); Lijphart (1975: 160, 166–72); Ragin (1987: ix–x).

often are in single case studies because of overdetermination, I added a case study on EU decision-making.

Moreover, organizational rules – the basic explanatory factor of this study – can be operationalized and measured in different ways, and these different ways require different kinds of sources and data. The IR literature distinguishes a formal, a behavioral and a cognitive or communicative conceptualization and operationalization of rules and finds virtue in each of them (Hasenclever, Mayer and Rittberger 1997: 14–21; Raymond 1997: 217–18). According to the behavioral conceptualization, the effects of rules are measured by the extent to which the relevant behavior of the actors is rule-governed. It requires behavioral data and lends itself well to quantitative studies. Yet, proponents of the cognitive or communicative conceptualization (Kratochwil and Ruggie 1986) argue that the effects of norms are above all seen in the communication between social actors and that rule-violating behavior does not indicate *per se* that a rule is invalid or rejected. This conceptualization calls mainly for the interpretation of textual data. The same is true for the formal conceptualization of rules as explicit and written (Keohane 1993).

In my research, I combined all conceptualizations. First, in order to show that the Western organizations constitute representatives of a community of liberal states, I used the formal indicator of explicit membership rules in the basic treaties of the organizations. For the test of the liberal community hypothesis, however, formal or cognitive indicators would have been insufficient. In order to find out whether the Western organizations *really treated* outside states according to their *factual adherence* to liberal norms, I used behavioral indicators for the implementation of liberal rules in the organizations' Eastern policies and in the domestic politics of the outsider states. These indicators were also suitable for statistical analysis. Finally, in the process analysis of NATO and EU decision-making, I included textual and discourse data alongside behavioral observations in order to show how community rules were used and referred to by the actors. Without a communicative conceptualization of rules, their rhetorical use would not even have been recognizable; but without a behavioral conceptualization, their effectiveness could not have been tested.[7]

Obviously, there is no end-point for increasing leverage in problem-driven research. There are always further alternative hypotheses, more cases, other kinds of observable implications, more data and other data

[7] On the need to combine discursive and behavioral evidence of norms, see also Kowert and Legro (1996: 484–85).

sources. However, having taken into account the major contending theories in the current IR debate on international institutions, analyzed the Eastern enlargement of the two most important regional organizations, extended the examination to other enlargement events, earlier enlargement rounds, and one more regional organization, and combined the analysis of outcomes and process, I felt sufficiently confident about my results.

Part I

Security, power or welfare? Eastern enlargement in a rationalist perspective

Rationalist theories of international institutions dominated the theoretical debate in International Relations throughout the 1980s. Moreover, club theory, the general rationalist theory of the size of organizations, is the best developed and most pertinent approach to explaining enlargement. For these reasons, I begin my analysis of Eastern enlargement with rationalist institutionalism. In the theoretical chapter (chapter 1), I describe the basic assumptions of rationalist institutionalism, present club theory, distinguish a security, power, and welfare approach to enlargement, and specify the conditions of enlargement for each approach. In the empirical chapters, I check to what degree these conditions were fulfilled in the Eastern enlargement of NATO (chapter 2) and the European Union (chapter 3). However, I will conclude that, whereas rationalist institutionalism accounts for the Central and Eastern European interest in joining the Western organizations, it does not convincingly explain why the EU and NATO member states agreed to expand their organizations.

1 Rationalist institutionalism and the enlargement of regional organizations

Rationalist premises

Rationalist approaches to the study of international relations and international institutions share the premises of individualism, state-centrism, materialism, egoism and instrumentalism:[1]

Individualism. Rationalist theories belong to the class of ontologically individualist theories which treat the individual actor (and not social structures) as the "ultimate source of social patterns" (Alexander and Giesen 1987: 13). Rationalist explanations of social interaction and its collective outcomes start with the actors whose identities, interests, and preferences they take as given and fairly stable over time.

State-centrism. IR rationalism differs from the individualist orthodoxy, however, in that it regards the state, a corporate actor, and not the individual, as the central actor in international politics. In a rationalist framework, this is not problematic as long as the corporate actor has a unitary will, a unitary behavior, and a degree of autonomy. These conditions are covered by the state-as-unitary-actor assumption commonly held by rationalist theories in International Relations.

Materialism. Rationalist institutionalism in IR conceptualizes the international environment as an anarchical and technical environment[2] characterized by the absence of hierarchical authority structures and by the predominance of material structures like the distribution of power and wealth. These material conditions are the most important explanatory factors for the processes and outcomes in international relations. The premise of materialism does not exclude that social norms or rules develop in the international system and effectively constrain states. After all, we are dealing with rationalist theories of international *institutions.*

[1] See, for instance, Baldwin (1993); Hasenclever, Mayer and Rittberger (1997: chs. 3 and 4). Whenever I use "rationalism" or "rationalist theories," I refer to the major rationalist approaches in International Relations (neorealism and neoliberalism), not to "rational choice" theories in general.

[2] The ideal-typical distinction of "technical" and "institutional" environments is taken from Scott (1991: 167).

According to this premise, however, such intersubjective structures are *not constitutive* for the international environment of the state actors (let alone for the state actors themselves). First, ideas and institutions are mostly treated as intervening variables between the material interests and the material environment of the actors, on the one hand, and the individual actions and collective outcomes, on the other. They provide constraints and incentives, not reasons, for action; they alter cost–benefit calculations, not identities and interests. Second, the establishment of normative institutions is itself explained as a result of material interests and rational action. Third, the effectiveness and stability of normative institutions ultimately depend on their utility for the actors. Compliance is a function of cost–benefit calculations.[3]

Egoism. Rationalist institutionalism in IR generally starts from the *homo oeconomicus* model. It assumes that actors act egoistically, that is, "the preferences of actors in world politics are based on their assessment of their own welfare, not that of others."[4]

Instrumentalism. Furthermore, in pursuing their self-interest, the actors behave instrumentally. They choose the behavioral option which promises to maximize their own welfare, or at least satisfy their selfish goals, under the given circumstances. The assumptions of egoism and instrumentalism combined meet the "rational actor" requirement as it is most widely used in rationalist approaches to the study of international institutions. Full, objective rationality is usually not regarded as a realistic assumption. Instead, most authors settle for some form of "bounded" or "subjective rationality" according to which actors do not have to be strict utility *maximizers* or to possess *full* information about the possible courses of action and their consequences or the capacity to process this information (see, e.g., Keohane 1984: 110–32; Zürn 1992: 78–92). However, rationalist approaches are "objectivist" in the sense that they do not pay systematic "attention to differences among individuals or biases in the way people think" (Jervis 1998: 976; cf. Hasenclever, Mayer and Rittberger 1997: 25–26).

These premises provide the theoretical foundation for the rationalist analysis of international organizations and their enlargement. In the rationalist account, *international organizations* are instrumental associations designed to help states pursue their own goals more efficiently (see, e.g., Koremenos, Lipson and Snidal 2001). According to Abbott and Snidal (1998), formal international organizations are attractive to

[3] See also Scott (1995) on the "regulative" conception of institutions.

[4] Keohane (1984: 66). To be sure, the assumption of egoism is no assumption of rational-choice theory as such (understood as a "thin theory"). It is most pertinent in economic theory and generally adopted in IR rationalism.

states because of two functional characteristics that reduce transaction costs: centralization and independence. International organizations render collective action more efficient, for instance, by providing stable negotiating fora, pooling activities, elaborating norms and acting as a neutral information provider, trustee, allocator or arbiter. Moreover, states pool and delegate authority to international organizations in order to "constrain and control one another" (Moravcsik 1998: 9). By removing the interpretation, implementation and enforcement of agreements from the reach of domestic oppositions and from the unilateral control of state governments, international organizations raise the visibility and the costs of non-compliance (Moravcsik 1998: 73–74).

Yet, rationalist IR theories generally do not regard international organizations as purposive and autonomous actors in international politics. They regard the states' concern for autonomy as too strong, and the power of international bureaucracy as too limited, for international organizations to represent anything but the *instruments of states*. Moreover, rationalist theories conceive international organizations as *clubs*, that is, *voluntary* groups "in the sense that members would not join (or remain in the club) unless a net gain resulted from membership" (Sandler and Tschirhart 1980: 1491). They assume that in an anarchical environment such as the international system, any cooperative institution must be self-enforcing on the basis of individual state interests (cf. Martin and Simmons 1998: 739). Finally, the club-theoretical assumption is also borne out by the decison-making procedures of international organizations which generally require a consensus on the admission of new members.

Although the enlargement of international organizations has not received much attention in rationalist theories of international institutions,[5] rationalist assumptions can easily be applied to this issue: decisions on membership in international organizations, then, are made according to criteria of instrumental rationality. They are based on the egoistic preferences of both members and candidates for membership, and they reflect the material conditions of the international system. Furthermore, the rationalist assumptions entail methodological guidelines for the formulation of hypotheses about enlargement. First, since rationalism is an individualist theory, hypotheses will be *actor-centric*. Second, since states are assumed to be the central and unitary actors in international politics, the appropriate *level of aggregation* is the *state*. By contrast, international

[5] See Bernauer (1995: 177) and Mattli (1995: 137) for this opinion (and as exceptions to this lack of attention).

organizations must not be treated as corporate actors with a unified political interest. Third, the assumption of rational states acting in a materially structured system and the rationalist indifference to actor-specific cognitions and individual as well as social meanings suggest an *objectivist* analysis – the telling of an "outside story" (Hollis and Smith 1990) – of enlargement decisions.

Club theory

The theory of clubs is the central rationalist approach to the problem of organizational size. It originated as a variation of the theory of public goods.[6] *Pure public goods* are defined by three characteristics: indivisibility, non-excludability and non-rivalry.[7] A good is indivisible if it cannot be consumed in parts; it is non-excludable if it is impossible or prohibitively costly for the provider to deny anyone the benefits associated with the good; it is non-rival "when a *unit* of the good can be consumed by one individual without detracting . . . from the consumption opportunities still available to others from that *same* unit" (Cornes and Sandler 1986: 6; cf. DeSerpa and Happel 1978: 100). Because of these characteristics, public goods create a high incentive for free-riding among rational actors. Therefore they are provided at suboptimal levels under market conditions. In order to correct this market failure, organizations are necessary.

Once an organization providing pure public goods is established, it is unproblematic to expand its size. As the good is non-rival, new members do not reduce the consumption opportunities of the incumbents. On the contrary, enlargement is usually desirable, first, because it is difficult to exclude non-member states from consuming the good in any case and, second, because as members these states would make at least a minimal contribution to the supply of the good or pay some fee for its consumption (Buchanan 1965: 2; Olson and Zeckhauser 1966: 274).

Pure public goods, however, are rare, and organizations that produce nothing but pure public goods are even more difficult to find. Real-world international organizations usually provide their members with *impure public goods* that are excludable as well as partially divisible and rival. As soon as impure public goods come into play, the size of membership becomes a major issue for the organization. On the one hand, additional members are a problem because they are not only additional contributors

[6] The seminal article is Buchanan (1965).
[7] Indivisibility and non-rivalry are often collapsed into one characteristic.

but also rival consumers. They cause crowding because the old members cannot use the public good as much or as often as before. On the other hand, however, the problem of size can be regulated thanks to excludability – formal membership being the exclusionary mechanism. Starting from the assumption of impure public goods, the theory of clubs seeks to determine the optimal size of organizations and to explain under which conditions they expand or reduce their membership.

A *club* is defined as a voluntary group deriving mutual benefit from sharing an impure public good.[8] This definition is held to fit most international organizations. NATO does not only provide (nuclear) deterrence to its members – which comes close to a pure public good – but also (conventional) defense. Conventional forces and weapons used for defense (or offense) are impure public goods which create divisible, rival, and excludable benefits (Russett 1970: 94–98; Sandler and Hartley 1999: 34–35). Conventional forces can be divided easily among allies, and those used to protect one particular alliance territory cannot be used at another border at the same time. If, because of enlargement, a larger border or area has to be protected, "conventional forces are subject to consumption rivalry in the form of force thinning" (Sandler and Hartley 1999: 34–35). Finally, states that do not contribute to common defense can easily be excluded from protection.[9]

In the European Union, tariff barriers and other legal boundaries are used to exclude states from the benefits of free trade and other economic freedoms. Moreover, EU market regulations as well as distributive and redistributive policies create divisible and rival benefits. The main policies are the Common Agricultural Policy (CAP) and the regional and structural policies which account together for about 80 percent of the budget. Thus, enlargement not only expands the internal market but also creates crowding costs because new members demand their share of the subsidies (see, e.g., Padoan 1997: 119–20).

Since the provision of impure public goods creates partial rivalry among the members of an organization, "the utility that an individual receives from its consumption depends upon the number of other persons with whom he must share its benefits" (Buchanan 1965: 3). Therefore, restrictions of membership size must be placed on clubs. Under which conditions do clubs enlarge their membership, then? The balance of costs and

[8] This definition is from Cornes and Sandler (1986: 7, 24–25). For an overview of club theory, see Sandler and Tschirhart (1980) and Cornes and Sandler (1986).

[9] Sandler, Loehr and Cauley (1978: 69) and Sandler and Hartley (1999: 35) further include private benefits such as the use of the jointly produced defense output for domestic order and national expansion. See Sandler's "joint product model" of alliances (1977). On NATO security goods and their behavioral incentives, see also Lepgold (1998).

benefits determines the choice.[10] According to Buchanan, for a given size of the club good, "the individual attains full equilibrium in club size only when the marginal benefits that he secures from having an additional member . . . are just equal to the marginal costs that he incurs from adding a member" (1965: 5). Since a club is a voluntary organization, this equilibrium condition applies to all members and candidates for membership individually. That is, for an international organization to expand, each member state must expect positive net benefits from enlargement in order to approve of expansion, and each state aspiring to membership must expect positive net benefits from joining the organization.[11]

It is Buchanan's achievement to have extended the analysis of public goods and their institutionalized provision from pure to impure public goods. His theory of clubs, however, is based on a number of simplifying assumptions. Briefly put, the "Buchanan club" operates without transaction costs, differentiates dichotomously between members and non-members and assumes homogeneous, non-strategic members and candidates (Sandler and Tschirhart 1980: 1483, 1487).

Transaction costs. Transaction costs consist of the decision-making and management costs that come with the establishment and the work of a club organization. These costs usually rise with the enlargement of an organization. First, the administrative workload of the organization increases, thus creating demand for more personnel. A higher number of international staff, in turn, requires more office space (in addition to that needed by the new member state's permanent delegation) and higher personnel costs. These factors raise the budgetary expenses of the organization. Second, communication and information exchange become more costly as membership expands. Efficient, direct face-to-face communication is increasingly replaced by more cumbersome, formalized procedures, and these formalized procedures become more time-consuming with each additional member that makes use of its right to speak or to table official documents. Moreover, documents and speeches have to

[10] More precisely, it is *marginal* costs and benefits, i.e., the costs and benefits of the last unit (member), that count. For the sake of simplicity, however, I will not write "marginal" each time I refer to these costs and benefits.

[11] This is also the basic idea behind the rare references to enlargement in the classical integration theories. Haas describes as "geographical spill-over" the development that outside states seek association or membership for "fear of isolation" or discrimination and in anticipation of benefits from a closer relationship to the regional organization (1968: 314–15; see also Schmitter 1969: 165). According to Deutsch, the desire to expand (or reduce) the size of a political community will "arise if a significant part of the population is coming to believe that major losses will follow from retaining the old size of their political community; or else if they come to expect major gains from adopting a new and larger one" (1970: 4).

be translated from and into further languages. In the EU, in particular, administrative costs rise disproportionately when additional official languages have to be interpreted and translated from and into all other official languages. In sum, the costs of communication and information exchange can be assumed to increase disproportionately with the expansion of membership.

Heterogeneity. In a homogeneous club, all club members have identical tastes or preferences and identical endowments (Cornes and Sandler 1986: 161). In reality, however, *heterogeneous* or *mixed clubs* are the rule. Any enlargement is likely to increase the heterogeneity of the membership because new national attitudes, traditions, institutions, and special interests become relevant for organizational policy-making. This is particularly true for Eastern enlargement as the CEECs bring with them the peculiar historical, political, economic, and social heritage and problems of their region. They have a comparatively low level of socioeconomic development and little experience with the capitalist market economy; they struggle with the problems of both economic and political transformation from a communist society; and they possess political traditions of authoritarianism and foreign domination. These characteristics distinguish them from the core of the old members and most of the newcomers of previous enlargement rounds (see, e.g., Huelshoff 1999: 63; Kreile 1997: 212–13).

Heterogeneity makes both the functioning and the analysis of clubs more difficult. First, heterogeneity increases decision-making costs. According to decision theory, "the costs of centralized decisions are likely to rise where more and more persons of differing tastes participate" (Sandler, Loehr and Cauley 1978: 69; cf. Nye 1971: 105–06). This theory also argues that "the addition of a new member will raise the costs of finding agreement in a *more than proportional* manner" (Fratianni and Pattison 1982: 252). Under the unanimity rule which is the most widespread decision rule in international organizations – it is the general rule in NATO and still applies to many important EU policies and all treaty revisions – enlargement will reduce the member states' capacity to reach decisions as increased heterogeneity will reduce the likelihood of consensus.[12] This capacity can be improved by moving from consensus to qualified majority voting as practiced in most EU policies connected to the internal market. However, even (qualified) majorities are more difficult to build in an enlarged organization because the number of potential blocking coalitions rises disproportionally (see Wilming 1995: 97).

[12] On the consequences of enlargement on control and capacity under different decision rules, see Kerremans (1998). If members were completely homogeneous, there would not be any capacity problem under the unanimity rule, since consensus would emerge naturally.

The joint-decision trap will be harder to evade; the opportunity costs of non-decisions will increase (see Scharpf 1985; Wilming 1995: 197). In addition, majority voting reduces the degree of control for each member state in an expanded EU, in particular that of the larger member states (see Kerremans 1998: 93; Raunio and Wiberg 1998).

Second, for a heterogeneous club to be in equilibrium, the membership charges or the fees for the utilization of the club good must vary according to the tastes (which will determine the utilization rate) and the endowments of the members. By contrast, in a homogeneous club, every member can contribute an equal amount to the club good (Sandler and Tschirhart 1980: 1491; Cornes and Sandler 1986: 182). Heterogeneity thus increases the costs of the club and its enlargement not only because decision-making becomes more difficult but also because either the distribution of membership charges has to be negotiated in view of the expected individual utilization rates, or the individual utilization rates have to be monitored and charged *post factum*. Similarly, Padoan argues that the higher the heterogeneity among members, the greater the asymmetric distribution effects and the greater the cohesion problems of the club. "Once the costs for cohesion management (i.e. the costs that must be borne to offset the asymmetry effects) exceed the benefits from integration the widening process will come to an end" (Padoan 1997: 109).

Finally, whereas the analysis of homogeneous clubs "can be carried out in terms of a representative member since everyone has the same identity" (Cornes and Sandler 1986: 161), the analysis of heterogeneous clubs must take diverging preferences and their distribution among the members into account. The introduction of both transaction costs and heterogeneity into the analysis of clubs leads to the common rationalist proposition that, *ceteris paribus, organizations with fewer members are preferable* to organizations with a higher number of members: "small is beautiful."

Other rationalist approaches support this hypothesis.[13] According to coalition theory, in order to avoid a diffusion of gains, "the players will form that grouping which is the smallest winning coalition, that contains just enough power to gain the decision, but no more than is necessary for the purpose" (Russett 1968: 286). Relatedly, the "marginal policy contribution" of an additional member "diminishes across all club sizes very rapidly beyond the initial few large countries" (Fratianni and Pattison 1982: 252). According to Mancur Olson's group theory, the likelihood

[13] These considerations are drawn from the economic theory of alliances and organizations. For a realist assertion of the virtue of small numbers in alliances, cf. Liska (1962: 27) and Waltz (1979).

of free-riding increases with group size so that "the larger the group, the farther it will fall short of providing an optimal amount of a collective good" (1971: 35; cf. Koremenos, Lipson, and Snidal 2001: 783). In sum, enlargement is seen to be subject to the law of diminishing returns to size: "Given that membership costs increase at an increasing rate, while membership benefits increase at a decreasing rate, there will be a finite optimal size of membership."[14]

Strategic action and bargaining. In the "Buchanan club," the members and candidates are considered to be non-strategic utility maximizers acting under (perfect) market conditions. In most regional international organizations, however, there is only a limited number of highly interdependent states whose actions affect each other directly and strongly. The number of potential candidates for membership in the regional environment of the organization is usually limited, too. Under these conditions, it is more plausible to assume, first, that the actors act *strategically,* i.e., in choosing their actions, they take into account the capabilities, preferences and strategies of other actors, and second, that the interaction outcome is a result of *bargaining.*[15]

How does bargaining affect enlargement decisions? If we assume heterogeneity, it is likely that individual member states incur losses as a result of enlargement, either in absolute terms or in comparison with other member states (relative losses). Under these circumstances, one of two conditions must be met lest enlargement be blocked. Either the winners fully *compensate* the losers through side payments and other concessions. (Of course, these concessions must not exceed the winners' benefits from enlargement and turn their cost–benefit balance from positive to negative.) Or the winners are able to *threaten* the losers credibly with exclusion (and the losses of exclusion exceed the losses of enlargement for the losers).

Whether the winners settle for compensation or issue threats depends on their bargaining power *vis-à-vis* the losers. The bargaining power of a state "is inversely proportional to the relative value that it places on an agreement compared to the outcome of its best alternative policy."[16] Let

[14] Sandler and Hartley (1999: 79). By contrast, Koremenos, Lipson and Snidal hypothesize that "inclusive membership increases with the severity of the distribution problem" (2001: 784–85). However, whereas an inclusive membership may indeed increase opportunities for trade-off, enlargement may also aggravate distribution problems depending on the nature of the issue and the characteristics of the new members. See the analysis of EU enlargement below.

[15] For the distinction of parametric and strategic action in neoliberal institutionalism, see, e.g., Milner (1998: 770–76) or Zürn (1992: 99–111). For a suggestion to introduce bargaining to economic studies of enlargement, see, e.g., Gylfason (1995: 53).

[16] Moravcsik (1998: 62). See his theoretical considerations on bargaining in the EC (1998: 60–67) and Snyder's similar analysis of alliance bargaining (1997: 74–77).

us assume the possible outcomes are: "enlargement," "no enlargement" (status quo), and a "new organization" excluding the losers. For the winners, enlargement is the best outcome; the losers prefer no enlargement. If the winners value "new organization" more highly than the status quo, they are able to issue credible threats of exclusion to the losers. These threats will be effective if the losers prefer enlargement to exclusion. Otherwise, if the winners prefer "no enlargement" to "new organization" or if the losers prefer "new organization" to "enlargement," the losers can successfully bargain for compensation or prevent enlargement altogether.

Variable relationships. In clubs, the variety of institutionalized relationships usually goes beyond the dichotomy of membership and non-membership. For instance, sports clubs often distinguish between "active" and "passive" members, the passive members being granted access to the social events of the club but not to its sports facilities. Differentiated membership reflects heterogeneous preferences and capabilities. For instance, "passive membership" is optimal for those members that are interested in the prestige of club membership or in meeting other members but not in consuming the club good. Partial membership, however, may also reflect asymmetrical bargaining power. Candidates will have to settle for a lower status if their interest in membership is considerably greater than the members' interest in admitting them.

In sum, a more realistic analysis of enlargement will not only have to take into account the characteristics of the goods provided by the organization and the balance between the crowding effects and the resource contributions of an expanded membership. It will also have to take into account increasing transaction or management costs, the heterogeneity of preferences and capabilities, their effects on the bargaining processes and outcomes among members and between members and non-members, and the variety of institutional solutions ranging from "no institutionalized relations" to "full membership."

Security, power or welfare: competing approaches to enlargement

Rationalist theories of international politics enter different costs and benefits into the club-theoretical equation or weight them differently. The major debate has taken place between neorealism and neoliberalism. More recently, realist theory developed into "defensive" and "offensive" variants (Frankel 1996b; Grieco 1997: 186–91). According to the most important goals that international actors are assumed to seek, these competing approaches can be termed the security approach (defensive realism), the power approach (offensive realism), and the welfare approach (neoliberalism). In this section, I present these approaches briefly and formulate the conditions under which (a) a state wants to become a member of a regional organization and (b) the regional organization is interested in enlargement.

The security approach

In his *Theory of International Politics* (1979), Kenneth Waltz formulated the core of neorealist thinking in International Relations. To this date, it remains the basic text of defensive realism and the security approach to enlargement. Waltz starts from the proposition that, "in anarchy, security is the highest end" (1979: 126). The security of a state is threatened if other states possess or are about to gain superior power. In this case, states will engage in balancing.

In general, states prefer to balance superior power by individual efforts to strengthen their national power base. Such *internal balancing* is most compatible with their interest in independence and autonomy (see Grieco 1997: 167–68, 170). Collective balancing reduces their freedom of action and entails the risk of long-term losses in autonomy and relative power. Moreover, internal balancing "is more reliable and precise" because "states are less likely to misjudge their relative strengths than they are to misjudge the strength and reliability of opposing coalitions" (Waltz 1979: 168).

Often, however, national efforts will not be sufficient. In this case, states take to *external balancing*, that is, they seek an alignment with other states against the superior state or coalition. When faced with a choice of alignments, balance-of-power theory predicts that states align with the weaker side:

> If states wished to maximize power, they would join the stronger side, and we would see not balances, but a world hegemony forged. This does not happen because balancing, not bandwagoning, is the behavior induced by the system. The first concern of states is not to maximize power but to maintain their positions in the system. (Waltz 1979: 126)

To be sure, even if states choose the weaker side for balancing purposes, they make sure that this alignment will not leave them less powerful, less secure or at greater risk than they were before, for the "weaker the ally *vis-à-vis* his adversary, the more one will have to contribute to his defense," and the "deeper his conflict with his adversary, the more likely he will be attacked or the greater the chance that, counting on one's support, he will precipitate a crisis or war himself" (Snyder 1990: 111).[17]

[17] See also Snyder (1984: 466–67) on the entrapment risk of the "secondary alliance dilemma."

These calculations also apply to "secondary powers." If "they are free to choose," they "flock to the weaker side; for it is the stronger side that threatens them. On the weaker side, they are both more appreciated and safer" (Waltz 1979: 127; cf. Liska 1962: 13). Although an alliance with the stronger side provides small countries with security against outside states, they risk being dominated or subjugated by their "protector." The only exception from balancing behavior that Waltz appears to concede is the case that the weaker coalition does not achieve "enough defensive or deterrent strength to dissuade adversaries from attacking" (1979: 127).

In order to come to terms with some of the anomalies which balance-of-power theory encounters in reality, Stephen Walt developed a *balance-of-threat theory* of alliances (1987; 1988). According to this theory, states seek allies to balance *threats*, not power. Whereas the overall capabilities emphasized by balance-of-power theory are an important ingredient of states' threat perceptions, alliance choices are determined by other factors as well: the higher not only a state's aggregate power, but also its geographical proximity, offensive capabilities and aggressiveness of perceived intentions, the stronger the tendency for a state to align with others to deter or defeat the threatening power (Walt 1987: 32). It is the factor of "perceived intentions" that makes the biggest difference to balance-of-power theory.[18] Although Walt expects "balancing behavior to be much more common than bandwagoning," he lists several conditions under which bandwagoning is probable (1987: 28–33).

The first condition is *weakness:* "In general, the weaker the state, the more likely it is to bandwagon rather than balance." This is because the weaker state is less able to add to the strength of a countercoalition, but will "incur the wrath of the more threatening states nonetheless" (Walt 1987: 29). Bandwagoning is also likely to occur if (sufficiently strong) *allies are not available.* This condition corresponds with Waltz's exception from the balancing rule. Both conditions are most convincing if they are combined. A weak state will balance against a threat if allies are available, which will effectively deter the threat or defend the weak state against aggression. It will choose to bandwagon, however, if it does not expect the available allies to be able to deter the threat or defend its territory. Thus, weak states may choose to bandwagon if, for instance, they are geographically so close to the threatening power that they would not survive its expansion in any case (Walt 1987: 31). In such a situation, only the perception that the threatening state or coalition cannot be accommodated

[18] Although Walt does not say clearly whether intentions outweigh capabilities in all instances, I will focus on this factor in order to stress the difference between both neorealist theories. In addition, note that, by emphasizing perceptions, Walt departs from the materialist foundations of neorealism (see Barnett 1996).

by bandwagoning will induce weak states to opt for balancing (Walt 1987: 33).

According to the security approach, enlargement will take place if it is necessary and efficient for both the non-member state (*S*) and the member states (*M*) of the organization (*O*) in order to balance the power or threat of another state or coalition of states (the rival *R*). The following specific conditions must be jointly present for a state to seek membership:

(1) *R* is (becoming) more powerful than *S* or threatens *S*.
(2) *S* is not capable of balancing the power or threat of *R* internally.
(3) *O* is less powerful or threatening than *R*.
(4) *O* is able to deter *R* from attacking *S* or to defend *S* effectively against an attack by *R*, or *R* is unalterably aggressive.
(5) The security benefits for *S* of membership in *O* are higher than those *S* would reap from any other relationship with *O*.[19]

In the case of the organization, we additionally have to take into account bargaining among member states and internal security costs and benefits.

(1) *R* is (becoming) more powerful than *O* or threatens *O*.
(2) *O* is not capable of balancing the power or threat of *R* on its own.
(3) *S* is less powerful or threatening than *R*.
(4) For each *M*, the accession of *S* enhances its net internal and external security, or those members that benefit from the membership of *S* possess the bargaining power or provide the compensation to make *M* agree to the accession of *S*.
(5) For each *M*, the security benefits of the membership of *S* are higher than those of any other relationship with *S*, or those members that benefit from membership more than from any other relationship with *S* possess the bargaining power or provide the compensation to make *M* agree to the accession of *S*.

The power approach

The balancing theories are based on the assumption that states are *defensive positionalists*. That is, they are primarily concerned with their own survival and security and therefore seek to prevent other states from increasing their relative capabilities (Grieco 1988: 498; 1990: 10; 1997: 167). Other ("offensive") realists do not share this assumption and postulate that states are *offensively positional* in general or under certain conditions.

[19] This condition refers to the point on "variable relationships" in the discussion of club theory.

Among offensive positionalists, bandwagoning and power-maximizing behavior is more common than defensive realists suggest.

Randall Schweller claims that the balancing proposition is not wrong but limited in scope. It omits a variable that is more fundamental than the balance of power or threat: the *balance of interests*. A state's balance of interests "refers to the costs [it] is willing to pay to defend its values relative to the costs it is willing to pay to extend its values." For satisfied states, the costs of value-extension are predominant. For revisionist states, however, they fall below the costs of value-defense. In Schweller's opinion, defensive realists view "the world solely through the lens of a satisfied, status-quo state" (1994: 85; cf. Schweller 1997: 929). Strong status-quo states ("lions") are defensive positionalists, indeed, whereas the exceptions from balancing behavior outlined by Walt hold for weak status-quo states ("lambs"). By contrast, rising revisionist powers ("wolves") are aggressors, and lesser revisionist states ("jackals") bandwagon with them "for profit," that is, in order to increase their power (Schweller 1994: 100).[20]

A different criticism of defensive positionalism is offered by realists like John Mearsheimer and Fareed Zakaria. In their view, states' interests invariably go beyond the defense of the status quo. States will, of course, balance defensively against threats and superior power, but they will not stop there. Instead, states seek to *maximize power* precisely in order to maximize security. According to Mearsheimer, "the greater the military advantage one state has over other states, the more secure it is. Every state would like to be the most formidable military power in the system because this is the best way to guarantee survival in a world that can be very dangerous" (1995: 11–12).

According to Zakaria, "the competitive imperative" of the international system and the state's predominant concern with survival produce "influence-maximizing" behavior "because anarchy and differentiated growth-rates ensure that 'survival' is never achieved and the state is never allowed to relax its efforts" (1995: 479, n. 43). It follows from this argument that not only revisionist states seek to maximize power. We would also expect unthreatened satisfied powers to take advantage of one another, increase their power, and strive for hegemony.

Benjamin Frankel reminds us, however, that "offensive realists do not argue that influence-maximization or power-maximization leads states to an ungovernable, maniacal pursuit of more and more power" (1996b: xviii). In particular, power maximization does not amount to maximizing the number of allies:

[20] The distinction between revisionist and status-quo states goes back to traditional realism (cf. Morgenthau 1973: chs. 2–3).

> In order to act "economically," alliance builders must not collect haphazardly all available allies and seek the most demanding commitments; they must consider the marginal utility of the last unit of commitment to a particular ally and the last unit of cost in implementing commitments. (Liska 1962: 27)

As instrumentally rational actors, states calculate the costs and benefits of each power-maximizing move and only pursue those that are efficient.

Offensive realists do not reject the balancing theories of defensive realism. They just regard them as too narrowly defined, because they assume that states do not only seek to join forces for *defensive* purposes. Rather, enlargement will also take place if it is necessary and efficient for both the non-member state and the organization in order to maximize their power. Therefore, the power approach does not contradict the conditions of the security approach but merely adds conditions under which even unthreatened states and organizations are interested in enlargement. The following conditions should be regarded as complementary to those of the security approach. For the outside state, these conditions are:

(1) *S* is not capable of increasing its power on its own.
(2) *O* is powerful enough to help *S* increase its power.
(3) The benefits for *S* of membership in *O* are higher than the benefits *S* would reap from any other relationship with *O*.

For the organization, the following conditions must be jointly present:

(1) *O* is not capable of increasing its power on its own.
(2) *S* is powerful enough to help *O* increase its power.
(3) For each *M*, the accession of *S* enhances its net internal and external power, or those members that benefit from the membership of *S* possess the bargaining power or provide the compensation to make *M* agree to the accession of *S*.
(4) For each *M*, the power benefits of the membership of *S* are higher than the benefits of any other relationship with *S*, or those members that benefit from membership more than from any other relationship with *S* possess the bargaining power or provide the compensation to make *M* agree to the accession of *S*.

The welfare approach

In the neoliberal perspective, the international system is not purely anarchical but increasingly characterized by *complex interdependence* as well (Keohane and Nye 1977). Due to increasing interdependence, states have become more sensitive to developments beyond their borders and, to achieve their goals, depend more strongly on international cooperation. Conversely, the effectiveness of military power has diminished. As a consequence, security and power are not the only and not even the main benefits that states seek by forming and expanding international organizations.

Instead of survival and security, states are concerned primarily with market failure; instead of maximizing power, or minimizing relative losses, they worry mostly about *achieving and maximizing absolute gains.* International institutions help them realize these gains by providing a remedy to market failure. As long as a state reaps net absolute gains from membership in international organizations or from their enlargement, it will prefer membership or enlargement to the status quo – even if other states achieve higher gains. If, as the welfare approach assumes, states need not worry about their survival and power losses, international organizations should be more likely to form, to persist and to expand than realism expects (see, e.g., Katzenstein, Keohane and Krasner 1998: 671–73).

The welfare approach resembles the power approach in its indifference toward third actors. Thus, the analysis can be limited to the properties of the members and the external state. Moreover, enlargement decisions are not dependent on the state's or the organization's inability to provide the desired good on its own. Efficiency is sufficient. Enlargement will take place if it is a cost-efficient means for both the non-member state and the member states of the organization, that is, if the gains from enlargement exceed the gains from any other form of relationship between the organization and the non-member state. Therefore, the list of conditions that have to be jointly fulfilled in order to explain a state's bid for membership is shorter than for the security or the power approach.

(1) The benefits for *S* of membership in *O* are higher than the costs.
(2) The benefits for *S* of membership in *O* are higher than the benefits *S* would reap from any other relationship with *O*.

The conditions for member states include bargaining:

(1) For each *M*, the benefits of the membership of *S* are higher than the costs, or those members that reap net benefits from the membership of *S* possess the bargaining power or provide the compensation to make *M* agree to the accession of *S*.
(2) For each *M*, the benefits of the membership of *S* are higher than the benefits of any other relationship with *S*, or those members that benefit more from membership than from any other relationship with *S* possess the bargaining power or provide the compensation to make *M* agree to the accession of *S*.

Generally, according to all rationalist approaches, the organization will expand if both the conditions for the state to seek membership and the conditions for the organization to admit the state as a new member are jointly fulfilled. However, once bargaining is taken into account, only one of the two sets of conditions must be true. If, on the one hand, a state that seeks to join the organization possesses the necessary bargaining power or the necessary resources to compensate the members for their losses, the organization will admit this state even if the internal process of interest aggregation worked against enlargement. On the other hand, if the organization possesses the necessary bargaining power or resources for compensation, it will be able to coerce or induce an unwilling external state to join.

Evaluating rationalist institutionalism

Any empirical analysis of the rationalist enlargement conditions is likely to become extremely complex. First, international organizations often are *multi-good clubs*. Second, under the assumption of *heterogeneity*, it is difficult to determine the actors' utilities theoretically and impossible to conduct the analysis in terms of a single, representative state. Third, *different kinds of costs and benefits* (e.g., transaction and crowding costs, financial benefits and power gains) have to be measured and compared. Fourth, the analysis has to take into account and compare *variable institutional relationships*. Ideally, we would have to measure, separately for each member and external state, for each club good and for different relationships between the organization and the external states, the value for each category of costs and benefits. These individual costs and benefits would then have to be compiled in order to find out whether the balance is positive for the members and the external states. Apart from the fact that this is already a highly complex operation, it does not even include the dynamics of bargaining. Moreover, most of the data concern *expected* costs and benefits, estimations of which are highly uncertain and often controversial. In addition, rational state actors also calculate the *reactions* of other states to their actions and the costs and benefits these reactions cause. Even if all items of the cost–benefit equation could be assessed and quantified with high certainty, they would still be hard to compare. The first issue is standardization – how do we, for instance, set off decision-making costs against financial contributions? The second issue is weighting – are some variables in the equation more important than others and, if so, by what factor?

Despite the precision suggested by the mathematical formulae put forward in club-theoretical analyses, these formidable empirical problems call for caution and modesty in applying club theory to enlargement decisions.[21] This modesty is not only justified for methodological reasons but also because it is unrealistic to assume that the political actors will base their decisions on such extremely complex cost–benefit assessments. I will therefore limit the analysis to a *qualitative* assessment of *major* costs and benefits and *refrain from any attempt at standardization and weighting.*[22] In order to further reduce the complexity of the analysis to manageable proportions and give rationalist institutionalism a fair chance to explain enlargement, I will take the following six analytical steps and decisions and apply the "principle of charity" wherever possible.

Theory selection. If a single approach produces a successful explanation, I count this as a confirmation of rationalist institutionalism as a whole. To arrive at a successful explanation, I will always use the most promising rationalist approach. On the other hand, whenever I argue that rationalist institutionalism fails to explain Eastern enlargement, I will apply all three competing approaches to show that the conditions of none of them were fulfilled.

Selection of club goods. As the Western regional organizations are generally multi-good clubs, I will limit the analysis to the most relevant goods – those that are listed as priority organizational goals in the constitutive treaties of the organization, have been the focus of the regulatory work of the organization, take up the highest share in the budget of the organization and in the contributions of the members and which require compulsory participation and implementation by the member states. In the case of NATO, therefore, the focus will be on nuclear deterrence and conventional defense; in the EU case, I will concentrate on the effects of enlargement on the internal market, on the one hand, and on the Common Agricultural Policy and structural funds, on the other.

Representative cost-benefit analysis. As a first step in the assessment of enlargement costs and benefits, I will treat the insiders and the CEE outsiders as two groups and estimate, for each of the most relevant club goods, whether the net benefits of enlargement are likely to be positive or not. In order to get around the problem of heterogeneity where divergent preferences or endowments are obvious, I will not only take a collective

[21] Good examples of detailed lists of costs and benefits involved in alliance decisions are Snyder (1997: 43–47) and Sandler and Hartley (1999: 60–88). Although Snyder makes an effort to arrange the costs and benefits in a formula, "No claim is made for empirical applicability" let alone quantification (1997: 47). Sandler and Hartley caution, "Given the wide range of costs estimates and the absence of benefit calculations, there is no way of knowing whether or not NATO expansion is an appropriate policy from an economic standpoint" (1999: 87).

[22] It may be, of course, that political actors use different simplifications and shortcuts and arrive at other conclusions.

perspective on these groups but also conduct the analysis in terms of the "easiest case": for the evaluation of the conditions for external states, I will choose the CEECs for which the net benefits of NATO and EU membership are most apparent. For the organizations, I will choose, first, the member state that would benefit most from Eastern enlargement and, second, the CEECs that would cause the least net costs if admitted to the organizations. This procedure is in accordance with the principle of charity. I will also follow this principle in the treatment of transaction or management costs: although these costs always rise with enlargement, I will disregard them if the balance for the provision and utilization of the relevant club goods is positive.

Heterogeneity and bargaining power. Even if the analysis under the assumption of homogeneity results in a successful explanation, it may not hold if heterogeneity, asymmetrical interdependence and unequal bargaining power come into play. I will, however, follow the principle of charity once again in disregarding these factors if the collective assessment of the enlargement conditions in steps (2) and (3) has resulted in a positive balance. If, on the other hand, the previous analysis has resulted in a negative or undetermined outcome, adding preference intensity and bargaining power may help to explain why enlargement took place nevertheless.

Institutional choice and candidate selection. After the overall assessment of whether a theory is able to explain Eastern enlargement in general, I will check whether it also accounts for the specific selection of new members or candidates for enlargement among the CEE outsiders and whether full membership is more efficient than intermediate forms of association.

Selection and interpretation of data. It is the goal of the analysis to explain the basic enlargement decisions of the EU and NATO in 1997. Therefore, I will focus on data that reflect the state of the organizations and the applicant states and the discussion of costs and benefits at that time. Moreover, whenever empirical results are not sufficiently clearcut to reject a theoretical statement, I interpret them in favor of the theory. Only obvious discrepancies between expectations and facts will count as a failure of the theory.[23]

[23] As a convenient by-product, this principle relieves me of the task of searching for high precision and going into detail whenever it is difficult to decide whether the theory's expectations are correct or not.

2 NATO enlargement

In this chapter, I analyze whether it was instrumentally rational for the CEECs to seek membership in NATO and for the NATO members to admit CEECs as full members to their alliance. If all states involved in the decision could expect to reap higher net benefits from the limited first round of enlargement than from other NATO–CEEC relationships, the rationalist explanation would be successful. I will argue, however, that rationalist institutionalism only succeeds in explaining the CEECs' bid to join NATO. It cannot account for NATO's enlargement decisions.

The CEECs and NATO membership

The security approach to enlargement, especially balance-of-threat theory, provides a largely convincing explanation of why the CEECs wanted to join NATO.

Russia was a potential threat to the CEECs. Although the Soviet Union ceased to exist, the Russian Federation has remained by far the most powerful country among the CEECs. It inherited most of the territory, population, and military forces of the Soviet Union and it is the only nuclear-weapon state and "great power" among the post-communist countries. Russia is not only more powerful than each individual CEEC but also poses a potential threat to them. An Eastern European state itself, Russia is located in the geographical proximity of the CEECs, and although Russia's offensive capabilities are not as high as those of the former Soviet Union, they remain considerable.

Although Central and Eastern European elites and societies generally did not fear an imminent resurgence of Russian power and aggressiveness, uncertainty about political developments in Russia and about future Russian intentions was pervasive. This uncertainty constituted the main ingredient to the perception of a Russian threat among the CEE elites and the most general motivation for their interest in NATO membership (see, e.g., Bedarff and Schürmann 1998: 114). Most CEE societies have had a long history of Russian rule, domination, or intervention. This traditional fear was kept alive by post-Soviet developments. Although the Russian Federation has respected the sovereignty of the former Soviet republics and Warsaw Pact member states and has abstained from outright military aggression beyond its borders, the Russian government has frequently expressed hegemonic aspirations and exerted more or less open pressure on its neighbors. The Russian military doctrine of 1993 defined the former Soviet republics, the "near abroad," as a zone of vital interest. The Russian government emphasized the protection of Russians living outside the Federation and the protection of the former Soviet external borders as major foreign policy goals. Russian troops were stationed in many successor states of the Soviet Union and play a Janus-faced role in their domestic and international conflicts. Although they often helped to stabilize the situation as peacekeeping forces, their presence has at the same time reinforced Russian influence.

Moreover, Russia's domestic political situation was a source of concern for the governments of the region. The attempted *coups d'état* of 1991 and 1993 as well as the electoral successes of left-wing and right-wing parties with openly neoimperalist programs demonstrated the frailty of Russia's democratization process and the unpredictability of its foreign policy.

The CEECs were not capable of internal balancing. Obviously, none of the CEECs possessed sufficient resources to balance Russian power. Although many of them were economically more advanced and more wealthy than Russia (on a per capita basis), none of them would have been able to develop military forces that could effectively deter Russia or defend the national territory against a Russian attack.

NATO was less threatening than Russia. Although NATO increased its relative power *vis-à-vis* Russia and was closer geographically to the Central European countries than Russia, it was not perceived as aggressive. In contrast to its Soviet counterpart in the East, US military hegemony in Western Europe had been benign and had excluded the use of force against allies. Therefore, it was reasonable for CEECs to balance a potential Russian threat by joining NATO – just as West European countries had flocked to the United States during the Cold War despite the fact that the Soviet Union had always been the weaker superpower.

NATO was able to deter Russia. The United States and NATO had proven throughout the Cold War that they were willing and able to deter the Soviet Union from attacking the members of the Western military organization or from undermining their autonomy otherwise. Given the even more favorable relations of military forces after the Cold War, this condition applied *a fortiori*.

The net benefits of membership for the CEECs were greater than those of any other form of relationship with NATO. First, by joining NATO as full members, the CEECs received a place under the US nuclear umbrella and the right to assistance by other members in the case of an armed attack (according to Article 5 of the North Atlantic Treaty). By contrast, in Partnership for Peace, NATO only promised to "*consult* with any active participant in the Partnership if that Partner perceives a direct threat to its territorial integrity, political independence, and security" (NATO 1994b: para 8, my emphasis). In addition, membership confers upon the CEECs the right to be represented in the North Atlantic Council, NATO's decision-making body, and in NATO's military command structure, and to fully participate in NATO intelligence processes.

On the other hand, the CEECs would be obliged to assist other NATO members in the case of attack. However, it was not only highly unlikely that NATO would be attacked, but the only country capable of threatening NATO in the treaty area was Russia. Therefore, the CEECs' individual interest in protecting their territory was hardly distinct from their obligation to protect the borders of NATO. In other words, they incurred virtually no entrapment risk. Second, CEE members would be urged to modernize and adjust their armed forces and military facilities to NATO standards. Studies on the cost of enlargement calculated that this upgrading would come to between US $10 and $42 billion to be paid mainly by the new members.[1] Yet by joining NATO, the CEECs acquired a degree of security that they could not provide on their own (given their non-nuclear status and their limited financial and personal resources) and that allowed them to spend less on defense than by relying exclusively on their own military.[2] Furthermore, NATO only demanded *interoperability* (NATO 1995: para 45) but did not set any concrete targets to be met by its new members in terms of quantitative or qualitative force levels. The Alliance expected them "to contribute their share" but "with a contribution level based, in a general way, on 'ability to pay'" (para 65).[3]

In sum, balance-of-threat theory explains the CEECs' interest in becoming NATO members as the only effective response to the potential or manifest Russian threat to their autonomy. Balance-of-threat theory,

[1] The lower figure stems from a Pentagon study, the higher figure from a study by the Congressional Budget Office (CBO). See Geipel (1999: 171).

[2] See the study of the Polish Euro-Atlantic Association quoted in Geipel (1999: 168). For Hungary, see "Budapest will auf die 'Überholspur'," *SZ* (*Süddeutsche Zeitung*), 14 June 1997.

[3] Note that the defense expenditures and capabilities of current NATO members also vary widely. Iceland has no armed forces at all; for the other member states, the estimated defense expenditures as percentage of GDP reached from 0.9 percent for Luxembourg to 5.7 percent for Turkey in 1999. See "Financial and Economic Data Relating to NATO Defence," NATO Press Release M-DPC-2(99)152, 2 December 1999.

however, has its limits. Up to this point, the CEECs have been treated as a homogeneous group. I have not taken into consideration that they were threatened by Russia to very different degrees or that not all of them were interested in NATO membership. Can balance-of-threat theory explain this variation? At first glance, it is puzzling that the most acutely threatened CIS countries, with Russian troops on their territory or with Russian involvement in their domestic or external conflicts, have at the same time been most reticent with regard to NATO membership, whereas many of the countries most interested in membership are situated beyond the "near abroad" and do not share borders with the Russian Federation. Walt's exceptions to balancing behavior, however, give a plausible account of this variation: the CIS countries may either have been under such strong Russian influence that they were not free to choose their military alignments, or they were so close to Russia and so far away from NATO that they did not expect effective NATO support in a crisis with Russia and preferred to adapt to a Russia that was not seen as unalterably aggressive.

This being granted, the puzzle does not disappear altogether. Take, for instance, the countries immediately bordering Russia in the West – the Baltic countries, Belarus and Ukraine. Although the objective Russian threat should have been equally high for all of these countries, their alignment policies could not have been more divergent. Whereas the Baltic countries strove to become NATO members, Belarus pursued a policy of reintegration with Russia, and Ukraine steered a middle of course of cooperation with NATO *and* Russia without openly bidding to join the Western organization before 2002.

In sum, even though balance-of-threat theory does not sufficiently account for the actual variation in CEE alignment policies, it explains why CEECs in general had an interest in NATO membership. Therefore, I take rationalist institutionalism to provide a satisfying explanation of the "demand side" of NATO enlargement.

NATO member states and Eastern enlargement

By contrast, the interest of NATO members in Eastern enlargement is difficult to account for by rationalist hypotheses. Whereas the security approach successfully explains why CEECs sought to become NATO members because of fear of a potential Russian threat, for the old members, enlargement was neither necessary nor efficient to increase their security, power, or welfare.

Russia neither threatened NATO, nor was it (becoming) more powerful than the Western alliance. For several reasons, the Russian threat to NATO was significantly reduced at the end of the Cold War.

The Warsaw Pact and the Soviet Union ceased to exist. As the main successor state to the Soviet Union, Russia inherited its nuclear forces but suffered a loss in territory, population, and allies.

The economic and political crisis in Russia strongly affected the military forces. Russia was not only unable to keep up with the "information revolution" in military technology, but the combat readiness of its armed forces and the morale of its troops decreased, too. Undoubtedly, the United States was by far the most powerful state – the only remaining superpower – and NATO by far the most powerful and effective military alliance in the international system.

Geographical distance between Russian and NATO forces increased. Whereas NATO and Warsaw Pact forces had formerly stood eye-to-eye at the inner German border and other East–West borders, the former western Soviet republics and Warsaw Pact members constituted a buffer zone of several hundred kilometers between NATO and the Russian Federation after the end of the Cold War.

Most importantly, the "aggressiveness of perceived intentions" was sharply reduced. Under the Yeltsin presidency of the 1990s, Russia was generally perceived as a country that had terminated the Soviet legacy of enmity to the West and sought a cooperative relationship including institutionalized relations with Western organizations. Already in its 1991 "Strategic Concept," NATO stated that "the threat of a simultaneous, full-scale attack on all of NATO's European fronts has effectively been removed" (NATO 1991a). Four years later, in its "Study on NATO Enlargement," the organization added, "Since then, the risk of a re-emergent large-scale military threat has further declined" (NATO 1995: §10).

Preclusion was not necessary at the time and would have required a different selection of new members. In the absence of an imminent threat, the security approach may still account for NATO enlargement as a policy of preclusion. According to the preclusion scenario, CEECs disappointed by Western rejection of their membership bids might join a different alliance, or Russia might regain strength in the future and return to its traditional hegemonic policy in Central and Eastern Europe. In that case, Eastern enlargement would either have deterred future Russian governments from a policy reversal or denied Russia the restoration of the former Soviet empire.

The first preclusion scenario is unrealistic because the CEECs would generally have preferred no alliance to renewing their security ties with Russia, and other alliances were simply not available to them. The second preclusion scenario is basically sound; its application to the case of NATO enlargement, however, meets with several problems and puzzles.

Even a reconstituted Soviet Union or Eastern pact would not be able to match NATO power and would not necessarily pose a threat to the West (see, e.g., Russett and Stam 1998: 367).

At any rate, there was no need to proceed with enlargement in the second half of the 1990s. There were no clear indications of Russian expansionism beyond the borders of the Russian Federation – in particular, Russia had kept its promises to withdraw its troops from the former Warsaw Pact member states and from the Baltic countries. It was not even clear whether Russia would ever return to its traditional ways (Reiter 2001: 46–47). Under these circumstances, a policy of preclusion could well have been delayed or used conditionally, that is, to signal to Russia that NATO was prepared to admit the CEECs if Russia exerted military pressure on them (see Brown 1995).

Christopher Ball argued that enlargement in the case of an actual threat might either come too late or exacerbate the situation (1998: 47–48). However, it was as likely that there would be considerable warning time before a revisionist policy would be in place and before Russia would have sufficiently strengthened its military capabilities to conduct a successful military campaign abroad (cf. Brown 1995: 36). Moreover, if Russia really was determined to expand militarily beyond its western borders, this would cause a crisis anyhow, and a firm commitment by a superior NATO to the protection of the CEECs might actually dampen it. Most importantly, defensive realists have generally held the opinion that premature enlargement may cause the disease it pretends to cure.[4] They feared that NATO enlargement would fuel Russian suspicions, strain the relationship between the West and Russia, urge Russia to pursue a stronger reintegration of the former Soviet Union under its leadership and to align itself with China, and thereby provoke the threat it was intended to prevent.

Finally, assuming that preclusion was the main objective of enlargement, it is difficult to understand the selection of new members. If the window of opportunity had really been so small that immediate action was required, NATO should either have completed enlargement in a single round or should have focused on Ukraine and the Baltic countries, the countries bordering on Russia and the main objects of Russian revisionism (cf. Mandelbaum 1995: 10). Instead, the first wave of expansion only included countries that could still have joined NATO *after* a potential manifestation of Russian expansionism in the former Soviet republics.

[4] See Brown (1995); Calleo (1998: 29); Gaddis (1998: 147); Reiter (2001: 48); Walt (1997: 173) and his general criticism of US postwar foreign policy in Walt (1988: 315).

In sum, neither the timing nor the scope of enlargement fits the preclusion hypothesis. Alvin Rubinstein aptly sums up the defensive realist case against NATO enlargement:

> Stripped of most of its former empire, severely weakened, increasingly ignored in key regional gatherings, and undergoing systemic decline, Russia has no prospects of regaining the commanding position it held in Central and Eastern Europe less than a decade ago. In sum, no threat to the structure of power that serves the NATO community exists, and it is difficult to imagine any strategic principle or concern so mighty as to justify jeopardizing the future of this irenic environment. (1998: 43–44)

Therefore, the search for a rationalist explanation of NATO enlargement must continue with the power approach.

NATO is able to increase its power on its own; the CEECs rather dilute it. NATO member states have not only gained in power as a result of the Soviet Union's collapse and Russia's decline. They also possess the economic resources and the technological capabilities to further increase their power without the assistance of outside states. Even if we assumed that NATO was interested in admitting additional members in order to increase its power, the CEECs would not have been a rational choice.

Of course, the new members increased the absolute power resources of NATO in terms of population, territory, economic output, and defense capabilities. Growth, however, was small. Taken together, the three new members increased the total population of NATO members by 8.3 percent but only added 2.1 percent of territory, 1.3 percent of GDP and around 1 percent of defense expenditures to the NATO power base. Their GDP per capita was around ten times lower than the NATO average and hardly matched that of Turkey, the poorest NATO member.[5] Moreover, the armed forces of the new members were in a poor state according to internal NATO reports.[6] Bringing them up to NATO standards would either take a long time given the limited financial resources of the new members or require the old members to invest the approximately

[5] Own calculation based on "Financial and Economic Data Relating to NATO Defence," NATO Press Release M-DPC-2(01)156, 18 December 2001 (1999 data for defense expenditures and GDP per capita); *CIA World Factbook* 1999 and 2001 (data for territory, population and defense expenditures); World Bank "World Development Indicators" (GDP at current market prices for 1998).

[6] See, for example, "NATO Concerned About Polish Military," *RFE/RL Newsline*, 20 January 1998, referring to a report from NATO headquarters. See also a 1997 RAND Corporation report judging Poland's army "a large force of low quality, in both readiness and modernness" (quoted according to Clemens 1999: 147). Note that Poland's military capacity is generally held to compare favorably with that of the Czech Republic and Hungary.

US $34 billion needed for that purpose.[7] Even interoperability was difficult to achieve in the short term. According to Klaus Naumann, chairman of the Military Committee at the time of the decision to enlarge NATO, "it will take perhaps up to ten years to fully integrate new members and achieve full inter-operability from a military perspective which does not include programmes to replace existing hardware by modern western equipment" (1997: 10).

Finally, even if NATO had really considered the small marginal benefits in absolute power resources and the comparatively poor military and economic state of the new members a step toward power-maximization, it is puzzling why the Western alliance opted for a limited enlargement and did not admit all CEECs desiring to become NATO members at once. In particular, it is unclear why it decided, in 1997, against the admission of Romania – bigger and more populated than the Czech Republic and Hungary together – and Slovenia, the CEEC with the highest GDP per capita.

In sum, NATO did not need the CEECs to increase its power. This fact alone severely weakens the power approach. Moreover, at least in the medium term, admitting the CEECs did more to dilute than to strengthen the resources and the effectiveness of NATO's collective defense. Thus, Eastern enlargement did not meet the realist supply-side conditions because it was neither necessary to increase security nor efficient to increase the power of NATO member states. Did it then provide net absolute benefits to NATO members, as required by the welfare approach? In order to meet this condition, Eastern enlargement would have had to produce either the same amount of security at a lower cost or greater security at a cost below the security benefits. Neither was the case.

Eastern enlargement did not produce net security benefits for NATO members as a whole. Crowding costs were to be expected from spatial rivalry and entrapment risks. As far as spatial rivalry is concerned, the inclusion of the Czech Republic and, above all, Poland lengthened the "Eastern front" of NATO. Hungary did not even share a single border with any other NATO country. As a result, NATO incurred, albeit rather modest, thinning costs from enlargement (Sandler and Hartley 1999: 72–73). Moreover, NATO benefited from a buffer zone of comparatively stable CEECs between its member states, on the one hand, and Russia and the Yugoslav crisis area, on the other. With enlargement, this buffer zone was

[7] This figure stems from the Cato Institute study prepared by Eland (1997) and represents the costs of upgrading to be paid by the new member states. This study is based on a more demanding upgrading of the new member states' military capabilities than other studies. For this reason, however, it is more in line with the power approach. Cf. Kay (1998: 117–18).

gone: Poland bordered on Russia's Kaliningrad enclave, and Hungary bordered on Yugoslavia. Instead, entrapment risks increased. The new members would be among the first to be affected by a renewed Russian expansionism or a spill-over of the Yugoslav crisis and, therefore, the first and the most likely to use the collective goods of deterrence and defense. It is true that Eastern enlargement provided NATO with forward-basing options and a better geographic position for its out-of-area operations in the Balkans (see Clemens 1999: 141). Yet these operations were neither core activities of NATO nor essential to the member states' own security. By contrast, a military threat to, or an armed attack on, a new member would be an Article 5 issue. Moreover, NATO could as well have used military bases in non-member states, as it did in Hungary before enlargement (Clemens 1999: 142).

The spatial rivalry and the entrapment risks will not be balanced by higher than average contributions of the new members. Contributions to NATO's civil and military budgets as well as special programs are generally based on "ability to pay" and roughly correspond to the economic capacity of member states. Since the economic capacity of the new member states is at the low extreme of NATO members, their contributions are small as well. The same is true for their contribution to the military power of NATO (see earlier discussion). Moreover, their economies and their state budgets do not allow for major military investments that would, over time, close the gap between their above-average likelihood of using the club goods and their below-average contributions to NATO's budgets and military forces.[8]

Rather, *enlargement was bound to cause additional costs for the old members.* These costs can be divided into three categories (Geipel 1999: 170): direct costs, upgrading costs and power projection costs.

Direct enlargement costs comprise all expenses necessary to adapt NATO's headquarters and staff as well as the common infrastructure (including C^3I systems and air defenses) to the greater number of member states and to build basic reception capacities in the new member countries to permit reinforcement in the case of crisis. According to NATO projections, these direct costs were estimated to amount to US $1.5 billion over ten years, whereas other studies calculated $10–11 billion (Geipel 1999: 171; Kay 1998: 117; Sandler and Hartley 1999: 71).

Upgrading costs concern the military forces of the new member states. NATO did not list these costs due to its October 1997 decision that,

[8] According to "Financial and Economic Data Relating to NATO Defence," NATO Press Release M-DPC-2(2000)107, 5 December 2000, the NATO average was 2.6 percent in 1999, whereas the figures for the CEECs were 2.2 percent for the Czech Republic, 2.0 percent for Poland and only 1.6 percent for Hungary.

for the most part, the new members would have to bear the costs of force modernization themselves. Critics pointed out, however, that the old member states would have to take over a share of these costs through bilateral loans and subsidies (see, e.g., Kay 1998: 117; Rubinstein 1998: 39). In fact, the US government alone authorized $1.2 billion in loans and grants in connection with NATO enlargement for the 1996–98 period (Granville 1999: 169).

The final category of costs affects the old member states directly. They include the means necessary to provide effective defense to the new members. Estimated costs reached from US $8 billion for minimal adjustments to $55 billion for a full forward presence of NATO forces. Again, NATO estimates did not include this category of costs because the alliance started from the assumption that such forward presence was not necessary in the absence of any imminent threat to the new member states (Geipel 1999: 171).

In general, the different cost estimates reflected different *a priori* positions on the desirability of enlargement and served to support the arguments of the proponents and opponents of enlargement. Yet, even the CBO study that fueled the debate with the highest estimates ($125 billion) acknowledged that, in the present benign security environment, "NATO can spend as much or as little as it likes to undertake expansion" (Geipel 1999: 163). Nevertheless, even under the best-case assumptions, the direct costs could not be avoided if NATO was to continue to operate as an effective alliance.

In sum, then, NATO members as a collective did not reap net benefits from Eastern enlargement. In addition to rising transaction and management costs, they incurred direct enlargement costs, force thinning costs and entrapment risks that were not balanced by the new members' contributions to NATO budgets and programs and to NATO's military capabilities.

The next question then is whether differences in individual member states' cost-benefit calculations and bargaining power explain NATO's decision to enlarge. There are two ways to approach an answer to the above question. The first approach is to look for states with net enlargement benefits and to ask whether these states possessed the bargaining power necessary to induce the other states to agree to enlargement. The second approach is to look for states that possess superior bargaining power and then to ask whether they had an egoistic interest in enlargement. Again, I argue that neither is the case.

As shown earlier, *the CEECs* generally benefit from membership in NATO. However, they *did not possess the material power to bargain their way into the Alliance.*

They had no credible alternative alliance options. A renewal of the Warsaw Pact would have harmed NATO but was beyond the set of acceptable outcomes for almost all CEECs. An alliance among the CEECs would have been feasible in principle but would have been a second-best alternative for all CEECs and difficult to bring about given the collective action problems among them. Above all, it would not have harmed NATO.

They could not credibly threaten the alliance with costs of non-enlargement that would have exceeded the costs of enlargement. Obviously, the CEECs did not possess the "positive power" to coerce NATO into enlargement. Alternatively, one might consider the argument that they had the"negative power" to threaten to disrupt NATO members' stability or security with the spill-over of domestic instability and civil as well as interstate wars in the CEE region, e.g., in the form of mass migration, terrorism or organized crime. Yet, "self-inflicted chaos" is no credible bargaining strategy for governments and state elites whose political power depended on the stability of their states and the success of transformation. It would not have been rational for them to lead their countries into domestic crisis and interstate war, and thereby to jeopardize their own political power, in order to get into NATO.

Most importantly, however, there is no evidence that negative "chaos power" has done anything to change NATO's cost-benefit calculations. First, NATO countries have been able to protect themselves effectively from the consequences of the wars in the former Yugoslavia. They were able to keep the refugee problem in manageable proportions. They were neither threatened militarily nor drawn into the wars by any of the participants. When they intervened militarily in Bosnia and Kosovo, it was not for collective defense but after long hesitation and for humanitarian and collective security reasons. Second, those states with high domestic instability (see Albania) or irredentist foreign policies (see Croatia under Tudjman) did not improve their odds of joining NATO (despite their strong desire to become members) but lost any chance to be considered as serious candidates.

The second category of states to look at are member states with a self-interest in Eastern enlargement. The one major member state that may fit this category is Germany. In the literature, a *German self-interest in NATO enlargement* is commonly attributed to its geographical position at the eastern border of NATO and the western border of Poland and the Czech Republic.[9] This location gives rise to both positive and negative interdependence.

[9] See, e.g., Kamp and Weilemann (1997: 1, 4); Schmidt (1996: 213, 219); Wolf (1996: 199).

First, Germany is the most important economic partner of the CEECs in trade and direct investments. In 1995, German–CEEC trade accounted for 52 percent of total EU–CEEC trade. In the 1990–95 period, Germany's share of foreign direct investment in the region was 19 percent, followed by the United States with 14 percent.[10] Furthermore, the CEECs have gained in importance for the German economy since the end of the Cold War. At the time of the enlargement decision, they accounted for about 10 percent of German foreign trade, the highest share among the major NATO member states. Against this background, NATO enlargement can be interpreted both as a means to protect German economic assets in the CEECs and as a way to increase German influence in NATO by bringing in "client" countries.

Second, due to its borderline position, Germany would be adversely affected by crises in the Central and Eastern European region to a higher degree than other member states. For this reason, Germany has borne the greatest share of bilateral, official aid to the CEECs – 17 percent for the 1990–96 period, followed by the United States (11 percent) and by France and Japan (7 percent each).[11] In this respect, NATO enlargement was useful for Germany to stabilize its Eastern glacis, to free itself of its frontline position in NATO and to distribute the stabilization costs for the CEECs more equitably among NATO members.

In order to determine whether Germany was self-interested in NATO enlargement, these benefits of enlargement have to be set off against the costs. Besides the transaction and crowding costs that all members have to bear, Germany had to be particularly concerned about the Russian reaction to enlargement given its position at the Eastern border of NATO and its important economic links to Russia (Wolf 1996: 200).

Even if we assume that Germany could expect to reap net benefits of NATO enlargement, *Germany did not possess the bargaining power necessary to make NATO agree to enlargement.* Although the specter of German unilateralism in Central and Eastern Europe played a certain role in the debate on NATO enlargement,[12] Germany could not credibly threaten the other NATO members with alternatives to NATO if they rejected enlargement. On the one hand, in a German–CEEC alignment Germany would have been without nuclear deterrence. Under these circumstances, Germany would have been less secure than within NATO and less able

[10] *Business Week*, 3 February 1997, 16. Belarus, Russia and Ukraine are not included in these calculations.

[11] *Business Week*, 3 February 1997, 16. The figures comprise bilateral loans, guarantees, and grants.

[12] See, e.g., Henry Kissinger, "Expand NATO Now," *Washington Post*, 19 December 1994, 27.

to compete with Russia over influence in Central and Eastern Europe. In addition, Germany's interest in stable relations with its Western partners was paramount to any interest in the CEECs. On the other hand, the CEECs would have been reluctant to align with Germany both for traditional fear of German dominance and because a non-nuclear Germany could not give them effective protection against Russia. Correspondingly, there is no evidence of Germany playing the card of unilateralism and of threatening the other NATO members to act on its own.

The final possibility for an explanation of NATO enlargement based on differential bargaining power is US interest. It is certainly plausible to argue that US bargaining power in NATO would have been strong enough to get the other NATO member states to agree to enlargement. Yet, *it is difficult to see the vital material interests that could have motivated the United States to use its bargaining power* in the absence of a need to prevent Russian dominance in the region. America is not only geographically far removed from Central and Eastern Europe but also little involved in the economies of this region. In 1995, trade with the CEECs (excluding Russia) accounted for less than 0.5 percent of US exports and imports. This share was lower than exports to and imports from the Russian Federation.[13] Finally, US security is much more dependent on the nuclear than on any conventional, land-based military threat. Correspondingly, nuclear arms control with Russia was more important than an additional, territorial glacis in Central Europe. Thus, if anything, the United States should have been less interested in enlargement for security or economic reasons than its European allies. To be sure, the United States *was* the main driving force behind NATO enlargement but this fact cannot be explained by the security, welfare, or power motives that realist or neoliberal theories ascribe to state actors. According to Kenneth Waltz, "the error of realist predictions" on NATO's enlargement "arose not from a failure of realist theory to comprehend international politics, but from an underestimation of America's folly" (2001: 34).

Conclusion

NATO Eastern enlargement is a puzzle for the rationalist approaches to enlargement. Whereas rationalism explains the CEECs' interest in joining NATO, it is unable to account for NATO's enlargement decisions. First, rather than facing a military threat or the growing power of an adversary in Europe, NATO enjoyed a higher degree of security and relative power

[13] Own calculation based on US government information, available at http://govinfo.kerr.orst.edu/impexp.html (28 July 2000).

than at any time before. Second, a preclusive enlargement to the three new Central European members was not only ill-timed and counterproductive but also focused on the wrong countries. Third, the new members diluted rather than strengthened NATO's military power and effectiveness; they increased the security risks and alliance costs of the old members. Finally, the country that was the most likely to have a self-interest in enlargement – Germany – did not have the bargaining power to impose enlargement, and the one country that would have had the bargaining power – the United States – did not stand to reap tangible security or economic benefits from enlargement.

Even the final rationalist enlargement condition was absent: Partnership for Peace was an alternative institutional form for NATO–CEEC relations that was likely to produce a higher net benefit than full CEEC membership. PfP allowed NATO to cooperate with the CEECs on security problems, consult with them in case of an imminent military threat, exert a stabilizing influence on the region, and draw on the CEECs' military resources for peacekeeping missions without extending a security guarantee to the CEECs, diluting the efficiency of alliance decision-making, incurring enlargement costs and risking tensions with Russia. To devise a "policy [that was] sufficiently flexible to adapt to on-going change" in "Europe's uncertain strategic landscape" and would not "draw new dividing lines" was the central premise behind the original PfP proposal, according to one of its proponents (Kupchan 1994: 10–11). And it is small wonder that scholars starting from rationalist assumptions arrived at the conclusion that PfP was "preferable to expanding NATO" (Walt 1997: 179, n. 55) and constituted the more "efficient institutional solution" (Bernauer 1995: 186–87) for NATO–CEEC relations.

By and large, this analysis also applies to the secound round of NATO enlargement. When NATO leaders, at their summit in June 2001, announced that the alliance would issue further invitations to membership at its Prague summit in November 2002, the basic parameters had not changed in favor of expansion.[14] First, NATO did not face a new military threat. The European security environment had improved rather than worsened after the Milošević regime had lost power and the situation in Kosovo and Macedonia was under control. Second, whereas the Baltic states were more sensible choices for a preclusive enlargement than the first new members, the actual need for preclusion was as low as for the first round. Third, the candidates for the second round were, on average, even poorer (except Slovenia) and smaller (except Romania) than

[14] Note that the decision in favor of a second round of enlargement was not a reaction to the 9/11/2001 terrorist attack on the United States and thus cannot be explained by the new military situation it created.

those of the first round. According to Philip Gordon of the Brookings Institution:

> Neither in quality nor quantity will the MAP states, collectively or individually, make a substantive difference in NATO's military potential. Their accession to NATO in the near-term would make the problem of interoperability and compatibility among the alliance's forces more acute, since it will enlarge the group of NATO countries within NATO that cannot meet the high levels of combat potential of the United States and a few other major allies.[15]

On the other hand, the second round would further lengthen the "Eastern front" of NATO and, with the inclusion of the Baltic countries, move the alliance into former Soviet territory and closer to the Russian Federation which, at the time, remained as opposed to NATO enlargement as before. In addition, the admission of seven new members would increase transaction and management costs to a greater extent than the first round (cf. Goldgeier 2002).

[15] "Testimony on Future of NATO and NATO Enlargement," The House International Affairs Committee, Subcommittee on Europe, 17 April 2002. See also Goldgeier (2002).

3 EU enlargement

As in the case of NATO enlargement, rationalist institutionalism accounts for the CEECs' desire to join the European Union but cannot explain why the EU members decided to start accession negotiations with the associated CEECs.

The CEECs and EU membership

The welfare approach to enlargement offers a largely convincing explanation of why the CEECs wanted to join the European Union.

The CEECs will reap net welfare benefits from membership in the EU. In general, the economies of the CEE candidates for EU membership will benefit both from integration into the Community market and from the redistributive policies of the EU.

(a) *The economies of the CEECs will grow as a result of accession.* In their study of the benefits of EU accession for the CEECs, Baldwin, François and Portes (1997: 138) come to the conclusion that the GDP of the CEECs will grow by approximately 1.5 percent as a result of the elimination of tariffs, the adoption of the EU common tariff and unrestricted access to the single market. If it is further assumed that membership in the EU will considerably reduce the risk of investments in the CEECs and thus help to attract foreign capital, the study even arrives at an 18.8 percent increase in real income for the CEECs (1997: 147). Although much less optimistic, the more recent enlargement study by the French Commissariat du Plan, which is based on a review of other studies, still comes to the conclusion that the growth effect of enlargement will be about 5–6.5 percent annually.[1]

Other authors are more sceptical. First, the economic gains are contingent on the use of correct policies by the new members (Rodrik in

[1] Cited according to *Le Monde*, 27 April 1999, 4. See also Bach, Frandsen and Jensen (2000: 175) who estimated a welfare improvement of 4.6 percent from integration in the CAP alone.

Baldwin, François and Portes 1997: 170). The growth effects of membership on the economies of states that joined the EU in earlier enlargement rounds were quite diverse (Dauderstädt 1998: 157). Second, trade liberalization will lead to a loss in state income from tariffs. In addition, it may result in stronger competitive pressure for the CEE economies and a higher trade deficit. Except for agriculture, export chances for Central and Eastern European goods will not rise significantly despite unrestricted market access. Rather, CEE economies will be forced to focus on their comparative advantages in labor-intensive and raw-material-intensive products instead of developing high-tech capabilities (Dauderstädt 1998: 151–52, 158). Third, a higher inflow of foreign capital and direct investments may result in balance-of-payments deficits and a revaluation of the local currencies. This would harm the competitiveness and export chances of CEE producers. Fourth, EU membership will increase pressure to adjust wages toward EU levels, thereby further undermining the comparative advantage of the CEE economies (Dauderstädt 1998: 158). Finally, the study by Baldwin and others does not pay attention to sectoral effects, the differentiation between enlargement losers and winners in the CEECs, and the political pressure that well-organized groups of losers may exert. EU membership may well fail to reduce, or might even increase, unemployment in the CEECs (see, e.g., Burda 1998).

(b) *All CEE members will become net recipients in the European Union.* Their wealth is well below EU average. In 1997, the average GDP per capita of the ten associated CEECs was at 40 percent of the member states. Even the wealthiest candidate country, Slovenia, attained only 68 percent of the EU average which was about the level of Greece, the poorest member state (69 percent). Bulgaria, Latvia and Lithuania were at 30 percent and less of the EU average.[2] In addition, the CEECs possess an agricultural sector that is, on average, two and a half times larger than that of the EU member countries (Baldwin 1995a: 32; Hyde-Price 1996: 203). The average agricultural share of total employment in the CEEC-10 is about four times as high as the EU average (22.5 percent as compared to 5.3 percent in 1995; Welfens 1999: 9–10). As a result, the CEECs will be entitled to high transfers under the CAP and the structural funds while contributing comparatively little to the Community budget.

Michael Dauderstädt cautions, however, that problems of absorption and providing matching funds may limit the actual transfers from the

[2] *FAZ* (*Frankfurter Allgemeine Zeitung*), 18 September 1998, 29 according to Eurostat. The basis of comparison is purchasing power parities at current prices.

Community budget to the new members. Bringing their economies up to EU environmental standards will cost the CEECs up to ECU 120 billion.[3] Moreover, the total costs of implementing the *acquis* are substantial and are estimated to go beyond the GDP of one year (1998: 152, 154).

Thus, even if autonomy costs are disregarded, the cost-benefit balance of EU accession for the CEECs is not unambiguously positive. However, most of the costs are a consequence of the region's general integration into the world market and its strong dependency on the EU. The EU share of the foreign trade of the former CMEA members was around 60 percent in 1997.[4] In the first half of 1998, Hungary even sold 72 percent of its exports to the EU.[5] Therefore, these costs will arise regardless of whether the CEECs join the EU or not. They have to follow EU rules if they want to export to their dominant export market; they have incurred trade deficits with the EU ever since the beginning of the 1990s; and they have specialized in labor-intensive and natural-resource-intensive products in any case.[6] If the CEECs do not have a choice but to adjust institutionally and economically, they may as well opt for membership and benefit from the EC funds, further gains from trade liberalization and a greater attractiveness for foreign capital.

This analysis is also reflected in the elite and public opinion of the CEECs. Although the CEE societies have become more aware and realistic concerning the risks and hardships of EU integration, there is still the expectation that it will be economically beneficial. Above all, however, EU membership is seen as necessary and inevitable (see, e.g., Fink Hafner 1999: 793–95; Kucia 1999).

The benefits of membership are higher than those of association. Generally, it is a problem of the Baldwin *et al.* study (1997) that it takes 1992 as the base year and does not offer a prognosis based on the continuation of the association regime. It is therefore difficult to gauge the *marginal* effect of full membership on the CEE economies. Critics have further pointed out that the CEECs could reap many of the benefits ascribed to EU membership under the conditions of association as well (see, e.g., Székely in Baldwin, François and Portes 1997: 173). They could lower their tariffs independently and institutionalize sound macroeconomic policies (e.g., by establishing currency boards as in the example of Bulgaria). Even Baldwin (1995b: 480) acknowledges, "An EEA-like arrangement that

[3] Jovanovic (1999: 483), quoting *European Voice*, 24 September 1998, 15. Environment commissioner Margot Wallström puts the figure at Euro 80–110 billion for the ten acceding countries (*EU Observer*, 22 January 2003).

[4] UN ECE, *Economic Survey of Europe 1999/1*, 145.

[5] UN ECE, *Economic Survey of Europe 1998/3*, 77.

[6] UN ECE, *Economic Survey of Europe 1998/1*, 133; *1998/3*, 76 and 89.

extended the Single Market eastward would permit the CEECs to secure most of the economic benefits of membership."

There are, however, important benefits that the CEECs could not reap as non-members. First, they would not be eligible to participate in the CAP and the structural policies of the EU. Second, they would continue to suffer from, or at least be under the constant threat of, EU anti-dumping measures, import restrictions (on agricultural products, steel and textiles where they are most competitive), and restrictions on the movement of labor, as they do under the Europe Agreements (cf. Jovanovic 1999: 478; Kawecka-Wyrzykowska 1996: 85–87). Third, EU membership makes the commitment to macroeconomic stability and trade liberalization more credible to investors than unilateral policies. Finally, in an overall assessment, the study of the Commissariat du Plan comes to the conclusion that the gains from full membership will be twelve times higher than the eventual benefits of simple association.[7]

In sum, although the welfare-based cost-benefit analysis does not produce a completely unambiguous result in favor of EU accession, it is plausible enough to conclude that rationalist institutionalism is able to explain why the CEECs want to join the EU.

The EU and Eastern enlargement

By contrast, rationalist approaches to enlargement ultimately fail to explain why the EU decided to start accession negotiations with the CEE candidates. First, Eastern enlargement does not produce net benefits for the EU. Second, member states that might profit from enlargement do not possess the bargaining power to make the other members agree to enlargement, and third, association would have been a more efficient institutional arrangement than enlargement. I start with the security and power approaches to enlargement and conclude with the welfare approach.

In contrast to NATO, which emerged from the Cold War uncontested and unthreatened, the EU had reasons to defend and improve its position in the international system. So the security approach is potentially able to contribute to the explanation of EU enlargement. Although the EU is one of the most powerful actors in the international economy, it is neither the leading nor an unchallenged economic alliance. The main defensive realist argument for enlargement is the one that Joseph Grieco put forward with regard to the Community's internal market and monetary union projects:

[7] *Le Monde*, 27 April 1999, 4.

[N]eorealists might argue that . . . the European nations, concerned not about their immediate security but as a matter of paying prudent attention to their relative position in the world economy, elected in the mid- to late 1980s to revive the EC in order to counter the continuing economic challenge of the United States, and especially the new and even more acute challenge of Japan. (Grieco 1996: 284)

Moreover, realists would expect US–EU economic rivalry to become more pronounced as Western Europe's security dependency on the United States lessens (see, e.g., Walt 1989: 1).

However, *the EU has proven capable of internal balancing*. The internal market program as well as monetary union have been successfully implemented and have arguably strengthened European competitiveness, autonomy and power in the international economy. Moreover, even if the EU had felt the need to strengthen itself through expansion, Eastern enlargement would hardly have been the instrumentally rational choice.

Eastern enlargement does not increase the economic power of the EU. In the perspective of the power approach to enlargement, it probably was useful to admit the former EFTA members, which are prosperous and highly developed economies and which could be expected to increase the EU's common resources. In contrast, the CEE economies will remain a drain on these resources for the foreseeable future. They are not capable of improving the global power position of the EU *vis-à-vis* the United States or Japan.

To be sure, Eastern enlargement will increase the internal market in terms of territory, population, and economic output. According to the Commission's 1997 impact study, the EU area will grow by 34 percent, its population by 29 percent but its total GDP only by 9 percent.[8] The GDP per capita of the CEECs reached only 18 percent (Latvia) to 59 percent (Slovenia) of the EU average at the time. According to the Commission's calculation, Eastern enlargement would result in reduction by 16 percent of the per capita GDP for the Community as a whole, constituting a substantial loss in wealth, "which is unprecedented and greater alone than that resulting from all the previous enlargements" (EC 1997b: 36). As a consequence, CEE members will not be net contributors to the Community budget. They neither add to the high-technology power base of the European Union nor do they possess strategically important raw materials.

Finally, *preclusion is not necessary.* The EU did not have to fear that Central and Eastern Europe could come under the control of its global competitors. First, even if the CEECs were interested in such an

[8] *European Commission* (1997b: 36), 1995 Data. GDP in purchasing power parities.

alternative, Western Europe's "gravitational pull" on the CEE economies could hardly be substituted by such geographically distant economies as the American or the Japanese. Second, there are no indications that the United States or Japan were interested in forming an economic bloc with the CEECs against the EU. Thus, Eastern enlargement was neither necessary nor helpful for the EU to balance other economic powers in the international economy or to increase its own economic power base. In view of this, what about the welfare approach?

Economists agree that *trade integration with the CEE region will benefit the EU economies in the aggregate.* It fully integrates a new market for Western European exports and investments in their close proximity. In addition, the supply of cheaper resources and cheaper but qualified labor as well as economies of scale will reduce costs and strengthen European competitiveness on the world market (von Hagen 1996: 6; Kawecka-Wyrzykowska 1996: 88). However, this positive outlook has to be qualified in two ways:

First, "Studies of the long-run output, employment, and welfare effects of increased CEE-EU trade in the EU commonly conclude that the overall impact will remain *relatively small*" (von Hagen 1996: 6, my italics). For instance, Baldwin, Francois and Portes (1997: 138) put the growth effect at 0.2 percent no matter whether reduced risks for investors in the CEECs are included or excluded. In its study, the French Commissariat du Plan concurs with this assessment.[9] On the basis of the EU's 1996 GDP at market prices (ECU 6,771 billion), a 0.2 percent growth would amount to ECU 13.5 billion.

Second, the effects of trade integration will be positive in the aggregate but *distributed unevenly* among sectors and countries. According to the simulations of Baldwin, Francois and Portes (1997: 148), Germany alone will gain one third of the economic benefits (that is significantly more than its 25 percent share of the EU's economic output), whereas the share of Italy, Ireland, and Greece will remain much below their share of the EU GDP. Portugal will even incur slight losses according to this scenario. The main reason is that EU agriculture, textile and leather as well as metalworking industries will be exposed to stiffer competition as a result of progressive market integration. EU member countries which specialize in such traditional and resource-intensive industries (like Spain, Portugal, Greece, and Italy) will face higher import pressures than others (von Hagen 1996: 6; Padoan 1997: 114–15). Moreover, Weise *et al.* expect political problems because the "burdens of adaptation are mostly concentrated on specific sectors in which actors are easy to mobilize politically. Profits, however, are spread more widely and, therefore,

[9] Quoted according to *Les Echos*, 21 April 1999.

less transparent" (1997: 26, my translation). Those countries that will benefit most from trade integration (in particular Austria and Germany) will, in turn, face migration pressures for which there is a high potential due to geographical proximity, high unemployment in the East and high wage differentials.[10]

Moreover, the budgetary effects of Eastern enlargement – and, again, their uneven distribution among member states – have to be taken into account. In its planning for the "Agenda 2000," the European Commission estimated the direct costs of preparing the CEE candidates for EU membership at around ECU 75 billion for seven years until 2006.

Eastern enlargement, however, will have more permanent effects on the Community budget. First of all, the *CEECs are expected to become net recipients*, that is, EU transfers will outweigh CEE contributions to the EU budget. More specifically, a full membership of the associated CEECs was generally expected to strongly affect those two policies that make up for around 80 percent of the budget: the CAP and the structural policies.

According to Stefan Tangermann (1995: 485), the CAP would be seriously affected because the ten CEE associates, whereas producing only 3 percent of the EU GNP, possess 44 percent of the EU productive land and attain 30 percent of the EU agricultural production. He expected that agricultural production would increase rather than diminish as a result of economic recovery, and that participation in the CAP would give the CEECs an additional incentive for agricultural production because EU prices in many areas of agriculture are well above world market prices. At the low end of estimates, the Commission calculated the budgetary impact of enlargement to be an additional cost "in the order of 11 billion ECU per year by 2005." Most other studies arrived at about the same sum for the admission of the Czech Republic, Hungary, Poland, and Slovakia alone; estimated CAP costs for all ten associated CEECs reached to over ECU 50 billion.[11]

Because of their low levels of wealth and income, the CEECs would benefit enormously from the structural funds. On the basis of the eligibility rules in force at the time of their application for membership, all ten CEE applicants would have received "assistance under Objective 1 of the Structural Funds in respect of the whole of their territory."[12] Under

[10] Weise *et al.* (1997: 18). This prognosis has been confirmed in a study on the consequences of Eastern enlargement on the European labor market commissioned by the *European Commission* (see *SZ*, 22 May 2000 and 25 May 2000, 26).

[11] See, e.g., Bach, Frandsen and Jensen (2000: 175); Baldwin, Francois and Portes (1997: 157), and the overview of other studies there (p. 155).

[12] *European Commission* (1997b: 38). Objective-1 regions are the most handicapped regions.

the assumption that the CEECs would receive as much assistance per capita as the poorest current members, Portugal and Greece, the structural funds would have to be increased by ECU 42 billion (Grabbe and Hughes 1998: 101). However, the CEECs would not be able to absorb, and provide matching funds for, transfers that, in some cases, amount to around one third of their GDP. Baldwin, Francois and Portes (1997: 154) correct this bias but still arrive at a "consensus estimate" of ECU 13 billion per year for the four Central European countries only. Note that this moderate estimate excludes the five poorest CEECs so that the actual sum for all ten candidates should be closer to ECU 20 billion.

Partial membership, excluding or limiting participation in the CAP and the structural policies, would reduce costs but only temporarily. The EU's negotiating position to limit direct payments to CEE farmers in the first years after accession reflects this strategy. However, as foreseen by some observers (Kreile 1997: 223–25; Tangermann 1995: 486), such a partial membership is very difficult to legitimate politically except as a temporary measure. Therefore, the accession treaties envisage direct payments to increase each year and reach the same level as for the member states after ten years.

Depending upon the enlargement scenario (timing and number of newcomers) and the calculation, then, the community budget would have to increase by 20 percent to two thirds of its current volume under pre-enlargement agricultural and structural policies.[13] One way to finance the extra costs would be to increase the Community budget. This strategy, however, would require member states to make additional contributions to the Community without the prospect of receiving additional transfers. The net contributors especially have therefore opposed any expansion of the budget to pay for enlargement, and the EU has agreed to keep its budget limit of 1.27 percent of the member states' GDP. Yet in this case, the CAP and the structural policies needed to be reformed and it was obvious that any reform would lead to income reductions for the EU farmers as well as to either lower transfers to the comparatively disadvantaged EU regions or a reduction in the number of regions eligible for financial support (cf. O'Neil 1999: 87–91). Precisely such reductions were the subject of the Commission's 1997 "Agenda 2000" reform proposals and of the budget negotiations at the Berlin European Council in March 1999. In Berlin, the structural funds were cut down to Euro 213 billion for the 2000–06 period and the CAP expenses were frozen at a level of Euro 40.5 billion per annum.

[13] See Baldwin (1994: 161–79; 1995a: 32); Baldwin, Francois and Portes (1997: 157); Hyde-Price (1996: 203); Weise *et al.* (1997: 258).

In sum, all the evidence – even if low-end estimates of EU costs are combined with high-end estimates of EU benefits – points to the conclusion that *the costs of enlargement exceed its benefits for the member states*, and that these *net costs will be unevenly distributed among the member states, with the poorer members being most likely to suffer both economic losses from full market integration with the CEECs and budgetary cuts.*

Three arguments might be put forward against this conclusion. First, it is sometimes argued that the current CAP and structural policies are so inefficient that cost-saving reforms would be rational anyhow. This, however, is a normative argument. In an empirically rationalist perspective, one must assume that current policies reflect the members' aggregated preferences and bargaining powers. Otherwise, rational actors would have changed them independently of Eastern enlargement. Second, it is true that, even without Eastern enlargement, the CAP would probably need to be reformed because of negotiations on agriculture in the context of the World Trade Organization (WTO). In that case, however, enlargement adds to the pressure on EU agricultural producers and will only make them more skeptical about the admission of CEECs.[14] Third, some more recent studies come to the conclusion that enlargement will not be a burden on the Community budget or only require modest additional funding by the old member states.[15] These studies, however, are already based on the EU's budget plans for 2000–06 and the cuts and caps decided in 1999. Any serious estimate of the marginal costs and benefits of enlargement must start from the policies in place *before* adjustments required by enlargement were made.

Two additional points confirm the conclusion that the decision to enlarge the EU to the East and begin accession negotiations with ten CEECs was not in the self-interest of the member states: first, the balance of costs and benefits for some form of association with the CEECs was much more favorable than for full membership. Second, the enlargement decision was not an outcome of the superior bargaining power or efficient compensation by states that presumably had an egoistic interest in the admission of CEECs.

Even if the full membership of the CEECs provided net benefits to the EU member states, it is highly doubtful that these benefits would exceed those that they reap under the current association regime. Already under association,

[14] Bach, Frandsen and Jensen (2000) include the effects of the Uruguay Round in their simulation and still come to the conclusion that the EU-15 will suffer a welfare loss from Eastern enlargement.

[15] See, e.g., the study by the French Commissariat du Plan, quoted in *Les Echos*, 21 April 1999 and *Le Monde*, 27 April 1999, and a study commissioned by the German Friedrich-Ebert-Stiftung (*SZ*, 6 April 2000).

economic integration has progressed significantly toward a free-trade area. Western corporations benefit from advantageous terms of trade, and, since 1991, the EU has realized a trade surplus with its Eastern neighbors each year. The surplus increased substantially in 1993 and 1994 after the association agreements had come into force. Baldwin, Francois and Portes (1997: 139) estimate that aggregate EU exports will rise by only 1.5 percent as a result of enlargement. In addition, mere association would allow the EU to continue to protect the sectors in which it is particularly vulnerable to competition and to prevent undesired migration more effectively than in an enlarged EU. What is more, association enables the EU members to reap most of the fruit of trade integration without incurring the transaction, autonomy, and budgetary crowding costs of political integration. The EU could continue to give assistance to the CEECs at its own discretion and to cooperate with them where it is in its own interest (e.g., in refugee policy) without granting the CEECs the right to participate in EU decision-making and in its redistributive policies.

As in the case of NATO enlargement, *the CEECs were not in a position to bargain successfully for admission* against the opposition of the member states. For the EU, the opportunity costs of non-enlargement were low. Interdependence between the CEECs and the EU was highly asymmetrical – whereas the share of EU exports and imports of the total foreign trade of the CEECs rose to between 50 and 70 percent in the 1990s, the CEECs' share of EU foreign trade remained below 5 percent. The inflow of Western capital was critical for the CEE economies whereas Eastern capital in Western economies was a negligible quantity. Since the EU market was critical to the CEECs whereas the CEE market was fairly unimportant for most EU member states (Baldwin, Francois and Portes 1997: 131), the CEECs could not credibly threaten to close their markets to the West and thus deprive the EU of the benefits of trade integration in case it rejected enlargement. By shielding their economies from integration with the Community market, the CEECs would have hurt themselves more strongly than the EU members.

Moreover, and also in correspondence with the NATO enlargement case, *the CEECs could not credibly threaten the EU with negative externalities* supposed to originate in economic crisis and domestic instability in the absence of enlargement (see, e.g., Kawecka-Wyrzykowska 1996: 97; Mattli 1999: 95–96; Saryusz-Wolski 1994: 24–25). Again, "self-inflicted chaos" is no credible bargaining strategy for CEEC governments. Moreover, the EU has proven able to defend itself efficiently against the spillover of Eastern European instability. For instance, in order to reduce the number of refugees and asylum-seekers reaching the West, EU members have successfully "passed the buck" to the CEECs via bilateral agreements and in the context of third-pillar intergovernmental cooperation (Lavenex 1998). (Such a cost-avoiding policy would probably become more difficult after the admission of CEECs.) In addition, in the analysis of Mattli (1999: 99), "the early market concessions of the EU were successful in warding off the threat of mass migration." Finally, as in the case of NATO, those CEECs that did not achieve internal stability on their own and exported instability beyond their borders have been excluded even from the benefits of association – let alone membership.

The last factor that could tip the balance in favor of enlargement was the superior bargaining power of those member states interested in the admission of CEECs for egoistic reasons. As in the case of NATO enlargement, *Germany* was the most likely candidate. In addition to the reasons discussed in the analysis of NATO enlargement, Germany has not only been the most important beneficiary of economic integration with the East among the major member states in the past but, according to Baldwin, Francois and Portes (1997: 148), it will also benefit disproportionately from full integration. Moreover, Germany was little affected by trade and budgetary competition with the CEECs. Even the costs of enlargement – above all, migration – would have to be borne primarily by weak border regions and underprivileged societal groups (low-skill labor) whereas producers would further benefit from better conditions for outward processing and direct investments in the CEECs.

Nevertheless, Germany's economic stakes in the East were small compared to those in the EU. Less than 10 percent of German exports went to the CEECs, compared to more than 55 percent to the EU. Hungary and Poland, the main target countries of German direct investments in Central and Eastern Europe, had a share of less than 3 percent of the total stock of German direct investments abroad at the beginning of 1999.[16] This was less than the share of Ireland alone. Under these circumstances, *Germany could not credibly (and did not) issue threats of pursuing a unilateral policy in the East or of building a German–CEE coalition against its EU partners. Neither is there any evidence of generous German offers for compensating the enlargement losers.* Quite to the contrary, the German government insisted that Eastern enlargement not increase the Community budget and, on the eve of the 1999 Berlin summit, even demanded that its net contributions to the budget be reduced.

[16] *Die Zeit*, 27 July 2000, 29 according to Deutsche Bundesbank data.

Conclusion: the rationalist puzzle of Eastern enlargement

Eastern enlargement constitutes a puzzle for the rationalist analysis of international institutions. The problem is not the interest of the CEECs in joining the Western organizations. Here rationalist institutionalism provided a plausible explanation in both the NATO and the EU cases. The puzzle is on the supply side. According to the security approach, enlargement was not necessary for an unthreatend and unrivalled NATO. In the EU case, it may have been useful for an economic organization in rivalry with the United States (and Japan); but then it was not efficient. This lack of efficiency also causes the power approach to fail – Eastern enlargement dilutes rather than strengthens the power of the Western organizations. Moreover, the auxiliary condition of preclusion proved unconvincing with regard to both the timing and the scope of Eastern enlargement.

Finally, even the welfare approach failed, although it is the least restrictive of the rationalist approaches and therefore the most likely one to be confirmed. First, the CEECs are poorer and located in a less stable environment than Western Europe. In addition to transaction and autonomy costs, enlargement was therefore expected to produce crowding costs that would exceed the CEECs' contribution to the club goods. NATO enlargement increases security risks for the old members and causes extra costs not balanced by the military or financial contributions of the new members. In the EU, enlargement provides welfare benefits to the old members but these are small, unevenly distributed and easily used up by the budgetary costs of enlargement. Second, both organizations had established institutional relationships with the CEECs (NATO's Partnership for Peace and EU association agreements), which were more efficient than full membership in that they allowed the members to pursue beneficial security cooperation and market integration with the CEECs without having to bear the transaction, autonomy and crowding costs of full membership. Third, enlargement cannot be attributed to the effects of differential bargaining power. In both cases, Germany was the major member state that was most likely to have a positive cost-benefit balance in Eastern enlargement. Yet Germany could not credibly (and did not) threaten the other member states with exclusion and unilateral policies because its security and the economic benefits of integration in the Western organizations clearly exceeded any benefits it might have reaped from alternative coalitions with the CEECs.

To conclude, I will deal with arguments in the literature on enlargement that appear in a rationalist format and seem to be able to explain the Western organizations' decision to admit CEECs. As I will show, however, they are subject to inappropriate "theoretical stretching." Basically, these arguments include the promotion of democracy and stability in Central and Eastern Europe among the interests of the Western organizations and their member states, the claim that enlargement, or the prospect thereof, does indeed strengthen democracy and stability in the CEECs, and that this effect adds to the benefits, and tips the cost-benefit balance in favor, of Eastern enlargement.

For instance, Sandler and Hartley (1999: 68) start their list of the benefits of NATO enlargement with the furthering of democracy and political stability in Central and Eastern Europe. Similarly, Andrew Kydd bases his analysis of NATO enlargement on the assumption that "stability" through the peaceful solution of ethnic conflicts and democracy was the most important goal of the member states (2001: 807). In the cost-benefit analysis of Becker (1998: 235–36), the expansion of the "European community of values" to the East, the "stabilization of the region," a "pan-European community of law," the "stabilization . . . of economic transformation processes in the CEECs," and the "provision of pan-European stability and conflict prevention" are the main components of the benefit side of EU enlargement.

Whereas these studies add the promotion of democracy and stability to the premises of the cost-benefit analysis, other studies turn to these items in their conclusions, that is *after* the analysis has shown that costs exceed benefits. For example, Baldwin, Francois and Portes (1997: 168) speak of "an extraordinarily low cost given the historic nature of the challenge in central Europe" and ask their readers to imagine "how eager Western Europe would have been in 1980 to pay ECU 8 billion a year in order to free central Europe from communism." Likewise, Grabbe and Hughes (1998: 107) consider the costs of enlargement "a very small price to pay for reuniting Europe and responding to post-1989 challenges" and submit that "the EU is attempting to achieve a historic step with remarkably low expenditure." And Bach, Frandsen and Jensen (2000: 178) conclude that the economic costs of Eastern enlargement "are, of course, dwarfed by the historical and political importance of creating a united and peaceful Europe."

The problem with these kinds of arguments, however indisputable they may appear, is that they add actor goals to the analysis which are beyond the scope of egoism and thus violate a fundamental assumption of IR rationalist institutionalism. As such, the promotion of democracy and stability in third countries is either an altruistic action – in that it benefits other actors, a value-rational action "determined by a conscious belief in the value for its own sake of" democracy and stability (Weber 1968: 25), or a norm-regulated action based on the social norms of the community of states to which the organization and its members belong. Therefore, it is not permissible under rationalist institutionalism to include democracy and stability in other countries, let alone an international community of values and norms, in the utility functions of the state actors in the same way as their own security, power, or welfare. Nor is it possible to explain an inefficient decision or action by some historic challenge or step that, on closer inspection, is also based on ideational values and normative obligations.

To be permissible and to make a difference in a rationalist explanation of enlargement, the "democracy and stability" argument needs to be integrated into an egoistic utility function (see Kydd 2001: 807). It would have to show, first, that instability and the failure of democracy in Central and Eastern Europe produce security and welfare costs in Western Europe that outweigh the enlargement costs; second, that the risk of instability and the failure of democracy in the candidate countries is high; and third, that enlargement is the most efficient instrument for controlling or preventing negative Eastern externalities in the West. As I have argued earlier, however, these conditions are not fulfilled.

On the one hand, pervasive instability and the return to authoritarian government would indeed produce negative externalities in the West such as undesired migration, organized crime, forgone opportunities of economic benefits and possibly even a new threat to Western security if Russia returned to expansionism. In the worst case, these costs would certainly outweigh the costs of enlargement.

On the other hand, however, the probability of this scenario is low in the candidate countries and the more likely a CEEC will become a member of NATO or the EU, the lower it is. The only country that could threaten Western security militarily – Russia – does not stand the slightest chance of joining the EU or NATO. The proven capacity of Ukraine to threaten the West with the radioactive fallout of its nuclear power stations did not earn it a top position among the candidates for membership. CEECs with a high potential of ethnic tension and unstable democratic systems will not be admitted to either NATO or the EU before these tensions are dissolved and democracy is consolidated. By contrast, the new NATO members and the candidates for EU membership are the most stable and democratic countries in Central and Eastern Europe, and there were no indications of instability in case they failed to accede to the Western organizations (see also Brown 1995: 37–38; Reiter 2001). In sum, the decision to admit a country to the Western organizations appears to be unrelated to its potential and its probability of doing harm to the West.

Finally, enlargement is neither necessary, nor does it seem to be efficient, for controlling the negative externalities produced by instability in the East. As argued above, the West has so far been able, without enlargement, to prevent instability and violence in Eastern Europe or their consequences (like refugees) to spill over into the West. Thus there has not been any need to take on the costs of enlargement. One might reply that enlargement would have been cheaper than the wars and the long-term military and civilian presence in Bosnia-Hercegovina and Kosovo. First, however, the violence in former Yugoslavia did not threaten the security or welfare of Western Europe, and the military interventions were not motivated by an egoistic interest to preserve the West from material harm. Second, it is highly doubtful whether the early admission of Yugoslavia to the EU and NATO would have prevented the dissolution of the federation and its consequences. To the contrary, it would very likely have disrupted the proper functioning of the Western organizations.

To be sure, rationalist institutionalism does not expect the EU and NATO member states to be indifferent to democracy and stability in the candidate countries. The admission of undemocratic and unstable countries would strongly increase the heterogeneity of the membership, the potential for serious intraorganizational conflict and the costs of decision-making. In the rationalist perspective, however, a community of basic political values and norms is at best a *necessary* condition of enlargement. In the absence of net economic or security benefits for the insiders, it does not create any *positive* incentive to expand the organization.

In a move of last resort, the rationalist analysis of enlargement could give up the assumption of egoism and start from a "thin theory" of rational choice and genuinely altruistic member state preferences. However, this new assumption also fails when confronted with the empirical evidence. As I will show later (Part IV), member states did indeed have egoistic preferences. The puzzle persists.

Part II

Expanding the Western community of liberal values and norms: Eastern enlargement in a sociological perspective

In the course of the 1990s, sociological approaches to the study of international relations have increasingly challenged the dominance of rationalist theories. The debate between "rationalism" and "constructivism" – as the sociological approaches are now usually referred to – constitutes currently the focus of theoretical controversy in International Relations. Since the rationalist theories failed to explain why the EU and NATO should expand to include the CEECs, I turn therefore to sociological institutionalism in an attempt to solve the puzzle of Eastern enlargement.

Constructivist approaches to the study of international relations are more united by their rejection of basic theoretical premises of rationalism than by common positions. The basic divide within the constructivist camp is the epistemological difference between "modernist" and postmodernist constructivism. Modernist constructivism does not, in principle, question the epistemological commitment of rationalism to an empirical and explanatory, causally oriented social *science*.[1] It should be clear from the purpose of this book, to explain enlargement by confronting competing hypotheses with the empirical evidence, that I take constructivist analysis to be compatible with modernist epistemology.

In the theoretical chapter (chapter 4), I discuss the basic premises of sociological institutionalism in International Relations, describe how sociological institutionalists theorize international organizations and their enlargement, and develop hypotheses. Subsequently, I describe the cultural foundations of the Western international community and probe the ability of sociological institutionalism to explain the Eastern enlargement of NATO and the EU (chapter 5). In an event-history analysis of the enlargement of West European regional organizations since their foundation, I submit the sociological-institutionalist liberal community hypothesis to an additional, statistical test (chapter 6). Finally, I will conclude that sociological institutionalism solves the puzzle Eastern enlargement presents to rationalist institutionalism.

[1] For these labels and differences, see Hopf (1998: 181–84); Katzenstein, Keohane and Krasner (1998: 675); Ruggie (1998: 35–36); Wendt (1999: 47).

4 Sociological institutionalism and the enlargement of regional organizations

Constructivist premises and concepts

In contrast to rationalism, sociological approaches to the study of international relations and international institutions are based on a social (structural) and ideational ontology and on the assumption of appropriate action.[1]

Idealism. Constructivists regard ideas, in the broadest sense of the term, as the most fundamental causes of social phenomena. They do not deny the causal influence of human nature or material conditions altogether but argue that "only a small part of what constitutes interests is actually material" (Wendt 1999: 115) and that "the manner in which the material world shapes and is shaped by human action and interaction depends on dynamic normative and epistemic interpretations of the material world" (Adler 1997a: 322).

Structuralism. Neither the ideas that shape the identities and interests of the actors nor social phenomena in general can be "reduced to aggregations or consequences of individuals' attributes or motives" (DiMaggio and Powell 1991: 8). Ideas have a structural, "intersubjective" quality; they are "collective representations" (Durkheim) or "institutional facts" (Searle).[2] Sociological institutionalists regard the environment of social actors as a cultural or institutional environment structured by collective schemata and rules.[3]

[1] I use the terms "sociological" and "constructivist" interchangeably. Cf. Hasenclever, Mayer and Rittberger (1997: ch. 5) for an overview of the constructivist analysis of international institutions.

[2] Note, however, that constructivists are not necessarily strong structuralists but ascribe an autonomous ontological status to individual agency, too. See, e.g., Wendt (1987) on this "structurationist" ontology.

[3] For the ideal-typical distinction of technical and institutional environments, see Scott (1991: 167); for an application of this distinction to international organizations, see Weber (1994). Jepperson, Wendt and Katzenstein (1996: 33) speak of "cultural and institutional" security environments.

Sociological explanations, therefore, do not start with actors and their exogenous corporate identities and interests. Rather, they problematize and endogenize identities, interests – and, ultimately, actors as well. That is, they analyze and explain them as products of collective ideational structures and social interactions that are subject to cultural variation and historical change. In principle, this "constructedness" also applies to the states that rationalist IR theories take as the central and unitary actors in international relations. In practice, however, many sociological approaches to the study of international institutions treat states as given actors and show the same state-centrism as rationalist approaches.[4]

In contrast to rationalism, constructivism attributes *primary* causal status to ideas and institutions. First, collective ideas and institutions shape the identity and the interests of the actors. Second, far from being reducible to material factors, they give meaning to material factors in the first place. Third, institutions empower actors. Fourth, actors do not confront institutions as external constraints and incentives toward which they behave expediently. Rather, social actors are assumed to internalize or habitualize institutional rules and rule-following behavior.

Socially constructed, value- and norm-based interests. Not surprisingly, sociological institutionalism starts from the *homo sociologicus* model according to which social actors act on the basis of internalized cultural values and social norms instead of their own, individual utility.

Appropriate action. Correspondingly, sociological institutionalism emphasizes non-instrumental and non-strategic logics of action. The most widely assumed logic of action is the "logic of appropriateness" according to which "political institutions are collections of interrelated rules and routines that define appropriate actions in terms of relations between roles and situations." Appropriate action, then, "involves determining what the situation is, what role is being fulfilled, and what the obligations of that role in that situation are" (March and Olsen 1989: 160). Actors do not judge alternative courses of action by the consequences for their own utility but by their conformity to institutional rules or social identities. According to James March and Johan Olsen, "ambiguity or conflict in rules is typically resolved not by shifting to a logic of consequentiality and rational calculation, but by trying to clarify the rules, make distinctions, determine what the situation is and what definition 'fits'" (1989: 161).

[4] This is most obvious for the English School and for Wendt who openly defends state-centrism (1992: 424; 1999: ch. 5). Moreover, *state* identities and *state* or *national* interests are the focus of much constructivist research (see, e.g., Finnemore 1996a; Jepperson, Wendt and Katzenstein 1996: 33; Katzenstein 1997a: 24).

To be sure, it would be misleading to characterize the logics of action assumed by sociological institutionalism as generally non-rational or irrational. Rather, they often imply a *different kind* of rationality as expressed, for instance, in the concepts of "value-rationality" (Max Weber) or "communicative rationality" (Jürgen Habermas). Appropriate action is purposeful but the "pursuit of purpose is associated with identities more than with interests, and with the selection of rules than with individual rational expectations" (March and Olsen 1998: 951).

Whereas rationalist institutionalism emphasizes the instrumental, efficiency-enhancing functions of *international organizations* in the service of state actors, sociological institutionalism sees them as autonomous and potentially powerful actors with constitutive and legitimacy-providing effects. International organizations are "community representatives" (Abbott and Snidal 1998: 24) as well as community-building agencies. The origins, goals, and procedures of international organizations are more strongly determined by the standards of legitimacy and appropriateness of the international community they represent (and which constitutes their cultural and institutional environment) than by the utilitarian demand for efficient problem-solving.[5] International organizations "can become autonomous sites of authority . . . because of power flowing from at least two sources: (1) the legitimacy of the rational-legal authority they embody, and (2) control over technical expertise and information" (Barnett and Finnemore 1999: 707). Due to these sources of power, international organizations are able "to impose definitions of member characteristics and purposes upon the governments of [their] member states" (McNeely 1995: 33; cf. Finnemore 1996a). For instance, they "define international tasks [and] new categories of actors . . . create new interests for actors . . . and transfer models of political organizations around the world" (Barnett and Finnemore 1999: 699). In that way, they do not simply *regulate* state *behavior* but *shape* state *identities and interests.*

Collective ideas play a central role in the sociological analysis of international institutions. "Identity," "values," "norms," "rules," "culture" and "community" are the core concepts in which sociological institutionalist explanations are formulated. Since these concepts are employed and related to each other in different ways in the literature, and sometimes used interchangeably, I begin with a brief conceptualization of ideational factors in order to lay the groundwork for the formulation of sociological institutionalist hypotheses about enlargement. The relationship between these concepts I propose is depicted in Figure 4.1. Identity, values, and

[5] See Barnett and Finnemore (1999: 703); Katzenstein (1997a: 12); McNeely (1995: 27); Reus-Smit (1997: 569); Weber (1994: 4–5, 32).

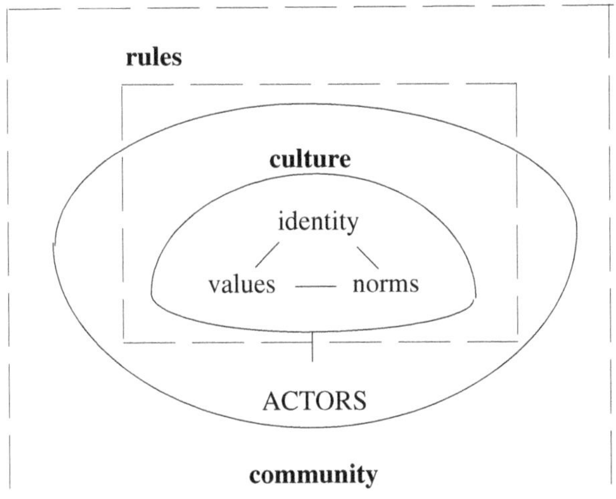

Figure 4.1 Basic sociological institutionalist concepts
Note: Non-institutionalized relations are symbolized by circles, institutionalized relations by broken, rectangular lines.

norms are interrelated and form a culture; a group of actors with a shared culture is a community. Rules are institutionalized culture; and a community organization represents an institutionalized community.

Identity. An identity is a set of ideas "that enable an actor to determine 'who I am/we are'" (Wendt 1994: 385). Typically, an identity also has a negative dimension and involves a sense of distinctiveness. It distinguishes the "self" from the "other," the "in-group" from the "out-group(s)," and defines their relationship.

Value. A value is an idea of the desirable. Political values describe the desirable characteristics of a polity and define the ultimate ends of social order that political actors pursue. The collective identity of political actors is usually (but not necessarily or solely) based on shared and distinct political values. Correspondingly, an identity implies values to be upheld and pursued by the actors sharing this identity.

Norm. A norm is an idea that defines a collective standard of proper behavior (cf., e.g., Finnemore 1996a: 22; Katzenstein 1996b: 5). Whereas a value refers to a desirable state of the world and defines the (ultimate) *ends* of action, a norm refers to the desirable behavior of actors and defines the appropriate *means* of action (to achieve those ends). Just as values, norms are interrelated with identity. On the one hand, norms constitute and shape identities (Jepperson, Wendt and Katzenstein 1996: 52) – they define the collective self by the way "we do things." On the other hand, they contain "behavioral prescriptions for the proper enactment of these identities" (Kowert and Legro 1996: 453).

Culture. I employ "culture" as the collectively held identity, values, and norms of a specific social group. Correspondingly, a political culture encompasses the totality of ideas about "who we are as a polity, what we desire and how we behave politically."

Community. A community is a social group that shares a culture. The members of a community identify themselves positively with each other, share common values and hold the same standard of appropriate behavior.

Rule. I define a "rule" as an institutionalized element of culture. Rules stabilize and regulate culture, that is, they define the proper or legitimate identity, values and norms of a community for its members.

Community organization. Community organizations represent the highest degree of institutionalization of a community. A community organization is a formal, rule-based structure capable of purposive action. Based on the community rules, it regulates community membership and acts to realize the community values and to uphold the community norms.

In the sociological perspective, *international organizations are community organizations* established by communities of states, structured by their common rules and acting on their behalf. Different international organizations can represent different communities, different layers of community and different community tasks.

International organizations can represent *different international communities* based on different collective identities, values, and/or norms. Regional organizations like the OSCE, OAU or ASEAN, for instance, consist of states that belong to different regions of the international system. From the sociological point of view, these regional communities are not so much constituted by geographical location and the concomitant security or economic interdependence but, just as nations in the constructivist analysis, they are "imagined communities" (Anderson 1991) and embody different constitutive values and norms. They are "socially constructed 'cognitive regions' or 'community-regions' whose people imagine that . . . borders run more or less where shared understandings and common identities end" (Adler 1997b: 250).

International organizations can represent *different layers, degrees, or "concentric circles"* (Buzan 1993) *of international community.* They can reach from organizations of weak communities that share only a "thin" identity and a few general rules to strong communities united by a "thick" identity and high rule-density. Typically, organizations with quasi-universal membership such as the United Nations represent an international community with a comparatively thin identity (basically, "we as states") and general rules (for instance, "state sovereignty"), whereas regional organizations are based on a thicker identity and more specific rules.

Finally, international organizations can fulfill *different functional tasks for the same community*. In the Soviet-dominated "socialist community of states," for instance, the Warsaw Treaty Organization specialized in military cooperation whereas the CMEA focused on the economic division of labor and coordination among the communist countries. Both organizations were based on the communist identity of the member states and the constitutive norms of "socialist internationalism."

Enlargement as community-building

In the sociological perspective, the enlargement of an international organization is inextricably linked to *international socialization*. In general, "socialization" means the internalization, by a social actor, of the rules of a community, and "internalization" consists in the adoption of social identities, values and norms into the actor's repertoire of cognitions and behaviors. In the case of states, "internalizing" can be defined as the process of transforming the rules of an international community into domestic rules, that is, into domestic institutions and discourses that effectively govern domestic and foreign policy-making. To be recognized as "one of us" by the community, a state must make the community's constitutive values and norms an integral part of its identity and act upon them independently of external stimuli.

For the *non-member states*, accession to an international organization primarily fulfills the needs of identification and legitimation. Being accepted as a member of an "aspiration group" of like-minded or "model" countries assures governments and societies of their identity and of the legitimacy of their political and social values. In addition, membership facilitates the assertion of these values against competing values in the domestic as well as in the international arena because it enhances both the material and immaterial resources for their defense. Aspirations to membership vary with a state's perception of and relation to the community culture. States that identify positively with an international community and share its values will also be willing to join the community organizations, to learn and follow their rules and to collaborate with other community members in and through them. The basic hypothesis about the enlargement preferences of outsider states follows these theoretical considerations:

If a non-member state identifies itself with the community and has internalized its rules – or, at least, if it perceives the community values and norms as legitimate and works toward institutionalizing them domestically – it wants to join the community organizations.

In the sociological perspective, the enlargement preferences of outsiders are not determined by egoistic cost-benefit calculations. Sociological institutionalism therefore hypothesizes in direct competition with rationalist institutionalism:

A non-member state that shares the community identity, values, and norms will strive for membership in the community organizations even if it incurs net material costs. Conversely, an outsider state that does not share the community culture does not desire to join the community organizations even if it could reap the net material benefits of membership.

For the *member states* of the community, community-building through international socialization also serves to strengthen their collective identity and legitimacy. The adoption of the constitutive values and norms of the community by outsider states is evidence of their social validity and persuasive power. It assures the community members of their cultural beliefs and practices, boosts their self-esteem and repels competing social ideas. There are two basic strategies of community-building and international socialization in which enlargement functions in different ways:

(a) The *inclusive strategy* of community-building aims at socialization *from within*. The community organizations first admit external aspiring countries and then teach them the community rules. Together with their accession to a community organization, the new members take on the obligation to learn and internalize its rules. On the condition that a community organization pursues an inclusive strategy,

a state is admitted to an international organization if it aspires to become a member of the international community the organization represents.

(b) The *exclusive strategy* of community-building consists in socialization *from the outside*. The community organizations communicate their constitutive values and norms to outsider states and tell them to what extent they have to internalize them before being entitled to join. After fulfilling the requirements, an outsider state is regarded as "one of us" by the community members and admitted to the community organizations. Accession to the community organizations as a full member then corresponds to a formal recognition that international socialization has been successful. Thus, on the condition that a community organization pursues an exclusive strategy of socialization,

> a state is admitted to an international organization if it has internalized the constitutive values and norms of the international community the organization represents.

Besides these two ideal-types, there are mixed strategies. Typically, some form of *association* with the community organization indicates that the community recognizes the desire of an outsider state to become part of the community and join its organizations. Furthermore, association serves to teach the community rules to the aspirant state and to put to a test its ability and willingness to learn them. The outsider state moves from associate to full membership after the learning process has been successfully completed.

Whatever the strategy pursued by a community organization, its enlargement decisions follow its membership rules and practices and are not determined by expedient interest-based calculations and by the distribution of material bargaining power among the member states. The membership rules of a community organization create an obligation to grant membership to all states which share or aspire to the collective identity of the community and are committed to their constitutive values and norms – even in the case of net transaction, crowding and/or autonomy costs to the members of the organization. If outsider states are recognized as legitimate members of the community on the basis of the values they uphold and the norms they follow, they are entitled to share the rights (but also obliged to share the duties) of a community member, to participate in the community activities, and to benefit from community solidarity.

> If an outsider state does not share the community culture it is not admitted to the community organization even if the members expect to reap net material benefits of accession. Conversely, a non-member state that shares the community identity, values, and norms will be admitted to the community organization even if the members incur net material costs as a consequence of enlargement.

To be sure, this obligation requires neither self-denial nor immediate enlargement. First, it does not extend to costs that are beyond the capabilities of the member states and would threaten the existence of the organization. Norms and rules create obligations only within acceptable parameters (see, e.g., Shannon 2000: 295). Second, non-member states may already apply on the basis of positive identification whereas the community organizations – in case they pursue an exclusive strategy – may only enlarge after outside states have internalized their constitutive rules and proven to be reliable community members. Depending on the speed and success of socialization, we therefore often observe a time lag between application and accession as well as different accession dates for states that applied at the same time.

In sum, according to the community approach to enlargement, an international organization expands if an outside state identifies itself positively with the international community represented by the organization, shares its fundamental values, and adheres to, or is willing to learn, its basic norms.

5 Eastern enlargement and the Western international community

In a constructivist perspective, NATO and the EU are community organizations. Consequently, the first step in the sociological institutionalist analysis of their enlargement is to determine the community culture. I claim that NATO and the EU are regional organizations of the Western international community. The members of this community share a liberal political culture – a postnational identity based on liberal norms of domestic and international conduct. Moreover, both NATO and the EU pursue a moderately exclusive strategy of international socialization that entitles outsider states to become full members only on the condition of advanced internalization. The second step in the analysis consists in showing that NATO and the EU decided to admit the (most) successfully socialized CEECs, indeed.

The Western international community

Both NATO and the EU are organizations of the Western international community which is characterized by three core features. It is an interstate, liberal, and postnational community.

The Western international community is an *interstate* community. States have established and further developed the community organizations through international treaties. Only states can become members, and it is states that decide whether or not an outsider state is admitted. Moreover, the size or power of political entities is not a criterion for membership as long as these entities qualify as states. States with well below one million inhabitants such as Luxembourg are members of the community; substate regions, let alone cities, with well above that population are not. This interstate quality may be a trivial characteristic but it is a necessary starting-point for the analysis of what constitutes the Western community.

The non-trivial defining feature of the Western international community is its *liberal* character. It is both a community of *liberal states* – member states must have a liberal internal order and behave according to liberal norms of domestic and international conduct – and a *liberal community* of states – that is, the community organizations are structured according to liberal principles, pursue liberal values and act according to liberal norms, too.

Liberal human rights – individual freedoms, civil liberties and political rights – are at the center of the Western international community's political culture. They are the "constitutive values that define legitimate statehood and rightful state action" in the domestic as well as in the international realm (Reus-Smit 1997: 558).

In the *domestic* realm, the *liberal principles of social and political order* – social pluralism, the rule of law, democratic political participation and representation, private property and a market-based economy – are derived from, and justified by, these liberal human rights. Only a state that bases its domestic political system on these principles and reliably follows these values and norms in its domestic politics is regarded as fully legitimate by the Western international community.[1]

In the *international* realm, liberal political culture shapes the institutions of peaceful conflict management and multilateralist collaboration. In both cases, domestic liberal norms are transferred to the foreign policy of liberal states and to the international interactions between them: "Democracies externalize their internal norms when cooperating with each other" (Risse-Kappen 1995a: 33).

The *democratic peace* – the fact that democratic states do not wage war against each other – has its roots in those domestic norms of liberal-democratic states that require political conflicts to be managed and resolved without violence and on the basis of constitutional procedures. As these norms are constitutive for the political culture and identity of liberal-democratic societies, they tend to be externalized out of habit or commitment. When democratic states interact, they perceive each other as sharing the same values, norms and practices. These perceptions foster positive identification between liberal states. In particular, the knowledge that other liberal states share their culture of non-violent, institutionalized conflict management enables liberal states to develop dependable expectations of each other's peaceful behavior.[2] In time, liberal democracies develop "pluralistic security communities" in which states positively identify with each other and neither expect nor prepare for organized

[1] As long as these norms are observed in principle, domestic systems are allowed to vary, e.g. with regard to presidential *vs.* parliamentary democracy, to the amount of direct democratic elements, or the degree of state interventionism in the economy.

[2] For the cultural or normative theory of the democratic peace, see Owen (1996) and Russett *et al.* (1995: 31–32). For the constructivist reformulation and extension of this theory, see Risse-Kappen (1995b) and Kahl (1999).

violence as a means to settle interstate disputes.[3] Conversely, if democratic states interact with non-democratic states, positive identification does not take place or is even replaced by negative identification. A stable peace will not be built.

The other basic international norm, *multilateralism*, is defined as a generic institutional form that "coordinates relations among three or more states on the basis of generalized principles of conduct: that is, principles which specify appropriate conduct for a class of actions, without regard to the particularistic interests of the parties or the strategic exigencies that may exist in any specific occurrence." These "generalized organizing principles logically entail an *indivisibility* among the members of a collectivity with respect to the range of behavior in question" and generate "expectations of 'diffuse reciprocity'" (Ruggie 1993a: 11).

Multilateralism corresponds to the basic liberal idea of procedural justice, "the legislative codification of formal, reciprocally binding social rules" among the members of society (Reus-Smit 1997: 577). When liberal values and norms of legitimate statehood spread among the dominant states of the international system in the second half of the nineteenth and the beginning of the twentieth century, they also redefined legitimate international practice:

> The principle that social rules should be authored by those subject to them came to license multilateral forms of rule determination, while the precept that rules should be equally applicable to all subjects, in all like cases, warranted the formal codification of contractual international law, to ensure the universality and reciprocity of international regulations. (Reus-Smit 1997: 578)

Multilateralist organizations in the Western international order have the effect of security and economic "co-binding." Liberal states "attempt to tie one another down by locking each other into institutions that mutually constrain one another." Again, co-binding corresponds to and is facilitated by the internal structure of liberal states whose domestic autonomy is constrained by the separation of powers and systems of checks and balances (Deudney and Ikenberry 1999: 182–83). Finally, multilateralism lessens the effects of power asymmetries between democratic states. They are "mediated by norms of democratic decision-making among equals emphasizing persuasion, compromise and the non-use of force or coercion . . . Norms of regular consultation, of joint consensus-building, and non-hierarchy should legitimize and enable" the influence

[3] See Deutsch *et al.* (1957) for the classical formulation of the concept of security community. For a more recent reformulation and application, see Adler and Barnett (1996) and Adler (1997b).

of smaller, weaker members of liberal community organizations (Risse-Kappen 1995a: 33).[4]

The liberal collective identity of the Western international community is a *postnational* or *civic* identity.[5] The Western liberal community does not possess any primordial quality rooted in natural or "naturalized" cultural characteristics. Its liberal identity is *universalistic*: liberal democrats claim that their values and norms are universally applicable and the only legitimate principles of political order and conduct. The liberal community seeks to expand its membership by disseminating its values and norms and by convincing other individuals and societies of their legitimacy. Accordingly, liberal identity is *acquirable and changeable.* Neither adherence to liberal values and norms, nor their rejection, is regarded as a "natural" or "immutable" characteristic of a state. The liberal identity is based on values and norms that can be taught and learned, adopted and rejected. Finally, it is subject to change. Constructions of the "West" and its "Others" as well as the boundaries of the Western community have changed considerably in the course of modern history (see, e.g., McNeill 1997), and many features of a nineteenth-century liberal state, like the rejection of female suffrage or the neglect of mass education and mass welfare, are not compatible with a liberal identity any more today.

Conversely, the Western community is *not a pan-national community.* "Pan-nationalism" reproduces the characteristic features of particularistic, ethnic nationalism at the level of an integrated, supranational community (see Cederman 2001). By contrast, a postnationalist liberal community "dissolves the historical symbiosis of republicanism and nationalism" and is not dependent on "a mental rootedness in the 'nation' as a prepolitical community of fate" (Habermas 1998: 116–17). It generally lacks and does not need "the historical and symbolic-cultural attributes of ethnic identity." It does not have a "myth of common ancestry"; to the extent that it conceives of itself as a "family" it does so as a "family of nations" whose family ties are common values and norms. It is not associated with "an historic territory" or a "specific 'homeland'" (Smith 1991: 14, 20–21). Rather, the "West . . . could be imagined as a civilization independent of locale" (McNeill 1997: 514). Finally, it is not based or dependent on a common religion or language. However, "notwithstanding the plurality of different cultural lifestyles," a liberal, civic community "requires

[4] Deudney and Ikenberry (1999: 185) furthermore attribute the weakening of power asymmetries in the liberal order to "liberal state openness and transnational relations" which create a "penetrated hegemony."

[5] See Cederman (2001) for a discussion of theories of supranational identity-formation. "Civic identity" and "civic community" are the concepts used by Brenner (1995: 8) and Deudney and Ikenberry (1999: 192–94).

the socialization of all citizens [or states, in the case of an international community, F.S.] in a common political culture."[6]

Finally, the liberal collective identity of the West is a *thin identity*. It is compatible with various ethnic or religious identities that are being "muted and diluted to the point where [they] tend to be semi-private in character" (Deudney and Ikenberry 1999: 194), with a pluralistic authority structure that combines regional, national, and supranational competencies, and with different varieties of democratic political systems and market economies. Its cultural content is limited to *political* culture; ethnic nationalism is replaced with "constitutional patriotism" (Habermas). This thin identity goes together with "an ethic of toleration, diversity, and indifference" that differs from "the chauvinism and parochialism of pre-modern and non-Western societies" (Deudney and Ikenberry 1999: 194).

NATO and the EU as community organizations

The origins, the basic treaties, and the membership rules of NATO and the European Union provide evidence of their identity and purpose as organizations of the Western international community. Moreover, both organizations pursue a moderately exclusive strategy of international socialization.

NATO is the main *security* organization of the Western community. During the Cold War, its most obvious purpose was to protect the liberal states of the Western community militarily against the rival "socialist community of states." However, as Mary Hampton has shown (1995; 1999), NATO's "creators [also] intended it to be the flagship institution for building a trans-Atlantic security community of likeminded democracies." In particular, it was designed to socialize (West) Germany to the liberal norms of the Western community and to forge a common identity between Germany and the West (Hampton 1999: 235).[7] This "Wilsonian impulse" even "preceded the American drive to balance against the Soviet threat" (Hampton 1995: 611).[8]

In the preamble to the *North Atlantic Treaty* of 1949, the signatory states declare the protection of their values, rather than just the preservation of national autonomy or the balance of power, as the basic purpose of NATO: "They are determined to safeguard the freedom, common

[6] Habermas (1994: 643). Deudney and Ikenberry (1999: 193) add a common business and commodity culture to the Western civic or liberal political culture.

[7] See also Wallander and Keohane (1999: 42) on the hybrid nature of NATO as an alliance and a security management institution.

[8] For a more critical perspective and instrumental interpretation, see Kurth (1997).

heritage and civilisation of their peoples, founded on the principles of democracy, individual liberty, and the rule of law." Article 2 refers to the "democratic peace" and adds another important strand of the liberal theory and strategy of peace – "commercial liberalism" or "peace through trade" (and the intensification of other transnational transactions):

> The Parties will contribute toward the further development of peaceful and friendly international relations by strengthening their free institutions, by bringing about a better understanding of the principles upon which these institutions are founded, and by promoting conditions of stability and well-being. They will seek to eliminate conflict in their international economic policies and will encourage economic collaboration between any or all of them.

Furthermore, NATO practices are governed by *multilateralist alliance norms*. Whereas a hegemonic US alliance organized as a "series of bilateral deals with each of the subordinates" would have been the most likely institutional form according to rationalist institutionalism (Weber 1993: 235), NATO is an institutionalized multilateral alliance. It "drew states into joint force planning, international military command structures, and established a complex transgovernmental political process for making political and security decisions" (Deudney and Ikenberry 1999: 183). According to Stephen Weber, "Within NATO, security was indivisible. It was based on a general organizing principle, that the external boundaries of alliance territory were completely inviolable and that an attack on any border was an attack on all. Diffuse reciprocity was the norm" (1993: 233). As Article 4 of the North Atlantic Treaty prescribes, "The Parties will consult together whenever, in the opinion of any of them, the territorial integrity, political independence or security of any of the Parties is threatened" and, in Article 5, they agreed that "an armed attack against one or more of them . . . shall be considered an attack against them all." Finally, due to the multilateralist norms of NATO and the transgovernmental political process, the much weaker European and Canadian allies have been able to exert a disproportionately high influence on US security policy and NATO decision-making (Risse-Kappen 1995a).

The written *enlargement rules* of NATO are vague. Article 10 of the North Atlantic Treaty reads, "The Parties may, by unanimous agreement, invite any other European State in a position to further the principles of this Treaty and to contribute to the security of the North Atlantic area to accede to this Treaty." Whereas the reference to the "principles of this Treaty" implies that affiliation with Western civilization and liberal statehood is a necessary condition of membership, the ability "to contribute to the security of the North Atlantic area" could mean that sharing the culture of the Western community is not sufficient. In principle, it could be used to exclude any applicant state that does not produce net security benefits for the member states.

In its beginnings, *European economic integration* also received a push by the US project of a liberal world order. Since the launching of Marshall Plan Aid and the Organization of European Economic Cooperation (OEEC) in the late 1940s, the United States has advocated and supported a multilateralist reorganization of West European international relations (see Ruggie 1993a: 27). Like NATO, the EU and its predecessor organizations have fulfilled a hybrid purpose. On the one hand, they have served to strengthen the West European states, their economies and welfare systems, at first in aiding them in their postwar economic reconstruction and in countering the communist challenge, later in order to hold their own in global economic competition.[9]

On the other hand, European integration was intended to create and stabilize a security community that would replace the traditional rivalry and bloody contests between the European powers, in particular between France and Germany. By establishing an institutional framework for economic integration, the European Community would, first, increase interdependence between the European states in a growing number of policy sectors, second, cause the political activity and loyalty of societal groups and organizations to shift from the national to the European level and, third and finally, create a supranational system of authority in which national identities and rivalries would be muted.[10]

In the preamble to the Treaty establishing the European Coal and Steel Community (ECSC) of 1952, the member states clearly stated the community-building purpose of integration when they expressed their resolve "to substitute for age old rivalries the merging of their essential interests; to create, by establishing an economic community, the basis for a broader and deeper community among peoples long divided by bloody conflicts; and to lay the foundations for institutions which will give direction to a destiny henceforward shared."

In the preamble to the Treaty establishing the European Economic Community (EEC) of 1958, the signatories declared themselves to be "determined to lay the foundations of an ever closer union of the peoples of Europe" and to be "resolved, by thus pooling their resources, to preserve and strengthen peace and liberty." In a passage that alluded to the culture-based enlargement rules of the Community, they further

[9] This corresponds to the "intergovernmentalist" story as told, e.g., by Milward (1994).

[10] This corresponds to the "neofunctionalist" story of European integration. See, above all, Haas (1968).

called "upon the other peoples of Europe *who share their ideal* to join in their efforts" (my italics). Finally, Article 6 of the Treaty on European Union (TEU) represents the most authoritative and clear statement of the constitutive liberal values of the Western community:

1. The Union is founded on the principles of liberty, democracy, respect for human rights and fundamental freedoms, and the rule of law, principles which are common to the Member States.

In the course of European integration, the community members have not only established a stable democratic peace among themselves but also a *unique multilateral and legal order*. The density and strength of the generalized rules governing the relations between the EU members as well as their delegation and pooling of sovereignty are unparalleled by other multilateral organizations. According to William Wallace, the "intensive multilateralism" involving government officials of the member states at all levels of the bureaucracy in negotiations on a quasi-permanent basis is the "most distinctive governmental characteristic of this regional system" (1999: 206). European law takes direct effect and possesses supremacy with regard to national law, and it is enforced by an independent supranational court, the European Court of Justice, whose decisions are binding upon the member governments.

From a constructivist point of view, the international relations of Europe have been thoroughly transformed in the process of European integration – not by the intentional erection or the gradual emergence of a European super-state, as the early federalists and neofunctionalists had envisaged it, and not only by the establishment of a unique multilateral governance system, but by the *Europeanization of state identities* (Katzenstein 1997a).

Respect for human rights, peaceful democracy, an economy based on private property and supported by a generous welfare state, and close connections with neighboring states and NATO as well as other European security organizations define what it means to be a "modern" European state. As institutionalized practices, these norms are so much taken for granted in northern and western Europe that they pass largely unnoticed. (Katzenstein 1997b: 262)

In addition, the Europeanization of state identities implies that "the constitutive processes whereby each of the [then] twelve defines its own identity . . . increasingly endogenize the existence of the other eleven" (Ruggie 1993b: 172). It is clear from these descriptions, however, that the Europeanized state identity is postnational in character and that identification with the European international community does not imply the supersession of national identities. Article 6 of TEU even states explicitly, "3. The Union shall respect the national identities of its Member States."

The liberal community culture is institutionalized in the *membership rules* of the European Union. The original Article 98 ECSC Treaty and Article 237 EEC Treaty accorded all *European states* the right to apply for membership and were therefore even less concrete than the corresponding article of the North Atlantic Treaty. Subsequent EU declarations and legal acts as well as EU practice, however, have established several more precise prerequisites for a successful application (Richter 1997; cf. Michalski and Wallace 1992: 33–36; Redmond and Rosenthal 1998b: 2–3). First, the EU requires its new members to be *democracies* which respect the *rule of law* and *human rights* (Preambles to the Single European Act (SEA) and the TEU, Article 6 TEU). Article 49 TEU makes this linkage explicit: "Any European State which respects the principles set out in Article 6(1) may apply to become a member of the Union."[11] Second, new members must conform to the *principle of an open-market economy with free competition* (Article 3a EC Treaty). However, this principle offers members a lot of leeway regarding the degree of state involvement and intervention in the economy and does not specify any necessary levels of economic development or capacity. Finally, new members must accept the entire *acquis communautaire*, that is, the entire body of EU law, as well as the *acquis politique* (from the "intergovernmental" pillars of the EU, the Common Foreign and Security Policy and Justice and Home Affairs).

Taken together, these prerequisites demonstrate the EU's predominantly *exclusive* strategy of international socialization. Although applicant states do not have to have institutionalized the entire *acquis* ahead of accession *negotiations*, they have to adhere to the constitutive liberal norms of the community.

Four objections may be put forward against the categorization of NATO and the EU as organizations of a single Western, liberal and postnational interstate community. The first concerns the regional instead of universal scope of both organizations, the second their different regional extension or identity. The third objection points to their different institutional order, and the fourth one claims that Western civilization is based on religious rather than political culture.

Regional organization. The first objection may be that Western, liberal identity is universalistic and not bound by any territory or "homeland" whereas both NATO and the EU have a defined treaty territory. Indeed, neither NATO nor the EU claims to represent the liberal or Western community in its entirety. For instance, Australia and New Zealand,

[11] For the wording of Article 6.1, see above.

undoubtedly "Western" countries, are beyond the scope of even the most ambitious enlargement projects. In contrast with the OECD, which includes these two countries as well as Japan and Korea, both NATO and the EU are *regional organizations of the Western international community*, and the region they focus on is *Europe*. However, in accordance with the postnational character of the community's liberal identity, "Europe" is not objectively defined by geographical or quasi-natural cultural borders. As the European Commission stated in its report on "Europe and the Challenge of Enlargement," Europe "combines geographical, historical and cultural elements which all contribute to the European identity. The shared experience of proximity, ideas, values, and historical interaction cannot be condensed into a simple formula, and is subject to review by each succeeding generation. The Commission believes that it is neither possible nor opportune to establish now the frontiers of the European Union, whose contours will be shaped over many years to come" (European Commission 1992: para 7).

Nevertheless, it is clear that a state without any European territory is not entitled to join the European Union or NATO even if it deeply shares the community's values and norms.

Regional identity. The second objection points to the puzzle that the NATO region includes the Northern Atlantic Ocean and the countries of North America which are not, and in all likelihood will not become, members of the EU. I contend, however, that NATO represents an *extended European – "Euro-Atlantic" – liberal community* rather than a separate international community. First, NATO was founded to defend Western Europe against the Soviet threat and to reorganize the security relationship among the Western European countries. It is clearly an organization of European security. Second, NATO has been liberal Europe's main security organization. There has not been an autonomous security organization of Western Europe competing with NATO. The West European Union (WEU) was clearly subordinated to and, for all practical purposes, inactivated by the establishment of NATO.[12] Third, the treaty territory includes the Northern Atlantic but excludes the Pacific Ocean and the Caribbean Sea which certainly are security-relevant zones for the North American members but not for Europe. Finally, according to Article 10 of the North Atlantic Treaty, NATO will only invite *European* states to join the alliance and, according to its "Study on NATO Enlargement," "NATO's enlargement will occur as one element of the broader evolution

[12] Whether the establishment of a "European defense identity" in the context of the EU and its merger with the WEU will change this relationship is difficult to judge at the moment.

of *European* cooperation and security" (NATO 1995: para 9, my italics). NATO considers its enlargement to "complement the enlargement of the European Union" (1995: para 4) and envisions "an eventual broad congruence of European membership in NATO, EU and WEU" (1995: para 20). In sum, then, it is plausible to argue that both the EU and NATO are organizations in the service of the same *European region of the Western community*. Canada and the United States are NATO members in order to contribute to the security of this region. At least as far as *enlargement* is concerned, the regional perspectives of both organizations coincide.

Institutional order. NATO and the EU also differ with regard to their institutional set-up. Both conform to the liberal norm of multilateralism but whereas NATO is more of a classical intergovernmental organization based on negotiations and agreements that leave state sovereignty formally untouched, the EU involves majoritarian decision-making, a far-reaching pooling and delegation of sovereignty, the establishment of autonomous competencies for supranational organs and the emergence of transnational public–private policy networks.

Again, however, the differences should not be overestimated in the case of enlargement because the EU's *finalité politique* is even more open and undecided than its borders. More than that, it is contested between member states some of which pursue the idea of federal statehood (as German representatives from Helmut Kohl to Joschka Fischer have done) whereas others would like to limit the EU as far as possible to an intergovernmental or economic organization (which is the reputation of Denmark and the UK). According to Marcussen *et al.* (1999: 618), two different identity constructions prevail in Europe, a "liberal nationalist identity . . . whereby the 'we' is confined to one's own nation state and where political sovereignty resides in the nation state" (exemplified by Great Britain) and a "modern Europe as part of the Western community based on liberal democracy and the social market economy" (represented by France and Germany). In the analysis of Jachtenfuchs *et al.* (1998), the "polity-idea" of a "federal state" is strong in the party spectrum of Germany and France whereas the two major British parties prefer the idea of an "economic community." Whatever may be the more adequate conceptualization, their richly documented historical analyses show that, whereas the basic liberal values and norms of the Western community are consensually shared by the member states, visions of the *finalité politique* have always differed and have been fairly resistant to change, let alone convergence, over time. For that reason, a commitment to any of the ideas of community *finalité* that goes beyond a general acceptance of "union" does not belong to the membership rules. By contrast, adherence to the liberal norms of domestic and international conduct is the "hard" and fundamental criterion for accession – for both NATO and the EU.[13]

Religious culture. A final objection concerns the exclusively political and postnational character of the Western community and its organizations and points to its deep roots in pan-national religious culture. Samuel Huntington (1993; 1996), the most prominent proponent of this perspective, claims that *civilizations*, that is, international and transnational communities based on religious culture, are (becoming) the fundamental entities and sources of collective identity in world politics. The fault lines between civilizations and the intercivilizational struggle for power are the most important sources of conflict in the post-Cold War world (Huntington 1993: 29).

According to Huntington, the Western community of states is based on Western civilization which, in turn, is rooted in and closely linked to Western Christianity. Because of this durable cultural core, the alleged universalism and multiculturalism of the Western liberal community is chimerical. Rather, the Western community has its quasi-natural border at the historical European fault line between Western "Latin" Christianity in both its Roman Catholic and Protestant variants, on the one hand, and Eastern "Orthodox" Christianity (as well as Islam), on the other. This fault line has its origins in the early medieval split in Christianity and runs from the border between Russia and Finland in the north through Belarus, Ukraine, Romania and former Yugoslavia, and ends south of Croatia at the Adriatic Sea.

In this view, the religious border marks the limits of the expansion of the organizations of the Western international community. In contrast to the liberal post-nationalist understanding, "Europe" therefore has a defined eastern border, and eastern enlargement will stop before the geographical boundaries of Europe are reached. Russia, Belarus, Ukraine, Moldova, Romania, Bulgaria, Macedonia, Yugoslavia, Bosnia-Hercegovina and Albania will not be able to become full members of the Western organizations because of their Orthodox or Islamic majority culture (see Huntington 1996: 255–59). However, the religious interpretation of Western community flies in the face of some simple facts about EU and NATO membership. First, religious civilization is not mentioned as an accession criterion in the formal membership rules or the programmatic texts on enlargement of any Western organization. Second, Orthodox Bulgaria and Romania conduct accession negotiations with the EU and will become NATO members in 2004; Orthodox Greece is a member

[13] But see, e.g., Michalski and Wallace (1992: 8, 35) and Redmond and Rosenthal (1998b: 3).

of both NATO and the EU; Islamic Turkey is a member of NATO and a candidate for EU membership.[14]

Community rules and Eastern enlargement

On the basis of the preceding discussion of the cultural foundations of NATO and the EU, I will now turn the general sociological enlargement hypotheses into more *concrete expectations*. In contrast with rationalist institutionalism, the organizations can be treated as *collective* actors because, in community organizations, membership decisions are typically based on collective identity, common values and social norms, not on the basis of individual preferences. Moreover, the conditions of NATO and EU enlargement can be treated as *identical* since they are assumed to be organizations of the same international community and to have the same regional scope as well as the same basic normative requirements for enlargement. Under the assumptions that the Western community is a liberal community and that the EU and NATO pursue an exclusive strategy of socialization, then,

> CEECs desire to join NATO and the EU if they identify themselves with the Western international community and have internalized its liberal norms or, at least, if they perceive these norms as legitimate and work toward institutionalizing them. NATO and the EU admit CEECs that share the liberal identity of the Western international community and have internalized the liberal community norms.

I will refer to these propositions as the *liberal community hypothesis of enlargement*. In more detail, we should be able to make the following observations:

(1) *The record of compliance with liberal norms of the CEECs selected for accession (negotiations)*
   (a) *matches that of the NATO and EU member states* – indicating not simply a verbal commitment to the community culture but a community of practices;
   (b) *has matched that of the NATO and EU member states for an extended time period* – indicating a stable and proven commitment to the community culture and a degree of internalization;
   (c) *is better than that of the CEECs not selected for accession (negotiations)* – indicating a selection of candidates based on different degrees of socialization to the community culture.

[14] I will take up this interpretation of the Western community again in chapter 6.

(2) *The selection of CEE candidates for EU and NATO membership is congruent* – indicating that NATO and the EU are organizations of the same international community and judge potential members according to the same normative standards.

Identity, legitimacy and the CEECs' desire to join

Most Central and Eastern European candidates for NATO and EU membership identify themselves positively with the Western international community, perceive their norms as legitimate, and work toward institutionalizing them. After the breakdown of the communist system, the CEECs have searched for a new place or "home" in the international system. The "return to Europe" – understood as the European region of the Western international community – has become their central foreign policy goal. Intensive cooperation with and, eventually, full membership in the Western organizations are the most important elements of this grand strategy. The "return to Europe" generally enjoys a broad consensus among the major political forces in the CEECs and has been pursued no less by postcommunist (e.g., in Poland, Hungary, Lithuania or Romania) than by centrist or right-wing governments. In the sociological perspective, the desire to join the Western organizations can be explained by the identification and the legitimation needs of the CEECs.[15]

The "return to Europe" results from a strong identification with Western values and norms as well as with the Western European international community from which these countries had been cut off under Communist rule. To be sure, only a few CEECs had traditionally been part of the Western liberal community so that the "*return* to Europe" in this sense is a euphemistic label. With a few exceptions, most notably Czechoslovakia, the CEECs had already been governed by authoritarian regimes before they fell prey to German expansion in World War II and to Soviet expansion into Central and Eastern Europe in its aftermath. At the end of the Cold War, however, the Western international community constituted for them the model of the "good" domestic and international order which inspired the Eastern European revolutions of 1989 and 1990 and which the CEECs have sought to emulate in their ongoing transformation processes. Membership in the EU and NATO represents for them the strongest indication that they successfully have transformed themselves into modern European countries and are recognized as a part of

[15] See Adler (1997b: 256); Alamir and Pradetto (1998: 136–37); Bedarff and Schürmann (1998: 115, 122); Hyde-Price (1994: 225; 1996: 197); Katzenstein (1997a: 30); Kierzkowski (1996: 15); Kolankiewicz (1994: 481–82); Neumann (1993).

the West by their role models. At the same time, it indicates that they have broken links with their communist past and cast off their "Eastern" identity.

Furthermore, the prospect of membership in the Western organizations serves as an important additional source of legitimacy for the proponents of liberal democratic reform in Central and Eastern Europe. First, it enhances their *international* legitimacy. Especially for the new states whose statehood may still be fragile and contested and whose territorial borders may be disputed, membership in the Western organizations is an important normative (and, of course, material) source of support. Second, membership enhances *domestic* legitimacy. Changes in domestic and foreign policy as well as the hardships of transformation are easier to justify and implement if they are demanded by Western organizations as a condition of closer cooperation and accession (or can be legitimized this way). The eventual accession to Western organizations confers political prestige upon the CEE governments, strengthens the self-esteem of CEE societies and makes authoritarian reversals more difficult (see Alamir and Pradetto 1998: 141–42; Hyde-Price 1994: 235). This broad-sweep sociological explanation of the CEECs' desire to join the EU and NATO, however, has to be differentiated.

CEECs that did not work toward institutionalizing Western liberal norms sought membership in the Western organizations, too. Identification with the values of the Western international community and the domestic institutionalization of liberal norms seems to be a *sufficient* condition for the CEECs' interest in EU and NATO membership. All CEECs with governments consistently pursuing the liberal democratic transformation of their domestic systems also sought close ties with and eventual membership in the Western organizations. However, commitment to Western values and norms has *not* been *a necessary condition.* CEE governments which exhibited authoritarian tendencies and defied Western norms and socialization efforts sought no less than liberal-democratic and reform-minded CEE governments to deepen their institutional relationships with the EU and NATO and to achieve full member status. This applies to Croatia under the Tudjman regime (until 2000), Romania under Iliescu (until 1996), Slovakia under Meciar (until 1998), and Ukraine under Kuchma.

In sum, the liberal community hypothesis about the CEECs' interest in joining the Western organizations is only partially convincing and, at any rate, does not sufficiently discriminate among cases. Commitment and adherence to the liberal norms of the Western community is a sufficient but unnecessary condition of a CEEC's interest in membership.

Obviously, there have been other motivations for acceding to the Western organizations.

Community rules and NATO enlargement

NATO documents on cooperation with the CEECs and Eastern enlargement confirm the sociological expectations about the *community-building motivation for enlargement* and about the *norm-based conditions* new members have to fulfill. Already the 1994 PfP Framework Document pointed to the liberal value basis of the entire process:

> Protection and promotion of fundamental freedoms and human rights, and safeguarding of freedom, justice, and peace through democracy are shared values fundamental to the Partnership. In joining the Partnership, the member States of the North Atlantic Alliance and the other States subscribing to this Document recall that they are committed to the preservation of democratic societies, their freedom from coercion and intimidation, and the maintenance of the principles of international law. (NATO 1994b: para 2)

In chapter 1 (para 2) of the "Study on NATO Enlargement" (NATO 1995), entitled "Purposes and Principles of Enlargement," NATO describes security, democracy, and enlargement as inextricably linked:

> The benefits of common defence and . . . integration are important to protecting the further democratic development of new members. By integrating more countries into the existing community of values and institutions . . . NATO enlargement will safeguard the freedom and security of all its members.

Adherence to the norms of multilateral and peaceful conflict management as a prerequisite of membership is explicitly demanded in paragraph 6 of the document:

> States which have ethnic disputes or external territorial disputes, including irredentist claims, or internal jurisdictional disputes must settle those disputes by peaceful means in accordance with OSCE principles. Resolution of such disputes would be a factor in determining whether to invite a state to join the Alliance.

Accordingly, US President Clinton plainly summarized which countries do not qualify: "Countries with repressive political systems, countries with designs on their neighbors, countries with militaries unchecked by civilian control, or with closed economic systems need not apply."[16]

Furthermore, US Secretary of State Albright made it clear that adherence to liberal norms is not only a necessary but also a sufficient condition

[16] <http://www.nato.int/usa/info/enlargement.htm> (17 May 2000).

of membership, since "no European democracy will be excluded because of where it sits on the map."[17]

Finally, corresponding with the sociological explanation of the CEECs' desire to join NATO, NATO Secretary General Solana (1997: 3) emphasized the identity- and legitimacy-building functions of NATO enlargement as "a means of reinforcing the new democracies with a confidence in their destiny and giving them a sense of belonging" and, in line with the logic of appropriateness, he referred to the "moral obligation for us to help them fulfil their legitimate aspirations."

NATO documents as well as statements by leading NATO officials further show that NATO conceived the path to membership in the Alliance as a process of *socialization*. According to US Deputy Secretary of State Asmus, this socialization process was "inspired by the way Western Europe benefited from Alliance policy in the 1950s." Just as NATO had helped to stabilize and defend democracy in Western Europe and to transform the international relations of the Western European countries into a security community, it was hoped that NATO could assist the CEECs in their liberal democratic transformation and the peaceful management and resolution of international conflicts in the area.[18]

Association in the Partnership for Peace program has served both as a *training program* and as a *probationary stage* for the CEECs aspiring to membership. In PfP, NATO teaches the values, norms, and practices of the Western international community and tests whether the candidates meet the learning objectives (cf. Adler 1997b: 256; Gheciu 2002; Risse-Kappen 1995a: 224). The "Study on NATO Enlargement" confirms this interpretation:

> Through PfP planning, joint exercises and other PfP activities, including seminars, workshops and day-to-day representation in Brussels and Mons, possible new members will increasingly become acquainted with the functioning of the Alliance . . . Possible new members' commitment to the shared principles and values of the Alliance will be indicated by their international behaviour and adherence to relevant OSCE commitments; however, their participation in PfP will provide a further important means to demonstrate such commitment as well as their ability to contribute to common defence. For possible new members, PfP will contribute to their preparation both politically and militarily, to familiarise them with Alliance structures and procedures and to deepen their understanding of the obligations and rights that membership will entail. (NATO 1995: paras 38–39)

[17] Speech at the North Atlantic Council Ministerial Meeting in Sintra, 29 May 1997, <http://www.nato.int/usa/state/s970529a.htm> (17 May 2000).

[18] Asmus (1997: 69). Cf. Morgan (1993: 345); Skålnes (1998: 45); Wallander and Keohane (1999: 45).

Since enlargement could put a great strain on the principle of consensual decision-making, NATO further stressed that "it will be important that prospective new members become familiar with the Alliance decision-making process, and the modalities and traditions of consensus and compromise, before joining." Finally, the "varying degree of participation is a key element of the self-differentiation process" (1995: para 46). NATO explicitly stated that countries participating in the "Planning and Review Process" (PARP) and ready to reinforce and deepen their "Individual Partnership Programmes," would distinguish themselves by "demonstrating their capabilities and their commitment" and enhance their prospects of NATO membership (1995: paras 40–41).

During the probationary period starting with Partnership for Peace, the aspiring countries have regulary received "grades" for their progress on the way to membership. For example, US Secretary of Defense Perry toured Central and Eastern Europe in September 1995, confirming that the Czech Republic met all prerequisites for NATO membership whereas Slovakia would have to intensify the democratization process.[19] According to the proponents of NATO enlargement, this socialization process has been a success. At the NATO Ministerial Meeting in Sintra (May 1997), Secretary of State Albright said that "we want to give the nations of Central and Eastern Europe an incentive to make the right choices about their future. We want to encourage them to resolve old disputes, to consolidate democracy, and to respect human rights and international norms. So far, that is exactly what the prospect of enlargement has done."[20]

Asmus (1996) concurred with the view that the "prospect of NATO enlargement has already contributed enormously to reform and reconciliation in Eastern Europe. From the Baltic to the Black Sea, foreign and defense policies are being reconstructed in order to bring these countries into line with alliance norms. Rarely has a Western policy had such an impact in eliciting such positive change."

The community-building approach not only provides a general rationale for NATO expansion but also accounts plausibly for the *selection of new members* for the first round of NATO Eastern enlargement. The Czech Republic, Hungary and Poland were more advanced than other CEECs in the adoption of Western liberal values and norms. They are closest to Western Europe not only in terms of geography but also in terms of common history and political culture. More than other CEECs, they can rightly claim to be a part of the "common heritage

[19] "Perry: Slowenien ist Vorbild für Mitteleuropa," "Perry ruft Slowaken zu mehr Demokratie auf," and "Perry: Prag erfüllt Bedingung für NATO-Beitritt," *SZ*, 19, 20 and 21 September 1995.

[20] <http://www.nato.int/usa/state/s970529a.htm> (17 May 2000).

and civilisation" of NATO countries. More importantly, they are the forerunners and paragons of liberalization and democratization in the region. Already under Soviet domination, reform movements in Hungary (in 1956), Czechoslovakia (1968), and Poland (1956, 1970, 1980) revolted against the communist system. Such movements did not develop in other CEECs before liberalization began in the Soviet Union under Gorbachev. In 1989, two of these countries led the way in the democratic transformation of the region: Poland invented the "round table" of peaceful transition and Hungary opened the "iron curtain" for GDR refugees.

Moreover, none of them has been engaged in major territorial and ethnic conflict with its neighbors or in major domestic ethnic conflict. All of them have shown the willingness and capability to manage such conflicts as there were by peaceful means. Poland granted minority rights to its German-speaking population and made no claims to Lithuanian, Belarusian and Ukrainian territory that had belonged to its prewar area. The Czech Republic used no force or pressure against Slovak separatism but agreed to a peaceful dissolution of Czechoslovakia. The Hungarian government has stayed away from irredentism despite sizeable Hungarian minorities abroad. In the face of considerable domestic opposition and repressive policies against the Hungarian minority in Slovakia and Romania, it has actively and successfully pursued the conclusion of basic treaties with both neighboring countries.

Arguably, the Czech Republic, Hungary and Poland not only matched the standard of NATO members but also distinguished themselves from the other CEE candidates with regard to the internalization of liberal values and norms when NATO made its decision on the invitation of new members. This can be shown on the basis of widely used comparative indicators of human rights and liberal democratic performance. In the context of this study, they are used to measure a state's adherence to the basic liberal norms of domestic conduct. Table 5.1 presents the relevant data for 1996, the year before NATO made its decision to invite the Czech Republic, Hungary and Poland to join the Alliance.[21]

Freedom in the World: "Freedom House" is a US based non-governmental organization publishing annual reports on "Freedom in the World." Its central indicators are ratings for "Political Rights" and "Civil Liberties" ranging from 1 (best) to 7 (worst). On their basis,

[21] See Karatnycky, Motyl and Shor (1997) for the Freedom House data; the "POLITY IV" database can be downloaded from <http://www.cidcm.umd.edu/inscr/polity>. The list of countries comprises the non-CIS NATO partners (and later participants in the Membership Action Plan), that is, the group of serious candidates for NATO membership.

Table 5.1 *CEEC compliance with liberal norms: the 1997 enlargement round*

	PR/CL	Freedom Index	Time	Democracy	Economy	Polity	Time
Czech Republic	1/2	free	7	1.38	1.88	10	7
Hungary	1/2	free	7	1.44	1.63	10	7
Poland	1/2	free	7	1.44	2.00	9	6
Albania	4/4	partly free	0	4.50	4.00	0	0
Bulgaria	2/3	free	6	3.81	5.38	8	7
Estonia	1/2	free	4	2.06	2.13	6	0
Latvia	2/2	free	3	2.06	2.50	8	6
Lithuania	1/2	free	6	2.06	2.50	10	6
Macedonia	4/3	partly free	0	3.88	4.50	6	0
Romania	2/3	free	1	3.88	4.63	8	1
Slovakia	2/4	partly free	0	3.81	3.38	7	0
Slovenia	1/2	free	6	1.88	2.38	10	6

Freedom House constructs a "Freedom Index" classifying countries as "free," "partly free" or "not free." "Time" represents the number of years a country has continuously been classified as "free."

Nations in Transit is a special report by Freedom House on the former communist countries of Eastern Europe. The "Democracy" rating is based on evaluations of "political process," "civil society," "independent media," "rule of law" and "government and public administration." "Economy" measures the progress in transformation to market economy. The report also contains an overall classification of countries as "consolidated democracies and market economies," "transitional governments and economies" and "consolidated autocracies and statist economies." Ratings are again from 1 (best) to 7 (worst).

Polity is an academic database measuring the democratic and autocratic characteristics of national political systems. Its main indicator is the Polity score ranging from 10 for the highest degree of democracy to −10 for the highest degree of autocracy. "Time" indicates the number of years a country has scored 8 or higher.

The data show, first, that the record of the new NATO members matches that of the incumbents. As for the Freedom House data, the ratings of 1 for political rights and 2 for civil liberties correspond to the standard ratings for the old NATO members.[22] The Polity scores of 9 or 10 for the new members are the standard scores for the old NATO

[22] Greece scored 3 for civil liberties. Turkey is the obvious outlier because it was only classified as a "partly free" country in 1996/97. All other NATO members were rated 1 for political rights and 1 or 2 for civil liberties.

members as well.[23] Second, all new members have a consistent record of compliance with liberal norms in their domestic politics. Ever since their democratic transitions in 1989/90, they have continously performed well in the Freedom House and Polity ratings (see the "time" columns). This indicates a high degree of consolidation and stability of their liberal-democratic systems.

The results are less clearcut with regard to the *differentiation among the CEECs*. On the one hand, the new members have been classified as "free" countries for a longer time than the other CEECs and scored higher in their ratings for the progress of democratic and economic transformation – indicating that the Czech Republic, Hungary and Poland were more advanced in the socialization process than the other CEECs. Thus, if only three countries were to be invited, the Freedom House data explain the actual selection correctly. On the other hand, however, nothing in the sociological institutionalist hypothesis determines that NATO should limit its initial round of enlargement to three countries in the first place. Lithuania and Slovenia matched both the "political rights" and "civil liberties" ratings as well as the Polity scores of the new members, and they even performed better on the Polity score than Poland. Given that their shorter period of socialization is due to their date of independence – Lithuania and Slovenia both became independent only in 1991 when the three new members already had had one year of liberal-democratic transformation – there did not seem to be any norm-based reason for NATO to exclude these two countries from its first round of enlargement.

At the Prague summit of November 2002, NATO invited seven CEECs to its *second round* of enlargement: the three Baltic states, Bulgaria, Romania, Slovakia, and Slovenia. By contrast, Albania and Macedonia as well as Croatia, the most recent candidate for NATO membership, were excluded from accession negotiations at this point. Table 5.2 shows that the selection of new members for the second round of NATO enlargement is fully in line with the data on compliance with the fundamental liberal norms of the Western community. First, the 2002 candidates generally attain the rating of 1 and 2 for political rights and civil liberties, which is the standard rating for the old member states and the accession countries of 1999. Bulgaria and Romania only deviate minimally from this standard. Moreover, Bulgaria, Latvia, Romania, and Slovakia have improved their ratings since the 1997 decision.

Second, the 2002 candidates have achieved some degree of democratic stability. Except for Slovakia and Romania, they have been rated

[23] The exception here is France with a score of 8 for 1996. However, due to the construction of the scores, the Polity ratings for France are notoriously low.

Table 5.2 *CEEC compliance with liberal norms: the 2002 enlargement round*

		PR/CL	Freedom Index	Time	Democracy	Economy
1997 Round	Czech Republic	1/2	free	12	1.81	2.00
	Hungary	1/2	free	12	1.94	1.92
	Poland	1/2	free	12	1.44	1.67
2002 Round	Bulgaria	1/3	free	11	3.06	3.50
	Estonia	1/2	free	9	2.00	1.92
	Latvia	1/2	free	8	1.94	2.50
	Lithuania	1/2	free	11	1.94	2.75
	Romania	2/2	free	6	3.31	4.00
	Slovakia	1/2	free	4	2.25	3.25
	Slovenia	1/2	free	10	1.94	2.58
Remaining candidates	Albania	3/4	partly free	0	4.13	4.17
	Croatia	2/2	free	2	3.25	3.58
	Macedonia	4/4	partly free	0	3.75	4.58

Data based on 2001/02 Freedom House ratings and "Nations in Transit" 2001 (http://www.freedomhouse.org). Polity data were not available for 2001 at the time of writing.

"free" for a longer time than the first round candidates when these were selected in 1997. Slovakia has the weakest record of reliability among the 2002 candidates, which is the main reason NATO made its final decision dependent on the outcome of the 2002 parliamentary elections.

Finally, there is a clear difference between the second round invitees and the remaining participants in NATO's Membership Action Plan. Only Croatia matches the ratings of the weakest accession country, Romania, but its shift toward liberal democracy after the end of the Tudjman regime has only been recent. Thus, the data for the second enlargement round corroborate the sociological approach to enlargement even better than those for the first round.

In sum, the community approach gives a convincing explanation of NATO's expansion to the East. It is congruent with the Alliance's officially stated reasons and makes a plausible case for the selection of candidates for the two rounds of NATO enlargement in 1997 and 2002. With regard to the first round, however, it is not fully determinate – NATO might as well have invited further CEECs whose record of compliance with liberal norms was not worse than that of the three front-runners. Moreover, the community approach does not explain the exact timing of the enlargement rounds. There is no theoretical reason why the second round should not have started in, say, 2000 instead of 2002.

The Eastern enlargement of the European Union

The European Union reaffirmed its general rules of enlargement in the early 1990s. In a report entitled "Europe and the Challenge of Enlargement" prepared for the Lisbon summit in June 1992, the European Commission responded to the request of the European Council in Maastricht (December 1991) to examine the implications of a future enlargement of the Community. First, it reiterated that a "state which applies for membership must . . . satisfy the three basic conditions of European identity, democratic status, and respect of human rights" (European Commission 1992: para 8). Second, an applicant state must accept the "Community system and its institutions" and must be able to implement the *acquis communautaire* (1992: paras 9, 11–12). Third, "Applicant states should also accept, and be able to implement, the Common Foreign and Security Policy as it evolves over the coming years" (1992: para 10).

The Commission proposals formed the basis for the Conclusions of the Presidency at the European Council in Copenhagen in June 1993. They not only established the accession of CEECs as an EU objective but also drew up a list of conditions to be fulfilled by the prospective members. These conditions came to be known as the *"Copenhagen criteria"* (European Council 1993). Basically, the EU requires "the stability of institutions guaranteeing democracy, the rule of law, human rights and respect for and protection of minorities" and "the existence of a functioning market economy." Candidates for membership must adhere to the aims of political, economic and monetary union as stated in the TEU (but do not have to meet the criteria of economic convergence required for joining the EMU).

Yet the Copenhagen criteria also contain provisions concerning the *capacities* of both the EU and the CEECs. While the candidates are required to have the capacity to cope with competitive pressure within the Union and the ability to adopt and implement the *acquis*, the Union must have achieved the capacity to absorb new members without endangering the momentum of European integration. At first sight, such conditions appear out of place in a sociological community perspective that emphasizes identity and legitimacy.

The condition of *Union capacity*, however, serves mainly as a demand on the current members to introduce the reforms necessary for an enlargement which the community rules oblige the EU to carry out.

According to the 1992 Commission report on "Europe and the Challenge of Enlargement," enlargement

> is a challenge which the Community cannot refuse. The other countries of Europe are looking to us for guarantees of stability, peace and prosperity, and for the opportunity to play their part with us in the integration of Europe. For the new democracies, Europe remains a powerful idea, signifying the fundamental values and aspirations which their peoples kept alive during long years of oppression. To consolidate their new-found liberty and stabilise their development, is not only their interest, but ours. (EC 92: para 40)

When, for instance, the 1996/97 Intergovernmental Conference left most reform issues undecided, the EU did not use this failure as a pretext for postponing formal accession talks. Instead, the negotiations began as planned in 1998. Rather than being made dependent upon progress in institutional and policy reforms, the enlargement project and timetable have created and increased the reform pressure.

As to the *capacity of the CEE candidates*, the Commission, in its 1997 "Opinions," evaluated the ability of the CEECs "to cope with competitive pressure and market forces within the Union," their "capacity to take on the obligations of membership," and their "administrative and legal capacity" *in the medium term*, whereas the institutionalization of basic liberal norms (democracy, human and minority rights, functioning market economy) was assessed *in its present condition*. This indicates that compliance with the constitutive liberal community rules is a "hard," non-negotiable criterion whereas economic and administrative capacities rank lower and do not have to be in place before a CEE candidate qualifies for opening accession negotiations.

Moreover, the EU committed itself to a process of socializing the CEECs to the rules of the Community and of preparing them for accession (see European Commission 1992). Association with its regular meetings of government officials and members of parliament, supplemented by a "Political Dialogue," served this purpose as well as the EU's more specific "pre-accession strategy" including a multilateral "structured relationship" between the CEECs and the EU institutions and a White Paper on the integration of the CEECs into the internal market (see, e.g., Mayhew 1998: chs. 2, 6; Sedelmeier and Wallace 1996). The European Commission furthermore constantly monitors and regularly assesses the learning results and the internalization of EU norms in the candidate countries. The first summary assessment was given in 1997, in the "Opinions" of the European Commission on the applications for membership of the ten associated CEECs. It resulted in a differentiated recommendation, to the European Council, to begin accession negotiations with some of the candidates and to postpone negotiations with others. Subsequently, all candidates have been subject to a screening process which serves to explain the Community rules to the CEECs and to evaluate the state of progress in their domestic adoption and implementation. Finally, the Commission has prepared annual Regular Reports on the candidates which have served to monitor the progress in the accession negotiations, to update the "Opinions" and to recommend the opening of negotiations with further applicant countries.

On the basis of the data used for the analysis of NATO enlargement, does the community approach explain why the EU decided, in 1997, to open accession negotiations with the Czech Republic, Estonia, Hungary, Poland and Slovenia and, in 1999, to expand these negotiations to Bulgaria, Latvia, Lithuania, Romania and Slovakia?

For the 1997 decision, see Table 5.3, an extended version of Table 5.1 on NATO's enlargement decision of the same year. The first extension is the inclusion of *all CEECs*. This allows me not only to evaluate the normative basis of the differentiation between the "fast-track" countries and "pre-ins" but also between the associated and the non-associated CEECs. The second extension is the inclusion of data provided by the European Bank for Reconstruction and Development (EBRD) in its annual transition reports. The *EBRD indicators* evaluate economic transition and are more technical in character than the indicators employed so far. For instance, "progress in transition" according to the EBRD does not exclude authoritarian political structures. I use the EBRD data mainly to assess to what extent capacity-oriented economic and technical criteria may have influenced the EU's selection of associated members and prospective full members.[24]

As in the case of NATO enlargement, the data confirm the liberal community hypothesis to a very large degree but do not sufficiently explain the exact choice of candidates for the "fast track" to membership. With the exception of Slovakia, all associated countries were categorized as "free" whereas all other CEECs were rated "partly free" or "not free." Since all "free" CEECs were associated with the EU, a political system in which democratic rights and civil liberties are basically guaranteed appears to be a sufficient (although not entirely necessary) condition of *association* with the EU.[25]

[24] The EBRD ratings are my calculations. The score is the average of eight ratings of progress in transition concerning "enterprises" (mainly privatization), "markets and trade," and "financial institutions." The best rating is 4.3 indicating "standards and performance typical of advanced industrial economies."

[25] Neither Romania nor Slovakia were "free" countries when they became associated with the EU.

Table 5.3 *Selection of CEECs for EU association and membership (1996/97)*

Status	Country	PR/CL	Freedom Index	Time	Polity	Time	Democracy	Economy	Class	EBRD
EU accession talks 1998	Czech Rep.	1/2	Free	7	10	7	1.38	1.88	CD	3.5
	Estonia	1/2	Free	4	6	–	2.06	2.13	CD	3.4
	Hungary	1/2	Free	7	10	7	1.44	1.63	CD	3.6
	Poland	1/2	Free	7	9	6	1.44	2.00	CD	3.4
	Slovenia	1/2	Free	6	10	6	1.88	2.38	CD	3.2
EU association	Bulgaria	2/3	Free	6	8	7	3.81	5.38	TS	2.8
	Latvia	2/2	Free	3	8	6	2.06	2.50	CD	3.1
	Lithuania	1/2	Free	6	10	6	2.06	2.50	CD	3.0
	Romania	2/3	Free	1	8	1	3.88	4.63	TS	2.7
	Slovakia	2/4	Partly free	–	7	–	3.81	3.38	TS	3.3
No association	Albania	4/4	Partly free	–	0	–	4.50	4.00	TS	2.6
	Belarus	6/6	Not free	–	–7	–	5.88	6.00	CA	1.6
	Bosnia-H.	5/5	Partly free	–	no data		no data			
	Croatia	4/4	Partly free	–	–1	–	4.25	3.88	TS	3.0
	Macedonia	4/3	Partly free	–	6	–	3.88	4.50	TS	2.6
	Moldova	3/4	Partly free	–	7	–	3.81	4.00	TS	2.6
	Russia	3/4	Partly free	–	4	–	3.75	3.50	TS	3.0
	Ukraine	3/4	Partly free	–	7	–	3.88	4.25	TS	2.4
	Yugoslavia	6/6	Not free	–	–7	–	no data			

In the column "class," "CD" means "consolidated democracy," "TS" means "transitional state," "CA" stands for "consolidated autocracy." For the EBRD data, see EBRD (1997: 14). For the sources of the other data, see the information on Table 5.1.

Furthermore, the more detailed figures for political rights and civil liberties reveal a *distinction* between the five CEECs that were invited to formal accession talks and the other associated countries. First, all countries of the top group received the best rating for political rights (1) and the second-best rating (2) for civil liberties, whereas Bulgaria, Latvia, Romania and Slovakia scored only 2 for political rights and 2 or worse for civil liberties. Second, the top five countries rank highest with regard to their achievements of democratic and economic transition as indicated by low "Democracy" and "Economy" values. Finally, the ratings for the invited countries *match the ratings for current EU members.* All EU members were rated 1 for political rights and 1 or 2 for civil liberties. (Only Greece scored 3 for civil liberties.) In the light of the liberal community hypothesis, it is puzzling only that Lithuania was not invited to formal accession talks even though its human rights record was as good as that of the first-rate candidates and the EU members. Except for a strongly deviant assessment of the Estonian political system, the Polity data reveal roughly the same picture.

A cross-check based on the economic and technical *EBRD indicators* of transition supports the general findings. Whereas political transition based on the liberal norms of human rights and democracy usually goes hand in hand with economic transition to a liberal market economy, there are three obvious exceptions. According to the EBRD rating, Slovakia (3.3) should have been among the first-rate candidates for accession to the EU, and Croatia and Russia (3.0) should have been among the countries associated with the EU. Neither was the case. As suggested by the data, the cause for this discrepancy was their human rights record which was below the standards of their economic peer group. This finding corroborates the expectation that the adherence to domestic liberal values and norms is a *conditio sine qua non* for membership and cannot be balanced by purely economic adaptation.

These findings – based on sources independent of the EU – are furthermore largely congruent with the European Union's own evaluation which can be found in the "Opinions" that the *European Commission* prepared for each of the candidate countries in 1997 (see Table 5.4). Generally, assessments by the expanding organization itself should be treated with caution as they might be used to rationalize *ex post* a selection of new members that was based on other than the publicly stated criteria. However, the Commission ratings and statements can be compared with the independent Freedom House and Polity data and checked for inconsistent and opportunistic justifications. In particular, it will be interesting to see how the Commission weights the normative criteria (liberal political and economic order) in comparison with the more functional criteria (the

Table 5.4 *The European Commission's 1997 "Opinions" on the associated CEECs*

Country	Political Criteria	Economic Criteria	*Acquis*
Czech Rep.	yes	yes	yes
Estonia	yes but accelerate naturalization	yes but not yet fully able to cope	considerable progress
Hungary	yes	yes	yes
Poland	yes	yes	yes
Slovenia	yes	yes	"has to make considerable efforts"
Bulgaria	"on its way"	limited progress/unable to cope	no
Latvia	yes but accelerate naturalization	considerable progress/serious difficulties in coping	some progress
Lithuania	yes	considerable progress/serious difficulties in coping	some progress
Romania	"on its way"	considerable progress/serious difficulties in coping	no
Slovakia	no	yes but lacking transparency in implementation	yes

Evaluations are based on European Commission (1997a; 1997c). Economic criteria are "Functioning market economy" and (after the oblique) "Ability to cope with competitive pressure in the medium term." "*Acquis*" refers to the capacity to transpose and implement the *acquis communautaire* in the medium term.

ability to cope with competitive pressure and the implementation of the *acquis*).

The Commission's evaluation of the political criteria was very similar to the Freedom House data. It regarded all countries that Freedom House rated 1 for political rights and 2 for civil liberties as fulfilling the basic political criteria for membership. This also held for Lithuania, and even Latvia scored as well as Estonia. By contrast, Bulgaria and Romania were judged to lag behind in the institutionalization of a liberal political system, and Slovakia failed completely on the political score. Although Slovakia fulfilled the economic criteria to a very large extent and has transposed and implemented the *acquis* no worse than the Czech Republic, Hungary and Poland, political non-compliance was sufficient to be dismissed as a first-rate candidate. This relegation is the more telling as, a few years before, Slovakia had been named, by the EU as well as in the literature, in the same breath as the Czech Republic, Hungary and Poland, as one of the most likely candidates for early membership. This evaluation underlines the constitutive character of liberal democracy for the EU as an organization of the Western international community.

According to the Commission, all countries of the top group had institutionalized a functioning market economy (the first economic criterion).

Interestingly, the Commission considered Estonia not fully able to cope with the competitive pressure of the internal market in the medium term (the second economic criterion) but still put the country in the top group. This may indicate that, in accordance with the community rules, the normative-institutional criterion trumped the capacity-based criterion. The economies of the countries on the waiting list (other than Slovakia) were found wanting on both accounts. The lack of a functioning market economy and "serious difficulties" of coping with the pressures of the internal market in Latvia and Lithuania seem to have been the main reasons why Estonia was preferred to its Baltic neighbors despite their political aptitude (see Bungs 1998: 26–30). Moreover, it is obvious that the capacity to transpose and implement the *acquis*, another technical criterion, was of little importance for the *opening* of accession negotiations. Although Slovenia's score on this point fell short of all associated countries except Bulgaria and Romania, it was admitted to the top group due to its good political and economic record.

In its Regular Reports of October 1999 – two years after the first decision to begin accession negotiations with a group of CEECs – the European Commission recommended that negotiations should be "opened with all candidate countries that fulfil the Copenhagen political criteria (democracy, the rule of law, human rights and respect for and protection of minorities) and have proved to be ready to take the necessary measures to comply with the economic criteria, i.e. Bulgaria, Malta, Latvia, Lithuania, Romania and Slovakia" (European Commission 1999).

The wording of this basic conclusion shows again the distinction the EU makes between the constitutive political norms of the community – which must be "fulfilled" – and the economic criteria which only require a "readiness to take the necessary measures to comply."

If this recommendation was in line with the liberal community hypothesis, the "pre-ins" of 1997, first, should have made progress in the internalization of the constitutive liberal norms of the community, second, should have reached a level of norm compliance that matches that of the current members but, third, do not necessarily have to have acquired the economic and administrative capacities to cope with market pressures in the internal market and to implement the *acquis*.

In Table 5.5, the most conspicuous cleavage among the CEECs is that between "free" countries, on the one hand, and "partly free" and "not free" countries, on the other. This cleavage is fully reflected in the cleavage between the CEECs that negotiate with the EU about membership and those that are not even associated with the Union. Moreover, the "Democracy" scores of the associated CEECs were generally higher than those of the non-associated CEECs (which is not true for the

Table 5.5 *Selection of CEECs for EU association and membership (1998/99)*

Status	Country	PR/CL	Freedom Index	Time	Polity	Time	Democracy	Economy	Class
EU accession talks 1998	Czech Rep.	1/2	Free	9	10	9	1.75	1.92	CD
	Estonia	1/2	Free	6	6	–	2.06	1.92	CD
	Hungary	1/2	Free	9	10	9	1.75	1.75	CD
	Poland	1/2	Free	9	9	8	1.44	1.67	CD
	Slovenia	1/2	Free	8	10	8	1.94	2.08	CD
EU accession talks 2000	Bulgaria	2/3	Free	8	8	9	3.31	3.75	TS
	Latvia	1/2	Free	5	8	3	2.06	2.50	CD
	Lithuania	1/2	Free	8	10	8	2.00	2.83	CD
	Romania	2/2	Free	3	8	3	3.19	4.17	TS
	Slovakia	2/2	Free	1	8	1	2.50	3.25	CD
No association	Albania	4/5	partly free	–	6	–	4.38	4.50	TS
	Belarus	6/6	not free	–	–7	–	6.44	6.25	CA
	Bosnia-H.	5/5	partly free	–	no data		5.13	5.58	TS
	Croatia	4/4	partly free	–	–1	–	4.19	3.67	TS
	Macedonia	3/3	partly free	–	6	–	3.44	4.58	TS
	Moldova	2/4	partly free	–	7	–	3.88	4.00	TS
	Russia	4/4	partly free	–	4	–	4.25	4.33	TS
	Ukraine	3/4	partly free	–	7	–	4.31	4.58	TS
	Yugoslavia	6/6	not free	–	–6	–	5.50	5.33	TS

See previous tables for data sources. Democracy ratings, economy ratings and country classifications are from "Nations in Transit 1999–2000" (<http://www.freedomhouse.org>). These scores reflect the period through June 1999.

Table 5.6 *The European Commission's 1999 Regular Report on the "pre-ins"*

Country	Political Criteria	Economic Criteria	*Acquis*
Bulgaria	yes but further efforts to strengthen rule of law	continued progress/not yet in a position to cope	determined efforts
Latvia	yes, significant progress in integration of non-citizens	yes	important progress
Lithuania	yes	continued progress/on the way to being able to cope	progress in most areas
Romania	still yes	no	partial progress
Slovakia	yes	close/should be able to cope	important progress

Evaluations are based on the conclusions of the country-specific chapters of European Commission (1999). Again, economic criteria are "Functioning market economy" and (after the oblique) "Ability to cope with competitive pressure in the medium term." "*Acquis*" refers to legislative alignment in the internal market area.

"Economy" scores). Thus, the intensity of institutional relationships between the EU and the CEECs generally corresponds to the level of compliance with liberal norms in the CEECs.[26]

The second observation is that, although Latvia, Romania and Slovakia received better ratings by Freedom House than in 1996–97 (Slovakia also attained a higher score in the Polity database), the scores of the "second tier" do not quite match that of the "first tier" and the standard values of the member states. Moreover, the EU invited two countries – Romania and Slovakia – to accession talks, which had only recently voted out of office governments with authoritarian tendencies and therefore could not yet be regarded as stable, consolidated liberal democracies. Thus, although the EU did not violate the rule to admit only norm-compliant states to accession negotiations, it slightly lowered its standards in comparison with the 1997 decision. In retrospect, and on the basis of these indicators, it is even less understable why Lithuania or Latvia were not admitted to accession talks in 1997. As before, this result points to the partial indeterminacy of the explanation for the exact choice of new members.

The *core assessments of the Commission's 1999 Progress Reports* (Table 5.6) confirm the basic findings on the 1997 "Opinions." First, the political

[26] Note that the Polity rating for Estonia deviates again from the overall picture.

criteria are the non-negotiable, *sine qua non* criteria for the opening of accession negotiations. All associated CEECs fulfilled these criteria in 1999, according to the Commission. Second, the 1999 Report demonstrates even more clearly than the 1997 Opinions that economic criteria and the implementation of the *acquis* are of secondary importance in the decision to open accession negotiations. Although all candidates had made some progress in meeting the economic, legislative and administrative requirement of the Union, variation was large – reaching from a clear "no" and only "partial progress" in legislative alignment in the case of Romania to a clear "yes" and "important progress" in the case of Latvia – and the overall picture was much less favorable than for the fast-track CEECs in 1997.

Conclusion

The community approach to enlargement gives a *plausible overall explanation* for the Eastern enlargement of NATO and the EU. It is, however, *not fully determinate* with regard to the differentiation between applicants and non-applicants and between (potential) members and (potential) non-members among the CEECs.

Identification with the Western international community and compliance with its liberal norms has been a sufficient but not a necessary condition of the *CEECs' desire to join the Western organizations*. On the one hand, all CEECs that have been successful in their liberal-democratic transformation or, at least, have seriously and persistently pursued liberal reform, have also declared their interest in NATO and EU membership. On the other hand, however, CEECs that deviated from basic liberal norms in their domestic and foreign policies did not shy away from applying for membership.

The community approach to enlargement generally explains *why the Western organizations expanded to Central and Eastern Europe*. The prospect of membership in the Western organizations serves to encourage liberal democratic transformation in this region, and by admitting CEECs to accession negotiations, the Western community formally recognizes that they have internalized its liberal identity, values and norms and that they are legitimate community members. This strategy of exclusive socialization is based upon the membership rules of the EU and NATO, has been reaffirmed in the official discourse on Eastern enlargement, and has been implemented in the association policies of both organizations.

The Western organizations' *selection of CEECs* to be invited to accession negotiations largely corroborates the liberal community hypothesis. Above all, compliance with community norms has been a necessary condition of membership. That is, no CEEC has been admitted to accession talks if it systematically violated basic liberal norms. To some extent, it also has been a sufficient condition of membership: CEECs with an outstanding record of socialization have not been denied accession negotiations and have not been discriminated against in favor of CEECs with a significantly worse record.

However, the liberal community hypothesis has not proven fully determinate with regard to either the *exact number* of invited CEECs or the *exact timing* of invitations to accession negotiations. For instance, NATO might as well have invited Lithuania and Slovenia to its first round of Eastern enlargement, and the EU might as well have added Lithuania to the "fast-track" group of CEECs. Otherwise, the EU could have relegated Estonia to the "pre-ins" in 1997 or postponed accession negotiations with Bulgaria and Romania in 1999 without contradicting the hypothesis of exclusive community-building. Finally, of course, the hypothesis does not predict the exact starting date for accession negotiations or the exact accession date. It demands that candidates have a consistent record of adherence to liberal norms indicating "internalization" but it does not specify whether the appropriate probationary period is three years or thirty.

Finally, *congruence between NATO and EU enlargement* has been moderate. Whereas NATO *admitted three* CEECs in 1999, the EU only *opened accession negotiations* but did so with *ten* CEECs. Although both organizations have similar membership rules, are committed to the integration of liberal-democratic CEECs, consider enlargement to be embedded in a process of international socialization, pursue an exclusive socialization strategy, started their formal enlargement procedures at approximately the same time in 1997 and differentiated among the CEECs according to their compliance with liberal norms, it is obvious that both the exact selection of CEE members and the timing of their accession follow specific organizational conditions and procedures rather than a common community rationale and a tightly coordinated enlargement schedule. After NATO's second enlargement round, however, it is likely that the eight most advanced CEECs will be both EU and NATO member states in 2004.

However, the sociological institutionalist explanation of Eastern enlargement also generates doubts and questions about its *generalizability*. Is it a specific explanation of *NATO* and *EU Eastern* enlargement because of the particularities of the CEECs, the post-Cold War situation, or the organizations in question? Or can it be generalized to the post-Cold War Northern and Southern enlargement processes of the EU, to earlier enlargement events of the EU and NATO, to the enlargement of other community organizations, and to enlargement events other than applications and accession?

Other post-Cold War enlargement processes. In the post-Cold War era, the EU not only embarked upon Eastern enlargement but also, in the first half of the 1990s, completed the so-called EFTA enlargement.[27] It further negotiated on the accession of Cyprus and Malta and has accorded Turkey candidate status. At first sight, the community-building and international socialization approach appears to be less suitable in most of these cases than for Eastern enlargement. First, the EFTA countries had long been liberal democratic states and part of the Western community before they applied for membership. To a lesser extent, this is true for Cyprus and Malta as well. Thus, whereas the analysis of Eastern enlargement showed that a country's commitment to the liberal community values and norms was *no necessary* condition of its application for NATO and the EU, the EFTA enlargement seems to demonstrate that it is *not even a sufficient condition*. Iceland, Norway, and Switzerland are still not prepared to join the EU (and, by the way, Austria, Finland and Sweden have still not decided to become NATO members). Second, the EFTAns are a group of advanced and wealthy industrial countries and therefore may have been attractive to the EU members for utilitarian reasons alone. In this case, a rationalist explanation would probably successfully account for the decision of the EU to expand to these countries.

Earlier enlargement events. The first enlargement which expanded the original EC-6 to Denmark, Great Britain and Ireland, raises similar questions. By contrast, the EC's Southern enlargement of the 1980s appears to resemble Eastern enlargement closely. Like the CEECs, Greece, Portugal, and Spain had transformed themselves from authoritarian to liberal democratic systems and were well below the Community average of wealth and economic capacity. But then it is puzzling that, whereas Spain joined NATO only in 1982, Greece and Portugal had already been NATO members when they were governed by authoritarian regimes. Turkey is another obviously deviant case.

Other organizations. As we have seen in the case of Eastern enlargement, NATO and the EU follow the same exclusive socialization strategy. Nevertheless, their timing of admisson and their selection of candidates have varied considerably. These differences are dwarfed, however, by the Eastern enlargement of the Council of Europe, another European organization of the Western community. By 1996, the CoE had admitted all CEECs except for Belarus, Bosnia-Hercegovina and Yugoslavia as

[27] EFTA is the European Free Trade Association, originally a rival organization to the EEC, established in 1960.

full members. Many of its members are only "partly free" and a far cry from consolidated liberal democracies. Obviously, the CoE has opted for an *inclusive* strategy of socialization. This observation, however, begs the question why organizations of the same community pursue different socialization strategies.

Other enlargement events. So far, the analysis has been limited largely to two kinds of enlargement events, the desire or application of outsider states to join an international organization and the decision of the organization to open accession negotiations and to admit outsider states. Broadly defined, however, enlargement encompasses other events, such as the establishment of institutionalized relations between the organization and the outsider state and associated membership, but also the exclusion or withdrawal of a member from the organization. Does the liberal community hypothesis hold for these events, too?

The anecdotal evidence provided above raises sufficient doubts about the generalizability of the sociological explanation to warrant a systematic study – of various enlargement events, over an extended time period, for several organizations and a large number of countries, and controlling for alternative causes – in order to test the significance of the community rules for the enlargement of the Western organizations. This will be the subject of chapter 6.

6 The event history of enlargement

In this chapter, I expand the analysis of NATO and EU Eastern enlargement in various ways: first, to a third European organization, the Council of Europe; second, to all European countries in the broad definition of the "OSCE region"; third, to the entire period since the foundation of the Western organizations; and fourth, to other enlargement events including the establishment of institutionalized relations between the organization and an outsider state and the withdrawal or exclusion of associated and member states. The rationale of these various extensions is to increase the number and variety of observations implied by the liberal community hypothesis about enlargement and, thereby, to put this hypothesis to a more demanding test than that of EU and NATO Eastern enlargement alone.

The tool for this test is event history analysis, a multivariate statistical analysis especially designed to analyze the conditions under which an event is more or less likely to occur. Before discussing the results of the event history analysis, I will specify the dependent variable "enlargement events," present some descriptive evidence about their occurrence, and explain the research design.

Enlargement events

To analyze the expansion of West European regional organizations, I developed the Enlargement Database (ENLABASE). ENLABASE contains data on the development of institutional relationships between the European Union, NATO and the CoE, on the one hand, and the (up to) fifty-three countries of the OSCE region, on the other.[1] ENLABASE provides a nearly complete dataset on the enlargement of the European organizations of the Western international community. First, the OSCE region, which includes the United States and Canada as well as the Transcaucasian and Central Asian successor states of the Soviet Union,

[1] ENLABASE and the codebook are available at <http://www.ifs.tu-darmstadt.de/regorgs/enlabase.htm>. The latest update (August 2002) covers events through 2001.

constitutes the broadest institutional articulation of "Europe" and comprises all states that are, in principle, eligible for membership in (at least one) of the Western organizations.[2] Second, the EU, NATO and the CoE are the core European organizations of the Western international community. Third, ENLABASE covers enlargement events starting with the establishment of these organizations in 1949 (NATO, CoE) and 1958 (EEC). The event data in ENLABASE cover the dates of membership applications for the CoE and the EU[3] and changes in the status of the institutionalized relationship between each state and organization. The annual status is observed on 31 December of each year.[4] Although the database distinguishes twenty-seven status levels for the EU and eleven for NATO and the CoE, in the following analysis I focus on four events only:

Institutionalization. The first event in the enlargement process broadly defined is the establishment of special institutional relations between the organization and an outsider state.[5] It requires at least the negotiation of a trade agreement with the EU and observer status in NATO's Euro-Atlantic Cooperation Council or the Parliamentary Assembly of the CoE.

Application. The application for membership is used as the indicator for a state's desire to join the organization. Although this indicator is reliable and easy to measure, two problems must be kept in mind. One is the fact that, in NATO, there is no formal application procedure at the beginning of the enlargement process. Candidates are invited by the organization. The other problem is that states may want to become members long before they formally apply but they wait for favorable circumstances.

Accession. Accession is the most important event in the enlargement process. However, just as "application" is used as an indicator for the principal decision of a state to join the organization, the variable of interest here is the principal decision of the organization to admit this state. In the EU and in NATO, this decision is made before accession negotiations start. I therefore use the beginning of accession negotiations (code 29) and not accession itself as the indicator event.[6] In the CoE, the accession

[2] The sample excludes the European micro-states of Andorra, Liechtenstein and San Marino as well as the Holy See.

[3] NATO has no formal application procedure. The relevant subset of ENLABASE is the table "APPLICATIONS." APPLICATIONS 2001 has 100 entries, 2 of which are uncertain.

[4] The relevant subset of ENLABASE is the table "STATUS." STATUS 2001 has 5,323 entries; 22 of them (or 0.41 percent) are uncertain. STATUS contains one annual data point for each state-organization dyad observed on 31 December of each year.

[5] Technically, it is indicated by the first time the status code reaches a value higher than zero.

[6] The broken-off accession negotiations between the EEC and the UK in 1963 is the only case in which either NATO or the EC ever retreated from their decision to admit a country with which they had entered into accession negotiations.

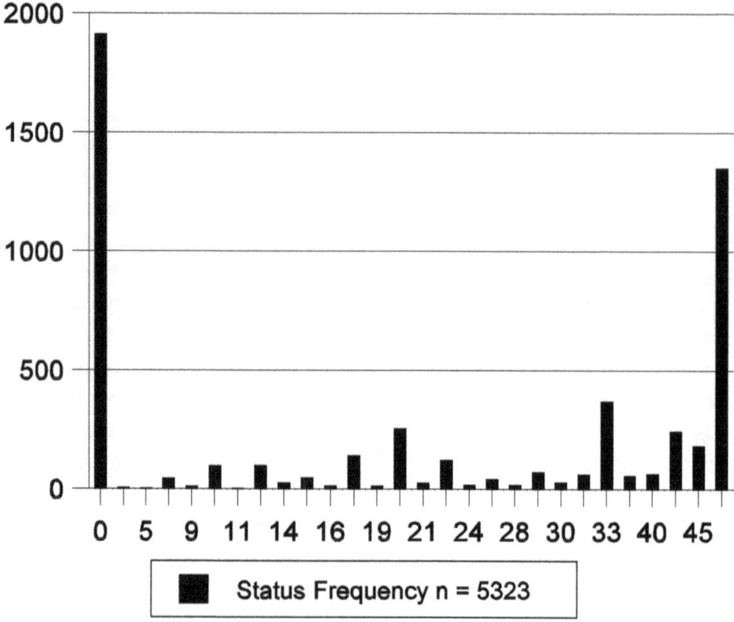

Figure 6.1 Status frequencies

procedure begins almost automatically after an application for membership. The decision to enlarge is then made at the end of a sometimes lengthy examination of the candidate. For this reason, the signing of the organization's Statute (code 30), which occurs shortly after the positive decision of the organization, is the most valid indicator.

Exclusion. An organization may also shrink as the result of the exclusion or withdrawal of a member state. Because this is a very rare event, I included those cases in which membership was frozen or in which the associate status of a non-member state was cancelled or suspended.

In the remainder of this section, I give an overview of the data contained in ENLABASE 2001. First, I take a look at the distribution of status values in the sample. Second, I describe the four major enlargement events to be analyzed here – institutionalization, application, accession and exclusion. The goal of this section is to make the reader familiar with the events to be explained and to bring out some basic features of the data and the enlargement history of the Western organizations.

Disregarding the time-series dimension of the data for the moment, the distribution of status values in the sample is strongly U-shaped with maxima at the lowest and the highest status values (see Figure 6.1). The

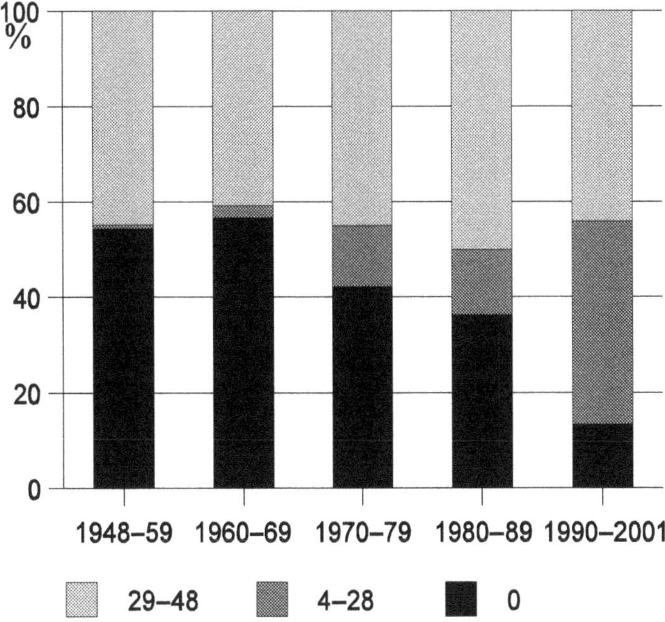

Figure 6.2 Status frequencies across time

minimal status of zero (no special status) accounts for 1,912, the maximal status of 48 (full membership) for 1,351 cases; taken together, both extreme categories cover over 61 percent of all observations. If we collapse the nine different categories for membership (codes 29 to 48) into one, less than 19 percent of all annual data points fall between "no special status" and "membership." This distribution indicates a dichotomous tendency of the status variable and justifies the selection of the four enlargement events for the subsequent statistical analysis. The major thresholds in the enlargement process seem to be the transition from "no special status" to (some kind of) an institutionalized relationship with the organizations and accession. The intermediate steps are of relatively minor quantitative importance.

The picture becomes more differentiated if we look at the changes in the distribution of status values across time. Figure 6.2 shows, first, that the polarization between members and states with no special institutional status was greatest in the first two decades. In the 1970s and 1980s, intermediate relationships became more important but were still underrepresented in comparison with the extreme categories. In the post-Cold War decade, however, this distribution has changed completely.

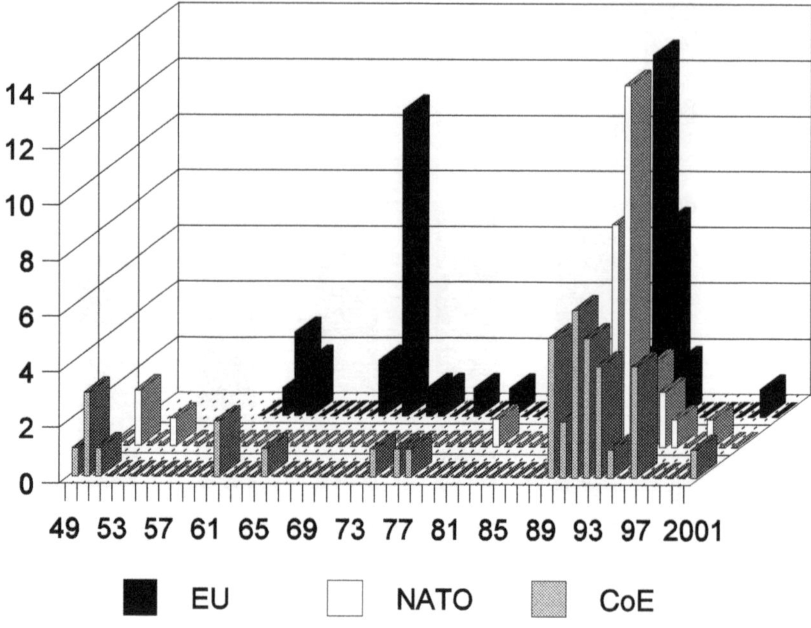

Figure 6.3 Institutionalization events

Whereas the "no special status" category has become marginal, intermediate relationships with the organizations have become almost as frequent as membership. It is becoming increasingly rare for an OSCE country not to have any institutionalized relationship with the Western organizations, and the Western organizations have developed a diversified array of institutionalized relationships with outsider countries short of membership.

Figure 6.3 shows the frequency of newly established institutionalized relations between the three organizations and outsider states for each year from 1949 to 2001. For each organization, there has been a short period of moderate activity immediately after their foundation. In the CoE and NATO, this short period was followed by a period of almost forty years with rare (CoE) or virtually no further establishment of institutionalized relations with non-member states. In contrast, the European Community embarked upon a signficant intensification of its relations with the EFTA members at the beginning of the 1970s leading to either membership or, at least, trade and cooperation agreements. This EC move toward institutionalization is the cause of the first major appearance of intermediate relationships between "no special status" and membership

Table 6.1 *Absence of institutionalized relations (July 2003)*

Organizations	Countries
EU	–
NATO	Bosnia-Hercegovina, Cyprus, Malta, Yugoslavia
CoE	Belarus, Kazakhstan, Kyrgyzstan, Tajikistan, Turkmenistan, Uzbekistan

in the 1970s and 1980s. The immediate post-Cold War years mark the apex of institutional expansion for all three Western organizations. After the mid-1990s, we can observe a new period of minor institutionalization activity which is mainly due to a saturation effect – almost all countries of the OSCE region have entered into institutionalized relationships with the three Western organizations. Table 6.1 gives an overview of the remaining countries.

Membership applications and accession are the most relevant events in the enlargement process. Table 6.2 gives a complete list of these events for all three organizations with the dates and names of the countries involved. Moreover, linked enlargement events and "enlargement rounds" are grouped in the table. From 1949 to 1956, NATO and the Council of Europe opened to a group of "latecomers" including the Federal Republic of Germany, Greece and Turkey. In the 1960s, the CoE was joined by a group of mainly newly independent countries (Cyprus and Malta in addition to Switzerland). Then a group of EFTA countries led by Great Britain sought to join the European Economic Community shortly after its establishment. After a failed attempt in the early 1960s, the Community's first enlargement was successfully completed in 1973. In the mid-1970s, the democratic transformation of the right-wing authoritarian systems in Greece, Portugal and Spain led to a Southern enlargement of all Western organizations. In the first half of the 1990s, the EU went through its second Northern or EFTA enlargement before it fully embarked upon the Eastern enlargement project together with the other two organizations.

Figure 6.4 shows the number of states that have applied, in each year, for membership in the CoE and the EC. As in the case of "institutionalization" events, applications are not equally distributed across time but tend to cluster around certain dates. A first wave of applications immediately followed the founding of the two organizations; in the EC case, this wave reappeared in 1967, four years after accession negotiations with the UK were broken off by the Community on the insistence of France. Then

Table 6.2 *Applications and accessions*

	EC/EU		NATO	CoE	
Year	Application	Accession negotiation	Accession negotiation	Application	Accession
Founding Members	Belgium France Germany (FR) Italy Luxembourg Netherlands		Belgium Canada Denmark France Iceland Italy Luxembourg Netherlands Norway Portugal UK US	Belgium Denmark France Ireland Italy Luxembourg Netherlands Norway Sweden UK	
1949				Greece Iceland Turkey	Greece Iceland
1950				Germany (FR)	Turkey
1951			Greece Turkey		Germany (FR)
1952–53					
1954			Germany (FR)		
1955					
1956				Austria	Austria
1957–60					
1961	Denmark Ireland UK			Cyprus	Cyprus
1962	Norway				
1963				Switzerland	Switzerland
1964				Malta	
1965					Malta
1966					
1967	Denmark Ireland Norway UK				
1968–69					
1970		Denmark Ireland Norway UK			
1971–73					
1974	Greece			Greece	Greece
1975					
1976		Greece		Portugal	Portugal
1977	Portugal Spain			Spain	Spain
1978		Portugal			
1979		Spain			
1980					
1981			Spain		
1982–86					
1987	Turkey				
1988				Finland	
1989	Austria			Hungary	Finland
1990	Cyprus Malta			Czechoslovakia Poland Yugoslavia	Hungary
1991	Sweden			Bulgaria Estonia Latvia Lithuania Romania	Czechoslovakia Poland
1992	Finland Norway Switzerland			Albania Croatia Russia Slovenia Ukraine	Bulgaria

Table 6.2 *(cont.)*

Year	EC/EU Application	EC/EU Accession negotiation	NATO Accession negotiation	CoE Application	CoE Accession
1993		Austria Finland Norway Sweden		Belarus Czech Republic Macedonia Moldova Slovakia	Czech Republic Estonia Lithuania Romania Slovakia Slovenia
1994	Hungary Poland				
1995	Bulgaria Estonia Latvia Lithuania Romania Slovakia			Bosnia-Hercegovina	Albania Latvia Macedonia Moldova Ukraine
1996	Czech Republic Slovenia			Armenia Azerbaijan Georgia	Croatia Russia
1997			Czech Republic Hungary Poland		
1998	Malta	Cyprus Czech Republic Estonia Hungary Poland Slovenia		Yugoslavia	
1999					Georgia
2000		Bulgaria Latvia Lithuania Malta Romania Slovakia			
2001				Yugoslavia	Armenia Azerbaijan
2002			Bulgaria Estonia, Latvia, Lithuania, Romania, Slovakia, Slovenia		Bosnia-Hercegovina
2003	Croatia				Yugoslavia (Serbia and Montenegro)

followed a period of low activity interrupted only by applications of the newly democratized countries of Southern Europe. Again, the number of applications increased enormously after the end of Cold War.

The chronological distribution of accession events shown in Figure 6.5 reveals the same pattern. The admission of new members or the beginning of accession negotiations is even more concentrated in time bringing about the typical feature of "enlargement rounds."

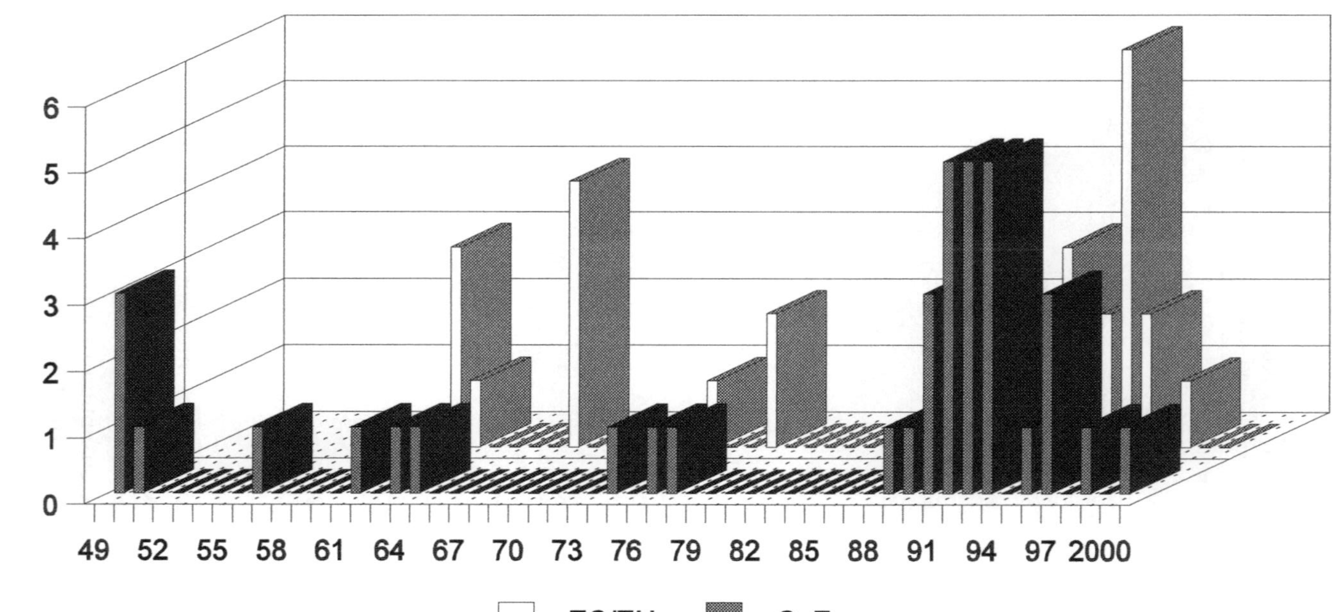

Figure 6.4 Applications for CoE and EC/EU membership

In the EU case, we see the beginning of the failed EFTA enlargement in 1961/62, the beginning of the successful first EFTA enlargement in 1970, the Southern enlargement starting in the second half of the 1970s, and the beginning of the second EFTA enlargement in 1993; finally, the start of the accession negotiations with the five fast-track CEECs plus Cyprus in 1998 and the follow-up with the remaining associated CEECs plus Malta in 2000. NATO is the organization with the fewest admissions. The admission of Greece, Turkey and Germany in the founding period of the alliance was followed by a long hiatus – to be interrupted only by the admission of Spain in 1982 – until negotiations with the first CEE candidates began in 1997. The expansion pattern of the Council of Europe shows the four phases highlighted in Table 6.2: post-foundation enlargement, accession of newly independent countries, Southern enlargement and Eastern enlargement. For all three organizations, Eastern enlargement marks the apex of expansion activity.

The events of exclusion or withdrawal are rare (see Table 6.3). As expected in a liberal Community perspective, most of these events are related to systematic violations of human rights and democratic rules – the military *coups d'état* in Greece and Turkey (1967 and 1980), the presidential *coup d'état* in Belarus (1996), Serbia's ethnopolitical aggression in former Yugoslavia, and Russia's (second) war in Chechnya (1999). In contrast, Belarus suspended its participation in PfP with NATO in 1999 as a sign of protest against NATO's military intervention in Kosovo.[7] Turkey suspended its active participation in the Association Council in 1997 because the EU refused to accord Turkey the status of a candidate for membership.[8]

This table also indicates when "the dog didn't bark," that is, when Western organizations failed to exclude a state in spite of systematic violations of liberal norms. For instance, NATO did not follow the other two Western organizations in excluding Greece and Turkey after the military *coups d'état*, or in suspending their membership in the alliance. In contrast to the CoE, neither NATO nor the EU formally suspended cooperation with Belarus or Russia.

Two general conclusions follow from the univariate analysis of enlargement events.

[7] Russia did the same but partially re-established cooperation with NATO under the NATO–Russia Founding Act before the end of the year. In 2000, Belarus resumed cooperation in the EAPC/PfP framework, too.

[8] In 1999, Turkey received official "candidate" status but has not yet started accession talks.

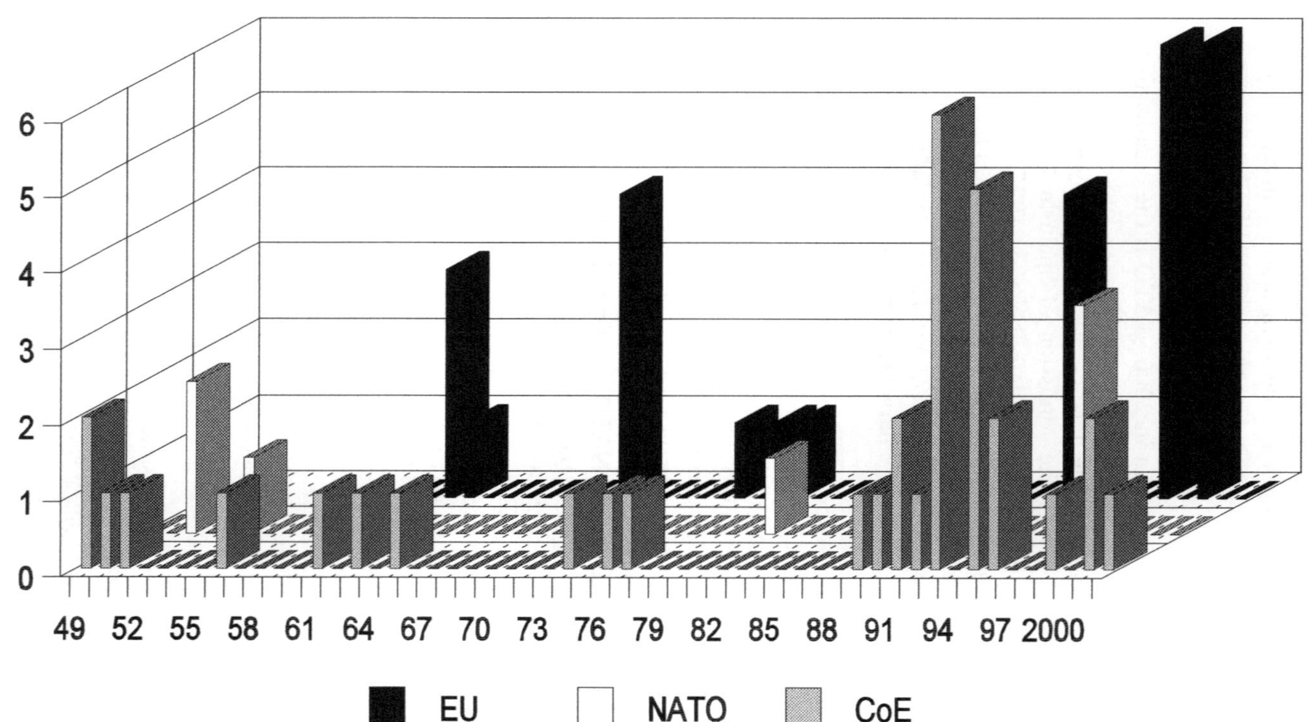

Figure 6.5 Accession events

Table 6.3 *Exclusion/withdrawal events*

Country	Organization	Year	Event
Greece	EC/EU	1967	association suspended
Greece	CoE	1969	European Human Rights Convention denounced
Greece	CoE	1970	withdrawal
Turkey	EC/EU	1981	association suspended
Turkey	CoE	1981	membership frozen (exclusion from Assembly)
Yugoslavia	CoE	1991	special guest status suspended
Turkey	EC/EU	1997	association frozen (no Council meetings)
Belarus	CoE	1997	special guest status suspended
Belarus	NATO	1999	partnership suspended
Russia	CoE	2000	membership frozen (PACE voting rights suspended)

First, the "positive" enlargement events – the establishment of institutionalized relationships, membership applications and accession (negotiations) – reveal a similar pattern: a clustered occurrence of events, an initial period of intensive enlargement activities after the founding of the organizations and a long period of moderate to low enlargement activities. This period ended together with the Cold War which brought about the organizations' apex of enlargement activity in the 1990s.

Second, several observations give rise to the expectation that enlargement events are time-dependent – the clustered occurrence of enlargement events, their apparent dependence on singular events like the establishment of the organization or the end of the Cold War, the growing importance of intermediate relationships between "no special status" and membership, and the saturation effect caused by the establishment of institutionalized relationships with almost all states of the region.

Event history analysis

Because of the structure of the data and the quality of the dependent variable, event history analysis (EHA) is the most suitable design for the statistical analysis of the enlargement process.[9] EHA deals adequately with pooled data as well as time dependence and, as the name implies, is specifically designed to analyze events: "qualitative changes that occur at a specific point in time" (Allison 1984: 9). Conventional linear or logistic regression is a problematic tool for the analysis of pooled data. Moreover, the static model on which it is based neglects both time-dependent

[9] See Allison (1984); Box-Steffensmeier and Jones (1997); Petersen (1991); Yamaguchi (1991) for an introduction to event-history analysis.

covariates and "censoring," that is, events that have not occurred during the period of investigation (see Box-Steffensmeier and Jones 1997: 1415–17). Finally, the length of the time series (up to fifty-one years) made it difficult to use a panel design.

Technically speaking, event history analysis is used to study "the duration for the nonoccurrence of an event" (Yamaguchi 1991: 3). Because of the origins of EHA in medical and engineering studies, this duration is called the "risk period." In the study of enlargement, the risk period for external states begins with the establishment of the international organization or with the establishment of the external state (in case it became independent after the organization was founded). All states that have not had the event in question at a given time are defined as the "risk set" of that time. When the event occurs, a state drops out of the risk set and of the sample of states to be analyzed. For the "institutionalization" event, the risk set comprises all states that have not entered into special institutionalized relations with the organization; for "application," it is the set of states that have not applied for membership. The risk set for "accession" is the class of non-member states that have not yet begun accession negotiations, and for "exclusion," it comprises all associated and member states. If, for instance, states withdraw their application or fail to join the organization after accession negotiations, they re-enter the risk sets for "application" and "accession."

Event history models first specify a "transition rate" (or "hazard rate") which determines the baseline likelihood of a unit to have the event at a given time regardless of any independent variables. This transition rate may be time-independent. In that case, the event is equally likely to occur at any time during the risk period. But, generally, event history models assume the baseline transition rate to vary with the time that has elapsed since the beginning of the risk period. For the purpose of this study, however, I am not interested in the transition rate and its time-dependence *per se* but focus on how it is affected by external factors that increase or reduce the likelihood of an enlargement event.

Event history models come in two basic variants: discrete-time and continuous-time models. For substantive and methodical reasons, enlargement will be analyzed with a *discrete-time model.*[10] Discrete-time models are based on the assumption that "the event of interest occurs only at discrete time-points" (Yamaguchi 1991: 15). This assumption holds for the most relevant events in the enlargement process. In

[10] Allison (1984: 14–22); Box-Steffensmeier and Jones (1997: 1423–42); Yamaguchi (1991: 15–27). See also the "grouped duration model" proposed by Beck, Katz and Tucker (1998: 1265–66).

general, international organizations make decisions about the beginning of accession negotiations or the admission of new member states at fixed, predetermined dates (for instance, the regular meetings of the heads of government and state). Treaties with external states enter into force on 1 January or, at least, on the first day of a month. Thus, there is always a real interval (and not just an observation interval) between the occurrence of two subsequent enlargement events of the same kind. Moreover, the most popular continuous-time model, the Cox proportional hazards model, leads to biased parameter estimates when several units experience an event at the same time (see Box-Steffensmeier and Jones 1997: 1424; Yamaguchi 1991: 16). This is often the case in the enlargement process, for instance, when agreements with external states enter into force at the same date or outsider states jointly begin accession negotiations. Finally, the data for most independent variables of interest are only measured annually so that it would not be possible to analyze smaller time intervals adequately. Discrete-time models in EHA are most often formulated as logit models[11] and estimated using binary logistic regression programs.[12] This is because the dependent variable is dichotomous: either the event has occurred at a given time (1) or not (0).

Liberal norms and their competitors: the independent variables

The independent variables presumed to increase or decrease the likelihood of enlargement events can be subdivided into five blocks: test variables (liberal norms), cultural control variables, material control variables, institutional factors and time dependence. Table 6.4 gives an overview of the variables, the theoretical concepts they are intended to measure, and the sources used.

Test variables. The test variables are indicators for the adoption of, and compliance with, the liberal norms postulated by the liberal community hypothesis as the main set of enlargement conditions. Domestic compliance with liberal norms is measured with the *POLITY* indicator built by subtracting a state's autocracy score from its democracy score according to the Polity database. Both the democracy and autocracy scores are derived from codings of the competitiveness and openness of executive

[11] Allison (1984: 17); Beck, Katz and Tucker (1998: 1266–68); Box-Steffensmeier and Jones (1997: 1425); Yamaguchi (1991: 15–19).

[12] I used the binary logistic regression program in SPSS 10. On logistic regression analysis, see Kleinbaum (1994); Menard (1995).

Table 6.4 *Independent variables*

Name	Indicator for	Calculation	Source
Test Variables (liberal norms)			
POLITY	compliance with domestic liberal norms	democracy score minus autocracy score of the POLITY database (+10 to −10)	POLITY IV http://www.cidcm.umd.edu/inscr/ polity
NEUTR	compliance with multilateralist norm	neutrality status (yes/no)	own research
MIDS	compliance with norm of peaceful conflict management	cumulated participation in militarized interstate disputes divided by number of years in the period of observation	MID database http://pss.la. psu.edu
Expectation	positive effect of POLITY and negative effect of NEUTR and MIDS on all events except "exclusion"		
Cultural Control Variables			
CIV	cultural identity	civilization according to Huntington	Huntington 1993
EURO	definition of "Europe"	location of a state in Europe narrowly or broadly defined	own definition
Material Control Variables (general)			
GDPTOT	economic output, resources	GDP at market prices in US Dollar	World Bank, *UN Statistical Yearbook*
GNPCAP	economic development, wealth	GNP per capita	World Bank, *UN Statistical Yearbook*, own calculation
GROWTH	economic performance	increase in GDPTOT since previous year	
PROX	geopolitical relevance and international interdependence	politico-geographical proximity (number of borders between organization and external state)	own calculation
Material Control Variables (specific)			
AGRIC	strength of the agricultural sector	share of agricultural production of total GDP	World Bank
EDUC	level of education	secondary-level school enrollment in percent of the eligible population	World Bank
DEFEXP	military resources	defense expenditures in US Dollar	IISS Military Balance
DEFCAP	military commitment	DEFEXP per capita	IISS Military Balance
Institutional Variables			
REL	institutional dynamics	existence of institutional relations before application or accession (yes/no)	ENLABASE
APP#, ACC#	influence of earlier events	repeated application, accession (negotations) (yes/no)	
Temporal Variables			
INST, APPT, ACCT, EXCT	time dependence	number of years in risk period for institutionalization, application, accession, and exclusion	ENLABASE, own calculation

recruitment, constraints on the chief executive, and competitiveness and regulation of political participation.[13]

In order to measure a state's compliance with the norm of peaceful conflict management, I used the Militarized Interstate Disputes database and calculated an annual dispute participation score (*MIDS*) by cumulating the number of disputes in which the state has participated since 1948, the beginning of the period of observation, and then dividing it by the number of years that have passed since 1948 (or the independence of the state). Note, however, that this is a relatively crude measure because hostility or fatality levels are not taken into account. It is based, furthermore, on a strict interpretation of the liberal non-violence norm because the norm is taken to apply to relations with all other states (and not only with other democratic states).

It proved most difficult to find adequate data for measuring compliance with the multilateralist norm. In order to avoid tautological reasoning, I discarded any indicator based on the number of memberships and the quality of participation in international organizations. The alternative used here is the dummy variable *NEUTR*. It distinguishes neutral and non-neutral states and serves as an indicator for an isolationist or multilateralist basic foreign policy orientation. Non-neutrality, however, covers only one aspect of multilateralism. There are countries like Sweden that pursue a policy of non-alignment in security affairs but are otherwise strongly engaged in multilateral international policy-making. Thus I only claim to test the effect of neutrality, not of adherence to multilateral norms in general. The hypothesis to be tested is:

> The higher the POLITY value, the lower the MIDS value, and if NEUTR equals 0, the more likely it is that a state will enter into institutional relations with the Western organizations, apply for membership, and be admitted (to accession negotiations), and the less likely it is that it will be excluded or withdraw from the organization.

Conversely, the null hypothesis postulates that neither POLITY nor MIDS nor NEUTR significantly affects the likelihood of the four enlargement events.

Cultural control variables. The cultural control variables cover the sociological alternatives to the liberal community hypothesis. First, in order to control for the rival conceptualization of the West as a religion-based

[13] In contrast with chapter 3, I did not use Freedom House data because they only date back to 1972 and thus cover only half of the period of investigation. Since Malta is not included in the Polity database, I calculated POLITY scores on the basis of Freedom House data. This is a justifiable procedure because Polity and Freedom House data are strongly correlated (Jaggers and Gurr 1995: 474).

civilization, the European states are categorized according to Huntington's (1993) classification into Western, Slavic-Orthodox, and Islamic states (*CIV*). Second, the analysis takes into account that, while all three organizations, in their basic treaties, restrict enlargement to "European" countries, Europe is a construction without objective, natural borders. Therefore, enlargement may be affected by the way in which Europe is defined. The liberal community hypothesis posits that Europe is defined by the spread of liberal values and norms in the OSCE area. The dummy variable *EURO* indicates a more narrow definition of Europe, excluding Central Asia, the Transcaucasian states, Russia, Turkey, the United States and Canada.

Material control variables. The general material control variables consist of three standard economic indicators and one geographical measure. The economic indicators are total economic output (*GDPTOT*), economic output per capita (*GNPCAP*), and economic growth *(GROWTH)*. These indicators cover different aspects of the economies of the states in the risk set – their size, their level of development and wealth, and their performance dynamics. The geographical proximity indicator (*PROX*) is an ordinal-scale proxy variable for geopolitical relevance and international interdependence. It is assumed that both factors decrease with growing distance between the organization and the state and that, therefore, proximity will increase the likelihood of institutionalization, application and accession. The distance is not measured in kilometers but by the kind and number of borders between the organization and the outsider state.[14]

In addition, I included *organization-specific* material control variables in the analysis. In the EU case, these variables are the strength of the agricultural sector of the economy (*AGRIC*) and the level of education (*EDUC*) in a given state. The share of the agricultural sector of a state's total economy is important because of the dominance of agricultural expenditure in the Community budget. Supposedly, the higher this share the greater the incentive for a state to join the EU but the greater the reluctance of the Community to admit this state. *EDUC* is a general indicator for the "modernity" of the state and, in particular, for the qualification of its workforce. Here, I assume that the level of secondary-school enrollment is positively correlated with both the external state's and the Community's interest in closer ties.[15] In the NATO case, data on total

[14] A direct land border is coded 1, a direct (territorial) sea border is coded 2. Two land borders are coded 3, three land borders 4. A distance of more than three land borders or a high sea border is coded 5.

[15] The level of unemployment in the external state would have been another important variable. Unfortunately, however, the data available from the World Bank for the entire country sample only cover less than a decade.

military expenditures (*DEFEXP*) and military expenditures per capita (*DEFCAP*) were added to the set of control variables.[16] Since the CoE does not provide material club goods, no specific material control variables were specified.

Institutional variables. The inclusion of institutional variables serves to control for the momentum that may be created by previous enlargement events. First, it may be that the existence of special institutional relations between the organization and a non-member state (*REL*) will, by itself, increase the likelihood of future applications and accession. Second, it may be that earlier (failed) applications or accession negotiations will influence the probability of later applications and accession negotiations (*APP#* and *ACC#*).

Temporal variables. In order to control for time dependence, a set of dummy variables (*INST*, *APPT*, *ACCT*, *EXCT*) was added to the specified logit models. They measure the amount of time a state has spent in the risk set for each event of interest.[17]

Finally, note that the main purpose of the EHA is to test whether liberal norms have a significant influence on the enlargement of Western organizations beyond the post-Cold War accession of CEECs to the EU and NATO. The other variables mainly serve as controls; it is not the goal of the analysis to evaluate competing theories, hypotheses, or explanatory factors.

Models and statistics: technical information

Missing data of some variables for certain time periods are a serious problem for EHA. For instance, whereas the general economic data were not available prior to 1960, the militarized interstate dispute data end with 1992. In order to maximize use of the available data, I specified *four models* for the analysis of each event.

Model 1 includes the *test variables* (plus controls for time dependence as well as institutional momentum). They cover the time period from the *establishment of the organizations to 1992* (because data on militarized interstate disputes are not available for the remainder of the 1990s). *Model 2* adds the *cultural control variables.* They are available for the entire period of investigation (1948–99). In order to be able to analyze the whole period, MIDS is dropped from these models. In turn, PROX is added.

[16] I did not include data on the total number of military forces because this variable is a poor indicator of military strength. It can indicate strong military power but also military inefficiency and an outdated military organization. Defense expenditures are the more reliable indicator.

[17] This is the procedure suggested by Allison (1984: 18) and Beck, Katz and Tucker (1998).

Model 2 thus *maximizes the period of investigation* and include all variables for which the necessary data are available.

Model 3 adds and focuses on the *general economic control variables*. For most of the countries, these data range from *1960 to 1998*. At the expense of excluding the foundational period of the organizations, Model 3 thus includes all general variables except MIDS and thus *maximizes the number of variables*. *Model 4* is designed to analyze the influence of the *organization-specific material variables* for the EU and NATO. In the EU case, this results in a shortening of the actual period of examination; it reaches from around 1975 to around 1996 depending on the availability of the data.

As a side-effect, this modeling strategy makes it possible to test the *robustness* of the correlations, that is, their statistical significance across models. It allows one to detect to what extent the significance of a given coefficient depends on the constellation of variables or on the time period under investigation. Tables 6.5–6.18 show the main results of the binary logistic regression analysis for each model.[18]

The row "model" provides information on *model significance* (Menard 1995: 19–24). G(M) is a measure of statistical significance for the entire model. It is calculated as the difference between −2LL (the log-likelihood multiplied by −2) for a model without explanatory variables and −2LL for the model examined. If G(M) is statistically significant, we can reject the null hypothesis and conclude that the independent variables taken together explain the event better than the intercept-only model. The following figure gives the percentage of cases that are classified correctly on the basis of the multivariate model. Note, however, that the statistics of model significance are of secondary importance because it is not the goal of the analysis to find the best model for the explanation or prediction of enlargement events but to test the liberal community hypothesis.

For each *independent variable* included in the model, the tables show the unstandardized logistic regression coefficients (β), their standard errors (S.E.) and a likelihood ratio test (G(X) and *p*).[19] G(X) represents the difference between G(M) and the −2LL for the model without the independent variable in question, p indicates the statistical significance of G(X).[20] The signs of the regression coefficients have been changed

[18] The data set used to estimate the models can be obtained from the author on request at <frank.schimmelfennig@mzes.uni-mannheim.de>.

[19] SPSS does not produce overall coefficients and standard errors for polytomous nominal-scale and ordinal-scale variables. Therefore, they are missing.

[20] One asterisk (*) indicates moderate significance (at the $p = .05$ level), two asterisks high significance (at the $p = .01$ level), and three asterisks extremely high significance (at the $p = .001$ level).

in some cases to improve readibility: positive signs always indicate a direction of the relationship between independent and dependent variable that is in line with the hypothesis; negative signs stand for relationships that contradict the hypothetically expected direction. Also note that the coefficients are unstandardized. Since they are based on different units of measurement, their relative strength cannot be assessed directly. It is not unproblematic to compare the coefficients for the same variable across different models because differently specified models will result in different degrees of bias affecting the size of the coefficients. The main interest is in statistical significance: is it justified to reject the null hypothesis that liberal norms do not systematically affect the enlargement events of the major Western organizations?[21]

Discussion of results: events

The presentation and discussion of the results of the event history analysis will be divided into two sections, one focusing on the enlargement events, the other on the independent variables.

Institutionalization. Which variables have a significant influence on the establishment of institutionalized relationships between the Western organizations and non-member countries? From the results of the statistical analysis, it appears that domestic compliance with fundamental liberal norms as measured by the POLITY indicator is the most robust explanatory factor. With the exception of the most specific model (4), POLITY coefficients are statistically significant and positive across all models and organizations. Thus, in accordance with the liberal community hypothesis, the democratic quality of national political systems seems to have mattered for the relationship of outsider states with the Western organizations already at this low institutional level.

The record for the other two test variables is mixed: whereas neutrality – unsurprisingly – has been a highly significant obstacle for the establishment of institutionalized relationships between NATO and the states

[21] In addition, I performed regression diagnostics. First, for each model, a tolerance statistic was calculated in order to discover collinearity. Except when mentioned in the tables, this statistic was above a value of 0.2 indicating no severe collinearity. The few cases of severe collinearity concerned two indicators that measure similar explanatory factors; in each of these cases, I let the program estimate two models, each of which included one of the two indicators. None of these indicators proved significant. Second, I performed a Box-Tidwell Test for non-linearity and a likelihood ratio test for non-additivity, that is, I tested the statistical significance of interaction effects for POLITY, the main independent variable (Menard 1995: 60–67). However, potential non-linear and significant non-additive effects were too few and not sufficiently robust to merit serious consideration and a respecification of the models.

Table 6.5 *Institutionalization Model 1 (test variables)*

	EU (N = 488)				NATO (N = 730)				CoE (N = 623)			
Var	β	S.E.	G(X)	p	β	S.E.	G(X)	p	β	S.E.	G(X)	p
POLITY	.091	.025	13.80	.000***	.158	.044	15.55	.000***	.157	.036	21.74	.000***
NEUTR	.819	.501	2.84	.092	3.89	1.11	24.15	.000***	1.28	.743	3.33	.068
MIDS	.314	.136	6.64	.010**	.188	.432	.21	.649	.252	.166	2.66	.103
INST			32.41	.001***			72.30	.000***			43.51	.000***
model	G(M) = 57.33 (.000), 90.8 percent				G(M) = 119.26 (.000), 96.6 percent				G(M) = 86.40 (.000), 95.8 percent			

* moderate significance
** high significance
*** extremely high significance

of the OSCE region, and to some extent also for the institutionalization of relations with the CoE, it did not consistently matter in EU external relations. By contrast, the EU is the only organization in which the peacefulness of outsider states may have been relevant.

Cultural affiliation does not exert any robust influence on institutionalization. Civilizational culture, the Huntington variable, is significant only in the EU case. On closer inspection, however, it turned out that this correlation contradicts the hypothesis of the West as a civilizational community: the statistical results indicate that Orthodox and Islamic countries have been significantly more likely to enter into institutionalized relations with the EU than Western states.[22] The other cultural control variable, the definition of Europe, has only been significant in one of the CoE models.

Among the general material control variables, proximity is significant in only half of the models, whereas the economic variables lack statistical significance throughout. By contrast, institutionalization proves to be strongly time-dependent. In sum, controlling for time, democracy is the most significant factor in the establishment of institutionalized relations between the Western organizations and the outsider states of the OSCE region.

Application. POLITY is again significant in the first three models for all organizations. Thus, the likelihood of application for membership appears to vary systematically with the regime of outsider states. This covariation remains significant if controlled for cultural, material, organizational, and temporal factors.

The evidence for the other two test variables is as mixed as for institutionalization: neutrality appears to have been an obstacle to applications for EU and CoE membership if we take the entire history of the organizations into account (Models 2 and 3). In the case of MIDS, states with lower involvement in militarized disputes have been more likely to apply for CoE membership. However, MIDS is not significant in the basic EU model.

The cultural control variables do not consistently affect the likelihood of applications for membership. Among the material control variables, proximity is the only robust influence. Ironically, economic per capita output is significantly correlated with applications for CoE but not EU membership.

As for the other variables, fairly robust and high significance for APPT indicates the time-dependence of application events. By constrast, prior

[22] Since SPSS does not produce coefficients for polytomous variables, I recategorized CIV as a dichotomous variable distinguishing between Western and non-Western states and reran Models 2 and 3.

Table 6.6 *Institutionalization Model 2 (cultural control variables)*

	EU (N = 497)				NATO (N = 783)				CoE (N = 688)			
Var	β	S.E.	G(X)	p	β	S.E.	G(X)	p	β	S.E.	G(X)	p
POLITY	.161	.036	24.06	.000***	.249	.054	33.55	.000***	.374	.064	57.90	.000***
NEUTR	.531	.548	.97	.325	2.40	.668	13.71	.000***	4.55	1.09	23.55	.000***
CIV			8.50	.014**			.45	.801			.25	.885
EURO	−.416	.549	.058	.445	−1.32	.871	2.34	.126	1.32	.837	2.57	.109
PROX			7.02	.135			13.24	.010**			21.79	.000***
INST			26.12	.010**			41.6!	.000***			36.12	.001***
model	G(M) = 72.13 (.000), 90.9 percent				G(M) = 151.99 (.000), 96.2 percent				G(M) = 149.95 (.000), 96.2 percent			

Table 6.7 *Institutionalization Model 3 (economic control variables)*

	EU (N = 256)				NATO (N = 370)				CoE (N = 296)			
Var	β	S.E.	G(X)	p	β	S.E.	G(X)	p	β	S.E.	G(X)	p
POLITY	.142	.053	8.64	.003**	.242	.101	8.20	.004**	.350	.091	25.16	.000***
NEUTR	.122	.697	.03	.861	3.18	1.31	6.46	.011**	4.69	1.70	10.57	.001***
CIV			7.49	.024*			1.61	.448			.076	.692
EURO	−.406	.890	.021	.646	−.353	1.52	.05	.815	3.34	1.42	7.35	.007**
GOPTOT	.000	.000	.00	.956	.000	.000	.01	.945	.000	.000	1.67	.196
GROWTH	−.047	.031	3.55	.110	−.054	.049	1.38	.240	−.02	.031	.22	.639
GNPCAP	severe collinearity with GDPTOT				.000	.000	.56	.453	.000	.000	.34	.562
PROX			7.57	.109			10.72	.013**			9.25	.055
INST			21.25	.047*			32.59	.002**			30.52	.004**
model	G(M) = 75.32 (.000), 89.8 percent				G(M) = 129.26 (.000), 95.9 percent				G(M) = 105.25 (.000), 94.9 percent			

Table 6.8 *Institutionalization Model 4 (specific material control variables)*

	EU (N = 57)					NATO (N = 304)			
Var	β	S.E.	G(X)	p	Var	β	S.E.	G(X)	p
POLITY	.311	.204	3.57	.059		.136	.081	3.25	.071
NEUTR	−32.74	782.18	8.03	.005**		3.54	1.55	6.16	.013**
GNPCAP	−.001	.000	3.48	.062		.000	.000	2.94	.086
GDPTOT	severe collinearity with GNPCAP					severe collinearity with GNPCAP			
GROWTH	−.090	.100	.96	.352		−.023	.046	.26	.609
AGRIC	.039	.101	.15	.697	DEFEXP	severe collinearity with DEFCAP			
EDUC	.858	.431	8.18	.004**	DEFCAP	−3.55	3.82	1.13	.287
PROX			9.38	.052*				10.71	.013**
INST			26.61	.001***				21.89	.025*
model	G(M) = 54.33 (.000), 86.0 percent					G(M) = 106.20 (.000), 96.1 percent			

Table 6.9 *Application Model 1 (test variables)*

	EU (N = 775)				CoE (N = 634)			
Var	β	S.E.	G(X)	p	β	S.E.	G(X)	p
POLITY	.158	.071	7.11	.008**	.187	.060	12.62	.000***
NEUTR	.077	.613	.02	.900	1.61	1.09	2.56	.109
MIDS	.089	.215	.18	.670	.693	.317	8.05	.005**
REL	−.238	.931	.07	.798	4.10	.840	38.37	.000***
APP#	1.37	.770	3.09	.079	2.94	1.41	3.23	.072
APPT			34.43	.001***			18.64	.135
model	G(M) = 56.27 (.000), 97.8 percent				G(M) = 128.45 (.000), 97.3 percent			

Table 6.10 *Application Model 2 (cultural control variables)*

	EU (N = 953)				CoE (N = 709)			
Var	β	S.E.	G(X)	p	β	S.E.	G(X)	p
POLITY	.311	.089	24.04	.000***	.279	.065	24.09	.000***
NEUTR	1.94	.619	10.96	.001***	4.31	1.33	14.69	.000***
CIV			1.65	.439			.90	.639
EURO	−.403	1.48	.007	.789	1.14	.988	1.43	.232
PROX			29.30	.000***			7.56	.109
REL	−.894	.685	1.73	.189	3.94	.936	29.46	.000***
APP#	−1.01	.695	2.24	.134	2.76	1.20	4.79	.029*
APPT			54.45	.000***			11.59	.561
model	G(M) = 121.63 (.000), 97.2 percent				G(M) = 167.67 (.000), 96.8 percent			

applications (APP#) do not significantly affect the likelihood of later applications. And whereas prior institutionalized relations (REL) with the CoE have significantly increased the chances of applications for membership, institutionalized relations with the EU have not had any systematic effect on the outsider countries' decision to apply. In sum, controlling for time, democracy (followed by proximity and neutrality) is again the most robust correlate of enlargement.

Accession. The accession models (Tables 6.13–6.15) reveal that POLITY is the only independent variable that is significant (and very highly so) across organizations, time periods and constellations of variables. As expected, "neutrality" did well in all of the NATO models. But its high significance in all models that cover the entire time period until 1999 demonstrates that it has also worked consistently as an impediment to membership in the "civilian" Western organizations. MIDS was only moderately significant in the basic CoE model.

Table 6.11 *Application Model 3 (economic control variables)*

	EU (N = 625)				CoE (N = 311)			
Var	β	S.E.	G(X)	p	β	S.E.	G(X)	p
POLITY	.308	.093	19.02	.000***	.289	.131	7.05	.008**
NEUTR	3.50	.992	16.47	.000***	6.24	3.51	3.94	.047*
CIV			4.57	.102			9.04	.011**
EURO	.049	1.69	.00	.977	−3.30	4.40	.62	.430
GDPTOT	.000	.000	.03	.855	.000	.000	1.08	.299
GNPCAP	.000	.000	.79	.487	.001	.000	4.68	.031*
GROWTH	.042	.049	.79	.375	.134	.116	1.69	.193
PROX			19.91	.001***			20.70	.000***
REL	.029	.906	.00	.975	35.50	138.69	29.56	.000***
APP#	−1.43	.931	2.46	.117	14.40	83.09	2.81	.094
APPT			19.98	.001***			22.56	.047*
model	G(M) = 99.00 (.000), 96.0 percent				G(M) = 144.86 (.000), 97.4 percent			

As in the analysis of the previously discussed events, the cultural control variables performed badly. Whereas CIV did not produce a single significant coefficient in six different models, there has been a tendency of the countries falling under a narrow definition of Europe to be more likely to be or more quickly admitted to the CoE than countries of the wider Europe.

The analysis of the material variables was severely hampered by failed model estimations owing to numerical problems (Model 3 for NATO and Model 4 for EU and NATO). The available results indicate that countries with high total economic output are more likely to accede to the EU and the CoE than countries with smaller economies; GNP per capita, however, is insignificant. Even proximity does not seem to matter as consistently for accession as it did for applications: it is significant in only one of the Models 2 and 3 for the EU and the CoE.

A prior institutionalized relationship with the organization is a bad predictor of accession. It is not only insignificant in the NATO and CoE models but, in the EU models, the significant coefficients even contradict the hypothetical expectation: the existence of an institutionalized relationship makes accession negotiations with the EU *less* likely to begin. Moreover, whether a state had conducted (failed) accession negotiations with the organization or had been a member before does not significantly affect the likelihood of its accession at a later date. Finally, accession seems to be less time-dependent than institutionalization and applications. ACCT is significant only in one third of the models.

Table 6.12 *Application Model 4, EU (specific material control variables)*

	POLITY	NEUTR	GNPCAP	GDPTOT	GROWTH	AGRIC	EDUC	PROX	REL	APP#	APPT
β	.260	3.99	.000	.000	.216	−.052	.034		12.50	4.17	
S.E.	.215	3.20	.000	.000	.120	.284	.057		85.60	44.66	
G(X)	2.24	1.84	1.07	.26	4.75	.42	.38	12.89	1.15	6.20	27.42
p	.135	.175	.301	.610	.029*	.519	.540	.012**	.284	.013**	.007**
model	N = 279, G(M) = 65.33 (.000), 96.1 percent										

Table 6.13 *Accession Model 1 (test variables)*

	EU (N = 806)				NATO (N = 738)				CoE (N = 645)			
Var	β	S.E.	G(X)	p	β	S.E.	G(X)	p	β	S.E.	G(X)	p
POLITY	.282	.164	11.03	.001***	.511	.369	13.96	.000***	.259	.089	17.21	.000***
NEUTR	1.12	.881	1.79	.180	13.02	105.5	10.74	.001***	.809	.840	.96	.327
MIDS	.159	.234	.50	.480	−1.65	1.80	1.036	.244	.567	.373	4.63	.031*
REL	−1.09	1.02	1.23	.268	−1.41	396.0	.000	1	1.07	.684	2.43	.119
ACC#	.614	.765	.63	.428	constant, no repeated accessions				4.77	1.91	5.45	.020*
ACCT			19.53	.108			20.24	.089			11.37	.580
model	G(M) = 41.43 (.001), 98.6 percent				G(M) = 35.1 (.005), 99.6 percent				G(M) = 56.65 (.000), 97.8 percent			

Table 6.14 *Accession Model 2 (cultural control variables)*

	EU (N = 1040)				NATO (N = 963)				CoE (N = 758)			
Var	β	S.E.	G(X)	p	β	S.E.	G(X)	p	β	S.E.	G(X)	p
POLITY	.418	.198	19.25	$.000^{***}$	.357	.203	10.80	$.001^{***}$	.419	.088	41.94	$.000^{***}$
NEUTR	1.62	.684	6.41	$.011^{**}$	12.67	65.06	17.69	$.000^{***}$	4.08	1.24	16.07	$.000^{***}$
CIV			1.15	.562			.41	.813			.08	.962
EURO	4.65	35.62	.14	.704	−1.67	2.04	.64	.422	2.24	1.10	4.97	$.026^{*}$
PROX			13.72	$.008^{**}$			3.38	.497			6.63	.157
REL	−1.73	.803	4.88	$.027^{*}$	−2.49	1.58	2.90	.088	.188	.697	.073	.787
ACC#	−.984	.773	1.71	.192	constant, no repeated accessions				3.46	2.79	1.89	.169
ACCT			31.36	$.005^{**}$			11.41	.653			22.95	.061
model	G(M) = 82.27 (.000), 98.1 percent				G(M) = 47.30 (.003), 99.4 percent				G(M) = 122.73 (.000), 97.4 percent			

Table 6.15 *Accession Model 3 (economic control variables)*

	EU negotiations (N = 691)				EU accession (N = 727)				CoE (N = 352)			
Var	β	S.E.	G(X)	p	β	S.E.	G(X)	p	β	S.E.	G(X)	p
POLITY	.489	.251	14.39	.000***	10.92	86.34	7.45	.006**	1.09	.404	36.22	.000***
NEUTR	3.27	1.31	7.65	.000***	.917	1.27	.52	.472	7.97	3.79	6.95	.008**
CIV			1.12	.944			.00	1			4.64	.098
EURO	19.73	51.85	2.51	.113	42.08	1345	.00	.984	14.37	6.00	15.71	.000***
GDPTOT	.000	.000	4.54	.033*	.000	.000	2.76	.097	.000	.000	5.70	.017*
GROWTH	−.074	.110	.44	.509	1.055	.666	3.96	.047*	.138	.132	1.25	.264
GNPCAP	.000	.000	.15	.699	.000	.000	.47	.493	.000	.000	.11	.741
PROX			2.79	.593			12.43	.014**			9.62	.047*
REL	−3.72	1.44	8.02	.005**	13.11	600.8	1.54	.214	−1.15	1.74	.42	.515
ACC#	−2.05	1.38	2.40	.101	constant, no repeated accessions				5.37	40.4	.11	.741
ACCT			23.61	.051*			28.32	.057			49.13	.000***
model	G(M) = 64.07 (.000), 98.0 percent				G(M) = 65.48 (.000), 99.0 percent				G(M) = 117.22 (.000), 97.2 percent			

Table 6.16 *Exclusion Model 1 (test variables)*

	EU (N = 395)				CoE (N = 784)			
Var	β	S.E.	G(X)	p	β	S.E.	G(X)	p
POLITY	122.49	40722	20.33	.000***	30.06	111.22	33.50	.000***
NEUTR	1245.6	9819.6	.00	.994	196.76	1484.1	.00	.987
MIDS	564.47	4130.5	2.77	.096	18.96	41.57	.21	.650
EXCT			.00	1			7.35	.289
model	G(M) = 25.13 (.003), 100 percent				G(M) = 41.05 (.000), 99.9 percent			

The estimation of EU Model 3 with actual accession as the dependent variable (Table 6.15, middle column) shows that choosing the beginning of accession negotiations as the indicator for the organization's decision to enlarge does not bias the analysis against the material control variables. Whereas GDPTOT loses its significance and GROWTH only turns barely significant, POLITY remains highly significant.[23] In sum and with the caveat that material control variables could not be thoroughly controlled, the decision of the Western organizations to admit, or to begin accession negotiations with, an outsider state appears to be most systematically related with that state's adoption of democratic norms in domestic politics and with its non-neutral status.

Exclusion. Because of the small number of exclusion events, the analysis of exclusion models was burdened with two problems. First, only one exclusion model for NATO could be estimated because there has not been any such event in NATO before 1999 (when Belarus suspended its participation in PfP), and this model proved insignificant. Second, the exclusion models classified the cases (almost) entirely correctly causing the problem of "(quasi)complete separation" and resulting in extremely high coefficients and standard errors. As a consequence, the estimated parameters are inefficient but not biased. That is, they can still be used to make accurate inferences about the variables (Menard 1995: 69).

The statistical results of the event-history analysis for exclusion are quickly summarized: POLITY is the only variable that proved significant in all the estimated models. Other variables were either significant in a single model only or had the wrong sign (EURO). These results indicate that exclusion or withdrawal from membership in, or association with, the EU and the CoE is systematically and inversely correlated with the states' compliance with basic liberal norms in domestic politics. The less

[23] Note, however, that NEUTR becomes insignificant.

Table 6.17 *Exclusion Model 2 (cultural control variables)*

	EU (N = 575)				NATO (N = 901)				CoE (N = 1058)			
Var	β	S.E.	G(X)	p	β	S.E.	G(X)	p	β	S.E.	G(X)	p
POLITY	25.5	597.8	17.00	.000***	2.73	193.3	5.74	.017*	9.40	77.6	21.52	.000***
NEUTR	52.3	3377	.00	.999	.531	8143	.00	1	53.46	5768	.00	.994
CIV			9.25	.010**			.00	1			.00	1
EURO	83.7	28476	.00	.999	−26.79	2264	.00	.994	−29.65	24992	4.15	.042*
PROX			13.92	.008**			2.77	.597			.00	1
EXCT			5.00	.543			6.03	.420			7.55	.273
model	G(M) = 37.52 (.001), 100 percent				G(M) = 15.61 (.409), 100 percent				G(M) = 51.39 (.000), 99.6 percent			

democratic a state is (or has become after accession or association), the more likely it is excluded or withdraws from the Western organizations. Neither compliance with the international liberal norms of peace and multilateralism, nor cultural and material factors, nor the duration of a state's membership or association affect this relationship consistently.

Discussion of results: variables

In the previous section, the focus of discussion has been on the four enlargement events and their determinants. I will turn now to the significance of different variable groups and individual variables across enlargement events.

Test variables. POLITY has proved to be by far the most robust variable in the analysis. In all models, the POLITY coefficients had the correct sign, and in thirty-one of thirty-four models, the POLITY coefficients were significant, mostly so at the 0.1 percent level. Insignificant coefficients for POLITY only appeared in the models testing organization-specific material variables for the EU and NATO, indicating that significance may be affected by short periods of examination. Generally, however, POLITY is an extremely reliable correlate of enlargement, and in the case of exclusions and withdrawals, it is even the only robust factor. Thus, the likelihood of an outsider state's establishment of institutionalized relations with, application for membership in, accession to, and exclusion from the Western organizations is robustly correlated with its adoption of fundamental liberal norms of domestic conduct.

The evidence for the other two test variables is less convincing. Unsurprisingly, the coefficients for *neutrality* are correct and significant in all NATO models (except exclusion) whereas the results for the EU and the CoE are mixed. The neutrality variable attained its best results in the application and accession models covering the full period of examination. This seems to indicate that neutrality is more important as an obstacle to applications for and the attainment of membership than for the establishment of institutionalized relations or exclusion from the organization. This is entirely plausible. Neutrality should hinder a state much less in establishing some low-level institutionalized relationship with a regional organization than in seeking and attaining membership. Once a neutral state is a member, however, neutrality should lose its relevance again.

MIDS is generally insignificant in NATO enlargement; it is significantly correlated with the establishment of institutionalized relations with the EU (but not with applications, accession and exclusion) and with applications for and accession to the CoE (but not with institutionalization and exclusion). Thus, there is only one unambiguous but also quite trivial

Table 6.18 *Exclusion Model 3 (economic control variables)*

	EU (N = 496)				CoE (N = 783)			
Var	β	S.E.	G(X)	p	β	S.E.	G(X)	p
POLITY	22.59	1049	1.2E+07	.000***	12.10	211.41	25.53	.000***
NEUTR	32.01	15733	.00	.999	−14.09	3339.7	.00	.999
CIV			.00	1			.00	1
EURO	60.22	21996	.00	1	−154.52	2117.7	1.5E+08	.000***
GDPTOT	−.000	.006	.00	1	.001	.008	.05	.816
GNPCAP	−.002	.901	.00	.999	−.000	.124	.00	.998
GROWTH	−3.56	1975.8	.00	1	−6.98	98.77	3.5E+19	.000***
PROX			.00	1			.00	1
EXCT			.00	1			16.07	.013**
model	G(M) = 36.63 (.004), 100 percent				G(M) = 60.51 (.000), 100 percent			

result for the liberal norms of foreign policy. Whereas the neutrality of an outsider state is an impediment to NATO enlargement, its involvement in militarized interstate disputes is not.

In sum, the liberal community hypothesis about the enlargement of Western organizations in Europe is partially corroborated by the statistical analysis. Adoption of and compliance with liberal norms in the domestic sphere is a robust factor in the enlargement process. The more democratic a non-member state, the higher its likelihood of establishing institutionalized relations, seeking membership and being admitted to the EU, NATO, and the CoE; the less democratic a member or associated state, the higher its risk of being excluded or withdrawing from the Western organizations. By contrast, the compliance of states with the foreign policy norms of non-neutrality and non-involvement in militarized interstate disputes is a less significant and reliable correlate of enlargement. It appears, however, that neutrality is a more significant obstacle than involvement in military conflict, in particular when it comes to applying for and being admitted to Western organizations.

Cultural control variables. The cultural control variables performed weakly in general. In the few cases in which CIV proved significant at all, a reanalysis based on a dichotomous categorization of states according to Western and non-Western cultural affiliation actually revealed that, in contradiction to the hypothesis of civilizational community, non-Western non-member states were more likely to establish institutionalized relations with the EU and to apply for CoE membership than Western states. The differentiation between a "wider" and a "narrower" Europe only seems to have mattered to some extent in CoE enlargement. At any rate, the large-*n* event history analysis supports the previous conjecture that, in contrast to political culture, religious culture does not matter systematically in the enlargement of the Western organizations. Nor do different conceptualizations of the borders of "Europe."

Material control variables. On the whole, the economic control variables perform no better than the cultural ones. None of them is statistically significant (with the correct sign) in more than two (out of thirteen) models. Of the organization-specific variables, only the level of secondary education had a significant coefficient in one of two models (EU institutionalization). Thus, the economic or military potential of outsider states does not seem to have any significant influence on their relationship with the Western organizations. In contrast, geographical proximity proved to be an important correlate of enlargement events. Being significant in more than half of the models, it is only outperformed by POLITY – however, by a wide margin. The significant coefficients are fairly evenly distributed across all three organizations but not across all four enlargement events.

Whereas outsider states are very likely to apply for membership the closer they are located to the organizations, this correlation is not robust for accession (negotiations) or exclusion events.

Institutional and temporal variables. Overall, the evidence for self-reinforcing or self-weakening institutional dynamics of the enlargement process is weak. First, whether a state had applied for membership or conducted accession negotiations before (APP#, ACC#) neither systematically increased or decreased the likelihood of subsequent applications and accession. Second, the effect of an institutionalized relationship on applications and accessions is non-uniform. Earlier association with the CoE increases the likelihood of a later application for membership but does not increase the chances of being admitted to the organization. In the EU case, earlier institutionalized relations (REL) do not increase the likelihood of applications for membership but appear to *decrease* the chances of being invited to accession negotiations. In the enlargement process of NATO, earlier institutionalized relations are not significantly related to the opening of accession negotiations at all.

The event history analysis detected significant time-dependence in more than half of the models. In general, the relevance of the time a state has spent in the risk set decreases with the progress of enlargement. It is significant in all institutionalization models, in most application models, in only a third of the accession models, and in only one of the exclusion models.

In sum, then, POLITY is the only variable that proved highly significant across all enlargement events, organizations, and estimated models. Domestic compliance with liberal norms thus seems to be a general condition of the central events in the enlargement process, from the establishment of institutional relations with external states and their membership applications to the admission of new members and their exclusion or withdrawal. The addition of cultural, material, institutional and temporal controls did not damage the robustness of this test variable. Provided that no important variables were omitted, it appears justified to conclude that outsider states' domestic compliance with liberal-democratic community rules is the single most important variable that drives and constrains the enlargement of Western organizations. Furthermore, the analysis gives no reason to doubt the negative corollary of the liberal community hypothesis: the entire enlargement process of the core Western organizations is *not* systematically affected by *other* factors than the spread of liberal values and norms in Europe.

Finally, there is no evidence that the enlargement processes of the three major Western organizations have differed systematically. To be sure, the significance of individual factors for individual events often varies across organizations but, on the whole, there is no discernible pattern to these variations except the trivial finding already mentioned: the neutrality of outsider states seems to have been a more serious obstacle to NATO enlargement than for the other two organizations. Above all, there does not seem to be any variation with regard to the central norms of liberal democracy – POLITY is a significant factor in the entire enlargement process of all three organizations.

Conclusion: the liberal community hypothesis confirmed

The case studies of EU and NATO Eastern enlargement cast serious doubt on the power of rationalist institutionalism to explain the expansion of Western regional organizations in Europe and produced evidence in support of the sociological-institutionalist liberal community hypothesis. The large-*n* event history analysis served to test this hypothesis further by expanding its observable implications to more countries, more organizations, more enlargement events, and a longer time-period, and by using rigorous statistical methods. With some qualifications, this test confirmed the result of the case studies and strengthened the liberal community hypothesis.

The democratic quality of state institutions and behavior proved to be a (in general, highly) significant factor in nearly all models representing various enlargement events of different Western organizations for different time-periods and controlled for cultural, material, institutional and temporal confounding variables. In light of this analysis, it is thus justified to reject the null hypothesis: that the enlargement of Western organizations is not systematically related to the basic liberal norms of domestic institutions and conduct. It is also justified to uphold the liberal community hypothesis in that respect: the more democratic a non-member state, the more likely it is to establish institutionalized relationships with the Western organizations, apply for membership in them, and be invited to join or to begin accession negotiations. Conversely, the less democratic a member state, the more it risks being excluded from the Western organizations (or the more likely it is to withdraw from them).

By contrast, the test of the liberal norms of *foreign policy* did not produce similarly convincing results. Neutrality and involvement in militarized interstate disputes were significant obstacles to enlargement according to only half of the models. Whereas neutrality at least appears to have been a general impediment to NATO enlargement as well as to the application for and admission to membership in the other two Western organizations, the evidence for the MIDS indicator is too weak to warrant any positive conclusions. To the extent that we accept that both indicators are valid operationalizations of the liberal norms of multilateralism and peaceful conflict management, then, the analysis suggests that liberal norms of foreign policy conduct are far less important than those of domestic conduct.

The results for the control variables support three conclusions. First, there is no apparent reason for bringing back in the rationalist hypotheses that were unable to explain NATO and EU Eastern enlargement. Although the event history analysis was not designed to test these hypotheses directly, the economic and military control variables proved so little significant that a serious reconsideration of the role of material interests in the enlargement process is not necessary. Only the relatively unspecific proximity variable was sufficiently robust to warrant the conclusion that the geographical distance between the member states of the organization and the non-members is a relevant condition of enlargement. This, however, holds mainly for applications. In contrast, accession, the most important event in the process, does not seem to be systematically conditioned by geographical distance.

Second, the competing sociological institutionalist hypothesis, emphasizing the causal relevance of religion-based civilizational culture for enlargement, appears to lack any empirical support in light of the event history analysis: the affiliation of a country with any of the three "civilizations" present in the OSCE region has not been a significant factor in enlargement.

Third, none of the other control variables was robust. There is no evidence that the enlargement process is generally time-dependent or subject to institutional momentum. Systematic time-dependence is limited to the events of institutionalization and application, and neither applications nor accession negotiations are generally an "automatic" follow-up of prior institutional relations with the organization.

It was the goal of the event history analysis of enlargement to demonstrate that liberal norms were a robustly significant factor in the entire enlargement process of the Western organizations if controlled for other variables likely to have an influence. The result that "democracy" was significant across all organizations, events and models *and* the *only generally robust* variable in the analysis goes far beyond the expected outcome of the statistical analysis and underlines the singular relevance of this factor for the expansion of Western organizations in the OSCE region.

To be sure, this finding does not sort out all the problems and questions raised at the end of chapter 5. After all, the correlations evaluated by event history analysis are probabilistic, not deterministic. Statistical analysis does not explain away individual outliers or deviant cases but shows only that they are not sufficiently important to render the correlations between two variables insignificant. Neither does the EHA explain divergence in the enlargement processes and strategies of the Western organizations. Again, however, it shows that these differences are not important enough to refute the liberal community hypothesis. In spite of the obvious variation in the speed and scope of the Western organizations' enlargement processes, "democracy" remains the only robustly significant condition they have in common.

Conclusion: the sociological solution to the enlargement puzzle

In this part, I have developed and applied a community approach to enlargement on the basis of sociological institutionalist assumptions. According to this approach, states seek to join and are admitted to regional organizations if they share the identity, values and norms of the international community these organizations represent. NATO and the European Union are European organizations of the Western international community. I therefore hypothesized that they would admit those CEECs which have come to share the liberal identity of the Western community and have internalized its liberal norms of domestic and international conduct.

To evaluate the community approach and the liberal community hypothesis, I have drawn on three kinds of empirical evidence. First, the *formal* rules of NATO and the EU show that liberal identity, values, and norms are constitutive for the organizations and their enlargement. Second, the official *discourse* on enlargement demonstrates the organizations' commitment to their community-building mission and the priority of the liberal community rules as criteria for the selection of new members. Third, on the *behavioral* dimension, the selective establishment of institutional relationships and the opening of accession negotiations with the CEECs seems to be strongly correlated with the degree to which CEECs comply with the community rules and have institutionalized liberal democracy.

On this evidence, the community approach is able to explain why the Western organizations are prepared to admit CEECs in spite of net material costs for their members. It attributes Eastern enlargement to the role of NATO and the EU as representatives and community-building agencies of the Western international community, not to their function as intergovernmental instruments for maximizing the gains of international cooperation. As community organizations, they are committed and obliged to disseminate the liberal community values and norms and to admit those states that share them reliably. Judged by the egoistic, materialist preferences of the member states, Eastern enlargement was not an *efficient* solution for institutionalizing the relationship between NATO or the EU and the CEECs. Judged by the community rules, however, it was the only *legitimate* solution, and if the community actors are assumed to follow a logic of appropriateness, therefore bound to become actual policy.

In the enlargement debate, the opponents of expansion have tended to caricature and dismiss its value-based and norm-driven logic. In the US debate on NATO expansion, for instance, Fred Iklé criticized the fact that NATO was regarded as a "nursery for the young democracies" of Central and Eastern Europe and that the proponents of enlargement failed to ask whether new members were security producers or consumers.[1] Ted Galen Carpenter deplored the "'feel-good' rhetoric about encouraging stability and incorporating the Central and East European countries into the Western community of nations" and the tendency "to portray the Alliance as primarily a political association" (1997: 162). Finally, Stephen Walt cautioned that "students of NATO are likely to exaggerate the importance of common ideologies and shared identities by taking the rhetoric of national leaders and foreign-policy élites too seriously" (1997: 170). Yet the empirical evidence suggests that NATO and the EU do indeed conceive of themselves as primarily *political* and *community* organizations and as socialization agencies and that the Eastern enlargement process cannot be explained if the influence of common ideologies and shared identities is underestimated.

Thus, by emphasizing ideational, cultural factors as the fundamental causes of international political outcomes, sociological institutionalism is capable of solving the puzzle Eastern enlargement constitutes for rationalist institutionalism. By conceptualizing international organizations as community representatives, and not merely as instrumental associations; by highlighting the causal relevance of social norms and institutionalized rules instead of individual interests and relative power; and by assuming norm-regulated instead of utility-maximizing behavior, the community approach gives a plausible explanation of NATO and EU enlargement, which must appear irrational in the perspective of egoistic, instrumental rationality.

The move from the sociological analysis of NATO and EU Eastern enlargement to the event history analysis of the core Western organizations' enlargement followed a *generalizing* explanatory strategy. As a result, we can regard the liberal community hypothesis as confirmed for the moment. The next step of the analysis will focus on the *processual*

[1] Statement at a NATO Roundtable organized by the Konrad Adenauer Stiftung, cited according to Josef Joffe, "Kinderhort für die jungen Demokratien," *Süddeutsche Zeitung*, 3 June 1995, 9.

implications of the liberal community hypothesis. Following a *reconstructive* explanatory strategy, I will ask *how* Eastern enlargement came about. Process analysis will show whether the constitutive liberal norms of the Western community really played the indispensable causal role in the decisions of NATO and the EU to expand to the East postulated by the liberal community hypothesis, and, if so, *in which way* these liberal norms shaped the collective behavior of the Western organizations.

Part III

Association instead of membership: preferences and bargaining power in Eastern enlargement

This part opens the second half of the book. In the first half, I analyzed and explained the *outcomes* of NATO and EU Eastern enlargement. In this and the following part, the focus will be on the enlargement *process* that brought about these outcomes. It is the central finding of the outcome analysis that Eastern enlargement is robustly correlated with the spread and consolidation of liberal democracy in the CEECs and that, therefore, it appears to be driven by the liberal values, norms, and collective identity of the Western international community. Here, the main research question will be: how did the community rules affect and produce the Eastern enlargement outcome?

As in the preceding chapters, the analysis will be theoretically informed by rationalist and sociological institutionalism. The theoretical assumptions of both schools lead not only to conditions of enlargement as such but also to hypotheses about the preferences of the actors, their political behavior, and the political process in which individual preferences and actions are transformed into collective outcomes. In chapter 7, I develop four process hypotheses based on different modes of action: habitual, normative, communicative, and rhetorical action. Since sociological institutionalism has so far provided the most convincing explanation of Eastern enlargement, I begin with the standard sociological hypotheses of habitual and normative action.

In chapter 8, I analyze state preferences and the initial decision-making process on Eastern enlargement and examine whether they conform to sociological institutionalist expectations. I will argue that this is not the case. The enlargement preferences were neither as uniform nor as rule-guided as sociological institutionalism predicted. Rather, they reflected, to a large extent, the material conditions and interests of individual states or policy-makers and thus correspond to rationalist expectations. The same is true for the initial enlargement decision-making and negotiating process and its preliminary outcomes – EU association and Partnership for Peace with NATO. In sum, this part brings up the "double puzzle" of

Eastern enlargement: on the one hand, the Eastern enlargement *outcome* is puzzling for rationalist theory but can be explained by the sociological-institutionalist liberal community hypothesis. On the other hand, however, the *preferences* of the member states (and the CEEC candidates) as well as the *initial* decision-making and negotiation *process* on Eastern enlargement are puzzling for sociological institutionalism but correspond to rationalist expectations.

7 Process hypotheses

Modes of action

The process hypotheses – postulating how the decision to expand NATO and the EU came about – draw on different modes of action and posit different conditions that produced the enlargement outcome. I will formulate and examine four such hypotheses: habitual, normative, communicative and rhetorical action. In this section, I classify these hypotheses according to an abstract criterion. In later sections and chapters, they will be explained in greater detail and translated into concrete expectations on NATO and EU enlargement. The criterion I propose for classifying the process hypotheses is the conceptual point at which the community rules are assumed to affect the decision-making process on enlargement. In other words, it is the point in the sequence of social action up to which the process is considered to be determined by individual choices and bargaining power alone.

In abstract terms, the process of social action can be conceived as a sequence of four stages or levels. The first is *cognitions*, that is, the set of beliefs or ideas actors hold about the world and the actors' ways of thinking and making decisions. The second level is the *goals* actors set for themselves and seek to attain through their actions. The third is the individual *behavior* actors choose in light of their goals and cognitions. Finally, two or more individual behaviors form an *interaction* that brings about a collective outcome. Social rules can become influential at each of these stages or levels. The earlier in the process they do, the deeper the institutional impact on social action. Each of the four modes of action is based on the assumption that rules have an impact on decision-making at different stages in the process of social action (see Table 7.1).

The *habitual mode of action* is the most structuralist and leaves the least room for individual agency. According to this mode, rules have the deepest possible impact because they already shape social action at the level of cognitions. If the actors' beliefs and thinking are

Table 7.1 *Modes of action*

	Rule impact on			
Logic of Action	Cognitions	Goals	Behavior	Outcome
Habitual	xxx	xxx	xxx	xxx
Normative		xxx	xxx	xxx
Communicative			xxx	xxx
Rhetorical				xxx

determined by social rules, then goals and behaviors are a matter of unreflective, habitualized rule-following; and if all actors act habitually, the collective outcome will necessarily correspond to collective rules.

With *normative action*, individual agency enters the picture. According to the normative mode of action, the goals of the actors are rule-based, too. But they are a result of the actors' normative reasoning and thus a matter of reflective and purposive choice, not of habit.

In contrast to habitual and normative action, the *communicative mode of action* does not postulate rule-based goals and preferences. It assumes, however, that actors with conflicting preferences enter into a discourse about legitimate political ends and means in which they argue according to normative standards of true reasoning and rational argument. In communicative action, social rules thus have their first impact at the level of behavior.

Unlike communicative action, *rhetorical action* starts from the assumption that both the preferences and the behavior of the actors are determined by individual and instrumental choices. According to this mode of action, social rules will, however, affect the process of interaction and, as a consequence, the collective outcome.

Finally, the pure *rational mode of action* serves as the null hypothesis for the analysis of the enlargement process. It is based on the assumption that the collective outcome will be determined by the constellation of actor preferences and their relative bargaining power alone and that social rules do not have an impact on the collective outcome.

This classification goes beyond the influential dichotomous conceptualization of logics of action proposed by James March and Johan Olsen (1989; 1998). Their "logics of appropriateness" and "consequentiality" are widely accepted as the basic distinction, at the level of theories of action, between sociological and rationalist institutionalism. In addition, the difference between a cognitive and a normative conception of the influence of rules on individuals and their actions has long been recognized in sociology (DiMaggio and Powell 1991: 14; Scott 1995: 35). Thomas Risse (2000) put the case for adding a "logic of arguing" based on the theory of communicative action to the dichotomy of appropriateness and consequentialism, and I proposed to differentiate rhetorical action conceptually from communicative action (Schimmelfennig 1997). As a result, the stark distinction between rationalist and constructivist logics of action is turned into a more continuous categorization starting with habitual action at the "sociological extreme" and becoming increasingly "more rationalist" as structural, social facts are assumed to affect social action later in the process and to leave more room for individual choice.

It is difficult to test the dispositional features and cognitive mechanisms assumed by the modes of action directly. However, they imply different verbal and non-verbal behavior that lends itself more easily to observation. To facilitate comparison and competitive evaluation, the observable implications that I will specify for each process hypothesis refer to a common set of phenomena: (1) the CEECs' enlargement preferences; (2) the member states' enlargement preferences; (3) the initial reaction of the organizations to the CEECs' bid for membership; (4) the decision-making process within the organizations; and (5) the effects of enlargement on later enlargement rounds.

Finally, note that, even though process analysis results in a more narrative form of presentation than the correlational outcome analysis of NATO and EU enlargement, I do not provide a full chronological account of the enlargement decision-making processes that one would expect in a historiographical perspective. Rather, I present "analytical episodes" focused on examining the empirical implications of the process hypotheses under scrutiny. These episodes sometimes violate the chronological order and regularly neglect those aspects of the enlargement process that are not relevant for hypothesis testing.

Habitual and normative action

The sociological-institutionalist liberal community hypothesis provided the most plausible explanation of the enlargement of West European regional organizations. For that reason, the process analysis begins at the sociological-institutionalist end of the modes of action. The hypotheses of habitual and normative action represent the microfoundations of sociological institutionalism most genuinely.

The habitual action hypothesis

The hypothesis of habitual action is based on a cognitive mechanism of the causal influence of rules which has been developed most explicitly in neoinstitutionalist approaches to the sociological theory of organizations (see, e.g., Powell and DiMaggio 1991). According to the cognitive mechanism, institutions shape individual action "by providing the cognitive scripts, categories and models that are indispensable for action, not least because without them the world and the behaviour of others cannot be interpreted" (Hall and Taylor 1996: 947). Social institutions define reality for the actors, give meaning to their perceptions, and provide the cognitive tools for thinking about decisions. The actors conform to social rules out of habit and cognitive necessity, not out of a conscious commitment or a sense of obligation. "For cognitive theorists, compliance occurs in many circumstances because other types of behavior are inconceivable; routines are followed because they are taken for granted as 'the way we do things'" (Scott 1995: 44). Habitual actors do not even (need to) deliberate on and choose between alternative goals and courses of action because they perceive and interpret their situation in rule-conforming frames to begin with. Thus, the mode of habitual action is the most radical in its departure from rational choice theory and in its rejection of the assumption of reflective and purposive actors (see DiMaggio and Powell 1991: 8, 10).

According to the hypothesis of habitual action, the central condition of Eastern enlargement was the existence of organizational rules and routines for the member states to follow in their enlargement decisions and negotiations and a set of cognitive scripts, categories and models toward which the CEECs could orient themselves. In the new, unexpected and uncertain situation of post-Cold War Europe, the habitual action hypothesis leads us to expect that member states fell back on established routines of dealing with outsider states and that the CEECs turned to Western templates for guidance. The hypothesis has the following observable implications for the processes of EU and NATO Eastern enlargement:

(H1) The CEECs' desire to join NATO and the EU was an automatic reaction to the post-Cold War situation.

(H2) The enlargement preferences of NATO and EU members were uniform and determined by the enlargement rules and routines of both organizations.

(H3) NATO and the EU offered membership or reacted favorably to the membership requests of rule-following CEECs.

(H4) The decision-making process within NATO and the EU was characterized by consensus about the timing of enlargement and the selection of new members as well as by the bureaucratic execution of organizational scripts for enlargement.

(H5) Further enlargement rounds are a matter of routine. They smoothly follow the trodden institutional paths of earlier rounds. With each enlargement, the process becomes more habitualized and taken for granted.

The normative action hypothesis

The mode of normative action is often associated with the "old institutionalism" in sociology represented by the classical work of Emile Durkheim, Max Weber, and Talcott Parsons.[1] It also comes closer to March and Olsen's "logic of appropriateness" than the logic of habitual action. Normative action is more reflective and purposive than the cognitive mechanisms of habitual action suggest. Moral commitment to social values, a sense of obligation toward social norms and a conscious identification with the community rather than taken-for-granted rules and routines motivate the actors. Rule-guided evaluation of the situation rather than rule-guided perception is the basis of decisions (Peters 1999: 103). Normative actors could in principle make a choice to violate rules; they will not make this choice, however, except in very special circumstances in which non-compliance is morally or normatively permitted or justifiable.

Socialization is the primary mechanism through which intersubjective structures are transformed into individual preferences and action. As a result of successful socialization, the values and norms that constitute the social identity and fabric of a community are internalized by its members, and, as a result of internalization, the individuals identify themselves with their community and commit themselves to its values and norms. Alternatively, we may say that individual actors become socialized into institutionally defined roles, learn the norms and rules associated with these roles and act appropriately by "fulfilling the obligations of a role in a situation" (March and Olsen 1989: 160–61).

Normative action does not imply the same degree of *automatic* rule-following as habitual action (Peters 1999: 29; Scott 1995: 39). Actors are assumed to reflect on the situation and to make conscious choices

[1] See, for instance, Parsons (1969: 440–56) or Weber's concept of "value-rationality" (1968: 25).

about their preferences and behavior. In doing so, however, they determine "what the situation is, what role is being fulfilled, and what the obligations of that role in that situation are" (March and Olsen 1989: 160). In making these assessments and choices, the actors do not start from their individual needs and interests and do not calculate how to advance them but reason normatively about what to want and what to do, remaining "within the parameters established by the dominant institutional values" (Peters 1999: 29). "The pursuit of purpose is associated with identities more than with interests, and with the selection of rules more than with individual rational expectations" (March and Olsen 1998: 951). As a result, the actors' preferences will be as rule-guided (under normal circumstances) as according to the hypothesis of habitual action but the process will have been different.

In the perspective of normative action, enlargement mainly depends on the commitment of the Western organizations and their members to their community culture and their community-building mission as well as on the CEECs' progressive internalization of the community's constitutive liberal norms.[2] The following implications for Eastern enlargement can be derived from the normative action hypothesis:

(N1) The CEECs' desire to become NATO and EU members was a corollary of their identification with the Western international community and its constitutive values and norms.

(N2) The enlargement preferences of NATO and EU member states were uniform and shaped by the constitutive values and norms of the organization and by their collective identity with the democratic CEECs.

(N3) The Western organizations offered membership to, or reacted favorably to the membership requests of, democratic CEECs.

(N4) Enlargement decision-making in NATO and the EU was characterized by general consensus about the timing of enlargement and the selection of new members as well as by a firm commitment to the admission of consolidated liberal democracies in the CEE region.

(N5) Further enlargement rounds are a matter of continued socialization. New members will be admitted after they will have internalized the community norms.

The main assumption the habitual and normative action hypotheses have in common – and that distinguishes them from the other process

[2] As indicated, for instance, by the extensive use of the terms "values," "norms," and "socialization," the introduction of sociological institutionalism in chapter 4 and the specification of the liberal community hypothesis implicitly followed the normative rather than the cognitive variant of this family of theories.

hypotheses – is that social values, norms and identities (which are usually institutionalized in the rules of a society, community, or organization) shape the actors' identities, interests, and preferences. In the terminology used above, they influence social action already at the level of individual dispositions (cognitions and goals) and not only at the levels of behavior and interaction. Therefore, in order to test these process hypotheses, the most important facts are the enlargement preferences of the member and applicant states. If these preferences are, in general, uniform among the relevant actors, follow the community values, norms, and identity and correspond to the enlargement rules of the organization, the analysis supports the sociological-institutionalist perspective.

8 State preferences and the initial enlargement process

CEEC preferences

Whereas the reform-minded Central European governments declared their interest in becoming EC and CoE members soon after coming to power, their bid to join NATO was neither an immediate nor an automatic consequence of their transition to democracy or the end of the Cold War. Rather, it was motivated by their concern about the security situation in Central and Eastern Europe. I will focus on Czechoslovakia, Hungary and Poland because they were the first CEECs to request membership in the Western organizations.

When the Soviet Union released the Central European countries from its sphere of control and communist rule collapsed, the new governments proclaimed the "return to Europe" as their paramount foreign policy goal and almost immediately announced their interest in joining the EC and the CoE. To quote only a few leading officials of the time, the Hungarian Foreign Minister Gyula Horn declared as early as October 1989, "Our political resolve is to develop very close relations with the European Community."[1] Hungarian MDF party chairman and later prime minister, Jószef Antall, affirmed in January 1990, "We are firm supporters of this idea [of European unification], and unconditionally advocate European integration. We want to prepare ourselves for the Council of Europe and the European Community."[2] Polish President Lech Walesa said in July 1991 that "nothing is more important for Poland than membership in the EC,"[3] and Czechoslovak Foreign Minister Jirí Dienstbier stated in a meeting with EC Trade Commissioner Frans Andriessen in March 1990, "I think all of us should be members of *one* European Community" and that "Czechoslovakia wants to join the EC as quickly as possible."[4]

[1] *Foreign Broadcast Information Service FBIS-EEU-89–204*, 24 October 1989, 5.
[2] *FBIS-EEU-90-016*, 24 January 1990, 43.
[3] *FBIS-EEU-91-135*, 15 July 1991, 20.
[4] *FBIS-EEU-90-043*, 5 March 1990, 11, my italics.

By contrast, NATO membership was initially not on the agenda of the new governments. They generally regarded NATO as a Cold War organization that should give way (together with the Warsaw Pact) to a pan-European, collective security system. During the period of communist rule, most democratic opposition groups did not want their countries to "change sides" but proposed to dissolve the adversary alliances and advocated a neutral or non-aligned status for their countries. They regarded the CSCE not only as an institution that promoted human rights in communist Europe but also as the nucleus for a new security organization for the entire continent. These ideas continued to dominate their thinking on security policy during the 1989–91 period.

The new Czechoslovak leadership represented by President Václav Havel and Foreign Minister Dienstbier was the most explicit among the CEEC governments in its vision of a new pan-European security organization based on the CSCE. Already, in January 1990, Havel promoted his idea of "Europe as a friendly comity of independent nations and democratic states, a Europe that is stabilized, not divided into blocs and pacts, a Europe that does not need the protection of superpowers, because it is capable of defending itself, that is of building its own security system." During a visit to the United States in February 1990, he even suggested that NATO be dissolved and US troops be withdrawn from Europe.[5] In Hungary, as a legacy of the 1956 revolution, the principle of neutrality received widespread support at the beginning and could be found in the programs of all parties ahead of the first free elections in the spring of 1990 (see Cottey 1995: 94).

About a year later, in the spring of 1991, indications of change abounded in all three Central European countries. They had not only come to regard NATO as an indispensable element in European security and to seek close cooperation with the Western alliance but also requested informal security guarantees and began to consider a future membership in NATO (see Cottey 1995: 37, 69, 94, 97). The change in the Czechoslovak position was most conspicuous. In his March 1991 address to the NATO Council, President Havel admitted that he had learned that a system of pan-European collective security was more difficult to realize than it had seemed in the early days of Central and Eastern Europe's transition to democracy. Without giving up this idea, Havel now emphasized the importance of cooperation with NATO, and, while admitting that his country could not become a full member of NATO at the moment, he argued that "an alliance of countries united by the ideals of freedom and democracy should not be forever closed to neighbouring

[5] See Cottey (1995: 65) for quote; Khol (2001: 148).

countries that are pursuing the same goals."[6] In the second half of 1991, the statements of interest in NATO membership became more concrete. At their summit in Cracow in October 1991, all Visegrád countries[7] demanded a security guarantee as well as a general commitment to Eastern enlargement from NATO. "Since then, joining NATO has remained the focus of the Visegrad countries' security policy" (Hyde-Price 1996: 244).

This *policy change* can be attributed to *three developments*. First, it turned out in 1991 that Eastern Europe's transition to democracy and national self-determination would not be as smooth and peaceful as its beginning. The Soviet crackdown in the Baltic republics in January and the *coup d'état* in August were a warning to the CEECs that the Soviet retreat from communism and imperialism was not irreversible. The war in Yugoslavia demonstrated the dangers of the nationalist revival that swept the entire region. Second, it became clear that the CSCE would not develop into a working system of collective security and that it could not effectively protect the CEECs against the threats that manifested themselves in the region. In this situation, the CEECs turned to NATO in order to obtain the security guarantees they desired, and since it had become obvious in the case of the Baltics and Yugoslavia that NATO would not provide these guarantees to non-members, they regarded NATO membership as the only viable option.[8] Finally, the CEECs had learned that EC membership, which they had declared their first foreign policy priority after the end of the Cold War, would take a very long time and required a difficult adaptation to the *acquis communautaire*. NATO membership appeared to be the less demanding way to achieve membership in one of the major Western organizations (see, e.g., Mattox 1998: 27).

Thus, the CEECs' desire to become NATO members was not an automatic, taken-for-granted response to the collapse of Communism and Soviet hegemony, as expected by the hypothesis of habitual action. If there was a habitualized response, it consisted in the calls for collective security or neutrality that had come to dominate the thinking of the democratic opposition in the CEECs in the 1970s and 1980s. Nor was the interest in joining NATO a corollary of the community of values that was developing

[6] See "NATO Headquarters. Brussels, March 21, 1991," available at http://www.hrad.cz/president/Havel/ speeches/1991/2103_uk.html (last visited 2 June 2000).

[7] "Visegrád" stands for the loose subregional framework of cooperation between the central European countries. The Hungarian town was the place of the first meeting of the governments of Czechoslovakia, Hungary, and Poland in February 1991.

[8] See, e.g., Eyal (1997: 700-01); Hyde-Price (1996: 242–44); Reisch (1994: 18–20). On Hungary, see Keresztes (1998: 18).

between East and West, as predicted by the hypothesis of normative action: in Havel's initial view, a democratic Europe ought to be organized as a system of collective security, not as an expanded alliance. Also, if the interest in NATO membership really reflected "a more fundamental and deep-seated historical desire to be part of the 'West'" (Larrabee 1997: 103), it should have manifested itself immediately after the democratic revolutions and in parallel with the early, strong, and explicit demands for EC membership.

The timing and the circumstances of the CEECs' desire to join NATO suggest that it was of an instrumental kind – to obtain the most (or, in fact, the only) efficient security guarantee for their states under the circumstances. This interpretation is supported by the statements in which CEE officials justified their interest in NATO membership. In his March 1991 speech in Brussels, President Havel based his turn towards NATO on the developments in the Soviet Union, the dangers of nationalism, and the deficits of the CSCE. As he recalled in his speech at the Bratislava summit of NATO candidates in May 2001, "allowing it [NATO] to disappear from the map of the world would have amounted to creating a security vacuum."[9] Foreign Minister Dienstbier considered NATO so important because it was the only European security institution that had "proved its effectiveness and viability."[10] In a collection of views by CEE officials published in 1995, NATO membership figured as "the most efficient and abiding way to hedge against future pressures from Russia" (Karkoszka 1995: 78) and "the crucial safeguard against the unknown" (Bajarunas 1995: 105), whereas the CSCE was considered "incapable of providing the continental security system that was needed under the new circumstances" (Pascu 1995: 89).

In sum, the empirical evidence regarding the Central European countries' development of enlargement preferences is not compatible with the hypotheses of habitual and normative action. It even goes beyond my skeptical assessment of the liberal community hypothesis as far as the CEEC candidates are concerned.[11] My earlier conclusion was that adherence to the rules of the Western community was a sufficient but not a necessary condition for a CEEC to seek membership in the EU or NATO. Now it seems that it was not even a sufficient condition. Even those new Central European governments whose democratic credentials were undisputed rejected NATO membership at first. Rather, their preference to join the alliance was an instrumental choice made in light of

[9] *RFE/RL Newsline* 15 May 2001.
[10] *FBIS-EEU-91-220*, 14 November 1991, cited in Cottey (1995: 69).
[11] See chapter 5.

changing and newly appreciated international circumstances in order to meet national security needs.[12]

NATO member state preferences

The enlargement preferences of NATO member states had two principal dimensions. The first question was *whether (and when)* NATO should commit itself to Eastern enlargement in general. Simply stated, the options were "fast enlargement," that is, an early and firm commitment to and preparation for the admission of CEECs to the alliance, and "no or slow enlargement," that is, rejection of Eastern enlargement or postponement of the decision. Depending on their preferences, member states can be categorized as "drivers" or "brakemen." The second question was *how many and which* states should be admitted. Here, the basic options were "limited enlargement," that is, a small first round of enlargement focusing on the Central European countries, and "extensive enlargement," that is, the admission of a larger group of CEECs including countries of southeastern and northeastern Europe.

The analysis of member state preferences is faced with three general problems. The first is the problem of *time*: what is the correct point in time for assessing state preferences? This problem would not exist if member state preferences had been stable throughout the enlargement decision-making process. This was not the case, however. I therefore propose that the right time to ascertain a government's "authentic" position is when the issue is on the agenda but has not been negotiated between governments. At this point in time, preferences are usually clearly developed but do not yet take into account the preferences of the other member states and the results of previous negotiations. For these reasons, I assessed the preferences on the general commitment to enlargement in the second half of 1993 when enlargement was established firmly on the agenda of NATO – the first intergovernmental negotiations among NATO members took place in the fall of this year. As for the selection of new members, the decision was open until the Madrid Summit of NATO heads of state and government in July 1997. For that reason, I analyzed the discussions preceding the summit.

The second problem is that of *representation*: whose preferences are the "member state preferences"? Again, representation would not be a problem if all governments had held unitary enlargement preferences. Yet, some governments were divided on the issue, at least temporarily.

[12] For a similar analysis of Slovenia's interest in NATO membership, see Bebler (1999: 126); Gustenau (1999).

The most important cases are those of the United States and Germany, two major NATO member states. The situation in these countries will be described in greater detail below.

The third problem pertains to the *authenticity* of preferences: what are the "true" preferences? To increase confidence in the validity of my findings, I used different kinds of sources. The main sources were newspaper reports about governmental statements and intra- as well as intergovernmental negotiations. Moreover, I drew on accounts by experts on the national security policy of the states in question. Finally, I conducted interviews at NATO headquarters, in Bonn (before the German government moved to Berlin), and Washington, DC, the capitals of those member states in which the issue of NATO enlargement initially generated major intragovernmental divisions.

The German government

In the first years after the end of the Cold War, the German preferences resembled those of the Central European states. On the one hand, Germany had been a leading advocate of EC membership for the CEECs early on. On the other hand, the German government did not promote a parallel enlargement of NATO but, under the aegis of Foreign Minister Hans-Dietrich Genscher, pursued the project of pan-European security structures. In addition to strengthening the CSCE, Germany actively supported the establishment and deepening of NATO cooperation with the CEECs. Yet, when the Central European governments brought up the issue of NATO membership, "Bonn's initial reaction was no warmer than that of any other member state" (Wolf 1996: 201).

In 1993, however, NATO enlargement turned into a divisive issue in the federal government. Defense Minister Volker Rühe became its leading proponent. In his Alistair Buchan Memorial Lecture at the International Institute for Strategic Studies (London, March 1993), Rühe demanded that the "Atlantic Alliance must not become a 'closed shop'. I cannot see one good reason for denying future members of the European Union membership in NATO." Going even further, Rühe asked "whether membership in the European Union should necessarily precede accession to NATO" (Rühe 1993: 135).

This strong pro-enlargement preference was not shared in other branches of the German government. Foreign Minister Klaus Kinkel, while also urging NATO to "think over its reticence toward the admission of Central and Eastern Europe in view of the conflicts in east and south-east Europe," did not see any "urgent need to decide" this issue. He feared that enlargement would threaten the cohesion of the alliance and its military credibility and warned that the isolation of Russia and Ukraine would put at risk the security gains from the end of the Cold War. Instead, he proposed a half-way house between full membership and loose cooperation and gave clear priority to the enlargement of the European Community.[13]

The controversy between Rühe and Kinkel became more pronounced in the second half of 1993 and throughout 1994 (Hacke 1997; Weisser 1999: 63–66; Wolf 1996: 205–09). Rühe continued to urge NATO to prepare for expansion ahead of the EC, denied Russia the right to a say in this matter, and, early in the process, already suggested limiting enlargement to the Visegrád countries. Kinkel criticized Rühe as being "too brash"[14] and openly disagreed with him in a speech before top Bundeswehr officers.[15] He constantly warned against an early decision on dates and candidates for enlargement and expressed his understanding of Russian misgivings about the expansion of the Western alliance. Furthermore, he proposed to develop NATO–CEE relations on a broader and less differentiated basis and indicated that NATO enlargement might wait until EU enlargement became more concrete. In part, this controversy developed and continued because Chancellor Helmut Kohl did not take a clear stance on the issue. In the later course of the enlargement debate, however, Kohl sided with Kinkel rather than Rühe. Faced with Russian opposition to NATO expansion, he tried to slow down the process and to placate Russia as much as possible (Wolf 1996: 202, 205).

In sum, there was no unitary German state preference for fast NATO enlargement in 1993 and 1994. Reinhard Wolf is right to stress that "Bonn never did speak with a single voice . . . The federal government as a whole was never as enthusiastic about this project as it might appear from Rühe's statements alone. In fact, it seems that on this issue, the defence minister was rather isolated . . . " (1996: 205). Consequently, whereas Rühe sought to commit NATO to the goal of Eastern enlargement at the Travemünde meeting of NATO defense ministers in October 1993 (Weisser 1999: 49–50), "the German delegation that Chancellor Kohl led to the 1994 NATO summit in Brussels had no intention of advocating any specific measures to proceed with expansion" (Wolf 1996: 203). Nevertheless, the position of the German government was more enlargement friendly overall than that of the other major European NATO members and the

[13] "Auf der Suche nach einem Mittelweg," *FAZ*, 6 March 1993, 5 (quote); "Verantwortung, Realismus, Zukunftssicherung – Deutsche Außenpolitik in einer sich neu ordnenden Welt," *FAZ*, 19 March 1993, 4; "'Rußland und die Ukraine auszugrenzen würde alles zunichte machen'," *FAZ*, 10 November 1993, 6.

[14] *Der Spiegel* 17/1995, 23.

[15] "Kinkel und Rühe uneins über Nato-Erweiterung," *FAZ*, 7 October 1994, 1–2.

German defense minister was the most outspoken enlargement advocate among his colleagues in the alliance in 1993.

There was stronger agreement in the German government that enlargement should be limited to the Central European countries. A position paper, drafted by an interministerial working group set up after the 1994 elections, named the Visegrád coutries as the preferential candidates for a parallel enlargement of the EU and NATO and rejected a collective admission of all aspiring countries (Hacke 1997: 240–41). Immediately ahead of the Madrid Summit, the German government again did not take a unified and clear position, but mainly for tactical reasons. Whereas Rühe explicitly stuck to the earlier consensus on three new members, Kinkel said he was content with "three, four or five new members." On the one hand, this was a tactical move of symbolic support for the French partners: the German government did not back France in its parallel controversy with the US administration on the AFSOUTH (Allied Forces South Europe) command and therefore thought it could show some cheap loyalty in the enlargement controversy, which it considered a done deal anyhow. On the other hand, Kinkel sought to make a mark for himself in his foreign policy competition with Rühe. Similarly, Chancellor Kohl had still supported the US position on a limited first round in talks with Clinton one month ahead of the summit. At the summit, then, he sought to occupy the position of a mediator between the camps and, in particular, between France and the United States.[16]

The US administration

The US administration was the second government among the major states of the alliance that was divided on the enlargement issue in the second half of 1993. However, the institutional lines between opponents and proponents ran differently than in Germany.

Leading Bush administration officials had already begun to suggest the possibility of NATO enlargement in the second half of 1992 without being able to turn enlargement into official policy ahead of the presidential elections of the same year (see Goldgeier 1999: 18; Solomon 1998: 19). When the Clinton administration took over in January 1993, NATO enlargement appeared to be even further removed from the political agenda given the strong domestic and economic focus of Clinton's campaign. However, National Security Adviser Anthony Lake and his collaborators

[16] Weisser (1999: 130–31); interviews Kamp and Stephen Szabo; "Kinkel: Umfang der Ost-Erweiterung noch offen," *SZ*, 7 July 1997, 1; "Kohl und Clinton auf einer Linie," *SZ*, 7 June 1997.

soon began to develop a foreign policy agenda for the new administration that came to be known as "democratic enlargement" (see Brinkley 1997) and was presented as a successor to "containment" in Lake's speech at the School of Advanced International Studies (SAIS) in Washington in September 1993. One of the "components to a strategy of enlargement" he listed was to "help foster and consolidate new democracies and market economies . . . where we have the strongest security concerns and where we can make the greatest difference." The "new democracies in Central and Eastern Europe" were a "clear example, given their proximity to the great democratic powers of Western Europe" (Lake 1993: 15–16). Although Lake did not explicitly call for NATO enlargement, he announced that "we will seek to update NATO, so that there continues behind the enlargement of market democracies an essential collective security" (Lake 1993: 16).

According to Lake, "Clinton embraced the enlargement concept almost immediately" (Brinkley 1997: 116) and was favorably inclined toward the idea of NATO expansion after the spring of 1993 (see Goldgeier 1999: 20). Within the bureaucracy, however, NATO enlargement initially was a minority position and met with considerable opposition. Not even the National Security Council (NSC) staff stood united behind the policy advocated by the national security adviser. Above all, the NSC's senior director for European Affairs, Jennone Walker, who chaired the Interagency Group that prepared the January 1994 NATO summit in Brussels, openly opposed it (Goldgeier 1999: 23–24). At the Department of State, only a small group of officials favored enlargement, and at the Department of Defense, such support was virtually non-existent. In both ministries and in the NSC, the dominant opinion was that NATO should develop cooperation with the CEECs along the lines introduced with the North Atlantic Cooperation Council.

In October 1993, the agencies reached a compromise that made Partnership for Peace the focus of practical NATO policy and included a statement about the basic openness of the alliance. This formulation was acceptable to all participants but did not reflect a genuine consensus. "From the moment the participants [of the Principals Committee meeting] went their separate ways, observers noticed that they interpreted the decision differently" (Goldgeier 1999: 42). Whereas the opponents of enlargement took the reference to NATO's openness as merely declaratory and without immediate policy implications, the few advocates of enlargement within the administration regarded it as a commitment to be implemented soon.

In sum, in the second half of 1993, there was no clear and undisputed US state preference on NATO enlargement. As in the case of Germany, there were forceful "drivers" as well as "brakemen" among the executive branches of government who, at that time, were only able to reach an ambiguous and unstable compromise on PfP as the next step in the development of NATO–CEEC relations. On the whole, however, both the German federal government and the US administration were significantly more favorably disposed toward the idea of NATO enlargement in 1993 than their major allies.

As Germany, the United States has also been a proponent of *limited* enlargement. It was the US administration that actively sought to commit the alliance to admitting only the Czech Republic, Hungary and Poland in 1999 and insisted most strongly on a small first round of enlargement on the eve of and during the final discussions at the Madrid summit in July 1997.[17]

The other allies

The other major NATO member states were both more unified and more reticent in their attitudes toward Eastern enlargement. Even before NATO enlargement was on the agenda, *France* had been opposed to strengthening the security cooperation between NATO and the CEECs in the framework of the North Atlantic Cooperation Council (see Boniface 1996: 185; Broer 1997: 303). In 1993, then, France actively pursued alternative plans for European security. In April, Prime Minister Edouard Balladur proposed a NATO-independent Stability Pact for Central and Eastern Europe, and in December of the same year, Foreign Minister Alain Juppé put forward the idea of associating the CEECs to the West European Union (WEU) instead of NATO. Finally, ahead of the Madrid summit, France was the most active proponent of an extended first round of enlargement. In particular, the French government advocated the addition of Romania.

In contrast with France, *Italy* did not explicitly criticize or oppose NATO enlargement. Nevertheless, the Italian government also favored a slow pace (Dassú and Menotti 1997: 5; Menotti 2001: 96). Later, it demanded a larger selection of candidates for the first round of enlargement and mainly supported Slovenia.

Finally, the "brakemen" coalition was reinforced by the *United Kingdom*. Regarding the scope of enlargement, however, Britain generally favored a small enlargement excluding the Balkan and Baltic aspirants

[17] See Goldgeier (1999: 118–19); "Albright on Potential New Members," RFE/RL *Newsline*, 30 May 1997; "Kohl und Clinton auf einer Linie," *SZ*, 7 June 1997.

Table 8.1 *NATO member state enlargement preferences*

	Limited enlargement	Inclusion of Romania and Slovenia
Fast enlargement or divided governments	US, Germany, Denmark, Netherlands, Norway	Belgium, Luxembourg
Slow enlargement	UK, Iceland	France, Italy, Canada, Greece, Portugal, Spain, Turkey

but, in contrast with Germany and the United States, the British government would have welcomed Slovenia in the first round as well.[18]

At the Travemünde meeting of NATO defense ministers in October 1993, Rühe's attempt to put enlargement on the short-term agenda was supported by his Belgian, Dutch, and Norwegian colleagues.[19] In addition, Denmark and Luxembourg declared themselves in favor of fast-track enlargement. In contrast, the southern or Mediterranean member states (Greece, Portugal, Spain, and Turkey) as well as Canada are on the record as further "brakemen" (see Broer 1997: 326). These states also constituted the core of the coalition that favored a first round of enlargement including Slovenia and Romania. In that regard, they were supported by Belgium and Luxembourg whereas Denmark and Norway advocated the membership of the Baltic states but did not develop a strong interest in including Romania and Slovenia.[20] The constellation of enlargement preferences is summarized in Table 8.1.

Obviously, the enlargement preferences of the NATO member states *contradict the implications of both sociological institutionalist process hypotheses*. Neither with regard to enlargement as a general goal, nor with regard to the selection of new NATO members was there uniformity or consensus among the member states. Consequently, collective organizational scripts, norms and values cannot have had a strong impact on the definition of state preferences. As the outcome analysis has shown, the liberal community hypothesis would indeed not have excluded a more extended NATO enlargement (including Slovenia but not Romania). But then, this hypothesis can explain neither why the member states were divided on this issue nor which member states favored limited or extended enlargement.

[18] Garden (2001: 77); Sharp (1997: 6); Taylor (1997: 221); "Major Backs Czechs in Alliance," *International Herald Tribune* (*IHT*), 19 April 1996; "Heftige Kritik an Clintons Plänen zur *NATO*-Erweiterung," *SZ*, 14/15 June 1997.

[19] "Partnerschaft für den Frieden," *FAZ*, 27 October 1993, 16.

[20] See Gallis (1997); Goldgeier (1999: 120) citing a *New York Times* report. See also Clemens (1997b: 191); Weisser (1999: 129). According to Gallis (1997: 18), the Netherlands joined its Benelux neighbors in supporting an extended first round of enlargement.

Most importantly, that many member states would have preferred not to expand NATO at all, in spite of the democratic transformation of the CEECs, cannot be reconciled with the community-building perspective on enlargement.

Can we go beyond this negative result and find a *positive explanation* for the divergence of state preferences? Table 8.1 indicates that enlargement preferences tend to vary with *geographical location*. Whereas the "drivers" cluster in the Northeastern sector of the alliance territory, the "brakemen" are generally located in its Northwestern and Southern sectors, and whereas the Northern member states were mostly in favor of limited enlargement, the Southern member states generally demanded the inclusion of Slovenia and Romania.

To explain this rough covariation, a "geopolitical" argument suggests itself. It starts with the observation that, although the exact composition of new members was uncertain until 1997, it had been clear all along that Poland and the Czech Republic would constitute the core of the enlargement area. The geopolitical explanation goes on to argue that countries located in the vicinity of these two states – the Northeastern members of NATO – were more favorably disposed toward enlargement than the others because *vicinity gives rise to negative and positive interdependence as well as influence*. First, member states in the Northeast would be more directly affected by instability and insecurity in East-Central Europe than more distant member states. The expansion of NATO to this neighboring region would help to control this negative interdependence. Second, geographical proximity increases trade and other useful cross-border exchanges. The accession of neighboring CEECs to NATO would help to protect and increase these beneficial exchanges. Finally, negative and positive interdependence may result in common interests and increased influence of the Northeastern countries of NATO on their Central European neighbors. Their admission to the Western alliance would then increase the power of the Northeastern member states in NATO coalition-building and decision-making.

In accordance with the first of these explanations, *Germany* figured as the vulnerable "frontline state" of the West in the German defense ministry's dominant mind-set. As a legacy of the Cold War, the strategic thinking of the defense establishment was preoccupied with the question of how to reduce the threat to Germany's eastern border and to maximize early warning times and mobilization periods. In this perspective, Central Europe was a strategic glacis. On the one hand, Central Europe's integration into NATO would stabilize the political situation of this glacis; on the other, it would move the border of the West further to the East, thereby relieving Germany of its frontline status. Finally, consideration for Russia did not figure prominently in either Rühe's personal or the defense ministry's collective outlook.[21]

Conversely, according to this reasoning, those NATO member states that were further removed from East-Central Europe and, therefore, subject to low negative and positive interdependence, had little interest in institutional expansion. Rather, they feared that expansion would, first, reduce the efficiency of NATO, second, divert its attention and resources from their own neighboring regions, and, third, shift the intraorganizational balance of power to their disadvantage.

The first consideration seems to have been the most important reason for *British* reticence toward enlargement. On various occasions, British ministers warned that NATO was not a "social club" and that membership was not merely "a political statement." Enlargement should enhance the security of the alliance as a whole and not just that of individual members.[22] Moreover, the British government was strongly concerned with the reaction of Russia to NATO enlargement in 1993 (see Mihalka 1994: 6; Taylor 1997: 218; Weisser 1999: 38).

Italy is a typical case for the second reason to be skeptical about Eastern enlargement. In the opinion of Dassú and Menotti, Italy's "lack of enthusiasm" can be explained by its dominant preoccupation with Mediterranean security. And when the decision to expand was made, "the only way to 'balance' NATO's inevitable drive eastward was to support some credible candidates in South Eastern Europe as an exercise in damage-control that moved Italy from the goal of slower to that of larger enlargement" (1997: 7; cf. Menotti 2001: 98).

Finally, the initial *French* opposition to NATO enlargement is generally attributed to concerns about power relations within the Western alliance.[23] On the one hand, the French government perceived NATO enlargement as a way to maintain US dominance in the new Europe. Since the time of de Gaulle, France had regarded NATO as an instrument of US military preponderance, refused to participate in NATO's integrated military structures, and sought to strengthen autonomous European military capabilities. Consequently, France viewed with suspicion all efforts to define new tasks for NATO, the CEECs' strong interest in US military presence and protection, and their preparedness to fully participate in NATO's military integration. On the other hand, France was concerned about the strengthening of German influence within the alliance. Due to Germany's strong economic involvement in its Eastern

[21] Background interviews Federal Ministry of Defense.

[22] See the statements quoted in Mihalka (1994: 6).

[23] See Boniface (1997: 5); Dannreuther (1997: 77); Manfrass-Sirjacques (1997: 202–03); Mihalka (1994: 6); Weisser (1999: 38–39, 78).

neighboring states, it regarded the Central European aspiring countries as natural allies of Germany. In this regard, the French preference for a larger first round of enlargement can be interpreted as a way to balance German influence in Central Europe by including Romania, which the French government regarded as "its" candidate and client.

In sum, both the overall "geopolitical" explanation proposed here on the basis of the distribution of enlargement preferences among the member states and the specific reasons given in the literature for the enlargement preference of major individual NATO members are clearly *rationalist*. They attribute state preferences to self-interested, national calculations of security interest based on the position of a state in a materially defined international environment.

Yet, there is one major exception to this pattern. Given its great geographical distance to and small interdependence with the CEE region, its leading position in the alliance, and its primary concern with Russian strategic forces, the United States should have been as reluctant with regard to enlargement as its Canadian neighbor initially was, and as preoccupied with the efficiency of the alliance as its close British ally. But whereas the initial majority positions of the major bureaucracies involved in NATO issues – the Departments of Defense and State – correspond to this rationalist expectation, the enlargement advocacy of Lake, and the support it received by President Clinton, are puzzling and call for further investigation.[24]

EU member state preferences

In the study of European integration, the rationalist explanation of state preferences is most prominently represented in the work of Andrew Moravcsik. Although he does not completely dismiss the influence of security-related geopolitical factors, he argues that state preferences in European integration are chiefly determined by "the economic incentives generated by patterns of international economic interdependence" (1998: 6).

As in the NATO case, the member state governments can be classified as "drivers" who advocated an early and firm commitment to Eastern enlargement and "brakemen" who were reticent and tried to put off the decision. Likewise, one group of member states pushed for a limited (first) round of enlargement focusing on the Central European states, whereas others favored an inclusive approach of "equal treatment" for all

[24] See below, chapter 10.

Table 8.2 *EU member state enlargement preferences*

	Limited enlargement	Inclusive enlargement
Drivers	Austria, Finland, Germany	Britain, Denmark, Sweden
Brakemen	Belgium, Luxemburg, Netherlands	France, Greece, Ireland, Italy, Portugal, Spain

associated CEECs. Table 8.2 shows the distribution of these preferences among the EU member states.[25]

Again, the distribution of enlargement preferences largely mirrors the *geographical position* of the member states. Except for Greece and Italy, the countries bordering on Central and Eastern Europe were the "drivers" of enlargement; except for Britain, the more remote countries were the "brakemen." The countries of the "central region" of the EU preferred a limited (first round of) enlargement, whereas the Southern and Northern countries, except Finland, favored a more inclusive approach.

The member states' geographical position *vis-à-vis* Central and Eastern Europe can be understood as a proxy variable for "the imperatives induced by interdependence and, in particular, the . . . exogenous increase in opportunities for cross-border trade and capital movements" that should determine national preferences (Moravcsik 1998: 26). Following the hypothesis that, all else being equal, international *interdependence* increases with geographical proximity, member states on the Eastern border of the EU are more sensitive to developments in Central and Eastern Europe than the more remote member states.[26] Crises and wars, economic and ecological deterioration in the region affect them more immediately and more strongly. Enlargement can be seen as an instrument to stabilize Central and Eastern Europe, to control the negative externalities of political and economic transformation in the East, and to expand the borders of the EU zone of peace and prosperity. For all of these reasons, EU border states have a strong interest in enlargement.

Second, geographical proximity creates *opportunities for economic gains* from trade and investment, for instance by reducing the costs of transport and communication. Member states close to Central and Eastern

[25] For largely mutually corroborative analyses of member state preferences, see Friis and Murphy (1999: 225); Grabbe and Hughes (1998: 4–6); Holvêque (1998); IEP/TEPSA (1998); Torreblanca (2001: 62–66, 286). As in the analysis of NATO, and for the reasons explained there, member state preferences on the general commitment to enlargement were ascertained before the Copenhagen European Council of 1993 (except for the 1995 entrants), those on the inclusiveness of negotiations before the Luxembourg European Council of 1997.

[26] On "sensitivity interdependence," see Keohane and Nye (1977: 12–15).

Table 8.3 *Member state shares of EU exports to CEECs and EU economic output*

	Export share percent	Output share percent
Disproportionately high share in exports		
Germany	41.2	27.4
Austria	8.8	2.7
Finland	3.1	1.5
Roughly proportional share in exports		
Italy	16.1	14.1
Netherlands	4.5	4.6
Belgium/Luxembourg	3.8	3.3
Sweden	3.1	2.9
Denmark	2.0	2.0
Greece	1.4	1.4
Disproportionately low share in exports		
France	7.4	17.8
Britain	5.6	13.4
Spain	2.0	6.8
Ireland	0.6	0.8
Portugal	0.2	1.3

A disproportionate share of trade is one that is 25 percent higher or lower in percentage points than a country's share of the EU's economic output (my calculation based on Eurostat data for GDP at market prices in 1996). For the shares in trade, see "EU trade in goods with CEECs," *Weekly Europe Selected Statistics* 1047 (23 March 1998); data for 1996.

Europe therefore stand to gain more from economic exchange with the East than more distant states. This is roughly reflected in the member states' shares of EU trade with the CEECs as compared to their shares of EU economic output (Table 8.3). All member states with a disproportionately high share in exports (Austria, Germany, Finland) are border states; all member states with a disproportionately low share (Britain, Ireland, France, Portugal, Spain) are not. We can further assume that those countries that are closest to and most highly involved in the CEE economies will also gain most from the membership of CEECs (e.g., through the further opening of markets and the better protection of their economic assets in the region).

Finally, in light of this argument, member states should be most interested in the membership of those countries with which they share a border or are in close proximity. This explains why member states in the center of the EU were content with the Commission's proposal to limit accession talks to the Central European candidates (plus Estonia) whereas the others wanted the talks to be more inclusive. It is also small wonder that France, Greece and Italy, all Southern states, gave their special support to Bulgaria and Romania, Southeastern candidates, whereas Denmark and Sweden, Northern states, most strongly advocated the cause of the Baltic states, the northernmost of the CEE applicants. That Finland did not join Denmark and Sweden in pushing for extended enlargement on the eve of the Luxembourg European Council of December 1997 may be explained by the fact that Estonia, Finland's direct neighbor and most important economic partner among the Baltic countries, was on the Commission's shortlist for fast-track accession negotiations.

The divergent state preferences are not fully explained, however, by different levels of gains from the control of negative, and the exploitation of positive, interdependence with Central and Eastern Europe. In this case, we would only see different degrees of enthusiasm for, but no opposition to, the EU's commitment to Eastern enlargement. In order to explain why most member states, including the border countries of Italy and Greece, acted as "brakemen" in the enlargement process, potential losses from enlargement must be included in the analysis. The unequal distribution of these losses mainly results from differences in *socioeconomic structure* among the EU member countries.

As discussed earlier, Eastern enlargement threatens to create particularly high costs, resulting from trade and budgetary competition, for the poorer, less highly developed and more agricultural members. To repeat the main points, because "less-developed" member states specialize in the same traditional and resource-intensive industries as the CEECs, they are likely to be more adversely affected by trade integration than more highly developed countries. And though rich border countries will, in turn, face migration pressures, in the history of the EU the movement of labor has been more strongly restricted and much lower than the movement of goods and capital. Moreover, since all CEE members will become structural net recipients, and under the condition that the Community budget will not be sufficiently expanded to cover the additional expenses for CEE members, the present main beneficiares of the budget were likely to be disproportionately affected. Correspondingly, all of them (Spain, Greece, Portugal and Ireland) were among the brakemen and later challenged the Commission's opinion that enlargement could be funded on the basis of the current budget limit.[27] Finally, as in the NATO case, the standard interpretation of French reticence toward enlargement points to French concerns that future CEE members would

[27] *Financial Times* (*FT*), 15 September 1997, 2; IEP/TEPSA (1998).

side with Germany and other border states in EU decision-making and thereby cause a power shift in favor of Germany and the North-eastern countries in general (see, e.g., Grabbe and Hughes 1998: 5; Holvêque 1998: 515).

Thus, the Northern border countries not only expected to reap the highest economic and security gains from enlargement; they were also little affected by trade and budget competition with future CEE members. By contrast, that Greece and Italy were among the brakemen, despite their geographical location, can be partly attributed to their specialization in traditional industries and, in the case of Greece, to concerns over budget competition. In addition, both countries were preoccupied more strongly with Mediterranean security than with the CEE region. Italy feared that the EU's focus on Eastern enlargement would divert its attention and funding from the Mediterranean region (Bardi 1996: 163–65), and Greece concentrated its efforts on the admission of Cyprus to the accession negotiations. The disincentives were highest for those states that could not expect any significant economic and security gains from enlargement but were likely to incur major costs from trade and budget competition (Portugal, Spain, and Ireland) or from a "geopolitical shift" of the Community (France). The Benelux countries fall somewhere in between – in economic terms, they had neither much to lose nor much to gain from enlargement.

Only the British preferences obviously deviate from this structural pattern, since Central and Eastern Europe is neither geographically close nor economically important to Britain. The early and strong British commitment to enlargement is generally attributed to the "europhobia" of the Conservative governments. It appears to have been based on the calculation that an extensive "widening" of the Community would prevent its further "deepening" and even dilute the achieved level of integration (see Garden 2001: 77; Grabbe and Hughes 1998: 5; Hayward 1996: 148).

In sum, no single factor explains the EU member states' enlargement preferences. The economic conditions emphasized by Moravcsik go a long way in giving a plausible account of state preferences but in some important cases (Italy, Britain, and probably France) geopolitical or ideological interests seem to have been decisive. At any rate, as in the case of NATO Eastern enlargement, the divergent state preferences are best understood as *individual* and *self-centered.* As rationalism would lead us to expect, they reflected egoistic calculations of, and conflict about, *national* welfare and security benefits or (in particular, in the British case) *national or party* attitudes to integration, not a collective, rule-based community interest.

The initial process

In this section, I describe the initial decision-making and negotiating process on NATO and EU Eastern enlargement which begins with the first CEEC demands for membership in the Western organization and ends with the first major outcomes of this process, PfP in the case of NATO and the Europe Agreements of association in the EC case. The preceding sections have shown that the community rules – which, according to the liberal community hypothesis, should be the main motivating force in the enlargement process – did not have any decisive impact on the enlargement preferences of the participating states. Rather, these preferences were driven in general by egoistic considerations of state security and welfare, as expected in a rationalist perspective. I argue that the same applies to the initial process: it was characterized by bargaining behavior, and its outcomes are plausibly accounted for by the constellation of state preferences and the international distribution of bargaining power.

NATO: NACC and PfP

When the Central European governments first expressed their interest in joining NATO in the course of 1991, they were confronted with a general reticence among the member states. Although NATO was prepared to establish and expand institutionalized cooperation with the former members of the Warsaw Pact, the expansion of NATO *membership* was rejected. In the apt wording of Paul Latawski, "the essence of NATO policy was a careful blend of functional cooperation and political dialogue devoid of any formal commitment" (1994: 62).

NATO had already declared its intention to redefine its relationship and enter into cooperative relations with the members of the Warsaw Pact before the Central European governments indicated their desire to become NATO members.[28] In a declaration agreed at NATO's London Summit in July 1990, the alliance offered to formally end confrontation, establish permanent diplomatic relations and base the future relationship on the principle of common security. In the new Europe, the security of each state was to be inseparably linked to that of its neighbors.

Faced with the first demands for membership, NATO immediately signalled the CEECs to abstain from applying for NATO membership. At the same time, however, NATO felt the need to offer them a stronger and more institutionalized cooperation. For this purpose, the US

[28] For an overview of NATO post-Cold War policy towards the CEECs, see Broer (1997: 298–300).

Secretary of State James Baker and German Foreign Minister Hans-Dietrich Genscher initiated, first, the "liaison concept" and, second, at a more institutionalized level, the North Atlantic Cooperation Council (NACC). *NACC* was established in December 1991 as an inclusive forum for consultation and exchange. Initially, it included the member states of NATO, on the one hand, and the former member states of the Warsaw Pact plus the newly independent Baltic states, on the other. In 1992, it was expanded to include the other successor states of the Soviet Union and to some formerly non-aligned CEECs, totalling a number of thirty-eight countries in 1993. Except under special circumstances, NACC was planned to meet once a year for plenary sessions of state representatives to discuss pan-European security issues. Moreover, NACC set up annual workplans which focused on programs of contacts and information exchange and continued the activities started under the "liaison concept" – for instance, meetings between officers and staff of the former adversary alliances including so-called "familiarization courses," fellowships for the study of democratic institutions, and seminars on defense conversion and the democratic control of the military. Conversely, NACC neither differentiated between the CEECs nor established direct military cooperation, let alone NATO security guarantees.

Critical observers like Jonathan Eyal therefore characterized NACC as "no different from the OSCE: a gigantic talking shop" and as a "prevaricating exercise, a mechanism for postponing decisions" (1997: 701). Obviously, the CEEC governments that had sought NATO membership out of disappointment with the CSCE were not satisfied with a NACC that mirrored this pan-European organization and, therefore, upheld their bid to join the alliance as full members.

At the beginning of 1993, an informal discussion in the North Atlantic Council at the level of ambassadors still came to the conclusion that the membership of CEECs was not on the agenda, for the time being (Weisser 1999: 23). Even after the German Defense Minister Rühe and US National Security Adviser Lake had put Eastern enlargement on the agenda, the pattern of NATO's initial reaction to the CEEC demands for membership – intensification of cooperation without commitment to enlargement – did not change. The next step was the Partnership for Peace program, mainly worked out by the US Department of Defense in 1993 and agreed by NATO in January 1994.

Besides continuing NACC activities, *PfP* contained some new elements. For the first time, it envisaged direct military cooperation between NATO and partner forces in military exercises and peacekeeping operations. The partner countries opened permanent liaison offices at NATO headquarters and NATO set up a separate organizational structure, the

Partnership Coordination Cell. Moreover, NATO promised to "consult with any active participant in the Partnership if that partner perceives a direct threat to its territorial integrity, political independence, or security" (NATO 1994a). Finally, PfP was based on the principle of differentiation. The Individual Partnership Programs (IPPs) negotiated between NATO and the partner countries allowed for varying degrees of cooperation, thus making it possible for the countries aspiring to NATO membership to establish closer ties with NATO than other countries and to prepare themselves for accession. Nevertheless, PfP did not promise the CEECs either military assistance in the case of attack or future membership. Translated as "Partnership for Postponement," "Procrastination," or "Prevarication" by its critics, PfP again failed to meet the interests of the CEEC aspirants and was heavily criticized in Central European capitals for falling short of committing NATO to Eastern enlargement. At one point, the Polish President Walesa even threatened to reject the program but, in the end, all CEECs interested in NATO membership signed the PfP Framework Document immediately.

Obviously, as in the case of the CEECs, enlargement was not an automatic, taken-for-granted response of NATO to the new international situation in Europe. Nor was it a close corollary of NATO's commitment to its constitutive values and norms which it reaffirmed on various occasions in the immediate post-Cold War period. As early as May 1990, the member states agreed, at a meeting of their foreign ministers, that NATO would have to develop into an instrument for the promotion of peace and democracy in Central and Eastern Europe (Broer 1997: 298). Second, on the occasion of President Havel's visit to NATO in March 1991, Secretary-General Manfred Wörner welcomed the successes of Czechoslovakia in building a pluralist democracy on the foundation of human rights, viewed these achievements as an important contribution to the creation of a Europe whole and free, and vowed to encourage and support reforms in all CEECs.[29] Third, in its Declaration on "Partnership with the Countries of Central and Eastern Europe" of June 1991, the North Atlantic Council stated that the division of Europe was over, that "our own security is inseparably linked to that of all other states in Europe," and that the "consolidation and preservation throughout the continent of democratic societies and their freedom from any form of coercion or intimidation are therefore of direct and material concern to us" (NATO 1991c). Finally, during the *coup d'état* in the Soviet Union

[29] "Erklärung des Generalsekretärs Manfred Wörner im Namen des Nordatlantikrats anläßlich des Besuchs des Präsidenten der Tschechischen und Slowakischen Föderativen Republik Vaclav Havel bei der NATO am 21. März 1991," *NATO Brief* 39: 2, 1991, 29–30.

in August 1991, NATO issued a Ministerial Declaration in which the alliance not only reiterated the wording of its June statements but added that the "security of the new democracies" was of particular concern to it (NATO 1991d).

On all of these occasions, however, NATO shied away from establishing a direct link between these references to its constitutive values and norms and a general commitment to the security of democratic CEECs, on the one hand, and their membership in the alliance, on the other. The kind of protection NATO had in mind at this time can be inferred from a statement by Secretary General Wörner that "NATO serves *as a security anchor in Western Europe* that helps the new democracies to develop their potential with the least instability and disorder and free from threat and intimidation" (Wörner 1991, my italics). Instead, in its June 1991 "Partnership" declaration, NATO stated that "we will neither seek unilateral advantage from the changed situation in Europe nor threaten the legitimate interests of any state." NATO wished neither to isolate a country nor to create new divisions in Europe and attached central importance to the CSCE process and its further strengthening (NATO 1991c).

Like the member states' enlargement preferences, the initial reaction of NATO to the CEECs' membership requests corresponds to the expectations of rationalist alliance theory (see Part I). Both initial outcomes, NACC and PfP, can be explained on the basis of the constellation of state preferences in the Alliance and the distribution of bargaining power between allies and candidates.

No NATO member government proposed enlargement before 1993. In 1993, leading representatives of major member governments like the US National Security Adviser Lake and the German Defense Minister Rühe broke the blockade. But since they could not even unite their own national governments behind enlargement, their chance to establish it as a NATO goal tended toward zero. Just as PfP "was in essence the lowest common denominator acceptable to the interagency process" in the United States (Mattox 1998: 31), it was generally welcomed at the NATO level as "a clever political fudge" that "papered over the cracks in the Alliance consensus on the issue of NATO's eastern policy" (Latawski 1994: 65), and, as a Canadian diplomat recalled, "helped us to get out of the hole we were digging on expanding NATO."[30]

For those NATO actors that opposed a commitment to enlargement, PfP was reassuring because it did not contain any concrete, binding commitment to Eastern enlargement, let alone a timetable or membership criteria. It gave neither the CEECs formal security guarantees nor formally

[30] Quoted in Solomon (1998: 39). See also Broer (1997: 308).

differentiated between them (in particular between Russia and the Central European countries). For the NATO actors in favor of enlargement, PfP was a progressive program compared to NACC because it reaffirmed that "the Alliance . . . remains open to the membership of other European states" (NATO 1991a), involved NATO more strongly in CEE security, "encourage[d] differentiation in practice" (Kupchan 1994: 15), and allowed NATO to prepare the aspirant countries for membership through military cooperation.

For NATO as a whole, NACC and PfP were efficient institutional solutions. They deepened and institutionalized cooperation with all CEECs, involved them in the task of peacekeeping, and burdened them with the costs of making their forces interoperable with those of NATO without, at the same time, creating any formal obligations to guarantee their security, antagonizing Russia, or weakening the cohesion and effectiveness of the alliance. These provisions reflect the strongly asymmetrical interdependence and bargaining power between NATO and the CEECs.[31] Whereas the CEECs needed NATO to satisfy their security needs and could not credibly threaten NATO with alternative alliance options or the prohibitive costs of non-enlargement, NATO did not need the CEECs to guarantee the security of its members. Despite their misgivings, they ultimately accepted NACC and PfP because a denial to participate in these institutions would have left them even worse off.

EU association

As in the case of NATO, the governments in Central and Eastern Europe, not the EC, were the first to raise the issue of Community membership and constantly pushed the member states for an explicit commitment to this goal. By contrast, in early 1990, the EC proposed to conclude association agreements without referring to, let alone promising, future membership.[32] In a preparatory communication to the Council, the Commission stated clearly that the associations "in no way represent a sort of membership antechamber" – "Membership will not be excluded when the time comes, but this is a totally separate question."[33] The Council, in turn, "advised the Commission simply to refer to Article 237 (EEC): any European state may apply for membership" (Sedelmeier and Wallace 2000: 438). Before and during the negotiations on the association agreements, the CEECs, the British and German governments (as

[31] See earlier discussion in chapter 2.
[32] For a detailed description of the negotiations, see Torreblanca (2001).
[33] *Europe* (Agence Internationale d'Information pour la Presse) 5185, 2 February 1990, 2.

well as Commissioner Andriessen) kept pressing for an explicit EC commitment to enlargement but failed to gain the support of the Council or the Commission. The only concession they achieved was a reference to future membership as their, but not the Community's, "final objective" (Sedelmeier and Wallace 2000: 438; see also Torreblanca 1997: 12; 2001: 105).

The first agreements with Central European countries were concluded in December 1991 and went into force in February 1994. The "Europe Agreements," as they came to be called, contained provisions on a political dialogue, the intensification of economic, financial and cultural cooperation, and the adaptation of (market-related) legislation in the CEECs to EC law. The substantive core of the association agreements, however, was a progressive liberalization of the movement of goods. Whereas the Community generally offered the CEECs a fast and asymmetrical liberalization of trade in industrial products, it reserved protectionist "anti-dumping" and "safeguard" measures for itself and made an exception of exactly those sectors (agriculture, textiles, coal, iron and steel) in which the CEE economies were competitive (Mayhew 1998: 23; Sedelmeier and Wallace 1996: 371). Portugal blocked a further liberalization of trade in textiles, France vetoed any concession on beef, and Spain blocked agreement on steel trade, leading negotiations to the brink of breakdown.[34] The negotiations about substantive policies were dominated by sectoral interest-groups and sectoral policy-makers in the Commission as well as in the member governments, and these actors were more concerned with the costs of trade liberalization in their domain of interest than with the general political goal of assisting the associated CEECs in their political and economic transformation (Sedelmeier and Wallace 2000: 439; Torreblanca 2001). As a result, Central and Eastern Europe ran into a permanent trade deficit with the Community.

Blocking tactics continued in later rounds of the accession negotiations. For instance, differences of view of the safeguard clause and defense measures delayed the interim agreement with Bulgaria for more than half a year;[35] and Italy blocked the opening of association negotiations with Slovenia for almost a year between 1994 and 1995, and the signing of the agreement for more than six months between 1995 and 1996 because of problems resulting from the nationalization of Italian property in the 1950s.

Furthermore, the EC as a whole, and some of the reticent members in particular, used diverse *delaying tactics* to deflect the CEECs' demands for

[34] *Europe* 5562, 7 September 1991, 8; *Europe* 5563, 9–10 September 1991, 9; Torreblanca (1997: 40–41).

[35] *Europe* 6079, 6 October 1993, 8.

full membership. On the one hand, they were offered alternative arrangements like French President Mitterrand's "European Confederation" or Prime Minister Balladur's "Stability Pact" for Europe as well as several ideas of "membership light" (that is, excluding the more cost-intensive Community policies). On the other hand, the urgency of other issues (such as the ratification of the Maastricht Treaty on European Union or accession negotiations with the EFTAns) has often provided a welcome opportunity to place the issue of Eastern enlargement at the end of the agenda.

The process and results of the EC's initial enlargement decision-making and negotiations *closely correspond to the case of NATO*. Martin Smith and Graham Timmins characterize the initial phase of EC and NATO policy toward the CEECs as one in which "the member states of both institutions were mainly concerned with debating and making changes to the mandates and workings of the institutions themselves" and, whereas both organizations "engaged in initial programmes of co-operation with CEE states," "these fell far short of offering a clear perspective of eventual enlargement" (2000: 21).

Moreover, both process and outcome conform to *rationalist expectations*. As I have discussed earlier (chapter 2), neither the drivers within the Community, mainly Britain and Germany, nor the CEECs possessed the material bargaining power to threaten the reluctant majority of member states credibly with alternative unilateral or multilateral policy options or prohibitive opportunity costs in case they failed to agree to Eastern enlargement. In this situation, association was the highest level of co-operation with the CEECs the member states could agree on. Through trade liberalization and regulatory adaptation, it enabled the potential winners of enlargement to intensify their economic involvement in CEE markets; and the political dialogue offered, in principle, an avenue to controlling negative externalities originating from the CEECs. At the same time, the association regime protected the potential losers of enlargement against the costs of trade and budget competition by equipping them with safeguard measures in those sectors in which they were particulary vulnerable to trade liberalization and by blocking the CEECs' access to the Community budget. Despite constant complaints about the EC's failure to commit itself to the goal of enlargement and to provide a more generous market opening, the CEECs accepted the Europe Agreements because association was still preferable to a weaker or no institutionalized relationship with the EC.

In game theory parlance, the initial outcome of the decision-making and negotiating process on NATO and EU enlargement corresponds to the "Nash solution" in a "suasion game" (Martin 1993: 104) or a "Rambo

Table 8.4 *Constellation of preferences in EU and NATO enlargement*

EU/NATO drivers and CEECs	cooperation with brakemen (C)	no cooperation with brakemen (D)
EU/NATO brakemen		
enlargement (C)	full membership (1,4)	no association (2,2)
no enlargement (D)	association (4,3)	no association (3,1)

game," as Michael Zürn (1992: 209–11) described this constellation of preferences (see Table 8.4). The "brakemen" in EU and NATO preferred a profitable association with the CEECs (DC), as realized in the Europe agreements and PfP, to "no association" (CD or DD) but would have accepted "no association" rather than full membership (CC). By contrast, the first preference of the CEECs and the "drivers" in EU and NATO was full membership but, just as the "brakemen," they preferred association (CD) to no association.[36]

In this constellation, the pro-enlargement forces had a dominant strategy of cooperating with whatever the "brakemen" saw as in their best interests. "Knowing this," the opponent camp could "achieve its most favored outcome by defecting" (Martin 1993: 104). Association is a "Nash equilibrium" because none of the actors would be better off after changing their strategy in light of the opponent's choice. If the "brakemen" switched to cooperation or if the "drivers" switched to defection, both would attain their least favored outcomes. Thus, the initial outcomes of the EU and NATO enlargement processes not only corresponded to rationalist expectations, they also promised to be stable given the structural causes of the member states' preferences and the structural asymmetry between Western members and CEEC candidates.

36 The preference orderings for both "no association" outcomes are somewhat arbitrary because the outcome is the same. I simply assume that actors prefer defection to cooperation if other actors defect. For the analysis of the game, however, these orderings do not matter.

Conclusion: the double puzzle of Eastern enlargement

The preferences of the states involved in Eastern enlargement and the initial EC and NATO decision-making process on enlargement strongly *contradict the expectations derived from the sociological-institutionalist process hypotheses of habitual and normative action.*

(H1 and N1) In the EC case, the CEECs' immediate and general request for membership corresponds to the hypothesis of habitual action but the membership bids of CEEC governments with authoritarian tendencies are not compatible with the hypothesis of normative action. The failure of the sociological-institutionalist process hypotheses is most obvious in the NATO case: even the most reform-minded CEEC governments did not regard joining NATO as a corollary of their democratic identity, values, and norms or as a taken-for-granted response to the post-Cold War challenges. Rather, initially they preferred neutrality or collective security to alliance membership.

(H2 and N2) The enlargement preferences of EU and NATO member states were not uniform. There was strong and persistent divergence with regard to the desirability of (fast) enlargement and the selection of new members both among and within the member states. Whereas a minority of actors may have been motivated by the community values and norms in their preference for a strong commitment to admitting democratic CEECs, the general distribution of preferences cannot be accounted for by collective rules.

(H3 and N3) In the immediate post-Cold War period, lasting roughly from 1989 to 1993, the Western organizations did not offer membership or commit themselves in principle to the admission of liberal-democratic CEECs. Instead, they proposed looser relationships that did not grant the CEECs the rights and benefits of full membership.

The enlargement preferences and initial enlargement decision-making process *correspond to rationalist expectations* which attribute actor preferences and behavior as well as collective outcomes to egoistic calculations of material interest and differential bargaining power and do not take into account the rules of the organizations. First, the CEECs' turn toward NATO membership was an instrumental choice based on security interests in light of the worsened situation in Russia and Yugoslavia and the inefficiency of the CSCE. Second, the enlargement preferences of the member states reflected divergent egoistic calculations of enlargement costs and benefits based on national security and welfare interests and on different degrees of positive and negative interdependence with the CEECs. Third, the denial of membership to the CEECs and the association and PfP agreements were the results of a bargaining process in which the member states, in particular the "brakemen" among them, possessed superior material bargaining power and were able to impose their preferred institutional form of CEEC–EC/NATO relations on the CEECs.

These observations deviate so obviously from the sociological-institutionalist expectations that neither a more precise differentiation between the cognitive and normative mechanisms of rule-following nor a test of the remaining implications of the hypotheses of habitual and normative action is necessary and justified. Eastern enlargement has not been a habitualized or morally conscious, rule-based response to systemic transformation in Central and Eastern Europe. Instead of falling back on organizational routines and reflecting their rule-based obligations as members of the Western international community, the member states of the EU and NATO defined the new situation in terms of a challenge to their own power, security and welfare and based their preferences on egoistic calculations of costs and benefits. Even for the founding states of the Alliance and the Community, decades of membership and prior enlargement rounds had not led to the internalization of enlargement rules or the habitualization to enlargement routines.

Thus, in the perspective of the rationalist-constructivist debate, Eastern enlargement constitutes a *double puzzle*. For both NATO and the EU, rationalist institutionalism largely explains the individual enlargement preferences of the state actors involved and the initial outcomes of the negotiating and decision-making process on enlargement. For an observer analyzing, from a rationalist point of view, the state of EC/NATO–CEEC relations in 1993, there was nothing puzzling about it. Rationalist institutionalism cannot explain, however, why NATO and the EU invited the first CEECs to accession negotiations only four years later.

By contrast, sociological institutionalism does account for the general decision of both Western organizations to admit CEECs and, with some degree of uncertainty, their selection of (potential) new members. Yet, the standard sociological process hypotheses of habitual and normative action are unable to tell us how this outcome was produced, as both the actor preferences and their initial behavior contradict the logics of script-following and appropriateness. If the community rules had any influence on Eastern enlargement, it was not through rule-based cognitions and preferences.

The analytical problem to be solved, then, is to explain how a process initially determined by egoistic preferences and strategic action resulted in a rule-conforming outcome. This is, of course, a very familiar theme for social scientists; the search for the causal link between "private vices" and "public virtues" and for normative order among selfish actors is at the core of modern social theory and has strongly motivated theory-building in International Relations since its beginnings. Put more concretely, how did the values and norms of the Western community intervene in a process of strategic action, upset the "association" equilibrium, and lead to Eastern enlargement? If, as Snyder concedes, the "logic of the Nash solution, or of bargaining power, may sometimes be dominated or considerably skewed . . . by normative . . . factors" (1997: 77), how do these normative factors become causally efficient?

Some empirical starting points for the search of an answer to this question are suggested by the preceding analysis. First, the geography- and interdependence-based rationalist explanation of enlargement preferences failed to account for the shift in US NATO enlargement preferences beginning in 1993. Did community values and norms play a role in this shift? Second, in spite of their unwillingness to commit themselves to Eastern enlargement, the Western organizations in their public declarations have repeatedly welcomed and acknowledged the liberal-democratic transformations in Central and Eastern Europe, pledged support for them, and reaffirmed in principle their openness to enlargement and to the admission of states that fulfilled the liberal accession criteria. Did these declaratory statements have any impact on the later process and outcomes, and if so, how?

Following the classification of process hypotheses developed at the beginning of this chapter, the theoretical starting points for the search for a solution to the double puzzle of enlargement are the two hypotheses that "lie in between" rule-independent rational action, on the one hand, and habitual and normative action, on the other: communicative and rhetorical action. Moreover, as suggested by the terminology of the "suasion game," some sort of moral or normative appeal was needed to persuade the "brakemen" to change their uncooperative strategy.

Part IV

From association to membership: rhetorical action in Eastern enlargement

"Rhetorical action" – the strategic use of rule-based arguments – solves the double puzzle of Eastern enlargement. It provides the causal link between the interest-based state preferences and initial stages of EU and NATO enlargement, on the one hand, and the rule-based final outcome, on the other. "Rhetorical action" draws on a strategic conception of rules that combines a social, ideational ontology with the assumption of rational action; it postulates that social actors use and exchange arguments based on identities, values, and norms institutionalized in their environment to defend their political claims and to persuade their audience and their opponents to accept these claims and to act accordingly. In NATO and the EU, the actors interested in enlargement used the liberal identity, values, and norms of the Western international community to put moral and social pressure on the reluctant member states and shamed them into acquiescing to the admission of CEECs.

In the theoretical chapter of this part (chapter 9), I discuss the conceptual and theoretical foundations of rhetorical action and specify hypotheses about the use and effects of arguments in decision-making. I do this in much greater detail than for the hypotheses of habitual and normative action because rhetorical action plays a pivotal role in my explanation of Eastern enlargement and has received less attention in the rationalist-constructivist debate than the other hypotheses. I introduce the strategic conception of rules on which rhetorical action builds, contrast rhetorical action with communicative action, and specify why and how political actors use, and are persuaded by, rhetorical arguments.

On this basis, I analyze, first, the decision-making process on NATO enlargement (chapter 10). This case study demonstrates the pervasiveness of rhetorical action at different stages and levels of decision-making. However, it does not conclusively reject the proposition that enlargement was merely a result of superior US bargaining power. I therefore examine the EU decision-making process as a control study (chapter 11). In the EU, the proponents of enlargement did not possess the bargaining power to overcome the opposition of the anti-enlargement coalition. Yet, by using rule-based rhetorical arguments, they silenced the reluctant member states and persuaded them to accept Eastern enlargement.

9 Rhetorical action

The strategic conception of rules: Goffman's social theory

The hypotheses of habitual and normative action started from the assumption that social actors take community and organizational norms and values for granted or internalize them.[1] By providing meanings and motives for action, norms and values affect social action at the dispositional level of cognitions and preferences. These hypotheses follow the cognitive and normative conceptions of institutions, rules and culture that have traditionally dominated sociological institutionalism. There is, however, an alternative, *strategic conception of rules*[2] in sociological theory on which the mode of rhetorical action is based.

In the account of Robert Edgerton (1985: 7–14), the strategic conception of rules originated in anthropology and sociology as a reaction to the "oversocialized view of man" and the "over-integrated view of society" (Dennis Wrong) that dominated social analysis following the normativist theories of Durkheim and Parsons. "From the slave of custom in the normative model, man came full circle to become the strategic master of rules – artful, dissembling, posing, deceiving and calculating for his own advantage" (Edgerton 1985: 12–13). In the strategic conception, rules are not motives for action, nor are they merely constraints, they are "resources for human strategies" in social interactions and they "are used not followed."[3]

The seminal work in this tradition is the social theory of Erving Goffman. Depending on the writings one draws on, Goffman's

[1] This section builds on, expands, and slightly revises, earlier conceptualizations and applications of the rhetorical action concept (Schimmelfennig 1995: 38–43, 292–302; 1997: 221–34).

[2] Note that, according to my earlier definition of rules as institutionalized culture, rules comprise values, norms, and identities (see chapter 3).

[3] Edgerton (1985: 14). For similar ideas on the concept and study of "culture," see Swidler (1986) and Laitin (1988).

conceptualization of actors varies between a highly socialized "self" with little personal autonomy and individuals who strategically calculate their behavioral moves and manipulate social situations for their own advantage. Likewise, his conceptualization of social interactions shifts between "rituals," i.e., highly structured situations and outcomes, and "games" in which the actors enjoy considerable freedom of action and the situation is mainly structured by the distribution of capacities and information among the actors.

In my reading, this variation is not necessarily an expression of theoretical ambivalence or inconsistency. Rather, it reveals a dialectical relationship between strategic action and cultural values and norms – between "manipulation and morality" (Branaman 1997). Goffman describes this "basic dialectic" in the following way: on the one hand,

> *qua* performers, individuals are concerned not with the moral issue of realizing standards, but with the amoral issue of engineering a convincing impression that these standards are being realized. Our activity . . . is largely concerned with moral matters, but as performers we do not have a moral concern with them.

On the other hand, however, "In their capacity as performers, individuals will be concerned with maintaining the impression that they are living up to the many standards by which they and their products are judged." As a result, "the very obligation and profitability of appearing always in a steady moral light, of being a socialized character, focuses one to be the sort of person who is practiced in the ways of the stage" (1959: 251).

In other words, the context of interaction is neither a true consensus nor a pure game. On the one hand, it is just a "veneer of consensus" or a "surface of agreement" (Goffman 1959: 9). Institutions establish "a framework of appearances that must be maintained, whether or not there is feeling behind the appearances" (Goffman 1959: 242). On the other hand, "in real-life situations," games always "occur in a context of constraining and enabling social norms" (Goffman 1969: 113–14). They are "socially mediated games" (Goffman 1969: 116).

According to Ann Branaman, Goffman's social theory points out that "manipulation and morality are not as separable as we might like to think":

> Morality does not reside within us or above us but rather is manufactured through performances and interaction rituals designed to affirm human dignity. Yet, on the other side, the seemingly manipulative and self-serving focus on enhancing one's self-image in the eyes of others is the most essential way in which we commit ourselves to the moral order of society. (1997: xlvi)

Goffman captures this dialectic in his metaphor of social life as a "drama" (1959: 249). In this "drama," the "presentation of self," "impression management," and "framing" are the core social actitivities. The central objective of the performer is to "control the impression" others "receive of the situation", and "to give them the kind of impression that will lead them to act voluntarily in accordance with his own plan" (Goffman 1959: 3–4, 15). Likewise, the framer tries to manipulate the frames of reference used by other actors to make sense out of events and define the social situation in which they are.[4]

The use and manipulation of rules by the performers and framers to influence their audience's impressions, definitions of the situation and actions is, however, only one aspect of social life as a drama. Equally important are constraints which often matter in ways the strategic users of rules neither intended nor fully control.

Cultural constraints. In order to act (and to act successfully), social actors must draw on the cultural and normative repertoires present in their environment. In keeping with the drama metaphor, actors-as-performers are constrained by socially determined roles and scripts; as framers, they must work with the concepts and beliefs of their audience. Even "fabrications . . . require . . . the use of something already meaningful in terms of primary frameworks" shared by the performers' audience (Goffman 1974: 84). In sum, social actors may manipulate rules but they cannot simply invent them or choose to ignore them.

Processual constraints. Strategic impression management and framing is embedded in an iterative "information game," that is, "a potentially infinite cycle of concealment, discovery, false revelation, and rediscovery" (Goffman 1959: 8). While the individual, through a "performance" including verbal and non-verbal behavior, seeks to create an impression in the audience that will help her to achieve her objectives, the audience checks her verbal and non-verbal expressions for clues to the sincerity and the consistency of her presentation of self. Knowing this, the individual will be careful to appear sincere and consistent, and so forth (cf. also Goffman 1969: 45).

As a result, to attain their goals, performers must pay attention to acting and speaking consistently and in correspondence with the rules they have chosen for their presentations of self and frames. Neither can they simply ignore these rules later in the process should they become inconvenient. Each performance entails a social commitment.

[4] Goffman (1974). The concept of strategic framing has subsequently been more fully developed in the sociological analysis of social movements. The seminal article is Snow and Benford (1988).

The individual's initial projection commits him to what he is proposing to be and requires him to drop all pretenses of being other things. As the interaction among the participants progresses, additions and modifications in this initial informational state will of course occur, but it is essential that these later developments be related without contradiction to, and even built up from, the initial positions taken by the several participants. It would seem that an individual can more easily make a choice as to what line of treatment to demand from and extend to the others present at the beginning of an encounter than he can alter the line of treatment that is being pursued once the interaction is underway. (Goffman 1959: 10–11)

Social constraints. Goffman does not assume that social actors internalize and are motivated by social rules. Even if they believe in the rightness of the rules and, in principle, accept the obligation to follow them, they may still try to manipulate or circumvent them for their own advantage. What is it then that makes performers and framers stick to their "lines" and comply with the rules on which they are based? Goffman suggests that, although actors may not be concerned about the rules as such, they are highly concerned about their image and esteem in their social environment. A positive image depends not only on public acceptance of the rules they refer to but also on credible performances. When a performer fails to remain faithful to her "initial projection" in presentations of self and framing, and is caught manipulating the rules, she causes a "disruptive event" likely to discredit her image and to lead to a breakdown of the interaction (Goffman 1959: 12).

On the part of the performer, the reaction to such a disruption is shame and embarrassment, a loss of "face" (Goffman 1959: 12; 1982: 11). To avoid or overcome these painful feelings, to protect their image, and to save their face, performers will be careful to remain within the accepted limits to their freedom of interpretation of their roles and scripts and to stick to their previously presented positions and lines. Individual norm compliance and the reproduction of social order are then "explained by our strategic determinations that we stand to lose more than we might gain by engaging in face-gaining maneuvers" and other manipulations (Branaman 1997: lxiii; see also lxx). Thus, for "the smooth working of society," the internalization of rules is not necessary:

Rather, each participant is expected to suppress his immediate heartfelt feelings, conveying a view of the situation which he feels the others will be able to find at least temporarily acceptable. The maintenance of this surface of agreement, this veneer of consensus is facilitated by each participant concealing his own wants behind statements which assert values to which everyone present feels obliged to give lip service. (Goffman 1959: 9)

To conclude, at the level of basic assumptions, the strategic conception of rules *combines the social and ideational ontology of constructivism – in a non-structuralist, processualist variation – with rationalist instrumentalism.*

Idealism. Like the cognitive and normative conceptions, the strategic conception of rules assumes that social action is embedded in a cultural and institutional "community" environment. It regards intersubjective ideas as the main stuff of which the social world is made up and as the most important causes of social phenomena.

Processualism. The strategic conception of rules treats intersubjective ideas in an expressly non-structuralist way. It rejects the view of culture and rules as given "substances" or "entities"[5] as well as the "oversocialized" view of actors whose identities and interests are determined by social structures. Rather, the intersubjective ideas that make up the social world provide the actors with reference points and repertoires that become effective in the course of social interaction. Processes of social interaction gather momentum independently of initial structures and the intentions of individual actors but produce patterns or configurations that cannot be reduced to either of them. This perspective fits under processualism, a metatheoretical position that gives ontological and explanatory priority to social processes.[6]

Self-defined goals. In contrast to cognitivism and normativism, the strategic conception of rules does not assume that the ends and goals social actors pursue are determined or shaped by collective culture and rules. First, even within a single community, its rules are open, and always subject to diverse interpretations, manipulations and debate. Second, the actors are assumed to be weakly socialized at best: they know the rules but they also know how to manipulate them. They use the rules but they do not necessarily follow them. Even if they conceive of themselves as members of a community and generally identify themselves with its values and norms, it does not follow that their issue-specific interests and preferences represent the "community interest" rather than their self-defined or self-interested goals. Beyond that, the strategic conception does not make any strong assumptions: strategic users of rules may strive egoistically for material gains in power and wealth but they may also have genuinely idealistic goals. In other words, the strategic use of rules is not defined by the kind of goals actors pursue but by the way they pursue them (cf. Goffman 1959: 6).

Instrumentalism. The strategic conception of rules shares the assumption of instrumentalism with rationalism. In a "community"

[5] For a critique of "substantialist" theories in IR, see Jackson and Nexon (1999).

[6] See Doty's (1997) "ontology of practice" and Jackson and Nexon's (1999) "processual relationalism."

environment, however, the main instruments that the actors (are forced to) use in order to increase their utility are of an ideational kind – for example, values, norms, identities, frames, symbols, and arguments.

In sum, the strategic conception of rules departs from the "oversocialized" view of actors, and the "overintegrated" view of society, typical for cognitivism and normativism. On the other hand, however, it equally distinguishes itself from the "underculturalized" view of society in rationalist institutionalism. In essence, social action is conceived as *strategic action in a community environment.* In the words of Paul DiMaggio, it moves us "beyond the polemical opposition of 'calculus' and 'culture' . . . to ask not *whether* people act strategically, but rather under what conditions and how they do so" (1998: 701).

In the following sections, I define rhetorical action as an argumentative mode of strategic action and show how "people act strategically" under the conditions of a community environment.

Rhetorical and communicative action

Rhetorical action is the strategic use of arguments.[7] In greater detail, it is the strategic use and exchange of arguments based on ideas shared in the environment of the proponents and intended to persuade the audience and the opponents to accept the proponents' claims and act accordingly. In the following, I will explicate the elements of this definition.

Strategic use. First, rhetorical actors use arguments instrumentally, that is they choose those arguments that they think will be (most) persuasive. Second, they use arguments strategically because they make their choices dependent on their perceptions of and assumptions on which arguments will be (most) persuasive given the beliefs and arguments of their opponents, the composition and beliefs of their audience, the cultural and institutional environment in their forum of debate and the history of the argumentative exchange. Rhetorical actors are assumed to be subjectively rational, that is, they do not possess objective knowledge about the effectiveness of their arguments and do not necessarily use the *most* effective argument (only). They base their choices on subjective perceptions and assumptions, choose arguments that appear sufficiently persuasive to them and often use multiple arguments out of insecurity about their effectiveness.[8]

Arguments. The basic situation in a debate consists in a proponent P making a claim c and an opponent O rejecting this claim. In addition,

7 Cf. Elster (1991: 85) on the "strategic uses of argument."

8 For an intentionalist conceptualization of rhetorical argument, see, e.g., Campbell (1992: 152–53).

debates are usually assumed to take place before an audience. The members of the audience do not argue themselves but evaluate the arguments of *O* and *P*. In order to persuade the opponent and the audience to accept the claim, the proponent puts forward an argument. According to Toulmin's terminology, arguments consist in the three core elements of "claims," "grounds," and "warrants." First, the proponent adduces grounds (or data) *g* supposed to provide a foundation for, and to give strength to, the claim. Second, in order to show that "these grounds really do provide genuine support for this particular claim," the proponent appeals to a warrant *w* assuming that *w* provides the ultimate justification for any claims (of this sort and in this context) and for the suitability of the grounds. Put differently, the warrant serves as a principle that enables *g* to defend *c* (Shi-Xu 1992: 271). In sum, *P* argues that *g* provides compelling reasons, validated by *w*, to conclude that *c*. This statement can be condensed to the basic argumentative formula – *P: "C because g according to w!"*[9]

The concept of rhetorical action is based on a broad understanding of "argument" and "argumentation":

(a) In the Aristotelian tradition, the rhetorical perspective on argument is not so much concerned with the argument as such and its internal validity as with its role in an argumentation process and the conditions under which it generates support for the claims advanced among the audience addressed. Arguments not only have demonstrative and inferential but also *emotive functions*. In the rhetorical perspective, the persuasiveness of an argument not only depends on whether it demonstrates the rightness of a claim (Aristotle's *logos*) but is also contingent on the quality of the arguer (*ethos*), the frame of mind and emotional state of the audience (*pathos*) and the context of the argumentation (Tindale 1999: 3–13; Triadafilopoulos 1999: 745, 749).

(b) Rhetorical action consists predominantly but *not exclusively of verbal behavior*. Rhetorical actors accompany their verbal arguments by nonverbal, *expressive actions*. They choose, for instance, their dress, their mimics and gestures, and the style and intonation of their presentation in view of their audience. To the same end, they carefully choose the media and fora of their presentations, and they use *symbolic actions* in order to enhance the persuasiveness of their arguments. It is in this respect that

[9] For an extensive explication of Toulmin's formula, see Toulmin, Rieke, and Janik (1979). The three core elements of argument are most often used in the literature, although there is no common terminology. See, e.g., Shi-Xu's (1992: 271) "standpoint" (for "claim") "datum" (for "grounds") and "warrant," or Öhlschläger's (1979: 99) "conclusion" (for "claim"), "argument" ("for grounds") and "inferential presupposition" (for "warrant"). Cf. Kopperschmidt (1989: 102–13) and Schimmelfennig (1995: 66–71).

the rhetorical use of arguments overlaps with dramaturgical action and "performances" as defined by Goffman.[10]

(c) I also subsume *framing* under arguing. Indeed, in order to formulate a persuasive argument, rhetorical actors frame their claims, grounds and warrants in a way that they think is most conducive to persuading their audiences and opponents. Powerful arguments depend on compelling frames.

(3) *Shared ideas.* Since Aristotle's "Rhetoric," it has been recognized that the persuasiveness of rhetorical arguments mainly depends on ideas (knowledge, beliefs) that are shared among the proponents, the opponents and the audience and serve as warrants for the argument. Aristotle referred to these ideas as *topoi.* These shared ideas can be formally institutionalized in the given forum of debate, as, for instance, the treaty norms of an international organization, or simply intersubjectively believed by the members of the audience. According to Burns (1999: 168), "rhetoric is 'situated' within a cultural context, and this cultural context in large part determines which symbols are used, as well as the rules constraining how they will be used."

Rhetorical actors use the ideas shared by the audience they address or privileged by their forum of debate in order to validate and support their claims, or they consciously choose an audience and forum in which their preferred warrants (and, as a consequence, their claims) will most likely be accepted. If there are multiple shared ideas in a given audience, proponents will appeal to those that they expect to support their claims most effectively, and if they address "diffuse" or "composite" audiences in which their warrants are not shared by all members, they must either search for other – common – ideas, amplify their arguments or "integrate, or interweave, appeals to diverse audiences" (Myers 1999: 56; see also Bleses, Offe and Peter 1997: 509, 519). Even a revolutionary discourse that seeks to disseminate radically new opinions "will rehearse old commonly shared stereotypes" (Billig 1991: 20) with which it must make new associations (Burns 1999: 179) and which it must direct towards new conclusions. Conversely, rhetorical action will be ineffective if the frames and arguments put forward by the proponents do not resonate with the shared ideas of the audience.

(4) *Persuasion.* Persuasion is the central, immediate goal of rhetorical action whatever the claims of the rhetorical actors and their motives for advancing them. Persuasion varies in *depth* and breadth. Persuasion is

[10] Goffman (1959: 15) defines performances as "all the activity of a given participant on a given occasion which serves to influence [here: persuade, F.S.] in any way any of the participants." For a radically open conceptualization of argument as "instrumental, symbolic behavior," see Bowers and Ochs (1971: 2).

deepest if the proponent succeeds in changing the cultural beliefs, that is, the identity, values, and norms, of the opponents or the audience. A change in situation-specific preferences can be located at an intermediate level of depth. However, persuasion can also result in mere cooperation. In that case, the opponents or the audience, although unconvinced of the proponent's claims, feel compelled to act according to her definition of the situation and preferences. With regard to *breadth*, the minimal goal of rhetorical actors in a debate is "self-persuasion" – they seek to defend and maintain their own claims and, in the case of corporate proponents, to preserve their unity. Beyond this minimal goal, rhetorical actors try to persuade and win over as many members of the audience as possible. Persuasion is broadest if it includes the (active) opponents as well.

How does rhetorical action thus defined differ from communicative action? Two paradigms or research programs are distinguished in argument theory. Following Aristotelian categories, Frans van Eemeren (1990) calls these paradigms the "dialectical" and the "rhetorical research program."[11] The dialectical research program has its disciplinary basis in philosophy and social theory and is mainly *normatively* oriented. It is concerned with the procedures required for a *legitimate consensus*. If real debates are studied at all in the dialectical research program, it is in a critical perspective (see, e.g., Eemeren 1986).

By contrast, the rhetorical research program is strongly represented in linguistics and has an *empirical* orientation. It studies "actual argumentation" (Klein 1980: 49) – the choice of arguments in real debates and the conditions under which they are persuasive and bring about a *factual consensus* based on the subjective beliefs of the actors participating in the debate (Kopperschmidt 1985: 153–54). Correspondingly, the rhetorical paradigm starts from the principle of the "arbitrariness of the collectively valid." Whereas the dialectical paradigm assumes a "universal audience" and an "ideal speech situation" to establish the conditions of legitimate consensus, and asserts that practical debates are capable of producing general, universalizable truths,[12] rhetorical argumentation is oriented towards the time- and context-dependent beliefs of a particular audience and denies the "truth-capability" of practical claims (Berk 1979: 105; Klein 1980: 46–47; 1985: 212; Perelman 1979: 97).

[11] Similar dichotomies can be found throughout the literature. See, for instance, Berk (1979: 14) and Campbell (1992) who distinguishes a "rationalistic" and a "rhetorical argument theory." Tindale (1999) differentiates the three perspectives of "product" (logic), "procedure" (dialectic), and "process" (rhetoric).

[12] *Wahrheitsfähig* according to Habermas; see, e.g., Habermas (1973: 132–34).

The dialectical research program entered the theoretical debate in International Relations via Jürgen Habermas' theory of communicative action.[13] In one way, however, this application deviates from the predominant orientation of the dialectical research program. According to Müller and Risse, the theory of communicative action is not only suitable as a normative theory for the critical analysis of international relations, it is also necessary to provide a full explanation of international cooperation (Müller 1994), and plausibly describes actual processes of argumentation and explains dispositional change in international politics (Risse 1999; 2000). As a result, the rhetorical and communicative action hypotheses become commensurable as *empirical* claims.

Both hypotheses have four more features in common. First, both assume a situation of *conflict between validity claims* as a starting point for debate. Second, both are *agnostic* as to whether these claims are based on egoistic or altruistic, material or ideational preferences (see also Eriksen and Weigård 1997: 230). Third, both emphasize *arguing* – the debate about validity claims – as a method of decision-making and are thus distinct "from both strategic bargaining – the realm of rational choice – and rule-guided behavior – the realm of sociological institutionalism" (Risse 2000: 1). Fourth, both assume that the arguers appeal to *shared ideas* in their arguments. But whereas Risse, following the dialectical paradigm and Habermas, equates the logic of arguing with "*truth seeking*," rhetorical action is equivalent to *persuasion*. Conversely, if rhetorical action is defined as the *strategic* use of arguments, communicative action is best characterized as the non-strategic, *appropriate* use of arguments.

(1) *Actor motivations.* At the most fundamental level, the modes of communicative and rhetorical action differ with regard to actor motivations. Although both hypotheses assume purposive action and do not presuppose rule-based preferences, the immediate goals the opponents seek to realize in debates stand opposed to each other. The communicative action hypothesis assumes that actors are truth seekers. They exchange arguments for the purpose of establishing a reasoned consensus. In this argumentative exchange, they put their claims to an open-ended argumentative validity test. They are open to being convinced by the better argument and prepared to change their ideational convictions – their factual and causal beliefs about the world, their values, norms and identities, and their interests and preferences.[14] By contrast, rhetorical actors are

[13] Habermas (1981). See the debate in *Zeitschrift für Internationale Beziehungen* beginning with Müller (1994). It was introduced to the English-speaking community by Risse (1999; 2000).

[14] This is Habermas' "consensus-oriented action" (*verständigungsorientiertes Handeln*). See Habermas (1986: 362, 364) and Risse (2000: 7, 9).

not engaged in a "cooperative search for the truth" but seek to prevail in argumentative exchange. Rhetorical actors want to persuade others; they themselves, however, are neither prepared to yield to the "power of the better of the argument" nor open to accepting their opponents' counterclaims.[15]

(2) *Argumentative behavior.* As a consequence of their divergent motivations and argumentative goals, rhetorical and communicative actors behave differently in debates. Briefly stated, rhetorical actors choose their arguments expediently whereas communicative actors follow normative standards and rules of appropriate argumentative behavior.[16] The regulative idea of appropriate argumentative behavior in the theory of communicative action is the "ideal speech situation" in which the participants do not restrict discourse with regard to other participants, topics and duration; recognize each other as partners in a cooperative search for truth and grant each other equal access to and participation in debate; behave in a way that facilitates mutual understanding and consensus-building; and, finally, only use verbal and sincere arguments (see Risse 2000: 10–11). In the perspective of rhetorical action, these behavioral standards are a matter of expediency. Rhetorical actors will stipulate or uphold them if they appear to further their own argumentative success; otherwise, they will ignore them.[17]

Although Risse emphasizes that the ideal speech situation serves as a "counterfactual presupposition" (1999: 535; 2000: 10, 17–18) and is not necessarily met in real debates, the argumentative behavior of rhetorically and communicatively oriented actors should differ significantly. The following observations would indicate that proponents engage in rhetorical rather than communicative action.

Mutual recognition. Proponents reject discussing an issue with their opponents, do not take them seriously, and refuse to listen to them. Proponents abuse, denigrate and ridicule their opponents.

Equality. Proponents deny their opponents (equal) access to the debate and interrupt them, "point to their rank or status" (Risse 2000: 18) or break off discussions arbitrarily and unilaterally.

[15] This is Habermas' "success-oriented action" (*erfolgsorientiertes Handeln*). See Risse (2000: 8).

[16] It is in that sense that I differentiated rhetorical and communicative action in chapter 7. Whereas rules affect communicative action at the level of behavior (not at that of issue-specific goals), in rhetorical action, they do not.

[17] Note that the absence of normative standards of argumentative behavior in rhetorical action is not Aristotelian. Aristotle, however, did not count on an ideal speech situation but on the virtue (*ethos*) of the orator to use his speech for morally sound purposes and "to appeal to what is best in the community" (see Triadafilopoulos 1999: 744–45, 750; cf. Tindale 1999: 17).

Sincerity. Proponents deceive, mislead or lie to their audience and opponents, use arguments they do not sincerely believe in or know to be false, or consciously misinterpret and twist the words of their opponents.

Consistency. Proponents change their arguments depending on the audience or the forum of debate or modify their claims, grounds and warrants over time in order to respond to changing argumentative challenges and situations (instead of sticking to their justifications and presupposing a universal, time-independent audience). Rhetorical actors also use multiple or mixed argumentative strategies based on divergent warrants. One reason for doing so may be uncertainty: subjectively rational arguers often do not know their audience well enough to choose the single, most effective argumentative strategy. They hope to reach a greater number of hearers, or strengthen their claims, by increasing the number and kinds of arguments. Moreover, they may calculate that a greater variety or a combination of arguments will increase support in diffuse or pluralistic audiences.

Warrants. Proponents appeal to the local values, identities or experiences of particular communities – instead of appealing to reasons that could convince anyone irrespective of time and place. They seek to move the audience by appealing to and taking advantage of emotions like pity, indignation, shame, fury, or pride – instead of counting on reasons alone (see Triadafilopoulos 1999: 752, 754).

Openness. Proponents do not give serious consideration to their opponents' arguments, refuse to admit argumentative defeat or switch to other arguments and make tactical concessions before having to do so.

(3) *Outcome of debate.* The communicative action hypothesis postulates that consensus-oriented opponents in a situation that approaches an ideal speech situation are likely to reach a true and legitimate consensus with "constitutive effects" (Risse 2000: 10). Typically, this consensus will be the result of a process of argumentation in which one of the opponents is convinced by the better argument of the other and changes her or his beliefs accordingly. Cooperation will then be a product of a consensual definition of both the characteristics of the situation and the appropriate behavior. Once the validity claims are no longer disputed and the decision-making situation has ceased to be problematic, the logic of action switches (back) to a logic of appropriateness.

In the rhetorical perspective, a true consensus voluntarily arrived at is a highly unlikely outcome. First, rhetorical actors are not open to being persuaded by the "force of the better argument" and to giving up their claims. Second, any consensus reached through rhetorical action is distorted – factual but not legitimate in the communicative perspective – because it is the result of strategic argumentation and systematic

Table 9.1 *Rhetorical and communicative action*

	Rhetorical action	Communicative action
Common assumptions	various actor utilities, decision-making by arguments	conflict about validity claims,
Rationality	strategic	communicative
Goals of the actors	success, influence, to persuade	consensus, understanding, to convince
Argumentative behavior	expedient	rule-based, approaching an ideal speech situation
Form of argument	including expressive and symbolic acts, emotive appeals	exclusively verbal, demonstrative
Audience	particular	universal
Truth capability of argumentation	arbitrariness of the collectively valid	rationality of the collectively valid
Consensus	factual, subjective	legitimate, objective

violations of the ideal speech standard. Third, rhetorical actors are not interested, *per se*, in changing the beliefs of their opponents and audience but primarily seek to induce cooperative or compliant behavior through the use of persuasion.[18] In other words, rhetorical actors are satisfied if the audience and opponents stop opposing their claims (whether or not they are really convinced) and behave accordingly (that is, *as if* they genuinely believed in their truth or rightness). Thus, in the rhetorical perspective, cooperation is more likely to be the result of social pressure or distorted speech situations than of legitimate consensus. Table 9.1 gives a summary overview of the main common and distinctive features of rhetorical and communicative action.

Rhetorical action and legitimacy

Why is rhetorical action relevant in politics? Because (1) political actors act in a cultural and institutional "community" environment; (2) they need legitimacy in order to be politically successful in such an environment; and (3) they use, and are sensitive to, rhetorical action in order to gain, maintain, and increase legitimacy.

[18] See Burke's definition of rhetoric: "the use of language as a symbolic means of inducing cooperation in beings that by nature respond to symbols" (1989: 188). See also Bleses, Offe and Peter (1997: 503).

(1) The basic condition for the relevance of rhetorical action is the cultural and institutional "community" environment that sociological institutionalism and the strategic conception of rules assume to characterize the social world. Political communities are defined by a shared political culture which consists of the constitutive values, norms and identity of the community. This community culture, in turn, determines the community's standard of legitimacy.[19] It defines who belongs to the community and what rights and duties its members have. It distinguishes rightful and improper ways of acquiring, transferring and exercising political power, and it determines which political purposes and programs are desirable and permissible. In doing so, the standard allocates different degrees of legitimacy to the actors' political aspirations, preferences and behaviors. To the degree that their institutional form, organizational goals, political programs and political behavior are perceived to correspond with this standard, political actors are regarded as legitimate actors pursuing legitimate goals.

(2) In the ideal-typical technical environment, the successful pursuit of political goals depends on the constellation of actor preferences and bargaining power alone. In a community environment, however, political actors need legitimacy whatever their political goals may be. In line with the strategic conception of rules, the rhetorical action hypothesis does not assume that political actors *internalize* the standard of legitimacy. They do not take it for granted or as a moral imperative that directly motivates their goals and behaviors. Rather, rational political actors confront the standard of legitimacy as an *external* institutional or cultural fact. Whether rational political actors act egoistically or altruistically, pursue value-based or interest-based goals, seek to come to and stay in power or propagate moral norms, they must take the standard of legitimacy into account in order to act effectively. Legitimacy is both a resource of support for legitimate actions and a constraint that imposes costs on illegitimate actions. *Ceteris paribus*, the more legitimate the actors and their goals are (or appear) in light of the community standard, the better they are able to realize their political objectives. Conversely, actors regarded as illegitimate and pursuing illegitimate goals by illegitimate means will face severe difficulties in inducing other actors to support them and cooperate with them.

(3) At the outset, the legitimacy of a political organization, its authority and its actions is nothing but a claim. The validity of this claim is

[19] For the use of this concept in International Relations, see Gong (1984). For an early article on the importance of "collective legitimization" in international politics, see Claude (1966). On the legitimacy of international rules, see Franck (1990).

challenged and must be justified against competing claims. Therefore, the issue of legitimacy gives rise to argumentation and is conducive to rhetorical action. In a community environment, *politics is a struggle over legitimacy*, and this struggle is *fought out with rhetorical arguments.*

On the one hand, political actors use arguments strategically in order to present themselves as legitimate and to persuade the audience of the legitimacy of their claims in order to elicit political support and induce political cooperation. By skillfully manipulating the community's standard of legitimacy through rhetoric, political actors are able to gain an advantage over their competitors and to reconcile contradictory legitimacy requirements. On the other hand, political actors come under pressure if their competitors are able to demonstrate, and to persuade the public, that they violate the community's standard of legitimacy. If the legitimacy costs become too high, political actors are forced to abstain from the incriminated goals and behaviors and to cooperate with their opponents, even though they may not be convinced by the opponents' arguments and claims and even though they may possess superior material or institutional power.

Put differently, in a community environment, legitimacy strengthens the actors' bargaining positions. By linking distributional conflict with the collective identity and the constitutive values and norms of the community, rhetorical action changes the structure of bargaining power in favor of those actors that possess and pursue preferences in line with, though not necessarily inspired by, the standard of legitimacy. Rhetorical action thereby has the potential to modify the collective outcome that would have resulted from constellations of interests and power alone.[20]

This argument, however, still begs the question of how it is that legitimacy and its rhetorical manipulation can have such powerful effects. In order to answer this question, we need to know more about how rhetorical actors choose and react to arguments, how rhetorical action becomes persuasive and how rhetorical actors can be made to comply with the "better," that is, the more persuasive and legitimate argument.

The rhetorical choice of arguments

In order to explain the rhetorical choice of arguments, the *argumentative roles of proponent and opponent* have to be distinguished. The proponent is the first to choose her argumentative strategy without knowing exactly how the opponent will react to it.

[20] For a similar analysis of the effects of norms on collective wage bargaining, see Elster (1989b: 215).

(H1) *P* chooses an argument based on the assumption that the audience and opponent accept the validity of the warrant *w* and that the grounds *g*(*w*) effectively support the claim *c*.

The result is an argument of the basic form *P: "C because g according to w!"* As the second mover, the opponent is, on the one hand, constrained by the argument *P* has chosen but, on the other hand, he knows *P*'s argument and is able to react specifically. Of course, *O* may choose to ignore *P*'s argument and refuse to enter into a debate if he considers this as his best available option. Otherwise, *O* can choose among three basic argumentative strategies in order to challenge *c*. These strategies are oriented toward the remaining three components of the argumentative formula (*P*, *g* and *w*):

(1) *Arguments against the proponent* (*O: "Not c because not P!"*) are intended to question the sincerity, impartiality, competence, or credibility of, or to denigrate and ridicule, the proponent. *O* thereby seeks to invalidate *P*'s argument without having to deal with its substance. Moreover, *O* tries to present himself as the more credible or authoritative arguer and source of information.

(2) *Arguments against the grounds* (*O: "Not c because not g!"*) are intended to refute the reasons and data *P* adduces to support the claim. By selecting such arguments, *O* accepts the warrant on which *P*'s argument rests but denies that the claim can be justified on this basis. For instance, *O* may argue that the data are false or falsified or that *P* interpreted them incorrectly.[21] In addition, *O* presents alternative or competing grounds ("true" and correctly interpreted data) that, in light of *w*, support his counterclaim.

(3) *Arguments against the warrant* (*O: "Not c because not w!"*) reject the warrant on which the argument is based. By using this kind of argument, *O* may well accept that *g* supports *c* given *w*. *O* nevertheless challenges *c* because he denies that *w* is a suitable principle of justification in the given situation or an acceptable principle at all, thereby undermining *P*'s assumption that *w* refers to a shared idea that will induce *O* to accept her claims. In response, *O* may propose a different warrant that strengthens his own claim.

The opponent chooses one or more of these counterarguments strategically and for the purpose of rejecting the proponent's claim. The main conditions in making this choice are, first, the *opponent's perception of the audience* and, second, the *opponent's perception of his own argumentative strengths and weaknesses*. If *O* thinks, for instance, he has the more

[21] In his study of the rhetoric of human-rights-violating governments, Cohen terms these strategies "literal denial" and "interpretive denial" (Cohen 1996: 523, 525).

persuasive grounds, he will join the debate on the basis of the warrant put forward by *P* and present his own data and interpretations. If, however, *O* does not expect to hold his own in this argumentation, he will reject *w*.

Yet it may be that *O* thinks he cannot afford to simply reject *w* – for instance, if this warrant is highly estimated in the audience. In this case, it would be rhetorically rational to interpret *w* in a way that allows *O* to adduce more persuasive grounds against *P*'s claim and for his own counterclaim. For instance, virtually all states characterize themselves as "democratic" because democracy has become a transnationally shared principle of legitimate political authority. The interpretations and implementations of the principle of democracy, however, vary widely. For the same reason, few states would openly reject "human rights." Instead, non-compliant states give precedence to "collective human rights," list "duties" alongside human rights, argue that "human rights" must be in the service of "development" or "socialism" and so on. Finally, *O* may choose an argument against the proponent in order to avoid a substantial argumentation at all.

(H2a) *O* chooses an argument against the proponent if he assumes that *P* lacks intrinsic support in the audience and that it will be easier to damage her reputation than to invalidate her argument.
(H2b) *O* chooses an argument against the grounds if he assumes that it invalidates *P*'s claim and supports his counterclaim or if he assumes that *w* is of central importance for the audience but expects to be able to reinterpret *w* successfully.
(H2c) *O* chooses an argument against the warrant if he assumes that he is not able to invalidate *P*'s claim on the basis of *w* and that *w* is not of central importance for the target group.

In making this choice, the opponent takes into account several context conditions that may modify the utility of the counterarguments:

Forum. Is it a public or private setting? In a private setting (*P* and *O* only), for instance, the beliefs of the audience do not have to be taken into account immediately. What are the cultural beliefs and rules in this forum? If they privilege the kinds of grounds and warrants advanced by the proponent, it will be more difficult for *O* to reinterpret *g*, or to adduce other kinds of evidence, and to challenge and reinterpret *w*. In a courtroom, for example, the opponents must frame their arguments in legal discourse, use legal warrants, grounds, and claims. In this forum, the opponent could not switch to a, say, religious strategy of justification without squandering his chances of persuading the audience.

Identity and authority of the proponent. Is it a member of the in-group or an out-group, friend or foe? If *P* is a member of an out-group, or even constructed as an enemy, whereas *O* is a member of the audience's in-group, counterarguments will generally be more effective than in the alternative case. How strong is her authority and cultural power in the forum? If *O* faces a culturally powerful proponent, the effectiveness of arguments against the proponent and the warrant will be reduced.

History. The past course of the debate, or the results of earlier debates, influence the choice of arguments at a later point in time. Some arguments are used typically at the beginning of a debate. For instance, arguments against the proponent are most effectively used before even beginning a substantial argumentation. By contrast, it is not very persuasive if *O* questions the credibility, integrity, or competence of *P* *after* having seriously responded to the grounds and warrants of her argument. The same applies to strategies of denial. Either they work immediately – then the data adduced by *P* are believed to be false or falsified and the argument is discredited – or they will not work at all with an attentive audience. *O* cannot question the grounds of *P*'s argument *after* having accepted them as correct in former rounds of debate. Generally, *O*'s persuasiveness will be reduced if he criticizes those aspects of *P*'s argument he implicitly or explicitly accepted earlier in the process or discards the grounds and warrants he used earlier to support his own arguments.

Depending on how the opponent treats the warrant of the proponent's argument, the argumentation results in one of three *argumentative constellations.*

If *O* accepts *w*, the argumentation is competitive. In a *competitive argumentation*, there is a consensus between *O* and *P* about the warrant, that is the *kinds* of grounds that are admissible and suitable to support a claim. The grounds themselves, however, are disputed.

If *O* does not accept *w*, the argumentation is controversial. In a *controversial argumentation*, *O* and *P* are in fundamental disagreement – on the validity of their claims, the grounds they adduce, and the ultimate principles of validation that could justify a claim.

Finally, there is the special case that *O* reinterprets or circumvents *w*. In such a *pseudo-competitive argumentation,* it appears as if all parties accept the warrant but, in reality, each of them interprets it differently. In essence, the argumentation is controversial.

These argumentative constellations have different *potential to persuade* the audience and the opponents. In controversial and pseudo-competitive argumentations, in which the opponents do not agree on the principle according to which the grounds for their claims must be evaluated, there is no such potential. As long as the opponents draw on different or differently interpreted principles of validity, the debate lacks a comparative standard that would provide evidence for the relative validity of the competing claims. In an audience in which the adherents of *P* accept the warrant for *P*'s claims and the adherents of *O* share the warrant for *O*'s claims, the opponents will not be able to win over adherents as long as they stick to their preferred warrant. Moreover, *P* and *O* will not have any argumentative influence *on* each other as long as they argue *past* each other.

By contrast, competitive argumentations have the potential to persuade. The competitive argumentation is the only constellation in which the opponents accept a common criterion for the validity and success of an argument and, therefore, face the possibility of argumentative defeat. If the grounds provided by *P* in a competitive argumentation are stronger than those of her opponent, she has the chance to win over the adherents of *O* as well as undecided members of the audience who share the warrant on which the debate is based. In this situation, *O* is under pressure either to come forward with alternative arguments for his claim or to accept *P*'s claim.

> (H3) Only competitive argumentations have the potential to persuade.

Finally, what are the conditions of *argumentative change* in the rhetorical perspective? As long as an argument or an argumentative strategy is, or promises to be, successful, the opponents have no incentive to change it. If an argument proves unsuccessful, however, it triggers a learning process that will be the deeper and faster the higher the costs of failure (in terms of loss of persuasive power and adherents). Argumentative strategies that do not persuade undecided members of the audience, the adherents of *O*, or *O* himself, but also do not damage the standing of *P* among her own adherents, may be upheld for a long time at low cost and maintained alongside new arguments. By contrast, an argument that also weakens *P*'s claims among her traditional followers will be abandoned quickly. If an argument proves unsuccessful, the opponents choose new arguments according to the strategic criteria described in H1 and H2.

Non-competitive argumentations will usually be *unsuccessful* but are also *unlikely to produce high costs* because they do not lead to defeat. As long as they help to unite and mobilize the opponents' own partisans, they will be continued. In addition, the opponents will try new arguments based on different warrants they expect to be shared by their audience. By contrast, new grounds based on the old, disputed warrants would not be persuasive and, therefore, will not be chosen by rhetorically rational actors.

Competitive argumentations without a decisive outcome will more likely result in a change of grounds. The opponents look for new, more persuasive data and evidence in order to demonstrate that their respective claims are (more) valid in light of the criteria specified by the commonly accepted warrant. If, however, the competitive argumentation does produce a clear result, the defeated opponent will either search for new arguments based on a different warrant or seek to reinterpret or reframe the warrant of the competitive argumentation in order to change the constellation to a pseudo-competitive argumentation and to avoid argumentative defeat.

(H4) The opponents change their arguments if they prove unsuccessful, and they change them more quickly and thoroughly, the more costly they are. New arguments are chosen according to H1 and H2.

(H4a) In a controversial or pseudo-competitive argumentation, the opponents keep arguments that persuade their own adherents and choose new warrants to win new adherents.

(H4b) In a competitive argumentation without a definite result, the opponents choose new grounds.

(H4c) In a competitive argumentation with a definite result, the loser chooses an argument based on a new warrant or reinterprets *w*.

Thus, even if rhetorical actors (objectively) lose a competitive argumentation with a definite outcome, they are not prepared to admit their failure but use rhetorical devices to evade defeat. They will question or reinterpret the grounds, reframe or reinterpret the warrant, or switch to new arguments based on alternative warrants. Even if they accept the claim of the opponent, they might only do so verbally and tactically, but refuse to act accordingly and renounce their acceptance at the earliest possibility. Therefore, and in contrast to communicative action, the question of compliance looms large in rhetorical action.

Rhetorical action and compliance

Mechanisms of compliance

Mechanisms of compliance with the "better," more legitimate and more persuasive argument can be distinguished in two dimensions. They can be coercive or non-coercive, formal or informal. Coercive mechanisms are based on the use of force or the credible threat to use force. Formal mechanisms have institutionalized procedures for ending a debate and

Table 9.2 *Mechanisms of compliance*

	Coercive	Non-coercive
Formal	institutional sanction	institutional decision
Informal	social mobilization	social influence

determining its result. A combination of both dichotomies produces the matrix shown in Table 9.2.

Institutional decisions. Typical examples for debates ended by "institutional decisions" are election campaigns and parliamentary debates. The opponents (presidential candidates or government and opposition) first exchange their arguments and try to persuade the audience (the electorate or the members of parliament). The audience then evaluates the arguments and casts a vote. Thus, the debate is decided in an institutionalized procedure by the audience. The mechanism of institutional decision does not assume that the defeated opponent will change his beliefs but requires that he accept the vote of the audience. In consolidated democracies, this is usually the case in elections and parliamentary debates in which the procedural rules have been observed.

Institutional sanctions. By contrast, institutional sanctions do not presuppose the defeated opponent to voluntarily comply with the vote of the audience. The typical case is a judicial trial where, again, the opponents (plaintiff and defendant or prosecuting attorney and defense counsel) use arguments in a highly institutionalized procedure to persuade an audience (judge or jury). The decision, however, is supported and executed by a coercive apparatus (the police).

Social mobilization. The mechanism of social mobilization comprises all forms of informal, non-institutionalized power (including coercive power) that force the defeated opponent to cooperate or give up. It may come into play, for instance, if a government loses an election but does not accept the outcome. In this case, the mechanism of "institutional decision" becomes ineffective but can be substituted by a popular uprising forcing the losers to comply.

Social influence. Finally, compliance can be a result of informal and non-coercive, "soft" mechanisms. They apply when there is no formal and institutionalized procedure for the audience to establish the outcome of the debate *and* the opponent cannot be coerced to accept, and comply with, the outcome. To be effective, social influence ultimately relies on cognitive and emotional reactions triggered by social rewards (such as popularity, respect) for compliance and punishments (such as shaming and shunning) for non-compliance.

Generally, rhetorical actors *use as many mechanisms as possible* simultaneously in order to increase their chances for success and to induce their opponents to cooperate. Social movement organizations, for instance, urge the electorate to vote for the candidates who support their demands; they take legal action about their cause; they mobilize their adherents to take part in informal activities like the occupation of government buildings and the disruption of conferences; and they seek to exert moral pressure on their opponents. The use of these mechanisms, however, also depends on their availability. In the context of international relations, this availability is limited:

(H5) Rhetorical actors can be made to comply with the more persuasive argument through four mechanisms: institutional sanctions, institutional decisions, social pressure and social influence.

(H5a) In international politics, institutional sanctions and decisions are usually not available or effective.

(H5b) In international politics, social mobilization is effective if the argument of state *P* is based on grounds that are perceived as persuasive and a warrant that is perceived as legitimate either by international actors or actors in the society of state *O* (salience) and if these actors are strong enough to make *O* accept the claim (strength).

(H5c) In international politics, social influence is effective if rhetorical action takes place inside an international community and refers to the rules of the community. It is the more effective, the more legitimate and resonant the rules and the more public the setting.

In international politics, the formal mechanisms are usually unavailable or of limited effectiveness. First, institutional sanctions understood as coercive means of ensuring state compliance are rare. For instance, although there are international courts, their rulings are often non-binding (see, e.g., the International Court of Justice), and if they are accepted as binding by the states, they still cannot be coercively enforced (see, e.g., the European Court of Human Rights). In the case of Eastern enlargement, there was no way for the CEECs or the "drivers" among the member states to take legal, let alone coercive, action in order to enforce the membership rules. NATO does not have any judicial organ, and the European Court of Justice does not have the competence to rule on enlargement decisions.

Second, institutional decisions in international politics are usually taken unanimously by the state governments. If these governments are the opponents in a debate, there is no third party occupying the role of "audience" and entitled to cast a vote after the exchange of arguments. This also applies to Eastern enlargement: member governments decide unanimously about the admission of new states. In the EU case, the European Parliament must confirm any enlargement decision of the member states but cannot overrule non-decisions on enlargement and decide to admit new members on its own. Generally, institutional decisions only come into play *after* the intergovernmental decisions, that is, when international treaties (including accession treaties) must be ratified by national parliaments. Consequently, in international relations, compliance is generally dependent on the informal mechanisms of social mobilization and social influence.

Social mobilization can take two avenues in international relations, one transnational, the other interstate. *Transnational* social mobilization requires that international debates be transformed into domestic debates. If a proponent government manages to persuade the public or powerful groups in an opponent state, the opponent government will come under pressure. The success of *P* in persuading social actors in *O* will depend on whether these social actors accept the warrant of *P*'s argument as valid or legitimate and regard *P*'s grounds as superior to *O*'s grounds. In the literature, this condition is discussed as "domestic salience."[22] In addition, the persuaded social actors must be strong enough to force the opponent government to accept *O*'s claim, for instance as a result of their institutional or coalition-building power in the political system, their ability to mobilize the electorate, or their capacity for staging anti-government or anti-systemic revolts. This variable is termed "domestic structure."

Transnational social mobilization conditioned by domestic salience and structure is the most prominent causal mechanism in studies on how international norms affect state behavior (see, e.g., Checkel 1997; Cortell and Davis 1996; Risse-Kappen 1995c). In the context of rhetorical action, it serves to establish a third-party audience with formal or factual decision and enforcement powers capable of making a rhetorically rational government comply with successful claims.

In the case of Eastern enlargement, however, the transnational social mobilization mechanism is not a plausible candidate for an account of how the reluctance of the "brakemen" in NATO and the EU was overcome. None of the reticent member governments was under domestic pressure worth mentioning to agree to Eastern enlargement, let alone faced electoral defeat if it opposed enlargement. The conflict

[22] See Cortell and Davis (2000) for a review of the literature on "domestic salience" and Checkel (1999) for highlighting "cultural match" as a factor conditioning the influence of international norms on domestic politics. Cortell and Davis (2000: 76) emphasize that cultural match "is dynamic and malleable" through political rhetoric.

about NATO enlargement generally met with public indifference in the "brakemen" countries and generated little debate beyond the expert communities and foreign policy elites (Mattox and Rachwald 2001). Indifference to EU enlargement was lower, mainly because the integration of the CEECs is perceived to affect the welfare of EU citizens. Yet, *Eurobarometer* public opinion polls suggest that public support for Eastern enlargement has generally been low and has waned over time.[23] "Less than 3 in 10 Europeans believed welcoming new member states should be a priority for the European Union" in 1999.[24] Even in those "brakemen" countries in which public opinion has been most favorably disposed toward Eastern enlargement – above all Greece, Ireland, Italy and Spain, in contrast to Belgium and France – there has not been any noticeable public pressure on the governments to give up their reticence.[25] In sum, Ulrich Sedelmeier and Helen Wallace note that "the advocacy alliance . . . has had little by way of outside support on which to draw, either from socio-economic groups that might stand to gain, or from broader political circles, or from public opinion" (2000: 457).

Interstate mobilization also depends on the conditions of (interstate) salience and (interstate) strength, but it is addressed to other state actors rather than societal actors – if state *P* is able to persuade a critical number of other states (for which *P*'s arguments are salient) to accept and support its claim, and if this coalition is capable of mounting sufficient bargaining power against *O*, *O* will be forced to comply. Again, in Eastern enlargement, the preconditions for this mechanism to succeed seem to be absent. As I discussed earlier, in the EU, the proponents of enlargement lacked sufficient bargaining power, and in NATO, no member state government took a unified stance in favor of enlargement in the early stages of the decision-making process. At any rate, this mechanism begs the question of how state *P* is able to persuade a critical number of other state actors in the first place.

Social influence, shaming, and rhetorical entrapment

Thus, to the extent that rhetorical action was indeed consequential in bringing about the decision to enlarge NATO and the EU to the East, the only plausible mechanism is *social influence*.[26] Social influence not only

23 See the following issues of *Standard Eurobarometer* 38/1992, fig. 5.2; 42/1994, fig. 6.2; 45/1996, figs. 4.4 and 4.5; 48/1998, fig. 4.4; 52/2000, fig. 3.9.

24 See *Standard Eurobarometer* 52/2000, quoted according to http://europa.eu.int/comm/dg10/epo/eb/eb52/highlights.html.

25 Interestingly, public skepticism in such pro-enlargement countries as Austria and Germany has been among the highest in the entire EU.

26 See Cialdini and Trost (1998) and Johnston (2001) for an overview of social influence mechanisms and the relevant literature, and Finnemore and Sikkink (1998: 902–04)

works in the absence of formal institutions choosing a winner after debate has ended, it can also be effective without superior bargaining power and coercive force. Social influence is based on the fact that human beings are social or "community beings." As community members, they *seek social approval and respect* from the other community members. In other words, they want to be recognized as legitimate. Conversely, they are *sensitive to social disapproval and disrespect.* They are concerned with their image and reputation in the community and do not want to be regarded as unreliable or illegitimate. If community member *P* is able to demonstrate that member *O* violates the community standard of legitimacy to which he subscribed, *O* will be induced to conform with the standard.

Several conditions affect the effectiveness of social influence.

Social influence is only effective *inside the actor's in-group or community.* Only the social rewards and punishments of a group to which an actor belongs or aspires to belong, and with which the actor identifies herself or himself, can have a conformity-inducing effect on the actor. If *P* is a member of an out-group or a community to which *O* neither belongs nor aspires to belong, *O* will react indifferently to *P*'s arguments.[27]

Social influence is only effective if the *goal or behavior in question is regulated by community culture or institutionalized in community rules* (see Johnston 2001: 501). If it lies outside the purview of the community's standard of legitimacy, social influence either will not be applied or not lead to the psychological reactions that induce conformity. Furthermore, social influence will be the more effective, the more fundamental or constitutive the issue and the concomitant rules are for the community. Rules that are directly related to the identity and the basic purpose of the community will exert the strongest compliance pull. Finally, the more clearly defined the community rules and the community actors' prior commitments, the more authoritative their source and the more accepted the procedure by which they have been established, the easier it is for *P* to demonstrate that *O*'s preferences and behavior violate the community standard. These conditions combined account for the *legitimacy* of the rule or commitment in question (see Franck 1990: 49, 142).

Third, just as for the social mobilization mechanism, *resonance* (or salience) is a helpful condition. Generally, social influence is most

and Shannon (2000) for applications to international politics. The conceptual relation between rhetorical action and social influence is loose. Rhetorical action is one possible way of exerting social influence but there are, of course, other uses of rhetorical action and other means of social influence.

[27] In their review of the social-psychological literature on social influence, Cialdini and Trost (1998: 161) report "that norms exert the greatest influence . . . when the source is similar to us, or when we are particularly concerned about establishing and maintaining a relationship with the source." See also Cialdini and Trost (1998: 166).

effective if actors truly believe in, or are seriously committed to the community values and norms – which does not mean that they always follow them in practice. In these cases, social rewards are most rewarding and social punishments are most embarrassing and painful. In the case of states, social influence to promote international rules will be easier also if a state's domestic values and norms match or harmonize with these rules.

Fourth, social influence is most effective if the acts of both the violation of the standard of legitimacy and social punishment are *public*, that is, observed by the other community members. If *P* argues in a private conversation that *O* violates the standard of legitimacy, *O* will feel less compelled to justify, let alone correct, his behavior than in a public setting. The prospect of being publicly stigmatized as a perpetrator is a stronger deterrent than a private and unpublicized sanction (see Cialdini and Trost 1998: 163, 166; Johnston 2001: 502).

Shaming – the public exposure of illegitimate goals and behaviors – is the most important mechanism of social influence in this context.[28] To be effective, shaming requires that actors have publicly committed themselves to the standard of legitimacy at an earlier point in time – either out of a sincere belief in its rightfulness or for instrumental reasons. When, in a specific decision-making situation, actors would prefer to deviate from the standard because it contradicts their self-interest, other members of their community can shame them into compliance by exposing the discrepancy between their declared commitment and their current preferences and behavior. (Of course, these other members may do so for entirely instrumental reasons in order to add legitimacy to their own self-interested preferences and behavior.)[29]

Members who sincerely believe in the community norms but could not resist the temptation of self-interested behavior will feel genuinely ashamed and will change their behavior in order to straighten things out with themselves and protect their self-image. Under these circumstances, rhetorical action and shaming serve to "shift attentiveness," "boost the salience" of the actor's internal norms, and induce the actor to shift from self-interested to normative action and thus back from a logic of consequences to a logic of appropriateness (see Busby 2002: 29). However, in a community environment and under the conditions of effective social influence, successful shaming does not depend on internalized norms. Even members who have committed themselves to a norm for mainly

[28] See Johnston (2001: 502). For an analysis of the European human rights regime based on the shaming mechanism, see Moravcsik (1995).

[29] On consistency and compliance, see Cialdini and Trost (1998: 176–79). Cf. Goffman (1959: 12–13).

instrumental reasons, who do not believe in its intrinsic qualities and do not change their preferences as a result of shaming, will be concerned with what the exposure of their illegitimate preferences and behavior will do to their standing and reputation in the community.

At the outset, however, shamed rhetorical actors will engage in rhetorical maneuvers to evade social disapproval without having to conform to the rules (see H4c). They may, for instance, downplay the community values and norms or reinterpret them to their advantage, question their relevance in the given context, or bring up competing community values and norms that back their own preferences.[30] There are, however, *limits to strategic manipulation*.

First, to the extent that the standard of legitimacy (w in the arguments against the non-compliant member) is clearly and unambiguously defined as well as internally consistent, it becomes difficult for the shamed member to shift to a pseudo-competitive argumentation or to rhetorically circumvent the conclusions of her opponents and their practical implications (see Franck 1990: 49; Shannon 2000: 294).

Second, actors must be careful not to lose their *credibility* as community members when manipulating social values and norms. Credibility is the single most important resource in arguing. The most authoritative warrant, the most impressive grounds, the most brilliant reasoning, and the best presentation do not help to persuade the audience if the proponent has lost her credibility. Conversely, a proponent who is regarded as highly credible is often able to invest comparatively little effort in her arguments and still persuade the audience.[31] Argumentative credibility is based on impartiality and consistency.[32]

The constraint of *impartiality* forces rhetorical actors to avoid obviously self-serving arguments and to present their claim as generalizable in principle and applicable to any actor under the same circumstances. "In argumentative situations, one *has* to phrase one's argument in impartial terms, as if one were arguing for the public good and not for one's own self-interest" (Elster 1992: 18). The audience can only be moved to accept a proponent's claim if it is based on a shared warrant, and a shared warrant must have the form of an intersubjective principle that

[30] See Goffman's "defensive practices" (1959: 13), that is, the strategies and tactics of individuals to protect the projection of their initial self-presentation.

[31] On the crucial role of credibility for social movements, see, e.g., Klandermans (1997: 49–50).

[32] The following is based on Elster (1989a; 1989b; 1989c; 1991; 1992). Although Elster distinguishes "rhetorical statements" from arguing because of their appeals to passion (1991: 37) and reserves "credibility" to the analysis of bargaining, his analysis of the strategic use of arguments and the "civilizing force of hypocrisy" covers rhetorical action and its unintended effects perfectly.

goes beyond saying "because I want it." Of course, in rhetorical action, impartiality is always relative to the audience; the intersubjective principle of justification does not have to be generalizable. For instance, before a national audience, it is sufficient to appeal to national identity, values, experiences and customs.

The constraint of *consistency* applies, first, to the match between arguments and actions, second, to the match between arguments used at different times and in different contexts, and third, to the internal consistency of arguments. Rhetorical actors that do not honor their argumentative commitments in deed, reject warrants and grounds they accepted in earlier stages of the debate, are caught making contrary arguments before different audiences or are perceived to appeal to contradictory ideas to persuade a diffuse audience, will lose credibility:

> Any given normative argument may, in any given situation, be used in an opportunistic manner. But once it has been used, the speaker is stuck with it. If he wants to retain his persuasive powers, he cannot simply disregard the argument if a later situation should arise in which it works against his self-interest.[33]

The "joint impact of the constraints of impartiality and consistency can be considerable" (Elster 1992: 19). If inconsistency and partiality are publicly exposed and the rhetorical actor is caught using the community rules arbitrarily and cynically, his credibility suffers. As a result, his future rhetorical actions will be less effective, that is, his ability to manipulate the standard of legitimacy to further his political goals will be reduced: "A participant who is seen as choosing norms à la carte, and discarding them whenever they work against him, will undermine himself in the long run" (ibid.).

To be sure, successful shaming requires that the shaming agent argue impartially and consistently, too. Only if the shaming proponent is perceived to argue in the interest of the community rather than merely in her self-interest and only if she sticks to her grounds and warrants, and follows, in her own actions, what she demands of others, will her arguments be credible and persuasive. If not, the shamed opponents will point to her partiality and inconsistency in order to question her credibility and to bring up an excuse for non-compliance. The logic of arguing

[33] Elster (1992: 19); see also Elster (1989a: 103). Note that Elster (1989b: 239; see also Elster 1989a: 104; Elster 1989c: 129) regards the constraint of consistency as an *internal* constraint imposed by the psychological need to preserve intrapersonal consistency. This is also the dominant view in social psychology (see Cialdini and Trost 1998: 176). The internal constraint, however, requires a degree of internalization not taken for granted in the perspective of rhetorical action. In this perspective, shaming ultimately relies on consistency as an *external* constraint. This constraint is effective because actors need to preserve argumentative credibility in their own interest.

can thus have an unintended impact on the behavior of both the shamed opponents and the shaming proponents.

In sum, even if rhetorical actors only use their community's standard of legitimacy opportunistically in order to justify their self-interested claims, they become *rhetorically entrapped* by their use of arguments. What appears to be a cost-free rhetorical commitment or a shrewd argumentative move in one situation, can turn into a costly constraint in another. Once rhetorical actors have publicly committed themselves to a claim and an argumentative strategy in their community, it is difficult for them to renege on this commitment. Likewise, once they have chosen a given forum, they are bound by its rules for the use of argument. The "shadow of the future" in a community environment is indefinitely long in principle, and so is the "shadow of the past": community members that were caught arguing deceitfully and self-servingly have a difficult time reestablishing trust in and respect for their arguments so that they will be taken seriously by, and able to persuade, their audience. Consequently, rhetorical actors are likely to be forced to stick to prior argumentative commitments and to act according to claims that run counter to their current self-interest.

I do not claim that rhetorical entrapment will always work. For instance, to the extent that they are able to anticipate such entrapments, rhetorically rational actors will seek to avoid them. However, their capacity to foresee future argumentative situations is limited. Moreover, in the end, rhetorical entrapment is a matter of cost-benefit calculations: there may be situations in which acquiring the reputation of being inconsistent and partial and breaking with the community is less costly for the rhetorical actor than paying heed to prior argumentative commitments.

To take up the classification of process hypotheses (chapter 7), it should be clear now why and how, in rhetorical action, norms *do* influence collective outcomes but not before the interaction process sets in. Rhetorical actors pursue individually defined goals by using arguments instrumentally and strategically. Up to this point in the process, norms are relevant only as a *contingent* source of individual goals and strategic arguments. Once social norms or rules have been introduced into the debate in order to support self-serving claims, however, they become causally influential in the further course of the debate as an argumentative resource for some actors, and an argumentative constraint on others, and this may often be in ways rhetorical actors do not anticipate or intend.

These are the binding effects of rhetorical arguments that give rise to Elster's "civilizing force of hypocrisy" and to Goffman's "basic dialectic" of manipulation and morality. To summarize, even among selfish actors and in the absence of coercive power or egoistic incentives to comply, rule-based collective outcomes are possible as a result of rhetorical action. Rule-compliance may be the unintended outcome of untruthful performances and arguments by uncommitted actors.

The outcome of rhetorical action may thus be the same as that of communicative action (or, for that matter, habitual and normative action) – rule-based cooperation. Only the process leading to this outcome will have been different. First, whereas in communicative action the actors are assumed to argue sincerely, consistently, impartially, and fairly *from the start*, in rhetorical action, they will be forced to approach standards of proper argumentation *in the course of the debate* by the constraints of impartiality and consistency and their interest in preserving argumentative credibility. Second, whereas in communicative action, the constitutive rules of the community will be invoked and accepted by all members of the community as a standard for the evaluation of arguments, in rhetorical action they will be invoked by those actors that are able to use them in order to support their self-defined claims and to put pressure on their opponents. Third, whereas, in communicative action, cooperation is the result of a consensus that all participants in the debate searched and worked for, in rhetorical action it will be an unintended outcome brought about by the "invisible hand" of the argumentative process against the will of some actors.

Thomas Risse criticized this account in what could be termed an "incompleteness argument," claiming that rhetorical action does not properly explain the outcome of argumentation processes either theoretically or empirically. At the *theoretical level*, Risse asserts, "If everybody in a communicative situation engages in rhetoric – the speaker, the target, and the audience – they can argue strategically until they are blue in the face and still not change anyone's mind" (2000: 8). If "changing one's mind" is understood as "convincing" and "changing beliefs," Risse is right. Yet rhetorical actors are not primarily interested in convincing their audience and their opponents but are satisfied when they induce them to cooperate. If "changing one's mind" is understood as "persuading to cooperate," however, Risse overlooks the fact that, in the rhetorical perspective, the skillful use of persuasive techniques can create sufficient social pressure to make unconvinced opponents cooperate and refrain from further challenges to the claims of the proponent.

At this point, Risse objects that, in order to create the social pressure inducing the opponents to cooperate, the audience must be "prepared to be convinced by the better argument." Consequently, rhetoric's "condition for success is . . . based on the logic of argumentative rationality" (Risse 2000: 8–9; cf. Müller 2002: 9). This is not necessarily so. First, the audience may have been favorably disposed to the claims of the proponent from the start. Then, the proponent's use of persuasive techniques was equal to "speaking to the convinced" (Bleses, Offe and Peter 1997: 503). The proponent may have intended to reinforce the beliefs of her partisans and to mobilize them so that *O* would either not dare to put forward his claims and arguments any more or decide to leave the forum. Second, the audience may indeed have been undecided or even opposed, in the beginning, to the claims of the proponent and persuaded to accept her or his claims as a result of rhetorical action. Yet, the fact that the audience was persuaded is not by itself sufficient proof of communicative rationality. The audience may not have yielded to the "force of the better argument" but may have been deceived, moved by appeals to emotion and particularistic warrants, or it may have calculated the individual costs and benefits of the opponents' claims. Finally, the audience itself may have been subject to social influence skillfully and persuasively applied by the proponent. As a result, it may have been shamed into supporting the claim of the opponent without being convinced. In sum, I submit that rhetorical action does not presuppose communicative action theoretically and both hypotheses can be treated as conceptually independent.[34]

At the *empirical* level, Risse and his collaborators propose a "spiral model" to describe the process by, and the conditions under which, repressive governments become socialized to international human rights norms (Risse 1999; Risse, Ropp and Sikkink 1999; Risse and Sikkink 1999). The model contains a sequence of progressive socialization starting with a phase of "denial" in which the governments deny human rights violations and seek to refuse to enter into a debate. Under increasing international and domestic pressure, the process moves to the phase of "tactical concessions" in which the repressive governments engage in rhetorical action (characterized by an only pseudo-competitive argumentation on the basis of the human rights norms) until, in the next phase, human rights attain "prescriptive status." Rhetorical maneuvers are substituted by the opponents' mutual recognition of each other as equal participants in debate, the mutual acceptance of a common warrant, and argumentative consistency (Risse 1999: 549–50): "The more they 'talk the talk' . . . the more they entangle themselves in a moral discourse which they cannot escape in the long run."[35]

The problem with this (strongly condensed) account is the theoretical conclusion Risse draws from it – that, as a result of "argumentative self-entrapment," "the logic of argumentative rationality and truth-seeking behavior" takes over (Risse 2000: 23; see also Risse 1999: 551). As I

[34] Conceptual independence does not exclude that, in real debates, we may often find elements of both modes of communication.

[35] Risse and Sikkink (1999: 16 (quote), 22–30). The full sequence starts with "repression" and ends with "rule-consistent behavior."

have tried to demonstrate, following Goffman and Elster, the behavior Risse describes for the later stages of the socialization process can be attributed to the unintended binding force and the entrapment effects of rhetorical arguments as well. It is not necessary to assume communicative rationality and a truth-seeking orientation to explain why actors come to argue consistently on the basis of a common warrant and to comply with the standards they invoked opportunistically. The claim that the opponents "behave *as if* they were engaged in a true moral discourse" (2000: 23, emphasis added) is not beyond the scope of dramaturgical action or the strategic use of arguments and does not require the introduction of a new "logic of action" or a shift in rationality. Put differently, the empirical case for communicative rationality would have been strong if the actors in the socialization process had behaved as consensus-oriented truth-seekers from the start (which they did not). In that case, the rhetorical action hypothesis would have been disconfirmed and the communicative action hypothesis would have been able to explain the entire process.

In sum, the problem with the Habermasian, communicative perspective on arguing is its assumption of truth-seeking actor orientations and behavior, not its claim that arguing is a distinctive mode of action that matters in international relations. Elster makes a similar observation at the end of his study on arguing in constituent assemblies:

> Actual political behavior . . . did not seem to live up to the ideals of truth, rightness, and truthfulness. Yet it would be wrong to say that politics, even at its most savage, had no relation to the norms identified by Habermas. I found the resolution of these tensions and puzzles in the idea of strategic uses of argument. (1991: 107)

Conclusion

In this chapter, I developed, defined, and discussed the concept of rhetorical action and demonstrated that, in theory, it provides a mechanism for causally linking egoistic individual preferences and rule-based collective outcomes. Thus, it offers the possibility of solving the double puzzle of Eastern enlargement. Put briefly, in an institutional community environment, rational actors must justify their goals, preferences and behavior on the basis of the community's standard of legitimacy. Community members whose (egoistic) preferences are in line with the basic community rules can add legitimacy to their preferences and mobilize social pressure or exert social influence on their opponents. They do this through rhetorical action, the strategic use of arguments based on the community's standard of legitimacy. Community members whose preferences contradict the community rules are thereby shamed into acquiescence in the rule-based policy and induced to cooperate with the (albeit hypocritical) defenders of the community values and norms. The following process analysis of NATO and EU decision-making on Eastern enlargement serves to examine this mechanism empirically.

The rhetorical action hypothesis has the following observable implications for the enlargement decision-making process:

(R1) The CEECs' desire to join NATO and the EU was not necessarily uniform and followed individual goals.
(R2) The enlargement preferences of NATO and EU members were not necessarily uniform and followed individual goals.
(R3) NATO and the EU did not immediately offer membership or react favorably to the membership requests of the CEECs.
(R4) The decision-making process within NATO and the EU was characterized by conflict about the timing of enlargement and the selection of new members as well as by the strategic use of arguments by which the member states and candidates sought to justify and realize their own enlargement preferences. Enlargement proponents shamed opponents into acquiescing to enlargement.
(R5) Further enlargement rounds are a matter of debate. They will again be contested because of divergent state preferences and depend on successful shaming.

Propositions R1–R3 were already confirmed in the analysis of enlargement preferences and the initial decision-making process (chapter 5). Therefore, the following analysis will focus on propositions R4 and R5 which will be examined in comparison with the corresponding implications of the communicative action hypothesis (propositions 1–3 are the same for both hypotheses based on a logic of arguing):

(C4) The decision-making process within NATO and the EU was characterized by conflict about the timing of enlargement and the selection of new members as well as by a truth-seeking discourse on the appropriate policy toward the CEECs in which the participants reached a reasoned consensus.
(C5) Further enlargement rounds are a matter of consensus. They will build on the consensual understanding reached between the members of the Western organizations as well as between them and the CEECs.

I conclude this section with a *methodological note*. Rhetorical analysis is naturally based on the interpretation of public speech acts. The *advantage* of this method is that rhetorical analysis is able to draw on an abundance of publicly available data for the analysis of argumentative behavior such as official documents, speeches, declarations and statements at press conferences. This advantage is all the more relevant as direct and reliable historical sources on the Eastern enlargement decision-making process (in the North Atlantic Council and the European Council) will not be accessible for a long time.

It is *not a disadvantage* of this method that public speech acts are notorious for their lack of reliability and validity as indicators for the actors' beliefs and intentions. Whether these sources reflect the "true motivations" of the actors is irrelevant for a rhetorical analysis. First, the rhetorical action hypothesis does not make any assumptions on the actors' utilities or motives. Second, it is a general tenet of rhetorical analysis that "discourse is relatively autonomous since its viability does not require the faith of its agents" (Cruz 2000: 283). Third, whether or not political actors really mean what they say, they will choose their arguments strategically. Finally, rhetorical action will affect community members regardless of whether they truly believe in the community norms or simply fear for their standing in the community: both opportunistic and truthful arguments have real consequences for their proponents and the outcome of the debate.

By contrast, it *is* a *disadvantage* of rhetorical analysis that I cannot adduce direct evidence for the psychological, social influence effects of rhetorical arguments and for the primacy of credibility and legitimacy concerns in producing compliance. I therefore chose the indirect strategy of examining whether the main observable features of the process are consistent with the mechanism of social influence and rhetorical entrapment and "make sense" in a rhetorical perspective. Moreover, in the NATO enlargement case, I conducted interviews in order to find out how participants in the process describe their argumentative strategies and evaluate their effects.

Finally, there are the well-known problems of *text interpretation*: the selection of speech acts as well as the interpretation of the selected speech acts may be biased. However, I followed a few guidelines and control procedures. First, I focused on the *authoritative speech acts of leading representatives* of the major actors in the process. These comprise, for instance, major foreign policy speeches by heads of government and state, the conclusions of the presidency on European Council meetings or NATO communiqués on NATO Council meetings and official documents of the European Commission or NATO. Second, I searched a few *complete bodies of texts* for enlargement-related discourse in my period of investigation: *Europe*, the daily bulletin of the Agence Europe press agency, *NATO Review*, the major forum for "official" public debate on NATO issues and

RFE/RL Newsline, the daily online news service on Central and Eastern Europe. These two procedures maximize the probability that the selected speech acts are indeed representative and typical for the argumentative strategies used in the enlargement process.

In sum, I am able to produce *direct descriptive evidence* for the omnipresence of rhetorical action in the enlargement process. On the other hand, however, I can only adduce *indirect evidence* for its causal efficiency. Consequently, the causal claims will have to be formulated in more cautious terms than the descriptive ones.

10 The decision to enlarge NATO

The decision to enlarge NATO and the EU took place in a community environment in which all state actors shared a liberal political culture and had subscribed to the constitutive organizational rules. In a rhetorical perspective, the problem of enlargement decision-making in this environment was not a conflict between competing validity claims. There was no controversy about, or controversial interpretation of, the criteria for legitimate membership; no member state openly challenged the principle that democratic European states were entitled to join the Western organizations. The problem was one of compliance with the practical consequences of this principle. For the CEEC aspirants, the question was how to induce the reluctant member states to acquiesce in Eastern enlargement; for their opponents, it was how to avoid or, at least, put off honoring their commitments as members of the Western community. In this situation (and given that transnational social mobilization did not promise to be effective), the rhetorical action hypothesis predicts that the proponents of enlargement use arguments based on the community culture to shame the opponents into compliance.

For three reasons, the NATO case study analyzes the US domestic decision-making process on NATO enlargement in addition to international interaction. First, the fact that the United States, in 1994, became the most determined advocate of Eastern enlargement in the Alliance was the only major puzzle for the rationalist explanation of enlargement preferences (see chapter 8). How then can we account for the change in US enlargement preferences? Second, the United States is the most powerful state in NATO and has the greatest influence on alliance decisions. Third, the United States was the only alliance member state in which the ratification of Czech, Hungarian and Polish accession to NATO stirred a major elite debate.

This chapter begins with a description of the rhetorical strategies of the CEECs. I then analyze the change in the US position on enlargement, the international decision-making process and the US ratification process. Finally, I briefly demonstrate that the process leading to the second round of NATO enlargement confirms the essential features of the first-round process.[1]

Central and Eastern European rhetorical strategies

In order to overcome the initial opposition of NATO member states to commit themselves to Eastern enlargement, the governments of the aspiring states appealed to the constitutive values and norms of the Euro-Atlantic liberal community. It has been the central argumentative strategy of the CEECs to portray themselves as part of the Western community, to stress the instability of democratic achievements in their region and to show that NATO's liberal values and norms as well as historical precedent obliged the member states to stabilize democracy in the CEECs and, for that purpose, to grant them membership in NATO (cf. Fierke 1999: 37–39; Radu 1997; Schimmelfennig 2000: 129–32). In argument-theoretical terminology, the CEECs referred to the constitutive values and norms of the Western community as a warrant and adduced their European identity, their democratic values and norms and their need of interdemocratic solidarity as grounds in order to validate their claim to become NATO members. This argumentative strategy was used publicly in speeches, interviews and articles addressed to NATO, its member states, and their societies. Already the first speech of a Central and Eastern European head of state at NATO, President Havel's address to the NATO Council in March 1991, incorporated all of these arguments and constitued a model for the CEE efforts to persuade NATO. I will therefore quote at length from this speech and complement it by other examples.[2]

Return to Europe. In a first step, the CEECs sought to define themselves as "European" and "democratic" countries and to detach themselves from their communist and "Eastern" past in order to show that they were part of the Euro-Atlantic liberal community. They framed the post-Cold War political changes as their "return to Europe," to a community to which they had traditionally belonged and from which they had been artificially cut off during communist rule. At the beginning of his speech, President Havel expressed his satisfaction that he could "address you today as a representative of a democratic and independent country that shares your ideals and wishes to cooperate with you and to be your friend." A few months later at the same place, the Polish President Walesa quoted from the preamble of the North Atlantic Treaty when he affirmed that

[1] For further rhetorical or discourse analyses of NATO enlargement, see Fierke (1999) and Williams and Neumann (2000).

[2] See "NATO Headquarters. Brussels, March 21, 1991," <http://www.hrad.cz/president/Havel/speeches/1991/2103_uk.html>.

"we are determined to safeguard the freedom, the common heritage and civilization, founded on the principles of democracy, individual liberty and the rule of law." He added that the Polish people had wanted to subscribe to these values for a long time and had stood up for them in World War II and in their repeated revolts against communist rule.[3]

The claim to belong to "Western civilization" and "Europe" in the emphatic, not just geographical, sense was not limited to the Central European countries but was put forward also by states for which it was far from self-evident. In an effort to purge Romania of its Eastern or Balkan image, the Romanian Minister of Defense Teodor Melescanu defined his country as a "Central European country close to the Balkans" (Melescanu 1993). Similarly, the Lithuanian Ambassador Stankevicius affirmed that the "integration of Lithuania and the other two Baltic states into the community of Western nations means a return to their natural places in the international community" and that "despite 50 years of suppression, the Lithuanian, Latvian and Estonian nations have managed to preserve their affinity to Western European civilization" (Stankevicius 1996).

In addition, critical observers have noted that "appeals to Western Europe on behalf of 'Central Europe' are consistently made by offsetting it against a barbarous East" (Neumann 1993: 367), and "that the state of the subject is not only European, but that the next state to the east is not European" (Neumann 1998: 406). For instance, "while all nations deny the Balkan label, they frequently use it to describe their neighbors" (Radu 1997: 49). Just as the Central European countries expected NATO to differentiate between them and the other CEECs (see, e.g., Cottey 1995: 38), Melescanu (1993) tried to detach Romania from the Balkans and Stankevicius asserted that "the Eurasian commonwealth represented by the CIS is foreign to most Lithuanians" (1996).

Democracy in danger. In a second move, the CEEC representatives depicted their return to freedom and democracy as unstable and endangered. In his speech before NATO, President Havel referred to unexpected "obstacles" to the "building of a democratic system and the transition to a market economy," the "unfortunate inheritance, which these countries must deal with," the "general demoralization" and the fragility and vulnerability of CEE democracies. As a result of these and other factors, Havel said, "our countries are dangerously sliding into a certain political, economic and security vacuum. . . . At the same time, it is becoming evident that without appropriate external links the very

[3] "Präsident Lech Walesas Besuch bei der NATO-Zentrale am 3. Juli 1991," *NATO Brief* 39:4, 1991, 33–35.

existence of our young democracies is in jeopardy." By pointing out that core Western values and norms were in danger, Havel sought to put moral pressure on the Western governments and to create a sense of urgency for NATO action.

Shaming NATO. In a third rhetorical step, CEEC representatives appealed to NATO's self-styled identity as the security organization of the Euro-Atlantic community of democratic countries and to its self-attributed mission to encourage and secure democracy in Europe. Against the preoccupation of the "brakemen" with military security and strategic concerns, Havel warned,

> The alliance should urgently remind itself that it is first and foremost an instrument of democracy to defend mutually held and created political and spiritual values. It must see itself not as a pact of nations against a more or less obvious enemy, but as a guarantor of Euro-American civilization.[4]

In a similar way, Ambassador Stankevicius deplored that

> Sometimes, in discussions on NATO enlargement, one hears voices in the West warning that the Baltic states are 'indefensible'. However, the concept of indefensible European states is in complete discord with modern principles of European democracy. (1996)

For the CEE advocates of NATO enlargement, their entitlement to join NATO followed logically from their European, liberal identity and their need for the protection of democracy, on the one hand, and NATO's identity as the security organization of the Euro-Atlantic community and its historical mission of promoting and protecting democracy, on the other. By refusing to commit itself to Eastern enlargement, NATO would betray its own identity, break its promises, and act inconsistently. Havel started out by reminding his audience of how the

> democratic West . . . succeeded for years in withstanding the expansion of the totalitarian system of the Communist type, sympathizing with the countries of the Soviet bloc and never ceasing to believe that these forces would be victorious. . . . Its commitment to the protection of democracy and human liberty was an encouragement and inspiration also for the citizens of our countries.

"From this," Havel concluded,

> arises a great responsibility for the West. It cannot be indifferent to what is happening in the countries which – constantly encouraged by the Western democracies – have finally shaken off the totalitarian system. It cannot look on passively at how laboriously these countries are striving to find their new place in the present world. The West, whose civilization is founded on universal values, cannot be indifferent to the fate of the East.

[4] *International Herald Tribune*, 15 May 1997.

These passages reveal a typical *shaming strategy*. First, Havel framed NATO members as the "democratic West," thereby appealing to their community identity. By framing NATO as a democratic community rather than a military alliance, he also defined enlargement as an issue of democracy promotion and protection rather than an issue of military deterrence and defense. Second, Havel positively invoked NATO's past value-based commitments and practices as consistent with the community culture. On this basis, he called on NATO to act consistently with its democratic identity and its past promises and behavior. By argumentatively locking NATO into the organization's own legitimacy claims, self-images and mission statements, Havel and other CEEC leaders sought to shame NATO into committing itself to enlargement.

Once more appealing to the constitutive values of NATO, inter-democratic solidarity and the democratic conscience of NATO members, Havel affirmed that "an alliance of countries united by a commitment to the ideal of freedom and democracy should not remain permanently closed to neighbouring countries which are pursuing the same goals" and expressed his firm belief that NATO–Czechoslovak cooperation,

> based on mutual trust and shared values, will strengthen the feeling of security in our society and will result in appropriate guarantees, thanks to which the Czechoslovak citizens will not have to fear the future and, in case of any threat, will not feel isolated and forgotten by the democratic community.

Likewise, the Hungarian ambassador to the United States, György Banlaki, exhorted NATO that "Temporizing on enlargement will raise doubts about the commitment of the West to that region" (in Clemens 1997a: 112). King Michael of Romania was even more explicit: "If having exerted all efforts to meet the criteria, new reasons are found to exclude Romania, the West will have little credibility not only in my country but . . . in the entire region" (1997: 9).

The CEE leaders reinforced this shaming strategy by invoking the *West's historical failures* and by creating the moral pressure to admit the CEECs either as a compensation for past mistakes or in order to avoid repeating them. Most often, they used the "Yalta" metaphor in order to remind the Western countries that they abandoned their allies after the Second World War and tolerated their Soviet domination and communist transformation. For instance, President Walesa bluntly denounced PfP as "Yalta II." More subtly, President Havel declared on the occasion of President Clinton's visit to Prague in January 1994: "At one time, the city of Yalta went down in history as a symbol of the division of Europe. I would be happy if today the city of Prague emerged as a symbol of Europe's standing in alliance" (quoted in Grayson 1999: 84, 87). Speaking at the British Royal United Services Institute, King Michael of Romania recalled how his father and he "got nice expressions of solidarity but, otherwise, a deafening silence" when asking for British assistance against the Third Reich and the Soviet Union (1997: 6).

CEEC representatives further appealed to the *multilateralist norms* of NATO – the principles of equality and indivisibility of security – but manipulated them self-servingly. The Central European governments that were the best-qualified candidates and the most likely new members of NATO did *not* refer to these norms but called for differential treatment of the CEECs: they did not want to see their admission delayed by being put in the same category as the more problematic candidates in the region. Conversely, the second-rate candidates appealed to equality and indivisibility to avoid being relegated to a lesser status and to support their claim for admission together with the stronger candidates. Whereas the Central European countries criticized the fact that PfP did not make any formal distinctions among the CEECs and asked for a timetable and a list of countries eligible for membership, the Balkan countries were "satisfied that the PfP program allows all nonaligned European states to participate on equal terms" and stressed that "the same rules and criteria must apply for all applicants" (Engelbrekt 1994: 38, 42; see also Solomon 1998: 35–36).

The Romanian Defense Minister Spiroiu referred to the multilateralist norm of "equal security" in order to reject "any type of discrimination."[5] The Ukrainian ambassador to the United States, Yuri Shcherbak, warned, "In order to avoid new dividing lines in Europe, the principle of the indivisibility of security should be observed" (in Clemens 1997a: 119). Starys Sakalauskas of the Lithuanian Embassy claimed that "all the new democracies should have the same starting points in terms of opportunities": "Including Lithuania in the NATO accession process would thus be an act of recognition that all of us together are members of the Western community of nations" (in Clemens 1997a: 122). Ambassador Stankevicius also referred to the principle of "indivisible security" in order to stipulate the Baltic states' inclusion in NATO enlargement. At the same time, however, the proponents of the indivisibility principle cared little about dividing lines running east of their countries. Witness Stankevicius: "The existing line between the European and Eurasian areas of political, economic and defence integration can hardly be regarded as a dangerous division of Europe" (1996).

Finally, CEEC officials adduced *historical precedent* as another way of invoking the consistency constraint to advance the cause of NATO enlargement. Ambassador Banlaki pleaded that "NATO has the chance to

[5] *FBIS-EEU-94-007*, 11 January 1994, 28.

do today in Europe's East what it did fifty years ago for the Western half of the continent" (in Clemens 1997a: 111). Moreover, Romanian Defense Minister Melescanu recalled the importance of "certain external factors . . . in securing both the consolidation and the irreversibility" of democratic transition in Southern Europe and pointed to German–French reconciliation and the avoidance of Greco-Turkish war as an example for how the relationship between Hungary and Romania would improve if not only Hungary but also Romania was admitted to NATO (Melescanu 1993; cf. Romania 1997).

What indicates the rhetorical, as opposed to a communicatively rational, quality of the CEECs' argumentative behavior? First, the CEECs used the value- and norm-based arguments in a self-serving, competitive, and opportunistic manner. They interpreted the values and norms in a way that served their own membership interest and emphasized their own qualifications for membership in contrast with other candidates. Second, in their shaming strategy, they appealed to emotions like guilt and remorse ("Yalta"). Third, CEEC advocates did not necessarily limit themselves to norm-based arguments. For instance, Melescanu not only sought to portray Romania as part of "Central Europe" and Western civilization but also alluded to material and strategic benefits of NATO enlargement when he referred to Romania's geographical position, population and territorial size.[6] This can be interpreted as a rhetorical move to enhance the persuasiveness of Romania's claim to membership in a pluralistic audience in which some members may share the warrant of "military utility." Or it could indicate a concern that the democratic credentials of Romania at that time were not sufficiently persuasive.

Finally, the CEEC advocates adapted their argumentative strategies to the audiences they addressed. For instance, Polish officials had initially focused on the "security vacuum" in Central Europe and the potential Russian threat in justifying their request for NATO membership (which was close to the "true" motivation; see chapter 8). During the US ratification campaign, however, Polish Ambassador Kozminski stressed the Western integration of Poland and argued that "enlargement would even strengthen Polish–Russian relations" (Grayson 1999: 138; see also 169). According to George Grayson, officials of the Polish Embassy "realized the importance of seizing the moral high ground. Thus, in public pronouncements and in exchanges with officials, the embassy reiterated that 'expansion would contribute to democracy [and] promote [European] stability'" (1999: 165). Similarly, Czech Ambassador Zantovský claimed

[6] Melescanu (1993). See also Moses (1998: 137). On a similar Bulgarian mix of arguments, see Engelbrekt (1994: 39).

that Czech "determination to join NATO . . . is rooted in [the] shared system of values, principles, and goals rather than threat-based" (in Clemens 1997a: 116). Michael Radu shows that this kind of argumentative adaptation was widespread:

> [U]pon being subjected to an avalanche of such arguments [that NATO expansion had nothing to do with a potential Russian threat] from NATO officials and respected Western analysts, most Central and Eastern European leaders have felt compelled to repeat them, often against their own beliefs and personal experience, and generally at the risk of sounding unrealistic at home. Hence, the claim that NATO's expansion is not directed against Russia but in fact enhances Russian security has been dutifully put forward by all the governments of Central and Eastern Europe. (Radu 1997: 44)

The argumentation of the CEECs clearly reveals the strategic use of arguments and corresponds to the form of rhetorical action (shaming) that was to be expected under the circumstances of non-compliant behavior in a community environment. But was it strong enough to persuade NATO members? Do we have evidence that they brought about a change, in NATO decision-making, from denial of membership to enlargement? To answer these questions, I will first analyze the change in US enlargement policy.

US preference change

During the Bush administration, the United States promoted expanded cooperation with the CEECs but not membership. Nor did President Clinton come to office with the avowed goal of expanding the Alliance to the East. Even after Clinton had become a proponent of enlargement, the pro-enlargement grouping initially held a minority position within the executive (see chapter 8). Given that NATO enlargement was hardly in the egoistic security or strategic interest of the United States (see chapter 2), can the change in US policy be attributed to the effects of rhetorical action? I argue that, in the United States, a coincidence of principled beliefs, personal persuasion and political interests brought about the beginnings of a pro-enlargement policy in the White House but the use of presidential authority was needed in order to turn it into official US policy. In order to explain the development of US enlargement policy, the role of President Clinton and key figures of his administration is of paramount importance.[7]

[7] Here, I follow Goldgeier (1999). Grayson (1999: 54) emphasizes that the ideas of the "RAND boys" (Asmus, Kugler and Larrabee) and the early enlargement advocacy of Senator Lugar "provided the main impetus for acceptance of NATO expansion." Szabo

Principled beliefs. James Goldgeier describes both President Clinton and his National Security Adviser Anthony Lake as "intellectual heirs of Woodrow Wilson, believing that the expansion of international institutions and the promotion of freedom . . . could increase global peace and prosperity" (1999: 20). These general beliefs inspired the foreign policy doctrine of "democratic enlargement" that Lake and his collaborators developed in the first months of the Clinton administration. Based on the Wilsonian insight "that our own security is shaped by the character of foreign regimes," he suggested that "we must promote democracy and market economics in the world – because it protects our interests and security; and because it reflects values that are both American and universal" (Lake 1993: 15). To "help foster and consolidate new democracies and market economies" was to be one of the central components of the enlargement strategy. According to Lake,"Clinton embraced the enlargement concept almost immediately" since it resonated with his liberal beliefs (Brinkley 1997: 116). These beliefs also shaped Clinton's and Lake's perception of NATO: neither of them seemed to be strongly interested in or committed to the Alliance or "Atlanticism" as such, but they regarded NATO as an instrument for the promotion of democracy and for the protection of an enlarged democratic community.[8] However, at this early stage, NATO enlargement was not an explicit component of "democratic enlargement."

Personal persuasion. These liberal beliefs about the value of promoting democracy, together with his positive attitude toward, and interest in, Europe stemming from his studies in England, may have made President Clinton particularly susceptible to the CEEC arguments for NATO enlargement. He was confronted directly with them when he met CEEC leaders, among them President Havel and President Walesa, privately in April 1993 on the occasion of the opening of the Holocaust Memorial Museum in Washington. Lake reported that Clinton was "impressed . . . with the passion with which these leaders spoke" and "inclined to think positively toward expansion from that

(1997) emphasizes the Rühe–Holbrooke connection. The available evidence suggests, however, that the enlargement preferences of the White House began to develop independently of these inputs, before the RAND article was published in the fall of 1993, and before Holbrooke returned from Germany to the United States in the fall of 1994. Finally, Smith and Timmins (2000: 37, 49) argue that US enlargement advocacy was motivated by the desire not to let the EU get ahead on the enlargement issue and overshadow NATO in relations with CEECs. However, this is a highly speculative thesis entirely based on the near coincidence of NATO and EU enlargement decisions in 1993 and 1994 and not corroborated by any of the studies, or by my interviews, on the US decision-making process.

[8] Interview Goldgeier.

day on" (Goldgeier 1999: 20; see also Warner 1998: 117). The emotionally charged atmosphere of a day filled with memories of Europe's darkest age may have added special weight to the CEE leaders' arguments on the need of promoting and protecting democracy in their countries.[9]

If it is correct – as this episode indicates without, however, providing "hard" evidence – that President Clinton was moved to endorse and advocate NATO enlargement as a result of his personal encounter with the most prominent representatives of the new Eastern Europe and his exposure to their rhetorical appeals, then an act of persuasion was indeed at the very origin of the change in US enlargement policy and, by extension, of NATO enlargement. Probably, however, extensive shaming on the part of the CEEC leaders was not necessary. First, even if Clinton's 1996 campaign statement that "*I came to office* convinced that NATO can do for Europe's East what it did for Europe's West,"[10] should be taken with a degree of skepticism, he had not been a declared opponent of enlargement either. Second, the claim of NATO enlargement to democratic CEECs resonated well with his general foreign policy beliefs. Finally, notwithstanding political maneuvering and tactical delays, Clinton appears to have been sincerely convinced of the CEECs' entitlement to NATO membership and determined to put it into action (see, e.g., Mattox 1998: 27). In addition, this policy also fitted in well with some domestic political concerns and interests.

Political interest. It would be too simple to attribute the US administration's "conversion" to NATO enlargement to the liberal beliefs of Clinton and Lake and to the power of the CEE leaders' arguments alone. The strategy of "enlargement" in general and the policy of NATO enlargement in particular also served instrumental, mainly domestic, purposes. First,

> Lake and others had developed democracy promotion as a Clinton campaign theme . . . also because they hoped to unite different wings of the Democratic Party around foreign policy, and in particular to bring conservative Democrats back into the fold after their defection during the Reagan and Bush years. (Goldgeier 1999: 21)

[9] John Lewis Gaddis, one of the fiercest opponents of NATO enlargement, also reports that the "most frequent explanation I have heard is that the Clinton administration, recalling the West's abandonment of these countries . . . felt an emotional obligation to them" (1998: 149).

[10] "The Legacy of America's Leadership as We Enter the 21st Century. Address by President Clinton to the People of Detroit, Detroit, Michigan, October 22, 1996," <http://www.state.gov/www/regions/eur/102296clinton_detroit.html> (29 October 1998), emphasis added. See also *New York Times* (*NYT*), 23 October 1996, A20.

Second, Clinton felt he needed to respond to the critics who accused him of lacking a clear direction in foreign policy and to devise a strategic doctrine if he was to enter the ranks of great American presidents. "Democratic enlargement" served these needs (Brinkley 1996: 113–14). NATO expansion, then, appeared to be a suitable policy to implement the new doctrine. "Concern about instability in central and eastern Europe" was widespread. The enlargement project demonstrated that "the administration had a NATO policy," "a Democratic president could conduct foreign and defense policy effectively," and that Clinton was willing and able to exert leadership in Europe (Goldgeier 1999: 9, 77 (quotes); see also Stuart 1996: 120; Warner 1998: 117).

Third, NATO enlargement was an important issue with Americans of Central European descent and could be pivotal for their voting behavior. It was not lost on both Democrats and Republicans that, in 1992, Clinton had carried twelve out of the fourteen states with the largest East European ethnic populations after several elections in which they had supported the Republicans (see Goldgeier 1999: 100–01; Stuart 1996: 121). "Since these states accounted for more than half of the electoral votes that Clinton received in that year, they were recognized as indispensable for a victory in 1996" (Stuart 1996: 121). In the competition for the "Polish vote," the Republicans regularly sponsored Congressional legislation in favor of a more determined enlargement policy and included the issue in the "Contract With America," their platform for the Congressional elections of 1994. In the Dole campaign of 1996, they tried to exploit the disappointment of voters of CEE descent with the slow progress in enlargement by naming candidates for and announcing dates of accession.

The Clinton administration, in turn, sought not let the Republicans get ahead on this issue and was thus under pressure to speed up the enlargement process. In this respect, it is no coincidence that the administration's NATO policy was first presented, in January 1994, to a domestic audience in Milwaukee, a city of numerous inhabitants with Central and Eastern European roots; that the administration publicly announced 1999 as the date for enlargement during the presidential campaign of 1996, and that it "chose Detroit, and its heavily Polish suburb of Hamtramck" to do so (Goldgeier 1999: 53, 78, 102, 106; Stuart 1996: 121). Thus, although domestic political concerns do not seem to have been at the origin of NATO enlargement,[11] there can be no doubt that ethnic and Republican

[11] This has been the claim of the proponents of enlargement in the Clinton administration. See Goldgeier (1999: 166) and my interviews with administration and CRS officials. This view is shared by Charles Kupchan who worked at the NSC in 1993 and was an opponent of enlargement (interview Kupchan).

pressure as well as electoral considerations moved the administration to remain on track and to speed up the implementation of enlargement within the Alliance.[12]

Presidential authority. Initially, NATO enlargement was a minority position and met with considerable opposition in the bureaucracy. The interagency compromise on PfP of October 1993 did not reflect a consensus. Whereas the proponents understood PfP as an initial step to enlargement, the opponents took it to be NATO's Eastern policy for the foreseeable future. And when President Clinton, on the occasion of his visits to Prague and Warsaw in 1994, declared that "now the question is no longer whether but when and how," this was seen as a call for action by the former and as placating rhetoric by the latter.

The ambiguity lasted until September 1994 when the US ambassador to Germany Richard Holbrooke returned to Washington as assistant secretary of state for European affairs and set out to enforce enlargement within the skeptical bureaucracy. The conflict escalated to a point at which Holbrooke charged the opponents of NATO enlargement with disloyalty to the president. It took a high-level meeting with the president in December 1994, called for by Secretary of Defense William Perry, to dispel any doubts that Clinton backed Lake and Holbrooke. In the end, even explicit enlargement skeptics such as Perry and Talbott fell in alongside the presidential policy and played an important role in its implementation. Thus, in the analysis of Goldgeier, "NATO enlargement emerged during 1994 as the central focus of the administration's NATO policy not because the proponents of the Partnership for Peace changed their mind, but rather as a result of the policy entrepreneurship of Anthony Lake and Richard Holbrooke" (1999: 44). It was not the outcome of an interagency debate leading to persuasion or consensus but, ultimately, resulted from hierarchical presidential authority.

A similar interplay of personal beliefs and contacts with political interests appears to have motivated the other high-ranking early proponent of NATO enlargement, German Defense Minister Volker Rühe. Already, before assuming office, the question of Central Europe's democratic transformation and integration into Western organizations had been on his mind. Long before the breakdown of communism, Rühe had established contact with Polish dissidents who were to become members of the new governing elite at the beginning of the 1990s. He felt that Germany had a special responsibility for the democratic consolidation and stability of Central Europe, and Poland in particular. Moreover, Rühe was not so

12 This has been the standard claim of the Republican proponents of enlargement (interview Brzezinski).

much interested in military affairs in the narrow sense. Having served as the foreign policy spokesman of the Christian Democratic Union's parliamentary caucus, he did not view himself simply as the *defense* minister but intended to use his position to make general *foreign* policy. His affinity to Poland and his beliefs about German responsibility in Central Europe made Rühe highly amenable to the demands and arguments of his Polish friends and acquaintances in favor of membership in NATO. Together with his political ambitions, these arguments may have induced him to make NATO enlargement his personal foreign-policy project.[13]

In sum, the Clinton/Lake and Rühe cases are similar in that the interplay of principles, persuasion, and politics produced a pro-enlargement stance. Both Clinton and Rühe held principled beliefs (democracy promotion and responsibility for Central Europe) that made them responsive to the arguments of their Central European interlocutors. It is doubtful, however, whether these beliefs and arguments were sufficient to make the difference. Many opponents or skeptics in Germany, the United States and other NATO member states shared these principled beliefs about the promotion and protection of democracy and were exposed to the same arguments of CEE officials. In order to explain why the Clinton administration and the Rühe ministery were the only NATO state actors that pushed "fast-track" enlargement, additional factors must have come into play. For both Clinton/Lake and Rühe, NATO enlargement was a welcome issue to define or sharpen their personal foreign policy agendas in political competition with other bureaucratic agencies (Rühe) and parties (Clinton). In addition, the Rühe initiative was supported by the specific geopolitical concerns of his ministry (which were shared by some proponents of enlargement in the United States but do not seem to have been central to Clinton, Lake and their collaborators), whereas the Clinton/Lake initiative was at least given additional momentum by electoral concerns (which were absent in the German case). Thus, it probably was some sort of egoistic political interest that tipped the balance and led Clinton/Lake and Rühe to pursue a policy that was consistent with but not determined by their principled foreign policy beliefs and the CEEC arguments.

Finally, the difference between Germany and the United States must be explained ultimately by power differentials. That Clinton, Lake and Holbrooke were able to make NATO enlargement official state policy – whereas Rühe was not – cannot be attributed to better or more persuasive arguments on the part of the American advocates of enlargement or less

[13] Background interviews, Federal Ministry of Defense; interview Kamp; Weisser (1999: 24–25).

American concern with NATO efficiency or Russian reactions. Rather, whereas US policy was pushed and backed by the highest political authority, Chancellor Kohl did not unequivocally support the initiative of his defense minister.

Rhetorical argumentation and entrapment in NATO

Like their Central and Eastern European counterparts, the advocates of NATO enlargement in the Alliance based their claims on the framing of NATO as a community organization and on its constitutive liberal identity, values, and norms. They presented the candidates for membership as legitimate members of the "family" of European democratic nations; they defined the rationale of NATO enlargement as the promotion and protection of democracy and liberal norms of international conduct; and they warned that a failure to enlarge would constitute a violation of the member states' obligations as community members. The rhetorical character of these arguments is indicated by two observations: first, the proponents tended to emphasize the normative aspect of their enlargement advocacy and to downplay their egoistic interests. Second, there are indications that they tailored their arguments to specific target groups.

The earliest piece of official enlargement advocacy, *German Defense Minister Rühe's speech* at the IISS, referred to both egoistic (geostrategic) and ideational motivations for enlargement. On the one hand, Rühe warned that "Germany alone cannot pay the bill for reforms in the East" and function "as a *cordon sanitaire* for the rest of Europe." On the other hand, he emphasized, in line with the arguments of the CEECs, the "shared values and common interests" of the Euro-Atlantic community. "It is this, not the presence of an existential threat that is the hub of the Alliance." He further urged that

> we must take full account of the vital security interests of our neighbours in the East and of the fact that these countries have always been members of the community of European nations. Now that democracy has prevailed in Central and Eastern Europe, we must work together to close the gap in prosperity and security that exists between Eastern and Western Europe. We must not disappoint people in the East. (Rühe 1993: 130, 133–34)

Later in the process, the egoistic security and financial interests were downplayed in the argumentation of Rühe and the defense ministry "because these arguments were problematic in the Alliance as well as *vis-à-vis* Russia."[14] Instead, they emphasized the value-based arguments of the

[14] Interview Federal Ministry of Defense.

IISS speech. In addition, Rühe argued that the democratic CEECs were entitled to membership according to the organizational rules stated in the North Atlantic Treaty. In their talks with other member states, Rühe and his collaborators even framed enlargement as an issue of "survival" for NATO: denying the CEECs their legitimate right to membership would destroy the alliance.[15]

Just as the German advocates downplayed their egoistic, strategic reasons for enlargement, *US proponents* have strongly rejected allegations of partisan domestic political considerations (Goldgeier 1999: 166). Rather, their argumentation mirrored that of the CEE governments. Strobe Talbott's August 1995 article in the *New York Review of Books* ("Why NATO should grow") set out the official rationale for enlargement based on the themes of "democratic community" and "promotion of liberal norms" that would be reiterated in the years to come (Talbott 1995: 27). First, "NATO should be open to the new democracies . . . that share common values, and that can advance the military and political goals of the Alliance," and, as Talbott would write later, "aspire and deserve to be part of the trans-Atlantic community" (Talbott 1997). President Clinton emotionally reinforced the "common values" theme by referring to President Havel and President Walesa as "men who put their lives on the line for freedom."[16] Second, the prospect of enlargement provides the CEECs "with additional incentives to strengthen their democratic and legal institutions" and "can also foster . . . a greater willingness to resolve disputes peacefully and contribute to peace-keeping operations" (Talbott 1995: 27). By contrast, the advocates discarded military or security reasons in the narrow sense as enlargement conditions. For instance, in his remarks to the Sejm (the Polish parliament) in July 1994, President Clinton affirmed "that expansion will not depend upon the appearance of a new threat in Europe."[17]

Moreover, the advocates of enlargement discredited criticism of enlargement by using *negative historical analogies*. In the same speech before the Sejm, Clinton declared "that we will not let the Iron Curtain be replaced with a veil of indifference" (*ibid.*). And they used American support for and NATO membership of Western European countries as a *positive historical analogy*. In his Detroit presidential campaign speech of October 1996, Clinton remarked that

[15] Interviews Federal Ministry of Defense; Wolf (1996: 206).

[16] "State of the Union Address by the President," 25 January 1994, <http://www.pub.whitehouse.gov/publications> (26 November 2000).

[17] "Remarks by the President to the Sejm," 7 July 1994, <http://www.pub.whitehouse.gov/publications> (26 November 2000). Clinton used the same wording during his visit to Budapest of that year (quoted in Goldgeier 1999: 88).

NATO defended the West by deterring aggression. Even more, through NATO, Western Europe became a source of stability instead of hostility. France and Germany moved from conflict to cooperation. Democracy took permanent root in countries where fascism once ruled. I came to office convinced that NATO can do for Europe's East what it did for Europe's West – prevent a return to local rivalries, strengthen democracy against future threats, and create the conditions for prosperity to flourish.[18]

The persuasive efforts and strategies of the US administration – linking the frames of "NATO as a democratic community" and "enlargement as the promotion of liberal norms" with appeals to intertemporal consistency – are nicely summarized in Clinton's speech before the Houses of Parliament in London, presumably strongholds of enlargement skepticism, in November 1995:[19]

Our cooperation with you through NATO, the sword and shield of democracy, can help the nations that once lay behind the Iron Curtain to become part of the new Europe. In the Cold War the alliance kept our nation secure, and bound the Western democracies together in common cause. It brought former adversaries together and gave them the confidence to look past ancient enmities. Now, NATO will grow and expand the circle of common purpose, first through its Partnership for Peace, which is already having a remarkable impact on the member countries; and then, as we agree, with the admissions of new democratic members. It will threaten no one. But it will give its new allies the confidence they need to consolidate their freedoms, build their economies, strengthen peace and become your partners for tomorrow.

Together with the rhetoric of the CEECs, this framing and justification of enlargement had the effect of *rhetorically entrapping the "brakemen"* in NATO. By presenting the policy of enlargement as a policy that was based on the fundamental values of NATO member states and on the membership rules of the Alliance, the proponents of enlargement made it *difficult for the "brakemen" to openly oppose this policy* without harming their credibility as community members.[20] First, they could not credibly question the values and norms on which the policy was based – that is, put forward an argument against the warrant – for this would have meant rejecting the very values and norms on which their own political legitimacy and authority rested, and unmasking NATO's official identity as

[18] "The Legacy of America's Leadership as We Enter the 21st Century. Address by President Clinton to the people of Detroit, Detroit, Michigan, October 22, 1996," <http://www.state.gov/www/regions/eur/102296clinton_detroit.html> (29 October 1998). Cf. Asmus (1996); Talbott (1995: 28).

[19] "Remarks by the President to the Houses of Parliament," 29 November 1995, <http://www.pub.whitehouse.gov/publications> (26 November 2000).

[20] This effect was strongly emphasized in my interviews with both proponents and skeptics (see, e.g., interview Kamp) of enlargement.

insincere. Second, it was difficult to deny the aptitude of the core candidates – that is, put forward an argument against the grounds – in light of the alliance rules. Whereas it would have been possible to call into question the liberal-democratic credentials of, say, the Meciar or Iliescu governments in Slovakia and Romania, the success in liberal-democratic transformation in the countries that were invited in 1997 was beyond dispute. Third, it was not promising to call into question the credibility of the "drivers" – that is, put forward an argument against the proponents. The moral authority of President Walesa and, even more so, President Havel was hard to undermine. Neither could the opponents of enlargement credibly question the commitment of the United States or Germany to the values and norms of the alliance. In the words of Stanley Sloan, a long-time observer of NATO affairs:

> Standing in the way of something that appeared to be logical in terms of the NATO Treaty and mandate I think would have been viewed as either a desire to maintain an old NATO that no longer was relevant or a lack of interest in the future of the alliance. Having the new democracies arguing so strongly on behalf of NATO and NATO membership, it would have been politically embarrassing for current members not to, in the end, take it very seriously, in spite of their concerns.[21]

As a result, the *French government* which purportedly criticized the push for enlargement vehemently behind the closed doors of the NATO Council, did not publicly reject the demands of the CEECs. The Central Europeans knew very well that France was opposed to NATO enlargement and began to criticize the French government in public. The French government, in turn, felt vulnerable to accusations of abandoning the CEECs as it had done in 1939, and fostering a "new Yalta." Moreover, it did not want to be identified in the CEE region as the spearhead of opposition to enlargement.[22] According to Paul Gallis (Congressional Research Service), moral pressure from Poland and other CEECs was more effective in silencing French opposition than any pressure from the United States.[23] Finally, at some point in the process, the French government realized that enlargement was irreversible and that it would be futile and too costly to continue to oppose it. If enlargement could not be prevented, "Why, then, give Eastern European countries the feeling that France alone wanted to keep them out of the club?" (Boniface 1997: 5; cf. Gallis 2001: 66). The effects of rhetorical action, however, did not go so far as to *convince* the French government, that is, to change its enlargement preferences. According to Boniface (1996: 182; 1997: 5), French

[21] Interview Sloan. [22] Interviews Gallis, Kamp. [23] Interview Gallis.

"reticence hardly gave way to enthusiasm" and "opposition continues to exist," but it was no longer expressed in public by French officials.

The same is true for Britain.[24] On the one hand, the British government was not convinced of the intrinsic value of NATO enlargement. As late as January 1996, Defense Secretary Michael Portillo admitted, "I don't see this as a great ambition of NATO to get bigger. What we are responding to is applications from other countries. We must take the time that is necessary to make wise decisions."[25] On the other hand, however, according to my interview partners, the Yalta analogy made a strong impact in Britain because Polish soldiers had fought for Britain in World War II and Britain was one of the powers responsible for "Yalta."[26]

Finally, a cable by the German ambassador to NATO, Hermann von Richthofen, that was written during the crucial decision-making period of fall 1994 and subsequently leaked to the press, provides insight into the shaming process. Von Richthofen complained that the US administration sent in-house studies on enlargement directly to the CEE governments without seeking the consent of the allies and that these studies were "being used to present the alliance with a *fait accompli* in the form of predetermined agreements, *non-compliance with which is bound to cause political damage*."[27] Whereas it might have been possible for the allies to slow down or water down a US initiative for rapid enlargement behind the doors of the North Atlantic Council, it was perceived to be too embarrassing to stop the initiative openly once it was out in public and known to the CEE governments.

Officially, NATO wanted to keep its enlargement options open as long as possible. As one member of NATO's international staff strongly involved in the drafting of the "Study on NATO enlargement" (1995) pointed out, it was never conceived as a rigid checklist but was carefully designed to eschew any automaticity and to preserve the primacy of political decisions by the heads of government. The allies did not want to produce any irresistible momentum.[28] According to this staff member, Paragraph 7 of the Study was the single most important one:

[24] See Dannreuther (1997: 78); Sharp (1997: 4); Taylor (1996); interviews British and German delegations to NATO.

[25] Quoted in Solomon (1998: 92). See also remarks by UK Ambassador John Goulden, quoted in Solomon (1998: 100–01).

[26] Some mentioned in addition that the British government feared that opposition to enlargement might drive Germany out of the alliance and damage the British special relationship with the United States.

[27] *SZ*, 1 December 1994; quoted according to Smith and Timmins (2000: 99), emphasis added.

[28] Interview member of NATO international staff.

Decisions on enlargement will be for NATO itself . . . There is no fixed or rigid list of criteria for inviting new member states to join the Alliance. Enlargement will be decided on a case-by-case basis and some nations may attain membership before others . . . Ultimately, Allies will decide by consensus whether to invite each new member to join according to their judgment of whether doing so will contribute to security and stability in the North Atlantic area at the time such a decision is to be made.

Yet three core features of the enlargement process helped to keep it on track and make progress toward the accession of the first CEE members: incrementalism, consistency constraints, and action-forcing events.

Incrementalism. Enlargement did not consist in a one-shot decision but in a sequence of small steps beginning with PfP in 1994. At the end of the year, NATO made the decision to go ahead with enlargement preparations and commissioned a study examining the principles and the "how" of enlargement without considering the "when" and the "who." The "Study on NATO Enlargement" was finished in September 1995. On the basis of the "Study," NATO then agreed to enter into bilateral "intensified dialogues" with its partners in 1996. At the end of the year, the "when" was decided in favor of 1999. Finally, in 1997, NATO made its decision concerning the "who."

At least until 1996, each of the intermediate decision steps was Janus-faced. On the one hand, they served as "substitute acts" for immediate enlargement. They bought time and were easier to accept for the enlargement skeptics among the member states because they implied that the decision was not imminent and created the impression that enlargement might not actually take place anytime soon. On the other hand, however, with each step in the process, NATO committed itself more concretely to enlargement. The proponents of enlargement made sure that this commitment was supported, at least verbally, by all member states and documented in the relevant communiqués. Finally, the substitute forms of cooperation also served to prepare NATO as well as the CEECs for eventual enlargement. As a result, it became increasingly difficult and costly (in terms of credibility and legitimacy) to stop the process.

For instance, already in the Partnership for Peace Invitation Document of January 1994, NATO reaffirmed its principal openness "as proved for in Article 10 of the Washington Treaty," and declared: "We expect and would welcome NATO expansion that would reach to democratic states to our East, as part of an evolutionary process, taking into account political and security developments in the whole of Europe" (NATO 1994a). Whereas the second part of this sentence was indeterminate enough for the reluctant member states to agree to a seemingly symbolic reaffirmation of NATO's constitutive rules, the first part established, for the first time, expansion as an official NATO goal.

It was subsequently used by the proponents of enlargement as evidence that NATO had put Eastern enlargement on track. First, when President Clinton visited Prague, in the immediate aftermath of the Brussels NATO summit of January 1994, he declared that "the question is no longer whether NATO will take on new members but when and how." This phrase had not been part of Clinton's prepared talking points but was added by Lake and his staff.[29] Second, whereas the skeptics within the US administration thought they could dismiss these statements as pure rhetoric, they were taken by the policy entrepreneurs as evidence of the president's commitment to enlargement and used to make the skeptics cooperate (Goldgeier 1999: 66, 69). Third, the abstract and ceremonial commitment of NATO to expansion in January 1994 was used by the CEECs to demand consistency. As one anonymous US official observed, "PfP was a non-policy to get everyone off the hook. It falls short of addressing a time-table and criteria. There is nothing behind it . . . But there is an opening through which some states will force NATO to let them come in" (quoted in Solomon 1998: 29).

Consistency constraints. The incremental enlargement process also gained momentum as a result of the consistency constraints produced by NATO's rhetorical commitments. First, these constraints limited the membership conditions NATO could legitimately impose on the candidates. Second, they helped the candidates keep up the moral pressure for enlargement.

NATO was *bound by the alliance norms and its official justification for NATO enlargement* in working out the details of the membership criteria. Having emphasized its identity as a community organization and deemphasized its function as a military alliance, NATO focused on the fulfillment of the political criteria of community membership rather than on military utility and efficiency. The alliance could not legitimately refuse to admit a state that was unable to provide net material and security benefits to the old alliance members as long as that state adhered to NATO's constitutive rules and was prepared to contribute to alliance activities according to its capabilities.

In its "Study on NATO Enlargement" as well as in the talks with the candidate countries, the political requirements – adherence to domestic and international liberal norms – proved to be the "hard criteria" for membership, whereas financial contributions and military power and efficiency played only a secondary role and were formulated in much "softer"

[29] Goldgeier (1999: 57); interview Kupchan.

language. NATO merely required "the ability of prospective members to contribute militarily to collective defence and to the Alliance's new missions" (NATO 1995: §75), but did not specify any quality or quantity of military contributions. NATO further demanded no more than financial contributions "based, in a general way, on 'ability to pay'" (§65), which was fairly limited in the case of the CEECs. As General Klaus Naumann – then chairman of the Military Committee of NATO – explained,

> Membership does not mean to have a free ride on defence. But this by no means implies that the new members have to embark on an ambitious armaments programme. NATO wishes to give the new members security so that they can concentrate on rebuilding their societies and economies which are the elements that stabilise democracies. . . . Enlargement remains . . . by and large a political process and I do not anticipate that military factors will weigh as the decisive factors in the Summit decision on which one or more nations will be offered NATO membership in the first wave. (Naumann 1997: 9–10)

The CEEC candidates, in turn, pursued a *two-pronged shaming strategy* exploiting the ambiguities of Partnership for Peace.[30] On the one hand, they took the vague promise of membership contained in PfP at face value and kept up the public, moral pressure on NATO in order to put this promise into action. In the drastic words of the Polish ambassador to the United States, Nicholas Rey, they sought to "embarrass the living daylights out of the United States and the West to gain admission to NATO" (quoted in Grayson 1999: 158). According to a member of a CEEC delegation to NATO, CEEC officials kept on "pestering NATO" with demands for membership "constantly, at all intergovernmental meetings at every level," implying that "we will make your life impossible if you don't admit us."[31] On the other hand, however, they were willing to make the most of PfP. According to one member of a CEEC delegation to NATO, the CEECs had no specific interest in PfP except as an instrument for advancing their membership aspirations: "Its beauty was self-differentiation" (1999), a basic principle of PfP, which allowed "partners to distinguish themselves by demonstrating their capabilities and their commitment with a view to possible NATO membership" (NATO 1995: §41). In sum, by keeping up the moral pressure and studiously fulfilling NATO's requirements, the CEECs hoped to maximize their chances for admission.

Action-forcing events. The enlargement process gained further momentum through two types of "action-forcing events" (Goldgeier 1999). On the one hand, NATO summits and the regular meetings of the North

[30] Interview member of CEEC Delegation to NATO.
[31] Interview member of CEEC Delegation to NATO.

Atlantic Council triggered initiatives and decisions. For instance, the 1994 NATO summit put pressure on the new US administration to demonstrate leadership and develop a NATO policy. The fiftieth anniversary of NATO in 1999 was a symbolic event that was well suited to admit the first members after the end of the Cold War. The regular meetings in between always served as occasions for the proponents of enlargement to call for the next step in the implementation of NATO enlargement.

On the other hand, visits to Central Europe served as action-forcing events. On these occasions, the leaders of Western countries stressed their satisfaction with the reforms in these countries, emphasized the community of values, and thus publicly committed themselves to the value foundation of the Western organizations. Moreover, they felt they had to address, and to be particularly reassuring on, the issue of NATO membership. In these situations, it would have been difficult for any opponent or skeptic to tell the CEEC officials to their face that he or she was not interested in enlargement. For instance, when NATO's January 1994 decision to launch PfP drew harsh criticism in the Central European capitals, "Americans were particularly sensitive to [the] charge [of Yalta II] as the Brussels summit was one part of a photo-opportunity filled road show for President Clinton that also included visuals in Prague and Moscow. The Central Europeans had to be placated if the pictures were not to be marred by political unpleasantness" (Latawski 1994: 69). In a similar vein, Jonathan Eyal describes the enlargement process in general as a story "of symbolic gestures made through 'photo-opportunities' which finally came back to haunt Western governments" (1997: 695).

Rhetorical action in US ratification

After the accession protocols with the three CEECs were signed, they had to be ratified by all member states. Apart from the fact that Turkey threatened to block NATO enlargement unless it was recognized as a candidate for membership in the EU, ratification was generally expected to be non-controversial once the US Senate had approved of enlargement. I will therefore focus on the US ratification process.

At first sight, it seemed that Senate ratification of NATO enlargement would not be in danger. NATO enlargement had not only been advocated by the Democratic administration but also pushed by the Republican majority in Congress. Moreover, Congressional legislation related to NATO enlargement had always attracted large majorities in favor. The administration, however, decided not to trust these signs and to hold back. It feared that the process might get caught in domestic, partisan politics or fall victim to post-Cold War isolationist tendencies. And it wanted a vote that would demonstrate broad support for enlargement with no strings attached.

In order to achieve these goals, the administration decided not to rely on existing bureaucratic structures but to create a special agency, the NATO Enlargement Ratification Office (NERO), to orchestrate the ratification campaign. NERO worked out the administration's strategy to address and deflect any concerns senators might have about NATO enlargement and reached out to the constituencies of the senators and to the major interest groups in society. The goal was to build up pressure from below in favor of enlargement and to prevent organized opposition against it. NERO's efforts were complemented by the US Committee to Expand NATO (USCEN). Bruce Jackson, a conservative Republican and a director of strategic planning at the Lockheed Martin Corporation, founded and presided over this non-profit organization, allegedly "to save the Clinton administration from defeat in the ratification debate."[32] The Committee united experienced national campaigners from both parties who were in favor of NATO enlargement for different reasons. It targeted mainly senators and elite opinion at Washington dinner parties. The activities of both organizations are most accurately described as rhetorical action, the strategic use of arguments to persuade various audiences to accept and support NATO enlargement.[33]

Generally, the *campaigners tailored their arguments to particular audiences* in order to address their most important concerns and to apply moral pressure and social influence where they were most vulnerable. The basic decision NERO had to make was whether to target the conservative or liberal critics of enlargement. After they had agreed that Republican support was more critical to success than that of the Democratic Left, and that Senator Jesse Helms was the crucial person to persuade, the argumentative strategy of the administration was refocused away from Wilsonian internationalism to fit the more conservative mind-set of leading Republicans. In addition to the previously dominant frame of NATO as a "community organization" and enlargement as "promotion of democracy," the enlargement proponents now also put a strong emphasis on NATO as an "organization of collective defense" and on its military effectiveness. A fact sheet released by NERO in February 1998 still argued that enlargement would "bolster stability and democracy in Central Europe" and "erase Stalin's artifical dividing line in Europe," but the top

32 Interview Jackson.

33 The activities of NERO and USCEN are described in Goldgeier (1999) and Grayson (1999). In addition, my findings are based on interviews with Bruce Jackson (USCEN) and Cameron Munter (NERO).

two reasons for enlargement listed in the sheet indicate the new emphasis on "strength":

Enlargement will make NATO stronger and better able to address Europe's security challenges. Europe has been a vital American security interest throughout this century. It remains so today. The addition of Poland, Hungary, and the Czech Republic to the Alliance will strengthen our common security [and] enhance NATO's ability to fulfill its core mission of collective defense . . .

Enlargement will strengthen NATO . . . These states will add over 200,000 troops to the Alliance as well as a willingness to contribute to the security of the surrounding region . . .. The military and strategic assets of these states will improve NATO's ability to carry out its collective defense and other missions.[34]

Moreover, at the Senate hearings, Secretary of State Albright sought to assure the senators that enlargement would not dilute NATO's military efficiency, that the NATO–Russia Founding Act would not give Russia a say in NATO's decision-making, and that the costs of enlargement would be small and shared fairly among the allies.[35]

Since they targeted an *American* audience in the ratification debate, the proponents also emphasized the *American* interest in enlargement, that is, they based their claim on a warrant that obviously would not have been effective in persuading the allies in the preceding intra-NATO debate. For instance, in his 1997 "State of the Union Address," President Clinton claimed that "when Europe is stable, prosperous, and at peace, America is more secure." "An expanded NATO is good for America."[36] Secretary of State Albright affirmed before the Senate Foreign Relations Committee that enlargement "can only be justified if it advances America's strategic interests" and then set out "to make the case that a larger NATO will serve our interests."[37] To be sure, the enlargement advocates of the Clinton administration did not present *other* grounds for enlargement than before, rather, their rhetorical move was to equate the community values and norms with the "American interest" and then to present the value-based

[34] "Top Ten Questions on NATO Enlargement. Fact Sheet Released by the NATO Enlargement Ratification Office, US Department of State, February 19, 1998," <http://www.state.gov/www/regions/eur/fs_980219_natoqanda.html> (26 November 2000).

[35] "Secretary of State Madeleine K. Albright, Statement on NATO Enlargement before the Senate Foreign Relations Committee, Washington, DC, February 24, 1998," <http://secretary.state.gov/www/statements/1998/980224.html> (29 October 1998). Cf. Goldgeier (1999: 124–28); Grayson (1999: 120).

[36] Quoted according to "The New Atlantic Community," <http://www.nato.int/usa/info/atlantic_community.htm> (28 November 2000).

[37] "Secretary of State Madeleine K. Albright, Statement on NATO Enlargement before the Senate Foreign Relations Committee, Washington, DC, February 24, 1998," <http://secretary.state.gov/www/statements/1998/980224.html> (29 October 1998).

reasons for enlargement as articulations of this American interest in order to persuade a national audience.

Further examples of target-specific argumentation abound. Veterans were assured of NATO's military efficiency. In order to put moral pressure on labor, President Walesa wrote a letter to labor leader John Sweeney reminding him of the labor union's long-standing support for the Solidarity movement. To assuage Jewish concerns about potential Polish anti-Semitism, it was argued that support for Polish democracy through NATO enlargement was the best prevention (see Goldgeier 1999: 134). USCEN warned Republicans who wanted to hit Clinton by opposing enlargement that "by doing so they would have hit Reagan."[38] The Committee further gained the backing of the Christian Coalition "on the basis that NATO enlargement broadened and strengthened the community of shared Western values" (Grayson 1999: 158). At every dinner organized by USCEN, the proponents of enlargement came from different communities in order to make sure that a variety of particular concerns was addressed and that NATO enlargement could not be identified as the "pet issue" of a specific interest-group.[39]

Besides these specific arguments targeted at particular audiences and their concerns, the general themes of the campaign were the community of values and the collective identity with the Central European candidates as well as the moral and historical obligation of the West to these countries. In Jackson's words, "what was selling was the values."[40] These themes were not only developed in the abstract but also personified. To demonstrate the existence of "community" and strengthen the idea of collective identity, the campaigners called up the Central European Embassies to send them good "communicators" (ibid.) and then brought along officials and intellectuals who "were cosmopolitan, well-dressed, and fluent in English" (Goldgeier 1999: 134). According to Jackson, officials like Bronislaw Geremek (Polish parliament) or Czech President Havel were the best witnesses and able to really persuade senators.[41] And in order to personify moral and historical obligations, the campaigners brought in Poles who had participated in the battle of Normandy and Americans who had fought together with them.[42]

According to the campaigners, the *strategic advantages of framing the issue as one of constitutive values, first principles, and high moral stakes* were manifold. First, in a strategy memorandum prepared by Jeremy Rosner, the head of NERO, one central element was to "define the issue in the broadest terms, and with the highest stakes" because "the broader the

[38] Interview Jackson. [39] Ibid. [40] Ibid. [41] Ibid.
[42] Interview Munter; Grayson (1999: 109–12).

lens and the higher the stakes, the stronger the President's hand on the Hill" (quoted in Grayson 1999: 114). The "pro-expansionists' continual stress on the West's moral obligation to Central Europe – for example, lawmakers responded to the theme of Poland's 'betrayal' at Yalta – cast the debate as one that transcended petty politics" (Grayson 1999: 125). This strategy made it difficult for Republican senators not only to deal with enlargement in a partisan perspective but also to attach other issues, like material gratifications for their states, to this "historic" decision.

Second, the "community of liberal values" theme was a unifying one. On the one hand, it could be tailored specifically in detail to address the concerns of many groups (see above the examples of the Jewish community, the Christian fundamentalists and organized labor). Most importantly, however, it was a theme that could not be identified with a single community (as, for instance, arguments that only appealed to Americans of Central European descent). Rather, it addressed the values that were constitutive for American society as a whole; or in Jackson's campaigner's way of putting it: by highlighting the value dimension of enlargement, "you could get all kinds of Americans to call their Senators."[43] "By stressing symbols and goals that unified rather than divided – 'democracy,' 'Yalta betrayal' 'integration of the West' – pro-expansionists rallied to their cause Big Business and Big Labor, Biden-style liberals and Helms-style conservatives, and Jewish and Polish groups" (Grayson 1999: 211). This use of the values warrant is also obvious in President Clinton's appeal to bipartisanship in the enlargement issue:

> From the start of my first administration, the United States worked to adapt NATO to new missions in a new century [and] to open its doors to Europe's new democracies . . . These are goals Republicans and Democrats alike share, building on the legacy of bipartisan leadership in Europe, begun after the war between President Truman, Secretary of State Marshall, and Senator Arthur Vandenberg.[44]

Finally, because the "community of liberal values" theme was basic to the collective identity of American society, it silenced any explicit opposition. To frame NATO as the military organization of a community of shared values and to describe its purpose as the defense of this community of values, was the "K.O. punch."[45] In sum, rhetorical action worked

[43] Interview Jackson.

[44] "Statement by the President on NATO Expansion. The White House, The Rose Garden, 14 May 1997," <http://www.nato.int/usa/president/s970514b.htm> (9 March 1999). Clinton referred back to this bipartisan tradition in a statement on senate approval of NATO enlargement on 30 April 1998, <http://www.nato.int/usa/president/s980430a.htm> (9 March 1999).

[45] Interview Jackson.

with skeptical senators and interest groups in basically the same way as it had with skeptical member governments.[46]

From first round to second

The second round of NATO enlargement initiated at the Prague Summit of November 2002 was not an automatic follow-up of the first one. It was not guided by an established rule-based routine or a normative consensus produced by the deliberations on the first round. Rather, it started from a constellation of individual preferences similar to the first round and depended on a similar set of factors and conditions to succeed. Indeed, after the accession of the first CEECs, many observers agreed that the second round would not come about easily.[47]

The "brakemen" of the first round remained enlargement skeptics ahead of the second round. The fact that *there has not been profound change in the enlargement preferences* demonstrates the rhetorical quality of the process. The British government, in particular, was strongly opposed to an early second round to be initiated at the Washington Summit in 1999 and continued to voice its traditional concern about NATO's coherence and efficiency (Larrabee 1999: 85; Peterson Ulrich 1999: 35). Moreover, Germany was not even the half-hearted enlargement advocate it had been in the mid-1990s. Already at the Madrid Summit of 1997, Germany had reservations about a too strong wording of the final communiqué on the membership prospects for Romania and Slovenia as well as the Baltic states. In 1999, it was as skeptical toward the Membership Action Plan (MAP) proposed by the US administration as the other European allies.[48] It was typical of the cautious and reluctant attitude of the German government that Chancellor Gerhard Schröder, during his visit to the Baltic states in June 2000, strongly supported their accession to the EU but did not commit himself to their admission to NATO. A few weeks later, Walter Kolbow, state secretary in the Federal Ministry of Defense, reaffirmed in Tallinn that Russian consent was needed before NATO could expand further.[49] According to the materialist analysis of enlargement preferences (chapter 8), the explanation for this more reticent position is straightforward: since 1999, Germany shares its Eastern borders with NATO members and has ceased to be a "frontline" state; furthermore, its main economic partners in the CEE region have become alliance members. As a consequence, Germany's fear about instability at

[46] Interview Sloan.
[47] Goldgeier (1999: 172); Grayson (1999: 212); interviews Jackson, Munter.
[48] Background interview Federal Ministry of Defense.
[49] *RFE/RL Newsline*, 8 June 2000 and 20 June 2000.

its eastern border was dispelled and its concern about Russia's reaction to enlargement became even greater than before.

Conversely, the *new members* that now constitute the Eastern "front-line" of NATO were the most openly in favor of a second round. For them, further enlargement would stabilize the region east of their borders at a price to be paid by the more wealthy and powerful member states. Moreover, following the pattern of the old members during the first round, they have focused on their immediate neighbors. Whereas Slovakia has been most important for the Czech Republic, the Baltic countries have been of primary interest to Poland.[50]

However, just as for the first wave, US leadership was crucial in launching the second enlargement round. During President Clinton's second term, enthusiasm for a second round had weakened considerably. First, the key policy entrepreneur for enlargement in the Clinton administration, National Security Adviser Lake, had already left his post before the first round was completed. Second, an amendment by Senator Warner proposing a three-year pause before future enlargement rounds came within ten votes of succeeding and signaled that Senate support for a quick follow-up to the 1999 enlargement was weak. Both factors contributed to the decision of the Clinton administration to leave future enlargement to the next administration. In this context, the Membership Action Plan – offered in 1999 to the remaining nine candidates – fulfilled a function similar to PfP five years earlier. It contributed to preparing the candidates for membership and signaled NATO's general commitment to the "open door" but offered no concrete perspective for and entitlement to accession.

On the other hand, just as in the first round, incrementalism, prior rhetorical commitments, and action-forcing events have created some momentum toward further enlargement. The promise of the Madrid Summit to keep the door open and the explicit reference to Romania, Slovenia, and the Baltic countries set a precedent which NATO could not ignore without the risk of losing credibility. Indeed, the "open door" has been invoked ceremonially at virtually every ministerial meeting of NATO – even if nothing else was done to implement this policy. Already at the Madrid Summit, NATO launched the "Enhanced Partnership for Peace" with "the aim of convincing the Madrid non-selectees that NATO's door remains open" (Peterson Ulrich 1999: 21). The Madrid promise to review the enlargement process at the next summit created a pressure on NATO "to deliver something" to the remaining candidates at the Washington Summit of 1999. As a result, MAP was established

[50] Interviews members of CEEC Delegations to NATO.

and "2002" was set as a date for reviewing NATO's enlargement project and as another action-forcing event. Finally, at each meeting with CEEC heads of state and government, NATO representatives have felt compelled to emphasize that NATO's door would remain open and to praise their progress on the way to membership.[51] Even British Defense Secretary George Robertson assured his Romanian and Bulgarian interlocutors in January 1999 that Britain backed their bid to join NATO – at a time when the UK was one of the most determined "brakemen" with regard to a new enlargement wave.[52]

Ronald Asmus and F. Stephen Larrabee, two authors of the early RAND study advocating Eastern enlargement, aptly characterized NATO's situation betweent the rounds. On the one hand, there was the widely supported but not officially articulated ("silenced") view that NATO should not expand to the Balkans or the Baltic states where member states had no vital strategic interests. On the other hand, however, "Opponents declare that enlargement to only a handful of states would be politically impossible to justify, could destabilize rejected countries, and in moral terms would amount to a 'new Yalta.' . . . Moreover, it would run counter to the rhetoric the alliance has employed up to now when making the case for enlargement" (Asmus and Larrabee 1998: 15).

Under these circumstances, the candidates continued to use the successful rhetorical strategies of the new member states. To give just a few examples, in February 1999, Romanian Defense Minister Victor Babiuc "warned that NATO might 'lose credibility' if no new countries are invited to join the organization"; President Emil Constantinescu continued the Romanian argumentative tradition by deploring NATO's discrimination among the CEECs and the "velvet curtain" that has replaced the "iron curtain" of the past, and warned that, in the absence of the West's support for reform, "the only alternative . . . is national communism."[53] Slovak Foreign Minister Eduard Kukan responded to US criticism of Slovak military combat readiness by saying that Slovak preparations were "unavoidably accompanied by technical problems, but we must not forget that the aim of the alliance is above all the protection and implementation of certain [democratic] values."[54]

Estonian President Lennart Meri "criticized what he considers the prevailing tendency to view NATO expansion in terms of the 'Cold War' rather than the new spirit of freedom,"[55] and Defense Minister Juri Luik urged NATO to "ignore Russian warnings against further expansion,"

[51] See, e.g., "NATO Secretary-General in Bulgaria," RFE/RL Newsline, 9 July 1999.
[52] RFE/RL Newsline 3, 13 and 14 January 1999. [53] Ibid., 8 February 1999.
[54] Ibid., 20 June 2000. [55] Ibid., 16 March 1999.

adding that "countries committed to defend common values should join together."[56] When Meri visited Washington in June 2000 to mark the fiftieth anniversary of the Baltic states' incorporation into the Soviet Union and to advocate a "big bang" second wave of enlargement in 2002 including all remaining applicants, he appealed to historical obligation and consistency by noting that the United States had formally refused to recognize Moscow's sovereignty over the three countries. "He said this gave Estonians, Latvians and Lithuanians the moral support to maintain their identities throughout Soviet domination and eventually to regain their independence."[57] Finally, the second round candidates appealed to NATO to honor their support in the Kosovo crisis by according membership.[58]

Again, the most elaborate plea for a second round came from Václav Havel, now president of a NATO member state, when he addressed the Bratislava Summit of candidates on 11 May 2001.[59] First, he invoked the "West" as a regional, "Euro-Atlantic" community of values. He claimed that the "European post-communist countries truly belong to the West," "that they were torn out of the Western community by force and that their natural place is within that community." Second, he tried to delegitimate consideration for Russia and to shame the reluctant member states into admitting the Baltic countries:

> I fail to understand why these three free countries should not be offered membership as soon as possible . . . Yielding to some geopolitical or geostrategic interests of Russia, or perhaps merely to its concern for its prestige, would be the worst thing that the alliance could do in this respect. It would amount to returning to the Ribbentrop-Molotov pact; . . . in short, to rededicating ourselves to the old principle of dividing the world and nations irregardless of their will.

Finally, he emphasized the symbolic meaning of choosing Prague as the venue for the 2002 summit and declared:

> I cannot imagine a NATO summit being held in Prague without extending an invitation for other applicants to join the alliance. Holding the meeting in Prague indirectly signifies a commitment to continued enlargement and is yet another proof that the "open doors" principle is not merely an empty phrase.

Within NATO, rhetorical entrapment, action-forcing events, and US entrepreneurship again worked together to initiate the second round. The action-forcing event was the Prague Summit of November 2002. Even

[56] Ibid., 24 June 1999.

[57] Andrew F. Tully, "Estonia's President Presses for 'Big Bang' NATO Expansion," RFE/RL Newsline, 19 June 2000.

[58] Michael Shafir, "The Kosova Crisis and the NATO Hopefuls," RFE/RL Newsline 3, 30 March 1999.

[59] Quoted according to RFE/RL Newsline, 15–17 May 2001.

though the Washington Summit of 1999 marked a pause in the process, the member states promised to review enlargement at their next summit. Throughout the 1999–2002 period, enlargement has been the most concrete agenda item for this summit. And as demonstrated by Havel's speech, the choice of Prague as the venue created additional expectations of an enlargement summit. Initially, NATO enlargement was not a priority issue for the new Republican administration under President George W. Bush; most of its leading representatives were on record as enlargement skeptics and did not share the strong Wilsonianism of the leading enlargement advocates in the Clinton administration (Kay 2001: 202–05). Nevertheless, as the Prague summit got closer, President Bush used a combined trip to NATO headquarters and Central and Eastern Europe to prepare the ground for the next round and adopted the enlargement rhetoric of his predecessor.

In May 2001, in a letter to a conference on Europe's new democracies held in Bratislava, President Bush wrote, "No part of Europe will be excluded because of history or geography."[60] At the North Atlantic Council meeting of 13 June, NATO decided that further countries would be invited to join at the Prague Summit. Two days later, in his speech at the Warsaw University Library, President Bush reaffirmed the liberal values and norms driving enlargement and referred to the negative historical analogies regularly invoked by the candidates:

> All of Europe's new democracies, from the Baltic to the Black Sea and all that lie between, should have the same chance for security and freedom and the same chance to join the institutions of Europe as Europe's old democracies have. . . . As we plan to enlarge NATO, no nation should be used as a pawn in the agendas of others. We will not trade away the fate of free European peoples. No more Munichs, no more Yaltas.

Furthermore, he framed enlargement as an issue of values instead of cost-benefit calculations and indicated a preference for an inclusive enlargement round:

> The United States will be prepared to make concrete historic decisions with its allies to advance NATO enlargement. . . . As we plan the Prague summit, we should not calculate how little we can get away with, but how much we can do to advance the cause of freedom. The expansion . . . of NATO has fulfilled NATO's promise, and that promise now leads eastward and southward, northward, and onward.[61]

60 "President Bush Letter to New Democracies Conference in Slovakia, 7 May 2001," available at <http://www.nato.int/usa/president/s20010507a.html> (24 September 2002). Bush repeated this message in a communication to the Bratislava meeting of the NATO candidates. See *NYT*, 12 May 2001.

61 *NYT* on the Web, 16 June 2001.

As in the first round, there was no open criticism of or opposition to this goal. Moreover, when it became clear that the Bush administration wanted to admit the Baltic states in line with NATO's liberal membership rules, even the more skeptical European allies (such as Britain, France and Germany) fell in line and publicly supported Baltic membership.[62] Finally, NATO's move toward the second round of enlargement was backed by domestic lobbying in the United States that mirrored the ratification campaign of 1997–98. It involved a network of experienced enlargement advocates – most prominently again the slightly renamed "US Committee on NATO" with at its head Bruce Jackson – who advised the representatives of the candidates on their performances and rhetorical strategies in the United States, sought to persuade the indifferent or skeptical segment of the public of the second round, and strove to build support for a smooth ratification in the Senate.[63]

Conclusion and alternative explanation

At the Madrid Summit of 1997 at which NATO decided to invite the Czech Republic, Hungary, and Poland to become alliance members, Czech Deputy Minister of Foreign Affairs Vondra approached a group of US senators participating at the summit on behalf of the Senate NATO Observer Group and asked them, "Why did you choose us?" The answer he got was, "We like you, we think you like us, and then you talked it into our heads for so long that we could not do otherwise."[64]

Has rhetoric been the key to NATO enlargement, as this little anecdote suggests? I tried to demonstrate in this chapter that the interpretation of enlargement decision-making as a process of effective rhetorical action is plausible. To begin with, enlargement decision-making was an elite process in a community environment in which neither public opinion nor organized interests played a crucial role. Under these circumstances, the rhetorical action hypothesis predicts that the argumentative process will be one of social influence.

Indeed, the decision-making process can be subdivided into five shaming episodes. First, prominent and respected Central European leaders persuaded US President Clinton of their countries' claim to join the Western alliance on the morally and emotionally charged occasion of the

[62] See, e.g., Taras Kuzio, "Western Support for Baltic Membership in NATO Increases," *RFE/RL Newsline*, 19 October 2001; "Germany More Favorable for Baltic NATO Entry – Paper," Baltic News Service, 2 February 2002.

[63] See, e.g., Pat Towell, "NATO Candidates Use Finesse, Persistence to Cultivate Hill Relationships," *Congressional Quarterly Weekly*, 9 February 2002.

[64] Interview member of CEEC Delegation to NATO.

dedication of the US Holocaust Museum. Second, the Clinton administration shamed the reluctant allies into acquiescing in enlargement by framing NATO as an organization of the Western liberal democratic community and presenting enlargement as the promotion and protection of its constitutive values and norms. Third, the CEECs induced NATO to stick to and put into action its membership commitment by appealing to its consistency and credibility and by fulfilling the legitimate membership conditions. Fourth, the Clinton administration rhetorically mobilized public opinion and put moral pressure on the US Senate to ratify the accession treaty. Finally, the second round of enlargement followed the same process pattern as the first round. The entire process has been characterized by the strategic use of arguments for self-defined goals and particular audiences. Thus, the observable features of the NATO decision-making process on enlargement – initial disagreement, rhetorical argumentation by the proponents and the silencing of unconvinced opponents – correspond to the expectations of the rhetorical action hypothesis. In sum, the rhetorical action hypothesis is capable of explaining how the rule-based policy of NATO enlargement came about despite a strategic constellation in which the member states generally held egoistic strategic preferences, the proponents of enlargement in NATO were few and without sufficient support in their own countries, and the CEECs did not possess the material bargaining power to induce NATO to embark on enlargement.

There is, however, an *alternative explanation* which attributes the decision-making process and its outcome to the use of *power*, not arguments, within the US administration and NATO (see, e.g., Goldgeier 1999; Rubinstein 1998).

For some stages in the decision-making process, the alternative explanation points out that persuasion was *unnecessary* or at least *easy* given the constellation of beliefs and preferences. First, the apparent persuasion of President Clinton by the CEEC leaders was an easy case given that Clinton had not opposed enlargement, held foreign policy beliefs that were in tune with the enlargement project, and could benefit from NATO enlargement in domestic politics. Second, in light of the consistent and broadly supported Congressional legislation in favor of NATO enlargement, Senate ratification was another easy case for rhetorical action.

In other cases, however, in which the constellation of preferences was truly adverse to enlargement, the outcome can or must be attributed to power. Initially, in 1994, threats based on presidential authority were necessary to bring the opponents of enlargement in the US administration into line. Once this was achieved, the acquiescence of the reluctant allies can be explained by US superior bargaining power within NATO. The United States is the preponderant military power in NATO on which the other member states ultimately rely for their own security and for pacifying their immediate neighborhood (such as on the territory of former Yugoslavia). In addition, NATO member states generally prefer a US-led alliance to alternative security arrangements dominated by one or more of the major European states. Under these circumstances, it is plausible that the NATO allies followed the US on enlargement out of strategic interest and did not need to be shamed into enlargement. Faced with the ultimate choice of either accepting enlargement based on the US timetable and selection of new members or risk reducing US interest in NATO and European security, the European allies went along with the Clinton administration.

Indeed, *US and NATO decision-making* on enlargement proceeded conspicuously *in parallel*. Each step toward enlargement was first discussed and decided by the US administration and then implemented at NATO level (see Goldgeier 1999: 119). First, it was the US administration that came up with the Partnership for Peace project in 1993. The thrust of this project – to deepen cooperation with the CEECs while avoiding a clear commitment to enlargement in the near future – reflected the state of the US interagency debate of the time.

Second, NATO was instructed to prepare a "Study on NATO Enlargement" in December of 1994, after the interagency debate had been decided in favor of fast-track enlargement. "Predictable grumbles followed from some Europeans about lack of consultation and American high-handedness" (Eyal 1997: 704). Even the German ambassador to NATO, Hermann von Richthofen, complained that there "was an abandonment at short notice, without any consultation, of the 'Russia First' concept" and that the United States was "applying political pressure for more speed in the expansion question, without paying attention to how this affects internal alliance positions on eastern policies."[65] When the study was finished in September 1995, it built on the criteria for membership developed by Secretary of Defense Perry (the "Perry Principles") in early 1995 (Goldgeier 1999: 95).

Third, it was not the North Atlantic Council but President Clinton in his 1996 reelection campaign who first announced that new members would be admitted at NATO's fiftieth anniversary in 1999. NATO agreed to this schedule in December of the same year. Fourth, the US administration came out publicly in June 1997 with its position to limit

[65] *SZ*, 1 December 1994; quoted according to Solomon (1998: 70). See also Broer (1997: 312); Goldgeier (1999: 85).

the number of new members to three. This corresponds to the decision NATO took at its Madrid Summit in July 1997 in spite of the preference of a majority of European member states for a more inclusive enlargement. Finally, it was the Bush administration that initiated the drive for a second enlargement round.

In this perspective, the couching of the US enlargement advocacy in "community" and "democracy" frames may have made it easier for the opponents to give in and comply. Community identity and alliance rules may have had a reinforcing, facilitating and smoothening effect on the decision-making process but they were not crucial in bringing about enlargement. In sum, the alleged effects of rhetorical action were either marginal or spurious.[66]

Yet, even though the process amply demonstrates that the United States was the main driver in NATO's enlargement decisions, it is not unambiguously clear whether US leadership on this issue was based on soft, normative or hard, material bargaining power. First, whereas there is abundant evidence of the US use of arguments based on the identity, values and norms of the Euro-Atlantic community, explicit bargaining was conspicuously absent from the process. At least, I could not find any evidence of US threats to the reluctant European allies in case they vetoed enlargement. Second, in the many cases of conflicting preferences between the United States and European allies, the allies are not usually silenced as effectively, and the United States does not get its way as easily, as in the enlargement cases. Moreover, as Risse-Kappen (1995a) showed in his analysis of alliance decisions in Cold War crises, the allies are indeed able to exert considerable influence on US foreign policy in spite of inferior material power – under the condition that their preferences and concerns are in line with alliance rules. Thus, we may still attribute successful US leadership on the enlargement issue to normative entrepreneurship and the congruence of US preferences and NATO rules; and we may explain the allies' acquiescence despite US unilateral decisions and political pressure by the fact that their preferences contradicted NATO rules and that they could not legitimately oppose the US moves.

In sum, however, the NATO case does not provide sufficiently strong evidence to exclude the "null hypothesis" that superior material bargaining power rather than norms (even if only strategically used in rhetorical arguments) brought about enlargement. To overcome this ambiguity or

[66] Note that this alternative explanation does not contradict my earlier rationalist analysis (chapter 2). It still remains difficult to see the vital security or economic US interest in, and the net US material benefits of NATO enlargement.

overdetermination, I need an enlargement case without the confounding influence of an intra-organizational material power structure in favor of pro-enlargement actors – a case in which the expected outcomes of shaming and bargaining are different.

EU enlargement is such a case. As I have argued earlier, the "drivers" within the EU did not have the bargaining power to make the reluctant majority of member states comply with Eastern enlargement. Whereas in the NATO case, the situation arguably ceased to be one of a "suasion game" once the US administration changed its preference on NATO enlargement in 1994, no such change of the game took place in the EU.

11 The decision to enlarge the EU

The EU case study will focus on the intergovernmental decision-making process. It is this process which proved most ambiguous theoretically in the NATO case, and it is here that the factor of interest – the structure of bargaining power – varies between NATO and the EU. This variation makes it possible to disentangle the potentially confounding effects of bargaining and shaming. The EU intergovernmental process is a hard case for rhetorical action because it needed to prevail against the material interests of most member states, a coalition with superior bargaining power, and an initial bargaining outcome (association) that was already put in treaty form and appeared to represent a stable equilibrium in light of the member state interests and power structure.

The chapter is divided into sections on "rhetorical commitment," "rhetorical argumentation" and "rhetorical entrapment" – the three main analytical phases in the shaming process. I seek to show that the Community has committed itself ideologically and institutionally to the integration of *all* European liberal societies since its beginnings and has continually confirmed this commitment in its rhetoric. This rhetorical commitment created the prerequisite for effective shaming during the enlargement process. The "drivers" among the member states as well as the associated CEE states regularly justified their demands for enlargement on the grounds of this commitment and of the community's collective identity. These arguments effectively silenced any open opposition to Eastern enlargement, allowed the "drivers" to make incremental progress with the preparation of Eastern enlargement, and ensured that enlargement policy has remained on track in spite of difficult practical problems and major distributional conflict. When rhetorical commitment was put to the test by rhetorical arguments, it led to rhetorical entrapment.

Rhetorical commitment

The *founding myth* of European integration starts with a definition of the European situation after World War II. Europe was devastated by the apocalypse of fascism and war, removed from the center of the international system, and threatened by Soviet communism. This development called for a break with the traditional pattern of European international politics: only a union of the democratic European states could create lasting peace, strengthen their domestic as well as international ability to resist totalitarianism, and make Europe's voice felt in international relations (see, e.g., Lipgens 1982: 44–57). European integration was thus based on a pan-European and liberal – both antifascist and anticommunist – ideology and identity.

The federalist congresses of the late 1940s appealed to *all* European peoples, rejected the division of the continent, and accepted integration in the West only as a core to be joined by the rest of Europe "in a free and peaceful community."[1] During the Cold War, however, the CEE peoples were represented only by politicians in exile, and the membership of the first organizations of the European international community – such as the CoE and the ECSC – had to be limited to west European countries.

When the European Economic Community was founded in 1958, the pan-European vocation was still present in the EEC Treaty in which the founding states declared themselves "determined to lay the foundations of an ever closer union among the *peoples of Europe*," called "upon *the other peoples of Europe who share their ideal* to join in their efforts,"[2] and accorded "any European state" the right to apply for membership (Article 237 EEC Treaty). It also surfaced regularly in ceremonial speeches of Community representatives, such as when, in 1968, the first president of the Commission Walter Hallstein invoked a "sentiment of pan-European solidarity"[3] or when, in 1980, French president François Mitterrand (who was to become the most prominent enlargement skeptic among the European leaders) stated, "What we term Europe is a second-best option which alone cannot represent all European history, geography and culture."[4] At the policy level, however, the pan-European orientation all but disappeared from the agenda. For all practical purposes, "Europe" came to be synonymous with "Western Europe."[5] In the détente period, problems of "peaceful coexistence" rather than community-building dominated the EC's approach to its Eastern neighbors. During the Cold War, to uphold

[1] Resolution of the Congress of Montreux of the Union Européenne des Fédéralistes (UEF), August 1947. This resolution and others are collected in Schwarz (1980).

[2] Preamble of the EEC Treaty (emphasis added).

[3] Speech before the "European Movement," 20 January 1968, quoted in Schwarz (1980: 415).

[4] Quoted in Sedelmeier (2000: 168)

[5] Even when the EC dealt with constitutive questions, as in its Copenhagen "Document on European Identity" of 1973 or in the 1975 Tindemans Report on European Union, its horizon did not reach beyond the "Nine."

their pan-European vocation was a cheap opportunity for the EC and its member states to reaffirm their allegiance to the community ideology. At the same time, however, this ceremonial reaffirmation created a public verbal commitment.[6]

The end of communist rule in Central Eastern Europe was greeted with enthusiasm in the West, since it signalled the victory of liberalism in the intersystemic conflict and promised to boost the West's international and domestic legitimacy. In line with their community values and their past rhetoric, the heads of state and government of the EC declared at their Strasbourg Summit of December 1989:

> The current changes and the prospects for development in Europe demonstrate the attraction which the political and economic model of Community Europe holds for many countries. The Community must live up to this expectation and these demands: its path lies not in withdrawal but in openness and cooperation, particularly with other European states . . . [T]he objective remains . . . that of overcoming the divisions of Europe.[7]

At the same time, however, the Community's pan-European ideology ceased to be a low-cost legitimacy-enhancing device because the new CEE governments demanded massive support for their transition to liberal democracy. More importantly, they interpreted "overcoming the divisions of Europe" as the promise of membership that was not explicitly mentioned in any of the EC's post-Cold War declarations.

Rhetorical argumentation

Both the CEECs and the Western supporters of Eastern enlargement counted on the impact of rhetorical action in order to achieve their goal. The CEE governments based their claims to membership on the standard of legitimacy of the European international community: European identity and unity, liberal democracy, and multilateralism. They invoked the Community's membership rules and took its ritualized pan-European liberal commitment at face value. They tried to demonstrate that these values and norms obliged the EU to admit them and that failing to do so would be an act of disloyalty to the ideational foundations of the European international community. They uncovered inconsistencies between the constitutive values and the past rhetoric and practice of the EC, on the one hand, and its current behavior toward the CEECs, on the other.

[6] On the role of Cold War "promises" in the enlargement process, see Fierke and Wiener (1999).

[7] European Council (1989). See the Conclusions of the Rhodes Summit (June 1988) and the Dublin Summit (June 1990) for similar statements.

In doing so, they have managed to "mobilize" the institutionalized identity and to make enlargement an issue of credibility. Finally, in order to advance their individual interest in accession, they have sought to show not only that they share the community values and adhere to its norms but also that they stand out from other candidates in this respect. Some typical examples for these rhetorical strategies follow. Obviously, they are highly similiar to those used to exert social influence on NATO.

Claiming European identity. The manipulation of collective identity consisted mainly in the claim by CEECs that they belonged not only to geographical Europe but also to the (informal) European international community. This claim was then linked to the formal membership rules of the EU in order to back up their demand for accession. CEE representatives argued that they traditionally shared the values and norms of European culture and civilization, were among the "founding fathers of a united Europe" (Stawarska 1999: 823), have always aspired to belong to the West during the years of the "artificial" division of the continent, and demonstrated their adherence to the European standard of legitimacy during and after the revolutions of 1989 to 1991 (cf. Neumann 1998).

The "return to Europe" became the battle cry of almost all CEE governments, including some improbable candidates. Not only did Hungarian Foreign Minister Geza Jeszenszky justify his country's official request for EU membership as the "return to this Community to which it has always belonged."[8] The Romanian ambassador to the EU, Constantin Ene, also asserted that "Romania has always been part of West European traditions" (1997), and even the head of a delegation of the Christian Democrat Union of Georgia visiting the European Parliament expressed the hope that Georgia would "return to Europe."[9] Finally, CEE state actors manipulated the European identity and the member states' ritualized commitment to "overcoming the divisions of Europe" in order to get a better deal in their negotiations with the EU. The Polish chief negotiator in the association negotiations with the EC, Olechowski, stated "that 'the technocratic approach' is not enough in these negotiations, which have a historic goal: give Europe back to Poland, and Poland back to Europe."[10] Correspondingly, the Western demonstration of its superior bargaining power in these negotations was denounced as an "economic Yalta" or a "new economic Iron Curtain" (Saryusz-Wolski 1994: 20–21).

Manipulating membership rules. Given that criteria of economic performance and the self-interest of most member states worked against Eastern enlargement, CEE governments pointed to the constitutive values and

[8] *Europe* 6204, 6 April 1994, 3.

[9] *Europe* 6065, 16 September 1993, 5.

[10] *Europe* 5456, 21 March 1991, 4.

norms of the Western community and the intentions "of the forefathers of European construction" or the "spirit of Jean Monnet" to support their demand that the member states base their decisions on *political criteria* and a *long-term collective interest* in European peace, stability, and welfare (see, e.g., Saryusz-Wolski 1994: 23; Stawarska 1999: 822).

On the basis of these criteria, CEE states have argued incessantly that they were, or would soon be, ready for Community membership. One representative of Hungary, for instance, claimed as early as 1990 that Hungary would be able to catch up with EC members within a few years; the Hungarian government has repeated this claim ever since.[11] In their race to membership, the candidate states furthermore sought to demonstrate their individual merits and achievements. The same Hungarian representative, for instance, pointed to Hungary's "pioneering role in the changes in central and Eastern Europe."[12] Reportedly, at a meeting with the EC in 1992, Hungary, Poland and Czechoslovakia "would have liked the joint statement to establish a clear distinction between themselves" and other candidates: "They do not believe Bulgaria and Romania are able to establish the same links with the EC as they do at this time."[13]

Moreover, CEE actors have sought to counter the Community strategy of postponing a concrete commitment to Eastern enlargement and its demands for the full adoption of the *acquis communautaire* ahead of accession. To achieve early admission and, possibly, water down the stringent admission criteria, they claimed that, in the absence of a concrete timetable for enlargement, the West risked the CEE societies turning away from liberal democracy. Full membership was the only means of securing liberal transformation and economic modernization.[14] The scenario for the decay of pan-European liberalism and the betrayal of the Community's founding myth was most dramatically outlined by Czech President Havel when he spoke about enlargement in 1994 before the European Parliament (EP):

> Anything else would be a return to the times when European order was not a work of consensus but of violence . . . For if the future European order does not emerge from a broadening European Union, based on the best European values and willing to defend and transmit them, the organization of the future could well fall into the hands of a cast of fools, fanatics, populists and demagogues waiting for their chance and determined to promote the worst European traditions.[15]

[11] See *FBIS-EEU-90–081*, 26 April 1990, 46; *SZ*, 30 March 1999, 45.
[12] *FBIS-EEU-90–081*, 26 April 1990, 46. [13] *Europe* 5827, 2 October 1992, 7.
[14] See *Europe* 6204, 6 April 1994, 3; Saryusz-Wolski (1994: 21). See the "democracy-in-danger" frame used in NATO.
[15] *Europe Documents* 1874, 16 March 1994, 3.

Exposing inconsistencies. The crucial element in the shaming strategy of the CEECs has been the argument that the EU failed to honor past commitments, match words and deeds and treat outside countries consistently. CEE state actors have repeatedly pointed to the *mismatch between political declarations* such as the Strasbourg declarations *and actual behavior*, such as protectionism and stalling tactics concerning enlargement (see, e.g., Saryusz-Wolski 1994: 23).

Moreover, CEE policy-makers compared the EU's Eastern policy with its *relations toward other non-members* and its behavior in *earlier rounds of enlargement* and demanded equal treatment. In the association negotiations, the Central European governments argued that a future membership clause had been included in the agreements with Greece and Turkey in the early 1960s. According to Peter van Ham, "in particular, the Spanish and Portuguese precedents have been major trump cards which could be played by the Central Europeans." Already in 1990, Hungarian Foreign Minister Kodolanyi argued that the Iberian enlargement "had been the result of a political settlement" (pushing economic problems into the background) and "that the Community would do the right thing now to take a similar decision" (Ham 1993: 196, 198). After the EU committed itself to Eastern enlargement, Central and Eastern Europeans still suspected that the Community would "discriminate against the transitional countries" by imposing *economic* conditions that would need to be met *prior to* accession negotiations, whereas "both Mediterranean enlargements were characterized mainly by political motives" and, in the earlier cases, the prerequisites of membership did not affect the beginning of negotiations (Inotai 1998: 159; see also Kumar 1996: 54).

These rhetorical strategies and arguments were echoed by the "drivers" among the member states and the Community institutions. In his 1990 Bruges speech, German President Richard von Weizsäcker first recalled the founding myth of European integration and the ideas of Schuman and Monnet and then appealed to the Europeans to follow their example under the present conditions. Like Havel, he argued that Europe was then and now faced with a clear set of alternatives: either integration or a return to nationalist and authoritarian destabilization.[16] Furthermore, the German government sought to deemphasize its self-interest in enlargement. Foreign Minister Kinkel, for instance, asserted that "we don't concern ourselves with these countries out of national interest. We feel we should take the opportunity to create a complete Europe."[17] British

[16] *Bulletin* 114, 27 September 1990, 1193–97.
[17] *Business Week*, 3 February 1997, 18.

Prime Minister Margaret Thatcher proposed in her 1990 Aspen speech that "the Community should declare unequivocally that it is ready to accept" the CEECs as members and based this claim on both identity and consistency: "We can't say in one breath that they are part of Europe, and in the next our European Community Club is so exclusive that we won't admit them."[18]

Furthermore, members of both the Commission and the EP invoked the standard of legitimacy against the egoistic preferences of member states. First, they emphasized *collective identity*. Already during his first visit to Prague after the "velvet revolution," Commissioner Frans Andriessen stated that "no one who has made the short journey between Brussels and Prague can be unaware that Czechoslovakia is our neighbour; its history is part of our history; its culture and traditions are part of our common European heritage."[19] Willy DeClerq, president of the EP's Committee on External Economic Relations, criticized those blocking the association negotiations by saying "he would have thought . . . that the Community was going to treat the countries concerned 'as European.'"[20]

Second, on various occasions, Commission President Jacques Delors publicly exposed the *inconsistency* between the Community's rhetoric and its practical behavior toward the CEECs. During the *coup d'état* in the Soviet Union in August 1991, he "launched a vigorous appeal to the Member States to show consistency between their actions and their statements."[21] "It's no good making fine speeches with a sob in your voice on Sunday and then on Monday opposing the trade concessions enabling those countries to sell their goods and improve their standards of living."[22] He further warned that "the perspective of the next enlargement is not clear" and that "it is not enough to send encouraging signals to the East European countries" (quoted in Torreblanca 1997: 14).

Third, the supporters of a generous policy toward the East have repeatedly addressed the *credibility* issue directly in order to exert pressure on the "brakemen." Commissioner Sir Leon Brittan affirmed that the blockage of association negotiations by some member states "could affect the Community's 'credibility.'"[23] Similarly, the EP requested in October 1993 that the European Council intervene to end the blockage of

[18] *FT*, 6 August 1990, 3. However, she could not help enlisting the CEECs for her own political agenda: "They have not thrown off central command and control in their own countries only to find them reincarnated in the European Community."

[19] *Europe* 5206, 3 March 1990, 5. [20] *Europe* 5566, 13 September 1991, 13.

[21] *Europe* 5549, 21 August 1991, 2.

[22] *FT*, 21 August 1991, cited in Ham (1993: 198).

[23] *Europe* 5564, 11 September 1991, 10.

the interim agreement with Bulgaria because "it is undermining the European Community's credibility in Eastern Europe."[24]

The most systematic and formal attempt to rhetorically commit the Community to Eastern enlargement can be found in the Commission's report, entitled *Europe and the Challenge of Enlargement*, to the Lisbon Summit in June 1992. Prepared shortly after the signing of the first Europe Agreements, it marked the starting point of the Commission's attempt to turn the association "equilibrium" into a concrete promise and preparation for enlargement. The Commission referred to the Community's vision of a pan-European liberal order as creating specific obligations in the current situation: "The Community has never been a closed club, and cannot now refuse the historic challenge to assume its continental responsibilities and contribute to the development of a political and economic order for the whole of Europe" (European Commission 1992: 2). By stating that for "the new democracies, Europe remains a powerful idea, signifying the fundamental values and aspirations which their peoples kept alive during long years of oppression," the report obviously meant to shame those members who betrayed "Europe" out of their narrow self-interest.[25]

Rhetorical entrapment

What indications do we have that these arguments stuck, and how did they influence the decision-making process? The evidence suggests that the rhetorical action of the "drivers" did not change the basic enlargement preferences of the "brakemen" but effectively prevented them from openly opposing the goal of enlargement and its gradual implementation. In other words, the "brakemen" became rhetorically entrapped.

For the enlargement skeptics, it was difficult to attack the pro-enlargement arguments on legitimate grounds. As in the NATO case, the "brakemen" could not and did not directly *dispute the warrant* of pan-European liberalism because this would have meant rejecting the very values and norms on which their membership in the Community rested, and admitting the hypocrisy of their former public pronouncements. They could and did, however, base their reticence on other, potentially competing values and norms of the Community's standard of legitimacy. The most widespread counterargument was that "widening" might dilute the achieved level of supranational integration and impede

[24] *Europe* 6094, 27 October 1993, 10.

[25] European Commission (1992: 8). On general Commission tactics (including "framing" and "co-optive justification") to generate support for controversial policies, see Tallberg (1999: 230–32).

its further "deepening." Since 1990, France had insisted that work on the Maastricht Treaty be completed before the Community dealt with the question of enlargement (see Deubner 1999: 96); and in September 1997 Belgium, France and Italy stated in a declaration to be included in the Amsterdam Treaty that a further institutional reinforcement of the EU was an "indispensable condition of enlargement."[26] However, whereas this norm-based counterargument might have compromised the British enlargement objectives, it was bound to fail with regard to Germany and the Commission, since both "drivers" had, from the start, demanded both widening and deepening (see, e.g., European Commission 1992: 2). Moreover, shaming obviously had already left its mark in 1997: the signatories of the declaration were careful to allay suspicion that they wanted to block enlargement, and other states hesitated to subscribe to the declaration because it might identify them as adversaries of CEE membership.[27]

The strategy of *destroying the proponents' credibility* was of limited use, too. As in the NATO case, the reputation of President Havel and President Walesa was beyond dispute. And, as I argued earlier, whereas it may have been possible to unmask the British advocacy of enlargement as an attempt to dilute the Community, the integrationist credentials of Germany or the Commission were difficult to undermine (cf. Torreblanca 2001: 151).

The strategy of arguing against the grounds, that is, of *calling into question the suitability of the warrant to support the claim*, would have consisted in denying that the candidate states truly belong to "Europe," adhere to the community rules and fulfill the accession criteria. This strategy was credible with regard to those countries that delayed reform or deviated from liberal transformation, and it was certainly correct that the CEECs were not ready for membership in the early 1990s. But the "drivers" never intended to admit authoritarian CEECs. Nor did they propose to begin accession negotiations immediately. Most importantly, the argument that these countries were not ready to join the EU did not preclude the EU from supporting their quest for membership early on. As Thatcher said in Aspen, "It will be some time before they are ready for membership; so we are offering them intermediate steps such as association agreements. But the option of eventual membership should be clearly, openly and generously on the table."[28] And the Commission argued that "we must respond with a strategy that is inspired not only by practical considerations of what is possible in the near future, but by a vision of the

[26] *Europe* 7058, 15–16 September 1997, 2.
[27] *Europe* 7058, 15–16 September 1997, 2.
[28] *FT*, 6 August 1990, 3.

wider Europe which must be imagined and prepared in the longer term" (European Commission 1992: 8).

Under these conditions, the "*drivers" were able to silence any explicit opposition to the general goal of Eastern enlargement* and to make the "brakemen" support the eventual membership of liberal-democratic CEECs – at least verbally. On various occasions, the "drivers" confronted the "brakemen" with the choice of either publicly subscribing to or openly opposing a step toward Eastern enlargement. These steps were usually small or involved no immediate costs or obligations, making them more difficult to reject. However, with each small or general public commitment, the credibility costs of non-enlargement rose.

According to the memoirs of President Mitterrand's advisor Hubert Védrine, Mitterrand considered himself in a morally awkward situation as long as he resisted the pressure of the German and the CEE governments to consent to enlargement. Therefore, the French government felt obliged – in its 1991 bilateral treaties with Czechoslovakia, Hungary and Poland – to declare its official support for their membership aspirations (Védrine 1996: 562; Deubner 1999: 96). Although France continued to obstruct any official commitment at the EC level, this move allowed Hungarian Prime Minister Antall to publicly raise French credibility stakes: "I have confidence in the French President's word."[29] Later, the French government felt compelled to soften its stance because it found itself accused of being the main obstacle to a pro-enlargement policy and feared losing the sympathies of the CEE societies (see Kreile 1997: 236; Sedelmeier 2000: 178).

Rhetorical entrapment worked similarly at the Community level. Here, the Commission, in particular Commissioner Andriessen and, later on, Commissioner van den Broek, played the most active role.[30] Already during the association negotiations the Commission went beyond its directives by inserting into the preamble of the draft agreements: "in the view of the parties these agreements will help this objective," that is, accession. None of the member states formally objected to this unauthorized move (see Sedelmeier 2000: 175). In a similar coup, the Commission's report to the Lisbon Summit "talked almost in a matter of fact way about accession as if it was already agreed as a common objective" (Mayhew 1998: 25). The report was largely ignored and certainly not endorsed by

[29] *Europe* 5568, 16–17 September 1991, 7.

[30] The Commission was not united either on its enlargement advocacy nor on its selection of candidates for the first round of negotiations but both Andriessen and van den Broek managed to gain a majority for their proposals in the college of Commissioners (Torreblanca 1997: 468; author's interview with member of Commissioner van den Broek's *Cabinet*, Brussels, 20 May 1999).

the member states at the Lisbon council (Torreblanca 2001: 306). But the fact that it was attached to the Conclusions of the Presidency accorded it official status as an EC policy document. At the following Edinburgh Summit (December 1992), it was again "barely discussed" and "hardly discussed by the Member States and certainly not disputed in the many hours of discussion and negotiation leading up to the" Copenhagen summit (Mayhew 1998: 25–27; cf. Sedelmeier and Wallace 2000: 440; Torreblanca 2001: 314–29). This peculiar process indicates that silencing was effective.

The rhetorical entrapment of the Community was aided by some of its formal *institutional features*. One was the Commission's proposal power. In elaborating the major documents defining the EU's policy toward Central and Eastern Europe, the Commission was able to frame the intergovernmental debate, to put the member states under pressure to make decisions, and to accelerate the process. Confronting the reluctant member states with a rationale for enlargement based on constitutive community rules severely limited their range of legitimate responses. The other institutional feature was the rotating European Council presidency which gives the country holding the presidency some discretion in the choice of, and the emphasis on, policy issues. In this perspective, it is small wonder that the most important initial steps toward enlargement were taken at the Copenhagen Council of 1993 and the Essen Council of 1994 when the presidency was held by Denmark and Germany respectively, two avowed supporters of a firm commitment to Eastern enlargement (cf. Sedelmeier and Wallace 2000: 440, 443). The Swedish government, another long-standing enlargement advocate, vowed to make enlargement, that is, the closing of as many chapters of the accession negotiations as possible, its first priority during its presidency in the first half of 2001 – although the Commission had originally planned to negotiate only a few chapters during this period.[31] And in the second half of 2002, it was the core ambition of the Danish presidency to ensure that enlargement came "full circle," that is to conclude the accession negotiations at the Copenhagen Summit of December 2002 – almost ten years after the Copenhagen Summit of June 1993 initiated the enlargement process.

As in NATO enlargement, *incremental lock-in* was another facilitating feature of the process. The Community's commitment to the objective of enlargement and the "brakemen's" consent in particular were certainly facilitated by the symbolic quality of this commitment at the beginning and by the expectation that it would not have to be honored for a long time. The membership perspective "was accepted only once it was

[31] *SZ*, 15 December 2000, 11.

ensured that it had no immediate political, institutional or budgetary consequences" (Torreblanca 2001: 329). However, each concession to the membership aspirations of the CEECs, from the very reluctant acknowledgment of these aspirations in the Europe Agreements by way of the general agreement to expansion at the Copenhagen summit to the pre-accession preparations decided in Essen, created a stronger commitment to enlargement – even if it was meant to be nothing but a tactical concession to accommodate the CEE states. Once the decision to enlarge was made, each further step toward preparing for the opening of accession negotiations was presented as a logical follow-up to this decision and difficult to oppose.

So the "brakemen" could only turn to the accompanying negotiations on treaty and policy reform in order to pursue their interests and retrieve some of their expected losses. This led to one of the most conspicuous features of the enlargement decision-making process; it is reflected in Alan Mayhew's observation at various European Council summits that "while there was little discussion or dispute on the common objective of accession, the minor trade concessions proved very difficult to negotiate" (Mayhew 1998: 164; cf. Torreblanca 2001: 316).

Furthermore, the enlargement process gathered momentum and was kept on track although the process of internal reform was delayed and has not met the objective of preparing the EU for the accession of the CEECs either at the intergovernmental conference leading to the Treaty of Amsterdam (1998), or at the 1999 Berlin Summit on Agenda 2000, or at the Nice Summit on institutional reform in 2000. According to Ulrich Sedelmeier and Helen Wallace, "The enlargement dimension set a considerable discipline on the positions of member governments." Despite sharp conflict about the budget and policy reform, the enlargement objective was not jeopardized because foreign ministers with their more "political" than "financial" perspective "shaped much of the final agreement" and because the member governments were mindful of "how much was at stake in Berlin in terms of the overall credibility of the EU" (2000: 453).

Even though the Nice summit failed to undertake the reforms deemed necessary to prevent the Union's decision-making processes from becoming too cumbersome after enlargement – the number of Commissioners was not reduced, the big leap toward qualified majority voting ended in a small step, and the new formula for calculating qualified majorities will probably make it more complicated to reach decisions than before – its results were greeted by member states and candidates alike as finally clearing the way for the first CEEC accessions. In May 2001, the Spanish government retreated from its threat to block the accession negotiations – if it did not obtain a guarantee for the continuation, after 2006, of its regional subsidies from the EU budget – after it had come under strong social pressure and had been isolated by the other member and candidate states, which accused Spain of lacking solidarity with the East and delaying enlargement out of narrow self-interest.[32] After the Irish rejected the Nice Treaty in June 2001, the referendum was repeated in October 2002, and, if they had voted against it a second time, the EU would have turned to contingency plans – like making the new voting rules part of the accession treaties – to be able to proceed with enlargement. Finally, after a long controversy, Chancellor Schröder and President Chirac cut a deal on the future of CAP spending just in time for the Brussels Summit of October 2002 to agree on the financial package to offer to future members and to assure that accession negotiations could be concluded until the end of the year. In sum, as a result of rhetorical entrapment, the policy of Eastern enlargement became safely locked in and effectively shielded from the "fallout" of the tough bargaining on internal reforms.

Finally, liberal membership norms and rhetorical action played an important role in *selecting* which CEE states would be considered for the accession negotiations. In order to justify its differentiation among these states, the Commission made every effort to present its "Opinions" on the applicants as an objective, neutral application of the norm-based Copenhagen criteria which left it "without a margin of political or geo-strategic assessment."[33] However, since the Commission's proposal strongly favored the central European countries, most northern and southern member states were not satisfied with it. In an effort to change this proposal, Denmark, Italy and Sweden did not bring up their national interests but acted rhetorically. They put forward an impartial argument that was both suitable to cover up the divergent subregional interests of their coalition and justifiable on the basis of the community's values and norms: the EU should open accession negotiations with all associated countries at the same time to avoid creating a new division of Europe and discouraging democratic consolidation in the "pre-ins." Minister Dini (Italy) pointed to "the responsibilities" of the EU to the "countries excluded," Minister Lund (Sweden) urged that they not "let the chance of establishing pan-European cooperation go by," and Minister Petersen (Denmark) warned "not to create new frontiers."[34] In the analysis of Lykke Friis, these arguments gained support, not because of Italian–Scandinavian bargaining power but because they "appeared more legitimate. These countries

[32] *SZ*, 18 May 2001, 8; 30 May 2001, 1 and 4.
[33] *Europe* 7019, 18 July 1997, 9. [34] *Europe* 7021, 22–23 July 1997, 8–9.

were . . . able to link their frame back to the core of the EU's self-image – the very fact that the EU has always presented itself as a club for all Europeans" (1998: 7).

In a parallel move, a great majority of the members of the EP, in their vote on the Oostlander/Barón Crespo report on 4 December 1997, declared themselves in favor of opening the formal accession process with all associated CEECs while beginning concrete negotiations with the five CEECs selected by the Commission. This vote is said to have made a considerable impression on the member states, and, in essence, anticipated their Luxembourg decision taken one week later (see Bailer and Schneider 2000: 31–32; Harris 1998: 7–9). As in the case of the Italian–Scandinavian coalition among the member states, this influence cannot be attributed to material or institutional bargaining power: Stefanie Bailer and Gerald Schneider argue that, although the EP has the formal power to reject any accession deal, it could not credibly threaten the member states with a veto given its strongly integrationist stance. It therefore had to turn to shaming: "When opting for an all-inclusive enlargement strategy, the EP could portray itself as 'an advocate of the Eastern European states' who considers long-term European interests much more than the more egoistic institutions of the EU." The EP was able to "embarrass the Commission and the European Council" because its vote signalled a "bipartisan" (Socialist–Christian Democrat) and transnational consensus of the MEPs and because the framing of the decision as one based on the Community's pan-European vocation rendered it difficult for the member state governments to openly argue against it (Bailer and Schneider 2000: 22).

Although the immediate consequences of the Luxembourg compromise were largely symbolic – after all, only the five most advanced CEECs entered into concrete accession negotiations with the EU in March 1998 – the official status of the "pre-ins" as participants in the accession process probably created some institutional momentum toward opening negotiations with them in the near future and against further differentiating between them. Indeed, only two years after the Luxembourg decision, the European Council meeting in Helsinki in December 1999 agreed to begin concrete accession talks with all of the five remaining CEEC associates.

Conclusion: solving the double puzzle of Eastern enlargement

The rhetorical mode of action is the causal link that solves the double puzzle of Eastern enlargement. Through a process of rhetorical action, the interest- and power-based initial outcome of the CEECs' association to the EU and NATO was turned into the rule-based outcome of "membership." In Part IV, I have tried to show both theoretically and empirically how a rule-based collective outcome is possible even if the individual actors pursue selfish and conflicting goals, the structure of bargaining power works against the rule-based outcome, and the rules cannot be enforced coercively. Drawing on the strategic conception of rules in sociological theory, I argued that, in a community environment, community members can be induced to refrain from pursuing their rule-violating preferences and to behave in a rule-conforming way when they are confronted with arguments that invoke their prior commitments, accuse them of acting inconsistently, call into question their reputation and credibility and thereby shame them into paying heed to their obligations as community members. In the empirical parts of the chapter, I showed how the mostly self-interested advocates of Eastern enlargement persistently appealed to the collective identity, the constitutive values and norms and the past promises and practices of the community organizations and how the no less self-interested "brakemen" in NATO and the EU were silenced – that is, they felt compelled to acquiesce in the enlargement initiatives of the "drivers" without being convinced of their claims.

The results of the NATO case study were inconclusive. Despite abundant evidence of rhetorical action, it could not be excluded that its presumed effects may have been spurious or redundant given superior US power in the alliance. By contrast, the EU case study demonstrated the effectiveness of rhetorical action in a decision-making situation in which the shamers held the inferior bargaining position. The pro-enlargement coalition – consisting of the CEECs, a group of those EU member governments that were most likely to benefit from enlargement and policy entrepreneurs in the Commission – strategically used arguments based on the identity, ideology, values, norms and past practice of the EU to shame the anti-enlargement coalition of member states, which expected individual net losses from Eastern enlargement and was in a position of superior bargaining power, into acquiescing in accession negotiations with CEEC aspirants. The EU study showed that rhetorical action can be effective without being backed by superior power and that it is capable of upsetting equilibrium institutional solutions which are not only based on structurally shaped constellations of material preferences and power but also formally institutionalized in international treaties (CEE association to the EU). It further demonstrated that the social influence effects of rhetorical action are strong enough to withstand the countervailing pressure by highly politicized and hard-nosed intergovernmental bargaining processes involving high material and institutional stakes (the internal negotiations on EU policy and institutional reform). To be sure, the EU case study does not prove that rhetorical action rather than US power paved the way to NATO enlargement. But it does show that rhetorical action is sufficient and capable of producing a rule-conforming decision in the absence of habitualization, internalization, a reasoned consensus or superior bargaining power.

Strategic action in the international community: concluding remarks

Material self-interest and power differentials shaped the reluctant Eastern enlargement process of NATO and the EU in its early stages. Ultimately, however, community rules and rhetorical action produced the decision of the major Western organizations to expand to Central and Eastern Europe.

Material self-interest in security and welfare goes a long way in explaining the initial preferences of the member and outsider states on the speed and scope of Eastern enlargement. By and large, the distribution of states' preferences mirrored the varying degree of interdependence with the countries of Central and Eastern Europe, and interdependence varied mainly with geographical proximity. Member states in the vicinity of Central and Eastern Europe regarded enlargement as an instrument to stabilize their neighborhood and to create favorable conditions for economic exchange. The other member states were more concerned about the effects of enlargement on the efficiency of the organizations and their own membership benefits and generally drew up a negative balance. By contrast, for the CEECs, EU and NATO membership promised to increase their security and welfare. At any rate, the enlargement preferences of the member and candidate states reflected self-interested calculations of individual, "national" utility, not collective identity, values or norms.

The *distribution of preferences and bargaining power* also accounts for the initial outcomes of the enlargement process: association to NATO through NACC and PfP and association to the EU through the Europe Agreements. Both institutional arrangements reflected the superior bargaining power of the enlargement skeptics in the organizations *vis-à-vis* the few supporters of enlargement and the power asymmetry between the Western organizations and the Eastern candidates. Both arrangements allowed the member states to deepen cooperation with the CEECs in fields of mutual interest such as peacekeeping and trade while denying them the decision-making power, the security guarantees and the material gratifications of full members.

Conversely, the distribution of preferences and power cannot explain why the EU moved from association to accession. And whereas the enlargement decisions of NATO may be attributed to US preponderance in the Alliance, the fact that the United States gave up its initial rejection of the CEECs' bid for membership and became the strongest advocate of enlargement among the allies cannot be explained by material conditions of the US international environment and US security interests. In sum, rationalist approaches to the analysis of international institutions help us to gain some theoretical insight into the (initial) process of Eastern enlargement but ultimately fail to explain the outcome, that is, the decision of the Western organizations to expand to Central and Eastern Europe.

By contrast, sociological institutionalism does provide a plausible explanation of the outcome of NATO and EU Eastern enlargement. In this perspective, NATO and the EU are organizations of the Western international community. Their *rules* are based on the liberal and post-national identity, values and norms of this community, and their organizational activities serve to defend and promote the community culture. The socialization of outsider states to the rules of the community is one of the central activities of the community organizations. When they have adopted the liberal community identity, values and norms, they are regarded as members of the Western community and entitled to join its organizations. In correspondence with this proposition, NATO and the EU embarked upon Eastern enlargement because its fundamental values and norms had spread to and taken root in Central and Eastern Europe since the Eastern European revolutions of 1989 and 1990. And although both organizations differ regarding the timing of enlargement and their choice of new members, both denied membership to CEECs that systematically violated the liberal community rules and selected, by and large, those CEECs that had made most progress in internalizing the Western community culture. In sum, the rule-based community approach to enlargement explains why NATO and the EU expand to the East in the absence of net material benefits for the organizations and in spite of unfavorable constellations of preferences and power among their member states.

However, *rhetorical action* was necessary to make the member states comply with the rules. The CEE governments and the proponents of enlargement among the member states used arguments based on the collective identity, values and norms of the Western community, and pointed to its past practice and promises, to demonstrate to the reluctant member states that they would act inconsistently, betray the values and norms to which they had committed themselves, and endanger their reputation as community members in good standing if they continued to oppose the expansion of the Western organizations. As a consequence, they shamed the skeptics and opponents into acquiescing in Eastern enlargement.

Is this a rationalist or a constructivist explanation? Does it support sociological institutionalism more than rationalist institutionalism? My analysis suggests that these questions are not only difficult to answer but also point in the wrong direction. Both theoretical perspectives help to explain Eastern enlargement but were found wanting in their "pure" form. Although rationalism explains most actor preferences and much of the initial bargaining process, it fails to account for the collective decision for enlargement. Sociological institutionalism, in turn, explains the outcome but not the input. The strategic conception of rules and the mechanism of rhetorical action are constructivist with regard to their social and idealist ontology but rationalist in their assumptions about the actors and their behavior. The problem with IR rationalist institutionalism was its materialist ontology, the problem with sociological institutionalism its assumption of normatively or cognitively appropriate action. Eastern enlargement was the result of social construction on the basis of intersubjective ideas but the construction was done by strategic actors using these ideas instrumentally for their selfish purposes.

My study suggests that one problem with the rationalist-constructivist debate in IR is the widespread exclusive "environment–agency link" on both sides, the combined assumptions of a materially structured international environment and a logic of consequences in IR rationalism and the combined assumption of a cultural international environment and a logic of appropriateness in IR constructivism. These exclusive links are not necessary for reasons of theoretical consistency (see, e.g., Finnemore and Sikkink 1998; Wendt 1999: 250). Moreover, they are empirically unconvincing generalizations.

On the one hand, and in line with constructivist assumptions, the international system has indeed become increasingly institutionalized – no matter whether the indicator is the number of international organizations, the number of their members, the range of issues covered by them or the frequency, density or intrusiveness of international political coordination and cooperation. And these activities and institutions not only serve to improve collective action for the benefit of each participating state but are also based on principles of legitimate statehood and state practice – most visibly in the field of human rights. To varying degrees, we can indeed describe the international system as a cultural and institutional environment for state action.

On the other hand, the growth of the international community has not superseded what one could call the primacy of subsystemic political influences. First, political actors on the international scene are generally politically socialized in national settings. Thus, even if they behave according to a logic of appropriateness, the norms they follow and the roles they enact will be primarily nationally defined. Second, it is in national settings that the most important and powerful political offices are allocated (e.g., through elections). Thus, political actors will usually be more responsive to domestic demands and pressures than to international norms and obligations. Third, for many political actors (such as in non-Western or weak states), internationally institutionalized values and norms do not reflect their own values and norms but the values and norms of other, powerful states. For all of these reasons, it is plausible to assume that political actors do not take the cultural values and norms institutionalized in their international environment for granted or internalize them but rather regard them as external constraints on, or resources for, domestically motivated action, and behave expediently and strategically toward them. In addition, the growth of a cultural and institutional environment of state action has not been accompanied by a shift toward centralized authority or coercive rule enforcement. Horizontal coordination and cooperation as well as decentralized enforcement remain the hallmark of international politics. If these empirical observations are valid, the "hybrid" environment–agency link of strategic action in a community environment put forward in this book promises to be a relevant approach to understanding contemporary international politics.

Moreover, this perspective and my explanation of Eastern enlargement offer a possibility of theoretical synthesis in the rationalist-constructivist debate. This synthesis works through "sequencing" rationalist and constructivist explanations and through specifying "domains of application" for effective rhetorical action (Jupille, Caporaso and Checkel 2003; Schimmelfennig 2003).

Sequencing. As one way of sequencing rationalist and constructivist explanations of international outcomes, Legro (1996) suggested a variation of the standard rationalist "international cooperation two-step" of preference formation and international interaction, according to which the first step – preference formation – is explained by domestic organizational culture instead of systemic material structure. "Strategic action in a community environment" also assumes a mixed two-step – but in reversed order. That is, a "rationalist" stage of preference formation is followed by a "constructivist" stage of international interaction in which organizational culture shapes the collective outcome. In the first step, community actors develop individual preferences on a policy issue resulting from individual cost-benefit analyses and based, for instance, on their position in the issue-area structure, their internal, domestic configurations of power and interest and their information. In the second step, the community identity, values, and norms are brought in by actors who use them argumentatively in order to legitimize their preferences and to increase their bargaining power in policy-making. These collective ideas are assumed to affect the interaction outcome by strengthening those actors that pursue policy goals in line with the community institutions and by constraining actors with illegitimate or less legitimate preferences. Whereas I contend that social and moral influence based on the community identity and its constitutive values and norms can be sufficiently strong to make "deviant" members refrain from pursuing illegitimate policy goals, I do not suggest that it will change their policy preferences. That is, in the next round of policy-making on the same issue or a related issue, their preferences are unlikely to be more "appropriate" then before.

Domains of application. In general terms, the applicability of the argument developed here and the presence and effectiveness of rhetorical action and shaming depend on the existence and strength of a community environment and its two core characteristics: a common ethos and high interaction density. The common ethos comprises the constitutive values and norms that define the collective identity of the community and its standard of legitimacy. It defines the argumentative grounds and warrants used by the actors in their arguments. Without such a common ethos, there would not be any need to engage in rhetorical action and the quest for legitimacy, and arguments based on the culture of the community would fail to have a persuasive effect on the audience. High interaction density is necessary for the process and social constraints on rhetorical action. The "information game," the detection of manipulative and inconsistent frames, arguments, and performances, and the concern about "face" and image work the better, the more frequent, the more long-term, and the more direct and personal interactions are. In the absence of a tightly knit community, there is a high incentive for an opportunistic or merely ceremonial use of the common ethos, and shaming will be less effective.

Furthermore, I expect community effects to vary across policy issues given the same degree of community. I propose four hypotheses based on issue-conditions of "constitutiveness," legitimacy, resonance and publicity.

(1) *The more closely an issue is related to the constitutive values and norms of the community, the stronger the community affects policy outcomes.* Obviously, the more constitutive a policy issue is or the more it involves fundamental questions of community purpose, the easier it is for interested actors to bring in questions of legitimacy and to frame the issue as an issue of

community identity that cannot be left to the interplay of self-interest and bargaining power.

(2) *The more consistent and determinate the pertinent community values and norms, the stronger the community effects on policy outcomes.* Even among issues that are constitutive or can be linked to constitutive issues, community effects may vary according to the values and norms in question. According to Thomas Franck, the degree to which an international norm "will exert a strong pull on states to comply" depends on four properties: "determinacy," that is, the transparency or textual clarity of the norm; "symbolic validation," that is, the ritual and pedigree conferring legitimacy upon the norm; "coherence," that is, "the degree to which a rule is applied coherently in practice"; and "adherence" to a norm hierarchy (Franck 1990: 49, 142). To the extent that the relevant community value or norm possesses these qualities, it becomes difficult for the shamed member to rhetorically circumvent its practical implications (cf. also Shannon 2000: 294).

(3) *The closer the match between national and community values and norms regarding an issue, the stronger the community effects on policy outcomes.* This is the condition of "domestic salience," a major explanatory factor in studies of the domestic impact of international norms (see Checkel 1997; 1999; Cortell and Davis 1996; 2000). Here, I suggest, however, that those community values and norms that reflect or match domestic ones will resonate more strongly with state actors when appealed to in the shaming process.

(4) *The more public the decision-making process, the stronger the community effects on its outcomes.* Publicity will increase the embarrassment and shame of non-compliant actors.

In this perspective, "Eastern enlargement" has been an "easy case" for effective community constraints on strategic state actors. Not only is the Western international community founded on a common liberal-democratic and pan-European ethos, its organizations also probably have the highest interaction density of all international organizations. Moreover, membership is a constitutive issue in any social group and organization, and in both the EU and NATO it was directly linked in a highly public process to the principles of human rights and democracy which fulfill the criteria of legitimacy to a high degree and are generally shared by the member states and their representatives. For these reasons, the Eastern enlargement of NATO and the EU was a useful case to establish that rhetorical action *can* produce compliance in the absence of deep internalization and in the face of adverse preference and power constellations. In order to test the argument further, however, it would be useful to analyze cases in which one or more of the conditions of strong community effects are relaxed or absent.

Finally, it should not be forgotten that the fundamental reasons for engaging in theoretical debates in IR are not metatheoretical but political. Ultimately the debate is (or, at least, should be) about the conditions of normative international order. The rigid environment-agency links in IR rationalism and constructivism lead to an overly pessimistic analysis of the possibility of such an order. Rationalism typically expects that a normative international order is just an epiphenomenon of power- or interest-based international cooperation. It will only be upheld if it is enforced by a hegemon or self-enforcing on the basis of individual interests. Constructivism postulates that a normative international order is possible in the absence of such a functional underpinning. But then it requires internalization and norm-regulated, "appropriate" behavior on the part of the international actors. The coincidence of morality and utility is as demanding a prerequisite as the internalization of international norms and rules. The strategic conception of rules and the story of Eastern enlargement draw a more optimistic picture. Under the condition of international community, international normative order does not have to wait for deep socialization or favorable interest constellations. As a result of rhetorical action and the constraints under which it operates, it also works among self-interested and strategic actors and in adverse constellations of material preferences and power.

Appendix Interviews (NATO decision-making study)

1 Washington, DC, 19 February – 5 March 1999

Ian Brzezinski, Office of Senator William V. Roth, Jr. (Delaware)
Paul E. Gallis, Section Head, Europe/Middle East/Africa, Congressional Research Service
James Goldgeier, George Washington University
Bruce Pitcairn Jackson, President, US Committee on NATO Enlargement
Charles Kupchan, Council on Foreign Relations
Cameron Munter, Office of the Counselor, Department of State
Stanley Sloan, Senior Specialist, Congressional Research Service
Stephen Szabo, Paul H. Nitze School of Advanced International Studies (SAIS), Johns Hopkins University

2 Bonn, 27–28 April 1999

Rafael Biermann, Planning Staff, Federal Ministry of Defense
Karl-Heinz Kamp, Konrad Adenauer Foundation
Heinrich Rentmeister, Federal Ministry of Defense

3 Brussels, 17–21 May 1999

Eitvydas Bajarunas, Lithuanian Mission to NATO, counsellor
Chris Donnelly, special adviser to the Secretary-General, NATO
Katerina Fialkova, counsellor, Czech Delegation to NATO
Isabelle François, NATO, Defense Planning and Operations Division
Armin Hasenpusch, Military Delegation of the Federal Republic of Germany to NATO
George Katsirdakis, NATO, deputy director, Defense Planning and Operations Division
R.P. Kirby, NATO, head, Euro-Atlantic Partnership & Cooperation Section, Political Affairs Division

Ivan Korcok, counsellor, deputy head of mission, Mission of the Slovak Republic to NATO
David Powell, UK Delegation to NATO, political counsellor
Robert Pszczel, Polish Delegation to NATO
Gheorghe Rotaru, Romanian Military Mission to NATO
Istvan Szabo, Hungarian Delegation to NATO
András Simonyi, ambassador, head of the Mission of the Republic of Hungary to NATO

References

Abbott, Kenneth W. and Snidal, Duncan 1998, Why States Act Through Formal International Organizations, *Journal of Conflict Resolution* 42: 3–32.

Adler, Emanuel 1997a, Seizing the Middle Ground. Constructivism in World Politics, *European Journal of International Relations* 3: 319–63.

1997b, Imagined (Security) Communities: Cognitive Regions in International Relations, *Millennium* 26: 249–77.

Adler, Emanuel and Barnett, Michael N. 1996, Governing Anarchy: A Research Agenda for the Study of Security Communities, *Ethics and International Affairs* 10: 63–98.

Alamir, Fouzieh Melanie and Pradetto, August 1998, Identitätssuche als Movens der Sicherheitspolitik. Die NATO-Osterweiterungsdebatten im Lichte der Herausbildung neuer Identitäten im postkommunistischen Ostmitteleuropa und in der Allianz, *Osteuropa* 48: 134–47.

Alexander, Jeffrey C. and Giesen, Bernhard 1987, From Reduction to Linkage: The Long View of the Micro–Macro Debate, in Jeffrey C. Alexander *et al.* (eds.), *The Micro-Macro Link*, Berkeley: University of California Press, pp. 1–42.

Allison, Paul D. 1984, *Event History Analysis. Regression for Longitudinal Event Data* (QASS 46), Newbury Park: Sage.

Ambrus-Lakatos, Lorand and Schaffer, Mark E. (eds.) 1996, *Coming to Terms with Accession* (Forum Report of the Economic Policy Initiative 2), London: CEPR and Institute for EastWest Studies.

Anderson, Benedict 1991, *Imagined Communities. Reflections on the Origins and Spread of Nationalism*, 2nd ed., London: Verso.

Asmus, Ronald D. 1996, Stop Fussing About NATO Enlargement and Get on With it, *International Herald Tribune*, 9 December, p. 8.

1997, NATO's Double Enlargement: New Tasks, New Members, in Clemens (ed.), 1997a, pp. 61–86.

Asmus, Ronald D. and Larrabee, F. Stephen 1998, NATO and the Have-Nots. Reassurance after Enlargement, *Foreign Affairs* 75: 13–20.

Bach, Christian F., Frandsen, Søren E. and Jensen, Hans G. 2000, Agricultural and Economy-Wide Effects of European Enlargement: Modelling the Common Agricultural Policy, *Journal of Agricultural Economics* 51: 162–80.

Bailer, Stefanie and Schneider, Gerald 2000, The Power of Legislative Hot Air: Informal Rules and the Enlargement Debate in the European Parliament, *Journal of Legislative Studies* 6: 19–44.

Bajarunas, Eitvydas 1995, A View From Lithuania, in Jeffrey Simon (ed.), *NATO Enlargement: Opinions and Options*, Washington, DC: National Defense University Press, pp. 101–20.

Baldwin, David A. (ed.) 1993, *Neorealism and Neoliberalism. The Contemporary Debate*, New York: Columbia University Press.

Baldwin, Richard E. 1994, *Towards an Integrated Europe*, London: CEPR.

1995a, Osterweiterung der Europäischen Union, *Internationale Politik* 50(6): 27–35.

1995b, The Eastern Enlargement of the European Union, *European Economic Review* 39: 474–81.

Baldwin, Richard E., François, Joseph F. and Portes, Richard 1997, The Costs and Benefits of Eastern Enlargement: The Impact on the EU and Central Europe, *Economic Policy* 24: 125–76.

Ball, Christopher L. 1998, Nattering NATO Enlargement? Reasons Why Expansion May Be a Good Thing, *Review of International Studies* 24: 43–67.

Bardi, Luciano 1996, Italy and EU Enlargement, in Kaiser and Brüning (eds.), pp. 155–66.

Barnett, Michael 1996, Identity and Alliances in the Middle East, in Katzenstein (ed.), pp. 400–47.

Barnett, Michael N. and Finnemore, Martha 1999, The Politics, Power, and Pathologies of International Organizations, *International Organization* 53: 699–732.

Bebler, Anton 1999, Slovenia and NATO Enlargement, *International Journal* 55: 125–36.

Beck, Nathaniel, Katz, Jonathan and Tucker, Richard 1998, Taking Time Seriously in Binary Time-Series-Cross-Sectional Analysis, *American Journal of Political Science* 42: 1260–88.

Becker, Peter 1998, Der Nutzen der Osterweiterung für die Europäische Union, *Integration* 21: 225–37.

Bedarff, Hildegard and Schürmann, Bernd 1998, *NATO und EU aus der Perspektive Ostmitteleuropas: Meinungsbilder der Eliten in Polen, der Tschechischen Republik, Estland und Lettland*, Münster: LIT Verlag.

Berk, Ulrich 1979, *Konstruktive Argumentationstheorie*, Stuttgart–Bad Cannstatt: Frommann-Holzboog.

Bernauer, Thomas 1995, Full Membership or Full Club? Expansion of NATO and the Future Security Organization of Europe, in Schneider, Weitsman and Bernauer (eds.), pp. 173–91.

Billig, Michael 1991, *Ideology and Opinions. Studies in Rhetorical Psychology*, London: Sage.

Bleses, Peter, Offe, Claus and Peter, Edgar 1997, Öffentliche Rechtfertigung auf dem parlamentarischen "Wissensmarkt" – Argumentstypen und Rechtfertigungsstrategien in sozialpolitischen Bundestagsdebatten, *Politische Vierteljahresschrift* 38: 498–529.

Boniface, Pascal 1996, NATO's Enlargement, France's Dilemma, in Haglund (ed.), pp. 181–96.

1997, *The NATO Debate in France* (Conference: NATO Enlargement: The National Debates over Ratification), Brussels: NATO, Academic Forum (http://www.nato.int/acad/conf/enlarg97).

Bowers, John Waite and Ochs, Donovan J. 1971, *The Rhetoric of Agitation and Control*, Reading, MA: Addison-Wesley.

Box-Steffensmeier, Janet M. and Jones, Bradford S. 1997, Time Is of the Essence: Event History Models in Political Science, *American Journal of Political Science* 41: 1414–61.

Branaman, Ann 1997, Goffman's Social Theory, in Charles Lemert and Ann Branaman (eds.), *The Goffman Reader*, Malden, MA: Blackwell, pp. xlv–lxxxii.

Brenner, Michael 1995, The Multilateral Moment, in Michael Brenner (ed.), *Multilateralism and Western Strategy*, Basingstoke: Macmillan Press, pp. 1–41.

Brinkley, Douglas 1997, Democratic Enlargement: The Clinton Doctrine, *Foreign Policy* 106: 111–27.

Broer, Michael 1997, Die Entwicklung der Politik der NATO zur Osterweiterung, in Pradetto (ed.), pp. 289–329.

Brown, Michael E. 1995, The Flawed Logic of NATO Expansion, *Survival* 37: 34–52.

Buchanan, James M. 1965, An Economic Theory of Clubs, *Economica* 32 (125): 1–14.

Bungs, Dzintra 1998, *The Baltic States: Problems and Prospects of Membership in the European Union*, Baden-Baden: Nomos.

Burda, Michael 1998, Les conséquences de l'élargissement de l'Union européenne sur les marchés du travail des PECO, *Problèmes économiques* 2593: 19–27.

Burns, Thomas Jerome 1999, Rhetoric as a Framework for Analyzing Cultural Constraint and Change, *Current Perspectives in Social Theory* 19: 165–85.

Busby, Josh 2002, *Listen! Pay Attention! Transnational Social Movements, Communicative Action and Global Governance* (Paper, Critical Perspectives on Global Governance Conference), Amerang, Germany, November 2002.

Buzan, Barry 1993, From International System to International Society. Structural Realism and Regime Theory Meet the English School, *International Organization* 47: 327–52.

Calleo, David 1998, Die Osterweiterung der NATO als Problem für die Sicherheit in Europa, *Aussenpolitik* 49: 27–31.

Campbell, J. L. 1992, An Applied Relevance Theory of the Making and Understanding of Rhetorical Arguments, *Language & Communication* 12: 145–55.

Carpenter, Ted Galen 1997, Wishful Thinking and Strategic Evasions: The Campaign for NATO Enlargement, in Clemens (ed.), pp. 162–80.

Cederman, Lars-Erik 2001, Political Boundaries and Identity Tradeoffs, in Lars-Erik Cederman (ed.), *Constructing Europe's Identity. The External Dimension*, Boulder, CO: Lynne Rienner, pp. 1–32.

Checkel, Jeffrey 1997: International Norms and Domestic Politics: Bridging the Rationalist-Constructivist Divide, *European Journal of International Relations* 3: 473–95.

1999, Norms, Institutions, and National Identity in Contemporary Europe, *International Studies Quarterly* 43: 83–114.

Cialdini, Robert B. and Trost, Melanie R. 1998, Social Influence: Social Norms, Conformity and Compliance, in D. Gilbert, S. Fiske, and G. Lindzey (eds.), *The Handbook of Social Psychology*, vol. II, New York: McGraw-Hill, 4th ed., pp. 151–85.

Claude, Inis L., Jr. 1966, Collective Legitimization as a Political Function of the United Nations, *International Organization* 20: 367–79.

Clemens, Clay (ed.) 1997a, *NATO and the Quest for Post-Cold War Security*, Basingstoke: Macmillan.

1997b, Political Options and Obstacles, in Clemens (ed.), pp. 183–206.

1999, The Strategic and Political Consequences of NATO Enlargement, in Sperling (ed.), pp. 139–59.

Cohen, Stanley 1996, Government Responses to Human Rights Reports: Claims, Denials, Counterclaims, *Human Rights Quarterly* 18: 517–43.

Cornes, Richard and Sandler, Todd 1986, *The Theory of Externalities, Public Goods, and Club Goods*, Cambridge: Cambridge University Press.

Cortell, Andrew and Davis, James 1996, How Do International Institutions Matter? The Domestic Impact of International Rules and Norms, *International Studies Quarterly* 40: 451–78.

Cortell, Andrew P. and Davis, James W., Jr. 2000, Understanding the Domestic Impact of International Norms: A Research Agenda, *International Studies Review* 2: 65–87.

Cottey, Andrew 1995, *East-Central Europe after the Cold War. Poland, the Czech Republic, Slovakia and Hungary in Search of Security*, Basingstoke: Macmillan.

Cruz, Consuelo 2000, Identity and Persuasion: How Nations Remember their Pasts and Make their Futures, *World Politics* 52: 275–312.

Dannreuther, Roland 1997, *Eastward Enlargement. NATO and the EU*, Oslo: Institut for forsvarsstudier.

Dassú, Marta and Menotti, Roberto 1997, *The Ratification of NATO Enlargement. The Case of Italy* (Conference: NATO Enlargement: The National Debates over Ratification), Brussels: NATO, Academic Forum (http://www.nato.int/acad/conf/enlarg97).

Dauderstädt, Michael 1998, EU–Osterweiterung: Wirkungen, Erwartungen und Interessen in den Beitrittsländern, *Integration* 21: 149–67.

DeSerpa, Allan C. and Happel, Stephen K. 1978, The Economics of the Olympic Games, in William Loehr and Todd Sandler (eds.), *Public Goods and Public Policy*, Beverly Hills: Sage, pp. 99–121.

Dessler, David 1999, Constructivism Within a Positivist Social Science, *Review of International Studies* 25: 123–38.

Deubner, Christian 1999, Frankreich in der Osterweiterung der EU, 1989 bis 1997, *Politische Studien* 50: 89–121.

Deudney, Daniel and Ikenberry, G. John 1999, The Nature and Source of Liberal International Order, *Review of International Studies* 25: 179–96.

Deutsch, Karl W. 1970, *Political Community at the International Level. Problems of Definition and Measurement*, : Archon Books.

Deutsch, Karl W. *et al.* 1957, *Political Community and the North Atlantic Area: International Organization in the Light of Historical Experience*, Princeton: Princeton University Press.

DiMaggio, Paul 1998, The New Institutionalisms: Avenues of Collaboration, *Journal of Institutional and Theoretical Economics* 154: 696–705.

DiMaggio, Paul J. and Powell, Walter W. 1991, Introduction, in Powell and DiMaggio (eds.), pp. 1–38.

Doty, Roxanne Lynn 1997, Aporia: A Critical Exploration of the Agent–Structure Problematique in International Relations Theory, *European Journal of International Relations* 3: 365–92.

Edgerton, Robert B. 1985, *Rules, Exceptions, and Social Order*, Berkeley: University of California Press.

Eemeren, Frans H. van 1986, Dialectical Analysis as a Normative Reconstruction of Argumentative Discourse, *Text* 6: 1–16.

1990, The Study of Argumentation as Normative Pragmatics, *Text* 10: 37–44.

Eland, Ivan 1997, *The High Cost of NATO Expansion. Clearing the Administration's Smoke Screen* (Cato Policy Analysis 286), Washington, DC: Cato Institute.

Elster, Jon 1989a, Social Norms and Economic Theory, *The Journal of Economic Perspectives* 3: 99–117.

1989b, *The Cement of Society. A Study of Social Order*, Cambridge: Cambridge University Press.

1989c, *Nuts and Bolts for the Social Sciences*, Cambridge: Cambridge University Press.

1991, Arguing and Bargaining in Two Constituent Assemblies (Storrs Lecture), New Haven: Yale Law School (unpubl. ms.).

1992, Arguing and Bargaining in the Federal Convention and the Assemblée Constituante, in Raino Malnes and Arild Underdal (eds.), *Rationality and Institutions. Essays in Honour of Knut Midgaard*, Oslo: Universitetsforlaget, pp. 13–50.

Ene, Constantin 1997, Romania Sets its Sights on NATO Membership, *NATO Review* 45 (6): 8–11 (quoted according to web edition, http://www.nato.int/docu/review).

Engelbrekt, Kjell 1994, Southeast European States Seek Equal Treatment, *Radio Free Europe/Radio Liberty Research Report* 3 (12): 38–43.

Eriksen, Erik Oddvar and Weigård, Jarle 1997, Conceptualizing Politics: Strategic or Communicative Action, *Scandinavian Political Studies* 20: 219–41.

European Bank for Reconstruction and Development (EBRD) (ed.) 1997, *Transition Report 1997. Enterprise Performance and Growth*, London: EBRD.

European Commission 1992, *Europe and the Challenge of Enlargement* (Europe Documents 1790, 3 July 1992), Agence Europe.

1997a, *Agenda 2000 – Volume I – Communication: For a Stronger and Wider Union* (DOC/97/6), Brussels.

1997b, *Agenda 2000 – Volume II – Communication: The Effects on the Union's Policies of Enlargement to the Applicant Countries of Central and Eastern Europe* (DOC/97/7), Brussels.

1997c, *Agenda 2000 – Summary and Conclusions of the Opinions of Commission Concerning the Applications for Membership to the European Union Presented by the Candidate Countries* (DOC/97/8), Brussels.

1999, *Regular Report from the Commission on Progress towards Accession by Each of the Candidate Countries* (http://europa.eu.int/comm/enlargement/report_10_99).

European Council 1989, Conclusions of the Presidency, Strasbourg, December 1989, *Bulletin of the European Communities* 22 (12).

1993, Conclusions of the Presidency, Copenhagen, June 1993, *Bulletin of the European Communities* 26 (6).

Eyal, Jonathan 1997, NATO's Enlargement: Anatomy of a Decision, *International Affairs* 73: 695–719.

Fearon, James D. and Wendt, Alexander 2002, Rationalism v. Constructivism: A Skeptical View, in Walter Carlsnaes, Thomas Risse, and Beth A. Simmons (eds.), *Handbook of International Relations Theory*, London: Sage, 52–72.

Fierke, K. M. 1999, Dialogues of Manoeuvre and Entanglement: NATO, Russia, and the CEECs, *Millennium* 28: 27–52.

Fierke, Karin and Wiener, Antje 1999, Constructing Institutional Interests: EU and NATO Enlargement, *Journal of European Public Policy* 6: 5, 721–42.

Fink Hafner, Danica 1999, Dilemmas in Managing the Expanding EU: the EU and Applicant States' Point of View, *Journal of European Public Policy* 6: 783–801.

Finnemore, Martha 1996a, *National Interests in International Society*, Ithaca, NY: Cornell University Press.

Finnemore, Martha and Sikkink, Kathryn 1998, International Norm Dynamics and Political Change, *International Organization* 52: 887–917.

Franck, Thomas M. 1990, *The Power of Legitimacy among Nations*, Oxford: Oxford University Press.

Frankel, Benjamin (ed.) 1996a, *Realism. Restatements and Renewal*, London: Frank Cass.

1996b, Restating the Realist Case: An Introduction, in Frankel (ed.), pp. ix–xx.

Fratianni, Michele and Pattison, John 1982, The Economics of International Organizations, *Kyklos* 35: 244–61.

Friis, Lykke 1998, "The End of the Beginning" of Eastern Enlargement – Luxembourg Summit and Agenda-setting, *European Integration online Papers* 2 (http://www.eiop.or.at/eiop/texte/1998a-007.htm).

Friis, Lykke and Murphy, Anna 1999, The European Union and Central and Eastern Europe: Governance and Boundaries, *Journal of Common Market Studies* 37: 211–32.

Gaddis, John Lewis 1998, History, Grand Strategy and NATO Enlargement, *Survival* 40: 145–51.

Gallis, Paul E. 1997, *NATO Enlargement: The Process and Allied Views* (CRS Report 97-666), Washington, DC: Congressional Research Service.

2001, France: NATO's "Renovation" and Enlargement, in Mattox and Rachwald (eds.), pp. 55–73.

Garden, Sir Timothy 2001, The United Kingdom: Making Strategic Adjustments, in Mattox and Rachwald (eds.), pp. 75–89.

Geipel, Gary L. 1999, The Cost of Enlarging NATO, in Sperling (ed.), pp. 160–78.

George, Alexander L. 1979, Case Studies and Theory Development: The Method of Structured, Focused Comparison, in Paul Gordon Lauren (ed.), *Diplomacy: New Approaches in History, Theory and Policy*, New York: Free Press, pp. 43–68.

Gheciu, Alexandra 2002, *Security Institutions as Agents of Socialization? NATO and Post-Cold War Central and Eastern Europe* (Paper, IDNET Workshop, EUI, Florence, February 2002).

Goffman, Erving 1959, *The Presentation of Self in Everyday Life*, Garden City, NY: Doubleday Anchor Books.

1969, *Strategic Interaction*, Philadelphia: University of Pennsylvania Press.

1974, *Frame Analysis. An Essay in the Organization of Experience*, New York: Harper Colophon Books.

1982, *Interaction Ritual. Essays in Face-to-Face Behavior*, New York: Pantheon Books.

Goldgeier, James M. 1999, *Not Whether but When. The US Decision to Enlarge NATO*, Washington, DC: Brookings Institution Press.

2002, Not When but Who, *NATO Review* 50(1) (quoted according to web edition, http://www.nato.int/docu/review).

Gong, Gerrit W. 1984, *The Standard of "Civilization" in International Society*, Oxford: Clarendon Press.

Grabbe, Heather and Hughes, Kirsty 1998, *Enlarging the EU Eastwards* (Chatham House Papers), London: Pinter.

Granville, Johanna 1999, The Many Paradoxes of NATO Enlargement, *Current History* 98: 165–70.

Grayson, George W. 1999, *Strange Bedfellows. NATO Marches East*, Lanham, MD: University Press of America.

Green Cowles, Maria and Smith, Michael (eds.) 2000, *Risks, Reforms, Resistance and Revival (The State of the European Union 5)*, Oxford: Oxford University Press.

Grieco, Joseph M. 1988, Anarchy and the Limits of Cooperation. A Realist Critique of the Newest Liberal Institutionalism, *International Organization* 42: 485–507.

1990, *Cooperation among Nations. Europe, America, and Non-Tariff Barriers to Trade*, Ithaca, NY: Cornell University Press.

1996, State Interests and Institutional Rule Trajectories: a Neorealist Interpretation of the Maastricht Treaty and European Economic and Monetary Union, in Frankel (ed.), pp. 261–306.

1997, Realist International Theory and the Study of World Politics, in Michael Doyle and G. John Ikenberry (eds.), *New Thinking in International Relations Theory*, Boulder, CO: Westview Press, pp. 163–201.

Gustenau, Gustav E. 1999, *Sloweniens Vorbereitungen auf die angestrebte NATO-Mitgliedschaft* (Bericht des BIOst 8/1999), Cologne: Bundesinstitut für internationale und ostwissenschaftliche Studien.

Gylfason, Thorvaldur 1995, Discussion, in Richard E., Baldwin, Pertti Haaparanta, and Jakko Kiander (eds.), *Expanding Membership of the European Union*, Cambridge: Cambridge University Press, pp. 48–53.

Haas, Ernst B. 1968, *The Uniting of Europe. Political, Social, and Economic Forces 1950–1957*, 2nd ed., Stanford: Stanford University Press.

Habermas, Jürgen 1973, *Legitimationsprobleme im Spätkapitalismus*, Frankfurt: Suhrkamp.

1981, *Theorie des kommunikativen Handelns*, 2 vols., Frankfurt: Suhrkamp.

1986, Entgegnung, in Axel Honneth and Hans Joas (eds.), *Kommunikatives Handeln. Beiträge zu Jürgen Habermas' "Theorie des kommunikativen Handelns,"* Frankfurt: Suhrkamp, 327–405.

1994, *Faktizität und Geltung. Beiträge zur Diskurstheorie des Rechts und des demokratischen Rechtsstaats*, 4th ed., Frankfurt: Suhrkamp.

1998, *Die postnationale Konstellation: Politische Essays*, Frankfurt: Suhrkamp.

Hacke, Christian 1997, Die Haltung der Bundesrepublik Deutschland zur NATO-Osterweiterung, in Pradetto (ed.), pp. 231–49.

Hagen, Jürgen von 1996, The Political Economy of Eastern Enlargement of the EU, in Ambrus-Lakatos and Schaffer (eds.), pp. 1–41.

Haglund, David G. (ed.) 1996, *Will NATO Go East? The Debate Over Enlarging the Atlantic Alliance*, Kingston, Ont.: The Centre for International Relations, Queens University.

Hall, Peter A. and Taylor, Rosemary C. R. 1996, Political Science and the Three New Institutionalisms, *Political Studies* 44, 936–57.

Ham, Peter van 1993, *The EC, Eastern Europe and European Unity. Discord, Collaboration and Integration Since 1947*, London: Pinter.

Hampton, Mary N. 1995, NATO at the Creation: US Foreign Policy, West Germany and the Wilsonian Impulse, *Security Studies* 4: 610–56.

1999, NATO, Germany, and the United States: Creating Positive Identity in Trans-Atlantia, *Security Studies* 8: 235–69.

Harris, Geoffrey 1998, *Enlargement of the European Union: The Parliamentary Dimension* (Paper, Joint International Relations Conference of ESGIR and ISA, Vienna, September 1998).

Hasenclever, Andreas, Mayer, Peter and Rittberger, Volker 1997, *Theories of International Regimes*, Cambridge: Cambridge University Press.

Hayward, Jack 1996, Britain and EU Enlargement, in Kaiser and Brüning (eds.), pp. 147–54.

Hollis, Martin and Smith, Steve 1990, *Explaining and Understanding International Relations*, Oxford: Clarendon Press.

Holvêque, Stéphanie 1998, L'Union européenne s'ouvre à l'est, *Revue du Marché Commun et de l'Union Européenne* 421: 514–23.

Hopf, Ted 1998, The Promise of Constructivism in International Relations Theory, *International Security* 23: 171–200.

Huelshoff, Michael 1999, CEE Financial Reform, European Monetary Union and Eastern Enlargement, in Sperling (ed.), pp. 63–80.

Huntington, Samuel P. 1993, The Clash of Civilizations?, *Foreign Affairs* 72 (3): 22–49.

1996, *Kampf der Kulturen. Die Neugestaltung der Weltpolitik im 21. Jahrhundert*, Munich: Europaverlag.

Hyde-Price, Adrian G. V. 1994, Democratization in Eastern Europe. The External Dimension, in Geoffrey Pridham and Tatu Vanhanen (eds.), *Democratization in Eastern Europe. Domestic and International Perspectives*, London: Routledge, pp. 220–52.

1996, *The International Politics of Eastern Europe*, Manchester: Manchester University Press.

Inotai, András 1998, The CEECs: From the Association Agreements to Full Membership, in Redmond and Rosenthal (eds.), pp. 157–76.

Institut für europäische Politik (in cooperation with Trans European Policy Studies Association) 1998, *Enlargement/Agenda 2000 – Watch. Pilot Issue* (http://www.tepsa.be).

Jachtenfuchs, Markus, Diez, Thomas and Jung, Sabine 1998, Which Europe? Conflicting Models of a Legitimate European Political Order, *European Journal of International Relations* 4: 409–45.

Jackson, Patrick Thaddeus and Nexon, Daniel H. 1999, Relations Before States: Substance, Process and the Study of World Politics, *European Journal of International Relations* 5: 291–332.

Jaggers, Keith and Gurr, Ted Robert 1995, Tracking Democracy's Third Wave with the Polity III Data, *Journal of Peace Research* 32: 469–82.

Jepperson, Ronald, Wendt, Alexander and Katzenstein, Peter 1996, Norms, Identity, and Culture in National Security, in Katzenstein (ed.), pp. 33–75.

Jervis, Robert 1998, Realism in the Study of World Politics, *International Organization* 52: 971–91.

Johnston, Alistair Iain 2001, Treating International Institutions as Social Environments, *International Studies Quarterly* 45: 487–515.

Jørgensen, Knud Erik 2000, Continental IR Theory. The Best Kept Secret, *European Journal of International Relations* 6: 9–42.

Jovanovic, Miroslav N. 1999, Where Are the Limits to the Enlargement of the European Union?, *Journal of Economic Integration* 14: 467–96.

Jupille, Joseph, Caporaso, James A. and Checkel, Jeffrey T. 2003, Integrating Institutions: Theory, Method, and the Study of the European Union, *Comparative Political Studies* 36: forthcoming.

Kahl, Colin H. 1999, Constructing a Separate Peace: Constructivism, Collective Liberal Identity, and Democratic Peace, *Security Studies* 8: 94–144.

Kaiser, Karl and Brüning, Martin (eds.) 1996, *East-Central Europe and the EU: Problems of Integration*, Bonn: Europa Union Verlag.

Kamp, Karl-Heinz and Weilemann, Peter R. 1997, *Germany and the Enlargement of NATO* (Conference: NATO Enlargement: The National Debates over Ratification), Brussels: NATO, Academic Forum (http://www.nato.int/acad/conf/enlarg97).

Karatnycky, Adrian, Motyl, Alexander and Shor, Boris (eds.) 1997, *Nations in Transit 1997. Civil Society, Democracy and Markets in East Central Europe and the Newly Independent States*, New Brunswick: Transaction Publishers.

Karkoszka, Andrej 1995, A View From Poland, in Simon (ed.), pp. 75–85.

Katzenstein, Peter (ed.) 1996a, *The Culture of National Security. Norms and Identity in World Politics*, New York: Columbia University Press.

Katzenstein, Peter J. 1996b, Introduction: Alternative Perspectives on National Security, in Katzenstein (ed.), pp. 1–32.

1997a, United Germany in an Integrating Europe, in Katzenstein (ed.), pp. 1–48.

1997b, The Smaller European States, Germany and Europe, in Katzenstein (ed.), pp. 251–304.

Katzenstein, Peter J. (ed.) 1997c, *Tamed Power. Germany in Europe*, Ithaca, NY: Cornell University Press.

Katzenstein, Peter J., Keohane, Robert O. and Krasner, Stephen D. 1998, "International Organization" and the Study of World Politics, *International Organization* 52: 645–85.

Katzenstein, Peter J., Keohane, Robert O. and Krasner, Stephen D. (eds.) 1999, *Exploration and Contestation in the Study of World Politics*, Cambridge, MA: MIT Press.

Kawecka-Wyrzykowska, Elzbieta 1996, On the Benefits of the Accession for Western and Eastern Europe, in Ambrus-Lakatos and Schaffer (eds.), pp. 85–107.

Kay, Sean 1998, *NATO and the Future of European Security*, Oxford: Rowman & Littlefield.

NATO's Open Door, *Security Dialogue* 32: 201–15.

Keohane, Robert O. 1984, *After Hegemony. Cooperation and Discord in the World Political Economy*, Princeton: Princeton University Press.

1993, The Analysis of International Regimes. Towards a European–American Research Programme, in Volker Rittberger (ed.), *Regime Theory and International Relations*, Oxford: Clarendon Press, pp. 23–45.

Keohane, Robert O. and Nye, Joseph S., Jr. 1977, *Power and Interdependence. World Politics in Transition*, Boston, MA: Little, Brown.

Keresztes, Lajos 1998, *Ungarns Vorbereitungen auf den NATO-Beitritt* (Berichte des BIOSt 8/1998), Cologne: Bundesinstitut für ostwissenschaftliche und internationale Studien.

Kerremans, Bart 1998, The Political and Institutional Consequences of Widening: Capacity and Control in an Enlarged Council, in Pierre-Henri Laurent and Marc Maresceau (eds.), *Deepening and Widening (The State of the European Union 4)*, Boulder, CO: Lynne Rienner, pp. 87–109.

Khol, Radek 2001, Czech Republic: A Pan-European Perspective, in Mattox and Rachwald (eds.), pp. 147–65.

Kierzkowski, Henryk 1996, Reforms in East-Central Europe – Preparing for EU Membership, in Kaiser and Brüning (eds.), pp. 15–37.

King, Gary, Keohane, Robert O. and Verba, Sidney 1994, *Designing Social Inquiry. Scientific Inference in Qualitative Research*, Princeton: Princeton University Press.

Klandermans, Bert 1997, *The Social Psychology of Protest*, Oxford: Blackwell.

Klein, Wolfgang 1980, Argumentation und Argument, *Zeitschrift für Literaturwissenschaft und Linguistik* 10 (38/39): 9–57.

1985, Argumentationsanalyse. Ein Begriffsrahmen und ein Beispiel, in Josef Kopperschmidt and Helmut Schanze (eds.), *Argumente – Argumentation. Interdisziplinäre Problemzugänge*, Munich: Fink, pp. 208–60.

Kleinbaum, David G. 1994, *Logistic Regression: A Self-Learning Text*, New York: Springer.

Kolankiewicz, George 1994, Consensus and Competition in the Eastern Enlargement of the European Union, *International Affairs* 70: 477–95.

Kopperschmidt, Josef 1985, *Rhetorica. Aufsätze zur Theorie, Geschichte und Praxis der Rhetorik*, Hildesheim: Georg Olms.

1989, *Methodik der Argumentationsanalyse*, Stuttgart/Bad Cannstatt: Frommann-holzboog.

Koremenos, Barbara, Lipson, Charles and Snidal, Duncan 2001, The Rational Design of International Institutions, *International Organization* 55: 761–99.

Kowert, Paul and Legro, Jeffrey 1996, Norms, Identity, and Their Limits: A Theoretical Reprise, in Katzenstein (ed.), pp. 451–97.

Kratochwil, Friedrich V. and Ruggie, John Gerard 1986, International Organization. A State of the Art on an Art of the State, *International Organization* 40: 753–75.

Kreile, Michael 1997, Eine Erweiterungsstrategie für die Europäische Union, in Werner Weidenfeld (ed.), *Europa öffnen. Anforderungen an die Erweiterung*, Gütersloh: Verlag Bertelsmann Stiftung, pp. 203–72.

Kumar, Andrej 1996, The CEE Countries' Aspirations for Enlargement, in Ambrus-Lakatos and Schaffer (eds.), pp. 42–84.

Kupchan, Charles A. 1994, Strategic Visions, *World Policy Journal* 11: 112–22.

Kurth, James 1997, NATO Expansion and the Idea of the West, *Orbis* 41: 555–67.

Kydd, Andrew 2001, Trust Building, Trust Breaking: The Dilemma of NATO Enlargement, *International Organization* 55: 801–28.

Laitin, David D. 1988, Political Cultures and Political Preferences, *American Political Science Review* 82: 589–93.

Lake, Anthony 1993, From Containment to Enlargement. Current Foreign Policy Debates in Perspective, *Vital Speeches of the Day* 60: 13–19.

Larrabee, F. Stephen 1997, East Central Europe: Problems, Prospects and Policy Dilemmas, in Clemens (ed.), pp. 87–108.

1999, NATO Enlargement After the First Round, *The International Spectator* 34: 83–85.

Latawski, Paul 1994, *The Security Route to Europe: The Visegrad Four*, London: Royal United Services Institute for Defence Studies.

Lavenex, Sandra 1998, "Passing the Buck": European Union Refugee Policies towards Central and Eastern Europe, *Journal of Refugee Studies* 11: 126–45.

Legro, Jeffrey W. 1996, Culture and Preferences in the International Cooperation Two-Step, *American Political Science Review* 90: 118–37.

Lepgold, Joseph 1998, NATO's Post-Cold War Collective Action Problem, *International Security* 23: 78–106.

Lijphart, Arend 1975, The Comparable-Cases Strategy in Comparative Research, *Comparative Political Studies* 8: 2, 158–77.

Lipgens, Walter 1982, *A History of European Integration*, vol. I, *1945–1947*, Oxford: Oxford University Press.

Liska, George 1962, *Nations in Alliance. The Limits of Interdependence*, Baltimore: The Johns Hopkins Press.

Mandelbaum, Michael 1995, Preserving the New Peace. The Case Against NATO Expansion, *Foreign Affairs* 74(3): 9–13.

Manfrass-Sirjacques, Françoise 1997, Frankreichs Position zur Osterweiterung, in Pradetto (ed.), pp. 181–209.

March, James G. and Olsen, Johan P. 1989, *Rediscovering Institutions. The Organizational Basis of Politics*, New York: Free Press.

1998, The Institutional Dynamics of International Political Orders, *International Organization* 52: 943–69.

Marcussen, Martin, Risse, Thomas, Engelmann-Martin, Daniela, Knopf, Hans Joachim and Roscher, Klaus 1999, Constructing Europe? The Evolution of French, British and German Nation State Identities, *Journal of European Public Policy* 6: 614–33.

Martin, Lisa L. 1993, The Rational State Choice of Multilateralism, in Ruggie (ed.), pp. 91–121.

Martin, Lisa L. and Simmons, Beth A. 1998, Theories and Empirical Studies of International Institutions, *International Organization* 52: 729–57.

Mattli, Walter 1995, Regional Integration and the Enlargement Issue: A Macroanalysis, in Schneider, Weitsman and Bernauer (eds.), pp. 137–52.

1999, *The Logic of Regional Integration. Europe and Beyond*, Cambridge: Cambridge University Press.

Mattox, Gale A. 1998, NATO: Past and Future, in Thompson (ed.), pp. 23–41.

Mattox, Gale A. and Rachwald, Arthur R. (eds.) 2001, *Enlarging NATO. The National Debates*, Boulder, CO: Lynne Rienner.

Mayhew, Alan 1998, *Recreating Europe. The European Union's Policy towards Central and Eastern Europe*, Cambridge: Cambridge University Press.

McNeely, Connie L. 1995, *Constructing the Nation-State. International Organization and Prescriptive Action*, Westport: Greenwood Press.

McNeill, William H. 1997, What We Mean by the West, *Orbis* 41: 513–24.

Mearsheimer, John J. 1995, The False Promise of International Institutions, *International Security* 19: 5–49.

Melescanu, Teodor 1993, Security in Central Europe: A Positive-Sum Game, *NATO Review* 41(5): 12–18 (quoted according to web edition, http://www.nato.int/docu/review).

Menard, Scott 1995, *Applied Logistic Regression Analysis* (QASS 106), Thousand Oaks: Sage.

Menotti, Roberto 2001, Italy: Uneasy Ally, in Mattox and Rachwald (eds.), pp. 91–107.

Michalski, Anna and Wallace, Helen 1992, *The European Community and the Challenge of Enlargement*, 2nd ed., London: Royal Institute of International Affairs.

Mihalka, Michael 1994, Squaring the Circle: NATO's Offer to the East, *Radio Free Europe/Radio Liberty Research Report* 3(12): 1–9.

Milner, Helen V. 1998, Rationalizing Politics: The Emerging Synthesis of International, American, and Comparative Politics, *International Organization* 52: 759–86.

Milward, Alan S. 1994, *The Frontier of National Sovereignty. History and Theory, 1945–1992*, London: Routledge.

Moravcsik, Andrew 1995, Explaining International Human Rights Regimes: Liberal Theory and Western Europe, *European Journal of International Relations* 1: 157–89.

1998, *The Choice for Europe: Social Purpose and State Power from Messina to Maastricht*, Ithaca, NY: Cornell University Press.

Morgan, Patrick M. 1993, Security Prospects in Europe, in Ruggie (ed.), pp. 327–64.

Morgenthau, Hans J. 1973, *Politics among Nations: The Struggle for Power and Peace*, 5th ed., New York: Knopf.

Moses, Alfred H. 1998, Romania's NATO Bid, *SAIS Review* 18: 137.

Müller, Harald 1994, Internationale Beziehungen als kommunikatives Handeln. Zur Kritik der utilitaristischen Handlungstheorien, *Zeitschrift für Internationale Beziehungen* 1: 15–44.

2002, *Arguing, Bargaining, and All That. Reflections on the Relationship of Communicative Action and Rationalist Theory in Analysing International Negotiations*

(Paper, Workshop "Arguing and Persuasion in International Relations and European Affairs," EUI, Florence, April 2002).

Myers, Frank 1999, Political Argumentation and the Composite Audience: A Case Study, *Quarterly Journal of Speech* 85: 55–71.

NATO 1991a, *The Alliance's Strategic Concept agreed by the Heads of State and Government participating in the Meeting of the North Atlantic Council* (http://www.nato.int/docu/basictxt/b911108a.htm).

1991b, *Declaration on Peace and Cooperation issued by the Heads of State and Government participating in the Meeting of the North Atlantic Council* (http://www.nato.int/docu/basictxt/b911108b.htm).

1991c, *Partnership with the Countries of Central and Eastern Europe. Statement issued by the North Atlantic Council Meeting in Ministerial Session* (http://www.nato.int/docu/basictxt/b910607a.htm).

1991d, The Situation in the Soviet Union. Statement Issued by the North Atlantic Council Meeting in Ministerial Session in Brussels on 21 August 1991, *NATO Review* 39(4): 8–9.

1994a, *Partnership for Peace Invitation Document*, (http://www.nato.int/docu/basictxt/b940110a.htm).

1994b, *Partnership for Peace Framework Document* (http://www.nato.int/docu/basictxt/b940110b.htm).

1995, *Study on NATO Enlargement issued by the Heads of State and Government Participating in the Meeting of the North Atlantic Council* (http://www.nato.int/docu/basictxt/enl-9501.htm).

Naumann, Klaus 1997, The Reshaping of NATO from a Military Perspective, *RUSI Journal* 142(3): 7–11.

Neumann, Iver B. 1993, Russia as Central Europe's Constituting Other, *East European Politics and Societies* 7: 349–69.

1998, European Identity, EU Expansion, and the Integration/Exclusion Nexus, *Alternatives* 23: 397–416.

Nye, Joseph S., Jr. 1971, *Peace in Parts. Integration and Conflict in Regional Integration*, Boston: Little, Brown.

Öhlschläger, Günther 1979, *Linguistische Überlegungen zu einer Theorie der Argumentation*, Tübingen: Niemeyer.

Olson, Mancur 1971, *The Logic of Collective Action. Public Goods and the Theory of Groups*, Cambridge, MA: Harvard University Press.

Olson, Mancur, Jr. and Zeckhauser, Richard 1966, An Economic Theory of Alliances, *Review of Economics and Statistics* 48: 266–79.

O'Neil, Patrick 1999, Politics, Finance and European Union Enlargement Eastward, in Sperling (ed.), pp. 81–99.

Owen, John M. 1996, How Liberalism Produces Democratic Peace, in Michael E. Brown, Sean M. Lynn-Jones, and Steven E. Miller (eds.), *Debating the Democratic Peace*, Cambridge, MA: MIT Press, pp. 116–54.

Padoan, Pier Paolo 1997, Regional Arrangements as Clubs: The European Case, in Edward D. Mansfield and Helen V. Milner (eds.), *The Political Economy of Regionalism*, New York: Columbia University Press, pp. 107–33.

Parsons, Talcott 1969, *Politics and Social Structure*, New York: Free Press.

Pascu, Ioan Mircea 1995, A View From Romania, in Simon (ed.), pp. 87–98.

Perelman, Chaim 1979, *Logik und Argumentation*, Königstein Athenäum.
Peters, B. Guy 1999, *Institutional Theory in Political Science. The "New Institutionalism"*, London: Pinter.
Petersen, Trond 1991, The Statistical Analysis of Event Histories, in *Sociological Methods and Research* 19: 270–323.
Peterson Ulrich, Marybeth 1999, *NATO's Identity at a Crossroads: Institutional Challenges Posed by NATO's Enlargement and Partnership for Peace Programs* (Paper, ISA Convention, Washington, DC).
Powell, Walter W. and DiMaggio, Paul J. (eds.) 1991, *The New Institutionalism in Organizational Analysis*, Chicago: University of Chicago Press.
Pradetto, August (ed.) 1997, *Ostmitteleuropa, Rußland und die Osterweiterung der NATO. Perzeptionen und Strategien im Spannungsfeld nationaler und europäischer Sicherheit*, Opladen: Westdeutscher Verlag.
Radu, Michael 1997, Why Eastern and Central Europe Look West, *Orbis* 41: 39–57.
Ragin, Charles C. 1987, *The Comparative Method. Moving Beyond Qualitative and Quantitative Strategies*, Berkeley: University of California Press.
Raunio, Tapio and Wiberg, Matti 1998, Winners and Losers in the Council: Voting Power Consequences of EU Enlargement, *Journal of Common Market Studies* 36: 549–62.
Raymond, Gregory A. 1997, Problems and Prospects in the Study of International Norms, *Mershon International Studies Review* 41: 205–45.
Redmond, John and Rosenthal, Glenda G. (eds.) 1998a, *The Expanding European Union. Past, Present, Future*, Boulder, CO: Lynne Rienner.
1998b, Introduction, in Redmond and Rosenthal (eds.), pp. 1–14.
Reisch, Alfred A. 1994, Central Europe's Disappointments and Hopes, *Radio Free Europe/Radio Liberty Research Report* 3(12): 18–37.
Reiter, Dan 2001, Why NATO Enlargement Does Not Spread Democracy, *International Security* 25: 41–67.
Reus-Smit, Christian 1997, The Constitutional Structure of International Society and the Nature of Fundamental Institutions, *International Organization* 51: 555–89.
Richter, Pascal 1997, *Die Erweiterung der Europäischen Union. Unter besonderer Berücksichtigung der Beitrittsbedingungen*, Baden-Baden: Nomos.
Risse, Thomas 1999, International Norms and Domestic Change: Arguing and Communicative Behavior in the Human Rights Area, *Politics and Society* 27: 529–59.
2000, "Let's Argue!" Communicative Action in World Politics, *International Organization* 54: 1–39.
Risse, Thomas and Sikkink, Kathryn 1999, The Socialization of International Human Rights Norms into Domestic Practices: Introduction, in Risse, Ropp and Sikkink (eds.), pp. 1–38.
Risse, Thomas and Wiener, Antje 1999, "Something Rotten" and the Social Construction of Social Constructivism: A Comment on Comments, *Journal of European Public Policy* 6: 5, 775–82.
Risse, Thomas, Ropp, Steve C. and Sikkink, Kathryn (eds.) 1999, *The Power of Human Rights. International Norms and Domestic Political Change*, Cambridge: Cambridge University Press.

Risse-Kappen, Thomas 1995a, *Cooperation Among Democracies. The European Influence on US Foreign Policy*, Princeton: Princeton University Press.

1995b, Democratic Peace – Warlike Democracies? A Social Constructivist Interpretation of the Liberal Argument, *European Journal of International Relations* 1: 491–517.

1995c, Bringing Transnational Relations Back In: Introduction, in Risse-Kappen, Thomas (ed.), *Bringing Transnational Relations Back In. Non-State Actors, Domestic Structures, and International Institutions*, Cambridge: Cambridge University Press, pp. 3–33.

Romania, King Michael of 1997, Romania and NATO: The Time for a Real Partnership, *RUSI Journal* 142(2): 6–11.

Rubinstein, Alvin Z. 1998, NATO Enlargement *vs.* American Interests, *Orbis* 42: 37–48.

Ruggie, John Gerard 1993a, Multilateralism: The Anatomy of an Institution, in Ruggie (ed.), pp. 3–47.

1993b, Territoriality and Beyond, *International Organization* 47: 139–74.

(ed.) 1993, *Multilateralism Matters. The Theory and Praxis of an Institutional Form*, New York: Columbia University Press

1998, Introduction: What Makes the World Hang Together? Neo-Utilitarian and the Social Constructivist Challenge, in John Gerard Ruggie, *Constructing the World Polity. Essays on International Relations*, London: Routledge, pp. 1–44.

Rühe, Volker 1993, Shaping Euro-Atlantic Policies: A Grand Strategy for a New Era, *Survival* 35: 129–37.

Russett, Bruce 1968, Components of an Operational Theory of Alliance Formation, *Journal of Conflict Resolution* 12: 285–301.

1970, *What Price Vigilance? The Burdens of National Defense*, New Haven: Yale University Press.

Russett, Bruce and Stam, Allan C. 1998, Courting Disaster: An Expanded NATO *vs.* Russia and China, *Political Science Quarterly* 113: 361–82.

Russett, Bruce *et al.* 1995, *Grasping the Democratic Peace. Principles for a Post-Cold War World*, 2nd ed., Princeton: Princeton University Press.

Sandler, Todd 1977, Impurity of Defense: An Application to the Economics of Alliances, *Kyklos* 30: 443–60.

Sandler, Todd and Hartley, Keith 1999, *The Political Economy of NATO. Past, Present, and into the 21st Century*, Cambridge: Cambridge University Press.

Sandler, Todd and Tschirhart, John T. 1980, The Economic Theory of Clubs: An Evaluative Survey, *Journal of Economic Literature* 18: 1481–521.

Sandler, Todd M., Loehr, William and Cauley, Jon T. 1978, *The Political Economy of Public Goods and International Cooperation* (Monograph Series in World Affairs 15), Denver: University of Denver.

Saryusz-Wolski, Jacek 1994, The Reintegration of the "Old Continent": Avoiding the Costs of "Half Europe," in Simon Bulmer and Andrew Scott (eds.), *Economic and Political Integration in Europe: Internal Dynamics and Global Context*, Oxford: Blackwell, pp. 19–28.

Scharpf, Fritz W. 1985, Die Politikverflechtungs-Falle: Europäische Integration und deutscher Föderalismus im Vergleich, *Politische Vierteljahresschrift* 26: 4, 323–56.

Schimmelfennig, Frank 1995, *Debatten zwischen Staaten. Eine Argumentationstheorie internationaler Systemkonflikte*, Opladen: Leske and Budrich.
1997, Rhetorisches Handeln in der internationalen Politik, *Zeitschrift für Internationale Beziehungen* 4: 219–54.
2000, International Socialization in the New Europe. Rational Action in an Institutional Environment, *European Journal of International Relations* 6: 109–39.
2003, Strategic Action in a Community Environment: The Decision to Expand the European Union to the East, *Comparative Political Studies* 36: 156–83.
Schimmelfennig, Frank and Sedelmeier, Ulrich 2002, Theorizing EU Enlargement: Research Focus, Hypotheses, and the State of Research, *Journal of European Public Policy* 9: 500–28.
Schmidt, Peter 1996, Deutsche Sicherheitspolitik im Rahmen von EU, WEU und NATO, *Aussenpolitik* 47: 211–22.
Schmitter, Philippe C. 1969, Three Neo-Functionalist Hypotheses about International Integration, *International Organization* 23: 161–6.
Schneider, Gerald, Weitsman, Patricia A. and Bernauer, Thomas (eds.) 1995, *Towards a New Europe. Stops and Starts in Regional Integration*, Westport: Praeger.
Schwarz, Jürgen (ed.) 1980, *Der Aufbau Europas. Pläne und Dokumente 1945–1980*, Bonn: Osang.
Schweller, Randall L. 1994, Bandwagoning for Profit. Bringing the Revisionist State Back In, *International Security* 19: 72–107.
1997, New Realist Research on Alliances: Refining, not Refuting Waltz's Balancing Proposition, *American Political Science Review* 91: 927–30.
Scott, W. Richard 1991, Unpacking Institutional Arguments, in Powell and DiMaggio (eds.), pp. 164–82.
1995, *Institutions and Organizations*, Thousand Oaks: Sage.
Sedelmeier, Ulrich 2000, Eastern Enlargement: Risk, Rationality, and Role-Compliance, in Green Cowles and Smith (eds.), pp. 164–85.
Sedelmeier, Ulrich and Wallace, Helen 1996, Policies Towards Central and Eastern Europe, in Helen Wallace and William Wallace (eds.), *Policy-Making in the European Union*, 3rd ed., Oxford: Oxford University Press, pp. 353–87.
2000, Eastern Enlargement. Strategy or Second Thoughts?, in Helen Wallace and William Wallace (eds.), *Policy-Making in the European Union*, 4th ed., Oxford: Oxford University Press, pp. 427–60.
Shannon, Vaughn P. 2000, Norms Are What States Make of Them: The Political Psychology of Norm Violation, *International Studies Quarterly* 44: 293–316.
Sharp, Jane M. O. 1997, British Views on NATO Enlargement (Conference: NATO Enlargement: The National Debates over Ratification), Brussels: NATO, Academic Forum (http://www.nato.int/acad/conf/enlarg97).
Shi-Xu 1992, Argumentation, Explanation, and Social Cognition, *Text* 12: 263–91.
Smith, Anthony D. 1991, *National Identity*, Reno: University of Nevada Press.
Smith, Martin A. and Timmins, Graham 2000, *EU and NATO Enlargement in Comparative Perspective*, Aldershot: Ashgate.

Snow, David A. and Benford, Robert D. 1988, Ideology, Frame Resonance, and Participant Mobilization, *International Social Movement Research* (Supplement to Research in Social Movements, Conflicts and Change) 1:197–217.

Snyder, Glenn H. 1984, The Security Dilemma in Alliance Politics, *World Politics* 36: 461–95.

1990, Alliance Theory: A Neorealist First Cut, *Journal of International Affairs* 44: 103–24.

1997, *Alliance Politics*, Ithaca, NY: Cornell University Press.

Solana, Javier 1997, Preparing for the Madrid Summit, *NATO Review* 45(2): 3–6 (quoted according to web edition, http://www.nato.int/docu/review).

Solomon, Gerald B. 1998, *The NATO Enlargement Debate, 1990–1997. Blessings of Liberty* (The Washington Papers 174), Westport, CO: Praeger.

Sperling, James (ed.) 1999, *Two Tiers or Two Speeds? The European Security Order and the Enlargement of the European Union and NATO*, Manchester: Manchester University Press.

Stankevicius, Ceslovas V. 1996, NATO Enlargement and the Indivisibility of Security in Europe: A View from Lithuania, *NATO Review* 44(5): 21–25 (quoted according to web edition, http://www.nato.int/docu/review).

Stawarska, Renata 1999, EU Enlargement from the Polish Perspective, *Journal of European Public Policy* 6: 822–38.

Stuart, Douglas T. 1996, Symbol and (Very Little) Substance in the US Debate over NATO Enlargement, in Haglund (ed.), pp. 117–45.

Swidler, Ann 1986, Culture in Action: Symbols and Strategies, *American Sociological Review* 51:273–86.

Szabo, Stephen F. 1997, Ein Projekt "Made in Germany." Was Rühes strategischer Logik entsprang, hat die Unterstützung der Regierung Clinton gefunden, *Frankfurter Allgemeine Zeitung*, 24 July, p. 9.

Talbott, Strobe 1995, Why NATO Should Grow, *New York Review of Books*, 10 August, pp. 27–30.

1997, Why the Transformed NATO Deserves to Survive and Enlarge, *International Herald Tribune*, 19 February, p. 8.

Tallberg, Jonas 1999, *Making States Comply. The European Commission, the European Court of Justice & the Enforcement of the Internal Market*, Lund: Department of Political Science, Lund University.

Tangermann, Stefan 1995, Osterweiterung der EU: Wird die Agrarpolitik zum Hindernis?, *Wirtschaftsdienst* 75: 484–91.

Taylor, Trevor 1997, Großbritannien und die Erweiterung der NATO, in Pradetto (ed.), pp. 211–30.

Thompson, Kenneth W. (ed.) 1998, *NATO Expansion* (Miller Center Series on A New World Order 6), Lanham, MD: University Press of America.

Tindale, Christopher W. 1999, *Acts of Arguing. A Rhetorical Model of Argument*, Albany, NY: SUNY Press.

Torreblanca, José I. 2001, *The Reuniting of Europe: Promises, Negotiations and Compromises*, Aldershot: Ashgate.

Torreblanca Payá, José Ignacio 1997, *The European Community and Central Eastern Europe (1989–1993), Foreign Policy and Decision-Making*, Madrid: Centro de Estudios Avanzados en Ciencias Sociales.

Toulmin, Stephen, Rieke, Richard and Janik, Allan 1979, *An Introduction to Reasoning*, New York: Macmillan.

Triadafilopoulos, Triadafilos 1999, Politics, Speech, and the Art of Persuasion: Toward an Aristotelian Conception of the Public Sphere, *Journal of Politics* 61: 741–57.

Védrine, Hubert 1996, *Les mondes de François Mitterrand. A l'Elysée 1981–1995*, Paris: Fayard.

Wallace, Helen 2000, EU Enlargement: a Neglected Subject, in Green Cowles and Smith (eds.), pp. 149–63.

Wallace, William 1999, Europe After the Cold War: Interstate Order or Post-Sovereign Regional System?, *Review of International Studies* 25, Supplement, pp. 201–23.

Wallander, Celeste A. and Keohane, Robert O. 1999, Risk, Threat, and Security Institutions, in Helga Haftendorn, Robert O. Keohane, and Celeste A. Wallander (eds.), *Imperfect Unions. Security Institutions over Time and Space*, Oxford: Oxford University Press, pp. 21–47.

Walt, Stephen M. 1987, *The Origins of Alliances*, Ithaca, NY: Cornell University Press.

1988, Testing Theories of Alliance Formation. The Case of Southwest Asia, *International Organization* 42: 275–316.

1989, Alliances in Theory and Practice. What Lies Ahead?, *Journal of International Affairs* 43: 1–17.

1997, Why Alliances Endure or Collapse, *Survival* 39: 156–79.

Waltz, Kenneth N. 1979, *Theory of International Politics*, New York: Random House.

2001, NATO Expansion: A Realist's View, in Robert W. Rauchhaus (ed.), *Explaining NATO Enlargement*, London: Frank Cass, pp. 23–38.

Warner, Margaret 1998, NATO Expansion: The Domestic Political Debate, in Thompson (ed.), pp. 115–35.

Weber, Max 1968, *Economy and Society. An Outline of Interpretive Sociology*, New York: Bedminster Press.

Weber, Steve 1993, Shaping the Postwar Balance of Power: Multilateralism in NATO, in Ruggie (ed.), pp. 233–92.

1994, Origins of the European Bank for Reconstruction and Development, *International Organization* 48: 1–38.

Weise, Christian, Brücker, Herbert, Franzmeyer, Fritz, Lodahl, Maria, Möbius, Uta, Schultz, Siegfried, Schumacher, Dieter and Trabold, Harold 1997, *Ostmitteleuropa auf dem Weg in die EU – Transformation, Verflechtung, Reformbedarf*, Berlin: Duncker & Humblot.

Weisser, Ulrich 1999, *Sicherheit für ganz Europa. Die Atlantische Allianz in der Bewährung*, Stuttgart: Deutsche Verlags-Anstalt.

Welfens, Paul J. J. 1999, *Wirtschaftliche Aspekte der EU-Osterweiterung* (Bericht des BIOst 7/1999), Cologne: Bundesinstitut für internationale und ostwissenschaftliche Studien.

Wendt, Alexander E. 1987, The Agent–Structure Problem in International Relations Theory, *International Organization* 41: 335–70.

1992, Anarchy is What States Make of It. The Social Construction of Power Politics, *International Organization* 46: 391–425.

1994, Collective Identity Formation and the International State, *American Political Science Review* 88: 2, 384–96.

1999, *Social Theory of International Politics*, Cambridge: Cambridge University Press.

Williams, Michael C. and Neumann, Iver B. 2000, From Alliance to Security Community: NATO, Russia, and the Power of Identity, *Millennium* 29: 357–87.

Wilming, Claudia 1995, *Institutionelle Konsequenzen einer Erweiterung der Europäischen Union. Eine ökonomische Analyse der Entscheidungsverfahren im Ministerrat*, Baden-Baden: Nomos.

Wolf, Reinhard 1996, The Doubtful Mover: Germany and NATO Expansion, in Haglund (ed.), pp. 197–224.

Wörner, Manfred 1991, NATO Transformed: The Significance of the Rome Summit, *NATO Review* 39: 3–8 (quoted according to web edition, http://www.nato.int/docu/review).

Yamaguchi, Kazuo 1991, *Event History Analysis* (Applied Social Research Methods Series 28), Newbury Park: Sage.

Zakaria, Fareed 1995, Realism and Domestic Politics: A Review Essay, in Michael E. Brown, Sean M. Lynn-Jones, and Steven E. Miller (eds.), *The Perils of Anarchy. Contemporary Realism and International Security*, Cambridge, MA: MIT Press, pp. 462–83.

Zürn, Michael 1992, *Interessen und Institutionen in der internationalen Politik. Grundlegung und Anwendung des situationsstrukturellen Ansatzes*, Opladen: Leske and Budrich.

Index